Restrictive Practices in Health Care and Disability Settings

Legal, Policy and Practical Responses

Edited by
Bernadette McSherry
and Yvette Maker

Routledge
Taylor & Francis Group
LONDON AND NEW YORK

First published 2021
by Routledge
2 Park Square, Milton Park, Abingdon, Oxon OX14 4RN

and by Routledge
52 Vanderbilt Avenue, New York, NY 10017

Routledge is an imprint of the Taylor & Francis Group, an informa business

British Library Cataloguing-in-Publication Data
A catalogue record for this book is available from the British Library

Library of Congress Cataloging-in-Publication Data
A catalog record for this book has been requested

ISBN: 978-0-367-37604-8 (hbk)
ISBN: 978-0-429-35521-9 (ebk)

Typeset in Galliard
by Apex CoVantage, LLC

Restrictive Practices in Health Care and Disability Settings

This volume explores different models of regulating the use of restrictive practices in health care and disability settings.

The authors examine the legislation, policies, inspection, enforcement and accreditation of the use of practices such as physical, mechanical and chemical restraint. They also explore the importance of factors such as organisational culture and staff training to the effective implementation of regulatory regimes. In doing so, the collection provides a solid evidence base for both the development and implementation of effective approaches to restrictive practices that focus on their reduction and, ultimately, their elimination across health care sectors. Divided into five parts, the volume covers new ground in multiple respects. First, it addresses the use of restrictive practices across mental health, disability and aged care settings, creating opportunities for new insights and interdisciplinary conversations across traditionally siloed sectors. Second, it includes contributions from research academics, clinicians, regulators and mental health consumers, offering a rich and comprehensive picture of existing regulatory regimes and options for designing and implementing regulatory approaches that address the failings of current systems. Finally, it incorporates comparative perspectives from Australia, New Zealand, the Netherlands, Germany and England.

The book is an invaluable resource for regulators, policymakers, lawyers, clinicians, consumer advocates and academics grappling with the use and regulation of restrictive practices in mental health, disability and aged care contexts.

Bernadette McSherry is the foundation director of the Melbourne Social Equity Institute and an adjunct professor of law at the University of Melbourne. She has degrees in law, arts and psychology, with a PhD from York University, Canada. She is the immediate past president of the Australian and New Zealand Association of Psychiatry, Psychology and Law and was a legal member of the Mental Health Tribunal of Victoria from 2001 to 2018. She has written widely in the fields of mental health law and criminal law and is currently a commissioner of the Royal Commission into Victoria's Mental Health System and a commissioner with the Victorian Law Reform Commission.

Yvette Maker is a senior research associate in the Melbourne Social Equity Institute at the University of Melbourne. Her work focuses on the disability- and gender-related dimensions of law, policy and practice. She has a special interest in disability human rights law, social security law and policy, and the design and regulation of social care and support systems. She holds bachelor of arts and bachelor of laws (hons) degrees from Murdoch University, and a PhD from the University of Melbourne. Yvette's sole-authored book, *Care and Support Rights After Neoliberalism: Balancing Competing Claims Through Law and Policy*, is forthcoming.

Biomedical Law and Ethics Library

Series Editor: Sheila A. M. McLean

Professor Sheila A.M. McLean is Professor Emerita of Law and Ethics in Medicine, School of Law, University of Glasgow, UK.

Scientific and clinical advances, social and political developments and the impact of health care on our lives raise profound ethical and legal questions. Medical law and ethics have become central to our understanding of these problems, and are important tools for the analysis and resolution of problems – real or imagined.

In this series, scholars at the forefront of biomedical law and ethics contribute to the debates in this area, with accessible, thought-provoking, and sometimes controversial, ideas. Each book in the series develops an independent hypothesis and argues cogently for a particular position. One of the major contributions of this series is the extent to which both law and ethics are utilised in the content of the books, and the shape of the series itself.

The books in this series are analytical, with a key target audience of lawyers, doctors, nurses, and the intelligent lay public.

Available titles:

Healthcare Ethics, Law and Professionalism
Essays on the Works of Alastair V. Campbell
Edited by Voo Teck Chuan, Richard Huxtable and Nicola Peart

Religion, Medicine and the Law
Clayton Ó Néill

Islam and Biomedical Research Ethics
Mehrunisha Suleman

Medical Treatment of Children and the Law
Beyond Parental Responsibilities
Jo Bridgeman

Restrictive Practices in Health Care and Disability Settings
Legal, Policy and Practical Responses
Edited by Bernadette McSherry and Yvette Maker

For more information about this series, please visit: www.routledge.com/Biomedical-Law-and-Ethics-Library/book-series/CAV5

Brief contents

Detailed contents

Figures

Tables

Table of cases

Table of statutes

Queensland

South Australia

Tasmania

Victoria

Western Australia

Germany

Netherlands

United Kingdom

United States of America

International instruments

Abbreviations

Akwa GGZ	Alliance for Quality in Mental Health Care
Bopz	Psychiatric Hospitals (Committals) Act (Netherlands)
BPSD	Behavioural and psychological symptoms of dementia
CRPD	Convention on the Rights of Persons with Disabilities
DGPPN	German Association for Psychiatry, Psychotherapy and Psychosomatic Medicine
DKG	German Hospital Federation
DoLS	Deprivation of Liberty Safeguards
ECHR	European Convention on Human Rights
GGZ Nederland	Dutch Association of Mental Health and Addiction Care
ICCPR	International Covenant on Civil and Political Rights
NDIS	National Disability Insurance Scheme
NHS	National Health Service
NICE	National Institute of Health and Clinical Excellence
PRN	Pro Re Nata (as needed)
PsychKG	Law on Support and Protective Measures for Persons with Mental Illnesses (Germany)
RACGP	Royal Australian College of General Practitioners
RANZCP	Royal Australian and New Zealand College of Psychiatrists
SBG	Stichting (or Foundation) Benchmark GGZ
SECREST NBEDS	Mental Health Seclusion and Restraint National Best Endeavours Data Set
UN	United Nations
Wvggz	Compulsory Mental Health Care Act (Netherlands)
Wzd	Care and Compulsion (Psychogeriatric and Intellectually Disabled Patients) Act (Netherlands)

Acknowledgments

This book is based on a research project funded by the Australian Research Council. The editors thank Andrew Simon-Butler for his invaluable research and editing assistance throughout the course of this project; Sandra Pyke for her excellent work compiling the Index and Tables of Cases and Legislation; Kathleen Patterson for her unstinting support in coordinating the overall project and Alex Callahan for her vital assistance with the workshop that brought the authors together to discuss their draft chapters. The editors also acknowledge the advice and support of all those at Routledge who've worked to bring this volume to fruition and are particularly grateful to all the authors for their dedication to exploring this complex topic and for their enthusiasm and good-natured responses to editorial requests.

Yvette Maker also extends her gratitude to Claire Spivakovsky for providing useful comments on a draft of Chapter 5, Robin Gardner and Anna Bohacova (Academic Research Service, Melbourne Law School) for research support and Alicia King for her advice and support.

John Allan wishes to thank his wife Jessie, who has encouraged and supported his efforts in seeking reform in mental health for many years.

Guy Cross thanks Lesley Savage and Yvette Maker for their patience and support.

Justine Fletcher acknowledges that Chapter 12 includes work towards a PhD which is supported through an Australian Government Research Training Program Scholarship. Justine Fletcher is supported by NHMRC PhD Research Scholarship 1133627.

Nathan Gibson would like to acknowledge his colleagues, of all persuasions, who work with complex, uncertain and distressing situations and yet try to maintain their humanity.

Amber Manwaring wishes to thank Shaun and Charlie who never fail to support, encourage and inspire her.

Margret Osterfeld and Martin Zinkler would like to thank Marina Langfeldt for her legal supervision of Chapter 10.

Cath Roper, Mary O'Hagan, Hamilton Kennedy and Helena Roennfeldt would like to acknowledge all people who have been detained and treated against their will, and in particular they would like to acknowledge the unique experiences of Indigenous peoples and people who identify as having a disability, as Rainbow or neuro-diverse, or who come from non-English-speaking backgrounds or are asylum seekers. There is work to be done in better understanding and repairing the intersectional trauma they have experienced.

Grant Sara expresses his thanks to Gary Hanson and Amy Young, Australian Institute of Health and Welfare, for comments on a draft of Chapter 9 and for their work in establishing and managing Australia's national seclusion and restraint data collection.

Lisa Waddington is grateful to the following people who provided background information or an interview or provided feedback on Chapter 7: Dr. Eric Noorthoorn of GGNet, Alexandra Kozarowitzy of the organisation Sevagram and Elles Ramakers of Maastricht University. She is also grateful to Juliane Dieroff for research assistance. All translations from Dutch to English in Chapter 7 were made by the author.

Contributors

John Allan

Associate Professor John Allan gained his Fellowship of the Royal Australian and New Zealand College of Psychiatrists (RANZCP) in 1987 after medical training in Queensland and psychiatry training in South Australia. He completed his PhD at the University of Queensland. He is the executive director of the Mental Health Alcohol and Other Drugs Branch in Queensland Health and has previously been Chief Psychiatrist in both Queensland and New South Wales. He is also an associate professor in the Faculty of Medicine, University of Queensland, and President of RANZCP. For 20 years he led the mental health services in Townsville, North Queensland. His current research and policy interests focus on mental health system reform, reduction in restrictive practices, human rights, recovery-oriented practice and smoking reduction strategies.

Peter Bartlett

Professor Peter Bartlett joined the School of Law at the University of Nottingham in 1993 and in April 2005 he was appointed to the Nottinghamshire Healthcare NHS Trust Chair in Mental Health Law. His research interests are primarily in the area of law relating to mental disability (including both psychosocial disability/mental illness and learning disability), both in England and Wales and internationally. His research interests include the *Mental Health Act 1983* (England and Wales), the *Mental Capacity Act 2005* (England and Wales), the *European Convention on Human Rights* and the United Nations *Convention on the Rights of Persons with Disabilities.*

Juanita Breen (previously Westbury)

Dr Juanita Breen is a senior lecturer at the Wicking Dementia Research and Education Centre in the Faculty of Health and Medicine at the University of Tasmania. With a strong background in pharmacy and aged care, she is passionate about reducing the use of psychotropic medication in older people, especially those with dementia. To that end, her research aims to understand the reasons behind psychotropic prescribing, map patterns of use and foster interdisciplinary working to ensure appropriate use of medication to manage behavioural and psychological symptoms of dementia and other mental health conditions.

Lisa Brophy

Professor Lisa Brophy has a professional background in social work and a career-long commitment to the mental health field of practice dating back to 1985. She is currently a professor and discipline lead in social work and social policy in the School of Allied Health, Human Services and Sport, College of Science, Health and Engineering at La Trobe University. She is also an honorary principal research fellow in the Recovery and Social Justice Unit, the Centre for Mental Health in the Melbourne School of Population and Global Health at the University of Melbourne. Since completing her PhD in 2009 Lisa's ongoing research focus has been on people experiencing mental illness and/or psychosocial disability and their recovery, social inclusion and human rights. She has been involved in local and international collaborations regarding mental health law and its implications for policy, law reform and direct practice. Lisa is a community member of the Victorian Mental Health Tribunal.

Kim Chandler

Dr Kim Chandler has researched and published in the area of restrictive practices, in particular the legal frameworks regulating the use of restrictive practices on people with intellectual and cognitive impairments. She holds a bachelor of arts, a bachelor of social work (hons) and a juris doctor from the University of Queensland, and a PhD from the Queensland University of Technology. Her PhD explored a rights-based approach to the authorisation of restrictive practices on people with intellectual and cognitive impairments.

Guy Cross

Guy Cross worked for 20 years at England's Department of Health. He initially focused on workforce-related issues. Moving into mental health, he worked on policy, service design and funding, including work on offenders and personality disorder. Later working on reducing restrictive practice, in 2014 Guy implemented 'Positive and Proactive Care: Reducing the Need for Restrictive Interventions'. He also coordinated the updating of Chapter 26 of the Mental Health Act Code of Practice entitled 'Safe and Therapeutic Responses to Disturbed Behaviour'. Since 2017, Guy has worked at the Care Quality Commission where his role includes initiatives to reduce restrictive practice.

Justine Fletcher

Justine Fletcher is a research fellow in the Centre for Mental Health in the Melbourne School of Population and Global Health at the University of Melbourne. Justine has worked on a number of evaluations of large-scale mental health programmes, most recently regarding the reduction of restrictive practices in mental health services. Justine is finalising her PhD which has evaluated the implementation of Safewards in 18 Victorian inpatient mental health wards. Justine completed a master's of clinical psychology and has worked as an independently practicing psychologist, with experience in working in mental health across various clinical and research settings.

Nathan Gibson

Dr Nathan Gibson trained in psychiatry in Tasmania, Scotland and Western Australia. He is a general adult psychiatrist and is currently the Chief Psychiatrist of Western Australia.

Bridget Hamilton

Associate Professor Bridget Hamilton is the director of the Centre for Psychiatric Nursing in the School of Health Sciences at the University of Melbourne. She leads a team of clinical nurse academics and consumer academics to build up the skills and contribution of mental health nurses in Victoria, for the benefit of people receiving mental health care. She is a registered mental health nurse with a 30-year career working as a clinician, manager, educator and researcher in public sector services.

Hamilton Kennedy

Hamilton Kennedy has been a user of mental health services over the past ten years. In the past five years, Hamilton worked as a peer support worker, consumer consultant, consumer academic and lecturer. Hamilton is currently a consumer academic in the Centre for Psychiatric Nursing at the University of Melbourne. Hamilton's writings and research have focused on improving safety, reducing restrictive interventions, furthering the field of peer support work and creating services which meet the needs of mental health service users. They use their firsthand knowledge of mental health services to inform their perspective and provide critical insights for others into the actual experience of service use.

Yvette Maker

Dr Yvette Maker is a senior research associate in the Melbourne Social Equity Institute at the University of Melbourne. Her work focuses on the disability- and gender-related dimensions of law, policy and practice. She has a special interest in disability human rights law, social security law and policy, and the design and regulation of social care and support systems. She holds bachelor of arts and bachelor of laws (hons) degrees from Murdoch University, and a PhD from the University of Melbourne. Yvette's sole-authored book, *Care and Support Rights After Neoliberalism: Balancing Competing Claims Through Law and Policy*, will be published by Cambridge University Press.

Amber Manwaring

Amber Manwaring holds bachelor of laws and bachelor of arts degrees from the Queensland University of Technology, and a graduate diploma of legal practice from the College of Law. She currently works in the Mental Health Alcohol and Other Drugs Branch at Queensland Health. Amber's experience and interest lies in person-centred approaches to improving social policy and legislation for vulnerable Queenslanders. Amber has led reforms relating to forensic disability, mental health, disability, the National Disability Insurance Scheme, child protection, the Royal Commission into Institutional Responses to Child Sexual Abuse, and domestic and family violence. Amber is currently leading the development of a national legislative scheme for the mutual recognition of civil mental health orders.

Bernadette McSherry

Professor Bernadette McSherry is the foundation director of the Melbourne Social Equity Institute and an adjunct professor of law at the University of Melbourne. She has degrees in law, arts and psychology, with a PhD from York University, Canada. She is the immediate past president of the Australian and New Zealand Association of Psychiatry, Psychology and Law and was a legal member of the Mental Health Tribunal of Victoria from 2001 to 2018. She has written widely in the fields of mental health law and criminal law and is currently a commissioner of the Royal Commission into Victoria's Mental Health System and a commissioner with the Victorian Law Reform Commission.

Mary O'Hagan

Mary O'Hagan was an initiator of the psychiatric survivor movement in New Zealand in the late 1980s and was the first chairperson of the World Network of Users and Survivors of Psychiatry. She has been an advisor to the United Nations and the World Health Organisation. Mary was a full-time Mental Health Commissioner in New Zealand between 2000 and 2007. Mary is the director of the international social enterprise PeerZone, which provides peer support and resources for people with mental distress. Mary has written an award-winning memoir called *Madness Made Me*. She was made a member of the New Zealand Order of Merit in 2015. She is currently manager mental wellbeing at New Zealand's Health Promotion Agency.

Margret Osterfeld

Dr Margret Osterfeld is a psychiatrist, psychotherapist, expert on German mental health law and expert on psychopharmacology. She is a member of the German National Agency for the Prevention of Torture, a member of Aktion Psychisch Kranke (Action Mental Health) Germany and a member of the German Association for Social Psychiatry.

Helena Roennfeldt

Helena Roennfeldt has master of suicidology, master of mental health, master of forensic mental health and master of social work degrees from Griffith University. She is currently a PhD candidate at the University of Melbourne writing on subjective experiences of mental health crises and alternatives to emergency departments. She is a lived experience researcher and academic, specialising in critical and alternative perspectives in mental health.

Cath Roper

Cath Roper is the senior consumer academic at the Centre for Psychiatric Nursing in the Faculty of Medicine, Dentistry and Health Sciences at the University of

Melbourne. She leads training, policy and workforce development initiatives in the mental health sector and has been influential in promoting co-production as an engagement methodology. Cath coordinates a core consumer subject in the graduate diploma in mental health nursing practice at the University of Melbourne. Her policy work and scholarship in the areas of supported decision-making, eliminating restrictive interventions and alternatives to biogenetic paradigms is influenced by experiencing multiple annual involuntary admissions.

Stephanie Sampson

Stephanie Sampson has worked as patient and public involvement coordinator with NIHR MindTech, at the University of Nottingham and as a systematic reviewer for Cochrane. She is now a freelance writer, researcher and CELTA qualified teacher of English.

Grant Sara

Dr Grant Sara is the director of InforMH, the unit responsible for data collection, analysis and reporting for the New South Wales Mental Health Services in the Ministry of Health and a clinical associate professor in the Northern Clinical School, Faculty of Medicine and Health, University of Sydney. He completed his medical degree at the University of Sydney, psychiatry training at Westmead Hospital and a PhD in public health at the University of Queensland. His research uses large administrative datasets to support better mental health care. Focus areas include comorbid psychoses and substance disorders, restrictive practices and reducing premature medical mortality in mental health service users.

Lisa Waddington

Professor Lisa Waddington holds the European Disability Forum Chair in European Disability Law at Maastricht University. Her principal areas of research are European and comparative disability law, the United Nations *Convention on the Rights of Persons with Disabilities*, and European and comparative equality law in general. Lisa is a member of the Maastricht Centre for European Law, the Berkeley Center on Comparative Equality and Anti-Discrimination Law and the Netherlands Network for Human Rights Research. She is a board member of the European Network of Legal Experts in Gender Equality and Non-discrimination and was a coordinator of the Academic Network of European Disability experts. Lisa has been a visiting professor at the University of British Columbia, the University of Melbourne and Leeds University.

Martin Zinkler

Dr Martin Zinkler is a psychiatrist and psychotherapist who is the head of the Department of Psychiatry, Psychotherapy and Psychosomatic Medicine at Kliniken Landkreis in Heidenheim, Germany. The service provides inpatient, outpatient and home treatment. He is co-editor in chief of *Recht & Psychiatrie*, the journal of law and psychiatry for the German speaking countries. He publishes mainly on human rights in mental health care.

Part I

Background

Rationales and options for reform

1 Restrictive practices

Options and opportunities

Bernadette McSherry and Yvette Maker

Introduction

In many health and social care contexts around the world, it is deemed acceptable and necessary to control service users' behaviour where that behaviour is considered to be risky, harmful, hazardous, challenging or otherwise unwanted. Various forms of restraint are used to control behaviour in a wide range of institutional and other settings. As explained later, in general terms, restraint may be 'physical', 'mechanical' or 'chemical' in nature.

The use of these different forms of restraint is controversial. Some forms are inherently dangerous and may involve serious deprivations of liberty, interference with physical and mental integrity and loss of dignity. The use of restraint may also cause injury and sometimes even death. Despite these hazards, different types of restraint continue to be used pursuant to varying levels and kinds of legal regulation and oversight.

There is growing impetus for reforms to either introduce effective regulation of restraint or improve its existing regulation in many parts of the world. A major driver of change internationally has been the United Nations' (UN) recognition of the use of various forms of restraint on persons with disabilities as breaching several human rights. The UN *Convention on the Rights of Persons with Disabilities* (CRPD) (2007), to which over 180 States are now party, protects a person's freedom from torture and cruel, inhuman or degrading treatment or punishment (Article 15) and emphasises that '[e]very person with disabilities has a right to respect for his or her physical and mental integrity on an equal basis with others' (Article 17). The UN Committee on the Rights of Persons with Disabilities, which monitors implementation of the CRPD, has repeatedly expressed its concerns about the use of restraint. It has recommended action to reduce or abolish restraint in its 'concluding observations' on reports submitted to it from many States Parties to the Convention including Slovenia, Luxembourg, the United Kingdom, Ethiopia, Thailand, Croatia, Germany, Denmark, the Republic of Korea, Mexico, Kenya and Australia.

It is therefore timely to consider the role and limits of regulation in relation to restraint across mental health, disability and aged care settings. This edited volume arises from a Discovery project funded by the Australian Research Council (DP160100679). It brings together authors from diverse backgrounds and disciplinary perspectives, including consumers, policymakers, public servants, clinicians and academics with expertise in law, social work, nursing, consumer perspectives, psychiatry, psychology and pharmacy. It discusses different models of regulating the use of restrictive practices, including legislation, policies and guidelines, as well as inspection, enforcement and accreditation, and explores the importance of factors such as staff training, availability of resources, data quality and organisational culture in relation to the effective implementation of regulatory regimes. In doing so, this volume is intended to provide an evidence base for the development and implementation of consistent and effective approaches to restraint that prioritise the minimisation, and ultimately elimination, of these practices across health care and disability settings.

Definitions and scope

Restraint is used across a wide range of health and social care settings, and on people with a variety of diagnoses and needs. This volume focuses on the use of restraint in mental health facilities, disability services (community and residential) and residential aged (or adult social) care in Australia, New Zealand, England, the Netherlands and Germany. Regulatory frameworks and cultural norms governing the use of restraint in these settings differ greatly across these jurisdictions and sectors. Restraint is also permitted or tolerated in a range of other settings worldwide, including forensic mental health services, hospital emergency departments, prisons, juvenile detention facilities, schools, homes and within communities.

Restraint can take many forms. The common feature of all forms of restraint is its purpose, namely, to control a person's behaviour. In this volume, we differentiate between three major forms of restraint: physical, mechanical and chemical restraint. Except where noted by the authors of individual chapters, we follow the broad definitions of those practices as they are used in England and Wales and the six states and two self-governing territories in Australia. We use 'physical restraint' to refer to the use of direct physical contact, where one or more staff members use their bodies to restrain a person (for example, Department of Health (UK) 2014). We use 'mechanical restraint' to describe the use of devices such as straps, jackets or belts to control a person's behaviour (for example, *Disability Act 2006* (Vic): section 3). We use 'chemical restraint' to refer to the use of a medication for the purpose of controlling or subduing a person's behaviour rather than for the purpose of treating an illness or medical condition (for example, *Mental Health Act 2013* (Tas): section 3).

Other terms may be used to describe similar interventions in other contexts and jurisdictions. In some cases, the same terms are used to mean different things. For example, the umbrella term 'bodily restraint' is sometimes used to refer to both physical and mechanical restraint (*Mental Health Act 2014* (Vic): section 3). The term 'prone restraint' refers to a specific form of physical restraint during which the person is held on the ground in a face-down position (see Cross in Chapter 6 in this volume). Terms such as 'rapid tranquillisation' or 'sedation' may be used instead of 'chemical restraint' (see Bartlett and Sampson in Chapter 3 in this volume). Other forms of restraint are also identified and regulated in some places. For example, 'environmental restraint' or 'restriction' may refer to restricting access to some parts of the person's environment, including items and activities by, for example, using physical barriers, locks or other means to stop the person entering particular places or accessing valued items or activities (National Disability Insurance Scheme (Restrictive Practices and Behaviour Support) Rules 2018: rule 6(e); NSW Government undated: 1). 'Emotional restraint' is sometimes used to refer to situations where people feel constrained from expressing their views openly and honestly for fear of the consequences (National Mental Health Consumer and Carer Forum 2009: 5).

Approaches to the regulation of restraint use in the mental health, disability and aged care sectors also vary within and across jurisdictions. Three main forms of regulation are discussed in this volume. The first is legislation, found in most Australian states and territories but not in all sectors (see, for example, Chandler in Chapter 4, Allan and Manwaring in Chapter 8 and Brophy, Fletcher and Hamilton in Chapter 12 in this volume). The second form of regulation is policy documents such as guidelines, codes of practice and procedures relied upon, for example, in England, Wales and Scotland (see Bartlett and Sampson in Chapter 3 and Cross in Chapter 6 in this volume). The third is regulation through a body with powers of inspection, enforcement and/or accreditation, as found in the Netherlands (see Waddington in Chapter 7 in this volume).

Even where regulation exists, legislation and policies may not reflect recent interpretations of international human rights law (see Bartlett and Sampson in Chapter 3 and Chandler in Chapter 4 in this volume, among others). Practices within settings may also vary greatly, with some instances of the overuse of restraint reflecting poor organisational cultures (see McSherry in Chapter 11 in this volume).

In light of the diversity of definitions and regulatory approaches, each chapter of this volume includes a definition of the forms of restraint and regulation addressed in that chapter. We draw connections between different systems in the introductions to the substantive parts of this volume.

Part I, which includes this chapter, introduces the key issues and questions about the use and regulation of restraint addressed in this volume. It also outlines the rationale for working towards elimination rather than just reduction. Parts II, III and IV address respectively what we consider to be the three key elements of regulatory reform to work towards this goal: regulation through legislation, policy or other means (Part II); implementing and monitoring regulatory change (Part III); and changing culture and practice (Part IV). A final, concluding chapter in Part V reviews the volume's major themes and identifies further research and practices that may support reform endeavours. While the chapters are organised into parts, they address interrelated issues and themes. We outline these common themes in this introductory chapter.

Several themes found in the wider literature on restraint and behaviour control in health and social care contexts are not addressed in this volume. They include the use of restraint in general medical settings, emergency departments and forensic psychiatry settings; the use of restraint on children and adolescents in schools, places of detention and other settings; and the use of restraint in homes and within communities. We acknowledge that restraint use is a global concern (see, for example, efforts to reduce the practice of 'pasung' in Indonesia: Daulima 2018) and that this volume addresses a relatively narrow band of high-income countries. The themes identified may resonate and serve as a starting point for efforts to reduce, if not eliminate, the use of restraint in other countries. We are mindful, however, of the dangers of homogenising the way that diverse cultures understand sickness, impairment or disability and health and efforts to control other people's behaviour.

The next section provides an overview of how the use of restraint reflects wider concerns about human rights and their limits.

Background: the wider context and options for reform

While there is growing awareness that prevailing approaches to the use of restraint and other restrictive practices are problematic and unsustainable, opinions vary as to whether reduction, minimisation or elimination should be the ultimate goal of reform. This diversity of opinion is reflected in the present volume. Some authors discuss reduction or minimisation of the use of restraint, with the assumption that restraint will continue to be necessary in some instances of last resort, for example, where there is a serious and urgent risk to the individual's health or life, or a risk to the safety of others. Other authors focus on the ultimate goal of elimination of the use of all forms of restraint on the basis that these practices are entirely inappropriate. There are several compelling rationales for working towards such elimination. Research evidence indicates that restraint can be counter-therapeutic (Bonner et al. 2002), as well as having the potential to cause serious, long-term harm including physical injury and death (Parker and Miles 1997; Evans, Wood and Lambert 2003; Mohr, Petti and Mohr 2003), in addition to fear, pain and psychological harm (Fish and Culshaw 2005; Frueh et al. 2005; Strout 2010; Rose et al. 2017). There is also evidence that restraint and other restrictive practices may be used for reasons that are not permitted by law or policy, for instance, to punish or because of a lack of awareness of alternatives (Muir-Cochrane, Holmes and Walton 2002; Bartlett and Sandland 2007; Foster, Bowers and Nijman 2007). Studies also suggest that restraint does not necessarily achieve safety goals, for example, in the case of the use of mechanical restraints such as belts and bedrails to reduce falls among aged care residents (Tinetti, Liu and Ginter 1992; Capezuti et al. 2002).

Several UN bodies have called for the abolition of the use of restrictive practices on the basis that they are a violation of human rights (see Maker and McSherry 2019). As touched on earlier, the UN Committee on the Rights of Persons with Disabilities has suggested that the use of restraint on persons with disabilities constitutes a violation of several of the CRPD's provisions, including its Article 15, which addresses the right to be free from torture or cruel, inhuman or degrading treatment or punishment; Article 16, which sets out the right of all persons with disabilities to be free from exploitation, violence and abuse; and Article 17, which affirms the right to respect for the physical and mental integrity of every person with disabilities on an equal basis with others (Kumble and McSherry 2010; Committee on the Rights of Persons with Disabilities 2015).

Similar statements have come from other quarters within the UN, including the High Commissioner for Human Rights and the Special Rapporteur on Health (Human Rights Council 2017; United Nations General Assembly 2017). The Special Rapporteur on Torture and Other Cruel, Inhuman or Degrading Treatment or Punishment, Juan Mendez (United Nations General Assembly 2013: para 63) has also called for:

> an absolute ban on all coercive and non-consensual measures, including restraint . . . of people with psychological or intellectual disabilities . . . in all places of deprivation of liberty, including in psychiatric and social care institutions.

The persistence of the use of restraint worldwide, in spite of the range and severity of concerns it raises, points to the extent to which coercion is embedded in mental health, disability and aged care service provision. In this regard, Cath Roper, Mary O'Hagan, Hamilton Kennedy and Helena Roennfeldt argue in Chapter 2 that the use of restraint and other restrictive practices is symptomatic of malfunctioning systems premised on coercion, oppression and discrimination. The authors, who have all used mental health services in New Zealand and Australia, offer an 'insider perspective' on restraint, arguing that it goes beyond direct restrictions on people's bodies, minds and freedoms and encompasses indirect impacts on self-hood including the constraint of self-expression, meaning-making, hope and trust. They link this with the primacy of Western medical (or 'biogenetic') understandings and responses to experience – and colonisation or rejection of indigenous world views and cultural practices – which ignores the wider social context in which people exist, dehumanises individuals and legitimises the use of restraint. Roper and colleagues argue that emerging alternative discourses, especially a human rights discourse that characterises restraint as a breach of fundamental rights rather than a safety issue, must be amplified in order to progress elimination efforts.

These authors furthermore point to consumer-led and consumer-endorsed initiatives (supported by a growing body of research evidence) as demonstrating the utility and effectiveness of alternatives to restraint and other coercive practices (Grey and O'Hagan 2015; Gooding et al. 2018). As with the literature on the use and regulation of restraint generally, most research on alternatives to restrictive practices has focused on mental health settings. For example, several studies have indicated the potential of the *Six Core Strategies to Reduce the Use of Seclusion and Restraint Planning Tool* released by the United States' National Technical Assistance Center for State Mental Health Planning (2005; National Association of State Mental Health Program Directors 2008; see for example Foxlewin 2012; Wisdom et al. 2015; Riahi et al. 2016). These six strategies, as outlined in a report prepared for Australia's National Mental Health Commission (Melbourne Social Equity Institute 2014: 13), are:

1 'Leadership towards organisational change' – articulating a philosophy of care that embraces seclusion and restraint reduction;
2 'Using data to inform practice' – using data in an empirical, 'non-punitive' way to examine and monitor patterns of seclusion and restraint use;
3 'Workforce' – developing procedures, practices and training that are based on knowledge and principles of mental health recovery;
4 'Use of seclusion and restraint reduction tools' – using assessments and resources to individualise aggression prevention;
5 'Consumer roles in inpatient settings' – including consumers, carers and advocates in seclusion and restraint reduction initiatives; and
6 'Debriefing techniques' – conducting an analysis of why seclusion and restraint occurred and evaluating the impacts of these practices on individuals with lived experience.

The research on alternatives to restraint use also suggests that changes to both regulation and practice are necessary to implement alternatives and move towards either a reduction or, ideally, elimination of the use of restraint across sectors (Gooding et al. 2018). Emerging initiatives like the World Health Organisation's 'QualityRights' programme provide comprehensive guidance for promoting the dual aims of regulatory reform and practice change in relation to restraint use and other practices that raise human rights concerns in mental health services (World Health Organisation 2012, 2019; Funk and Drew 2017).

The remaining parts of this edited volume explore the potential and limitations of existing regulatory approaches, and some of the challenges and opportunities in implementing regulatory reform and changing culture and practice on the ground.

The role of regulation and its limits

Part II comprises four chapters that explore and assess the main features of regulatory frameworks in two countries where the use and regulation of restraint has come under increased scrutiny in recent decades – England and Australia. In these systems, policy and/or legislation govern the use and oversight of various forms of restraint in multiple settings. The discussions in Part II point to positives of each approach, as well as limitations.

In Chapter 3, Peter Bartlett and Stephanie Sampson raise a number of ethical and practical problems with policies addressing the use of one form of restraint to control the behaviour of elderly persons and persons with learning disabilities in England, namely, rapid tranquilisation. Through a close analysis of policies from 120 NHS Trusts in England, they introduce several themes that recur throughout this volume. This includes the diversity and inconsistency of regulatory approaches within jurisdictions or health systems; the possibility that, where they do exist, the complexity and sheer volume of institutional policies and lack of clarity about the legality of different practices makes regulation ineffective at the service level; and doubt about the extent to which human rights considerations – even where they are named as relevant matters – actually inform policies and their implementation. Like Roper and colleagues, these authors note that the English policies tend to be based on a biomedical approach to treatment and behaviour control, with a focus on practical questions of *how* rapid tranquilisation should be administered rather than a real contemplation of the appropriateness and necessity of the practice.

Kim Chandler further elaborates on the limits of existing regulation, and the potential of a genuinely human rights-based approach, in her discussion of Australian legislation and policy in Chapter 4. Common law protections (at least theoretically) exist to prevent or respond to deprivations of liberty and false imprisonment in Australia. As Chandler notes, the common law doctrine of necessity has often been invoked to authorise detention and restraint of people with disabilities. Australian courts have been less inclined than their British counterparts to accept necessity arguments in the case of long-term restrictions, meaning formal authorisation through legislation is necessary. Legislation may have the advantage of prescribing formal processes for the authorisation and use of restraint and – at least by implication – prohibiting use outside these parameters. However, as Chandler points out, incomplete and complex legislative and policy schemes in different Australian jurisdictions and sectors raise concerns about the extent to which this more formal regulation protects the rights of people with disabilities and older persons. She accordingly proposes a human rights-based approach, incorporating procedural safeguards, that would de-centre the authorisation function of existing legislation and policy and prioritise what is necessary to support the exercise and enjoyment of the rights of those subject to restraint.

The need for regulation to be sensitive to the circumstances and needs of the diversity of service users is the focus of Chapter 5. Drawing on international research on the needs and experiences of women service users, Yvette Maker analyses the extent to which Australian legislation and policy addressing restraint use in disability and mental health services is 'gender sensitive'. Maker argues that regulatory instruments must be amended to promote gender awareness, foster strong relationships and relational security, and contemplate and respond to service users' experiences of trauma, while ensuring that they are not subject to new trauma. An intersectional lens must inform these changes in order to ensure that the multidimensional identities and experiences (including experiences of marginalisation and oppression) of service users are adequately recognised and accounted for.

The final chapter in Part II takes up a theme that is alluded to in the preceding chapters and explored in detail in the rest of this volume, namely, the relationship between the formalities of regulation and its implementation by services and individuals. In Chapter 6, Guy Cross draws on his experience as a civil servant in England's then-Department of Health (now the Department of Health and Social Care) to discuss the development and implementation of a series of policy measures designed to support the reduction of restrictive interventions in health and care services for adults. While noting that the policy emphasis on positive changes to practice through, for example, the introduction of individualised support plans for all service users was largely welcomed, Cross highlights difficulties with implementation, monitoring and reporting of the use of restrictive practices under successive policies. He attributes these difficulties to the use of imprecise definitions of permissible and impermissible forms of restraint, insufficient information and support for staff to implement alternatives, and inadequate attention to the wider context and resource implications of reform. Perhaps in consequence, concerns about the use of restraint and other restrictive practices have persisted. Cross argues that effective action will require better recognition that restraint use and reduction is not a 'stand-alone issue' and must be understood and addressed in relation to factors like resources, staff capabilities and the potential of new approaches to support monitoring and training efforts.

Implementing and monitoring regulatory change

Part III of this volume delves into issues that arise during the implementation and monitoring of regulation and regulatory reform. In Chapter 7, Lisa Waddington examines the relationship between regulation, monitoring and reduction in the use of involuntary treatment and restrictive practices in the Netherlands. Waddington describes recent legislative reforms to the regulation of involuntary treatment (including restraint) in relation to mental health service users, people with an intellectual disability or people with 'psychogeriatric conditions' receiving health treatment, noting that the new legislation is apparently more human rights-compliant than prior instruments. A key element of the Dutch regulatory system is an obligation on services to report all instances of involuntary treatment and restraint to a central register. Data collection has been identified as an important first step in recognising and responding to restraint use worldwide (National Technical Assistance Center for State Mental Health Planning 2005; National Association of State Mental Health Program Directors 2008), although Waddington's chapter highlights some of the challenges for data collection, including privacy and data protection laws and concerns about the accuracy of reporting. The data available in the Netherlands suggests that the wide range of coercion reduction interventions used by Dutch institutions has had some success, although research indicates that this data is not necessarily being used optimally to inform and guide efforts within services (Voskes, Theuniseen and Widdershoven 2011: 42).

A different set of reforms, introduced with the express purpose of addressing high rates of restraint use and moving towards minimisation or elimination, is explored in detail in Chapter 8. John Allan, current President of the Royal Australian and New Zealand College of Psychiatrists, played a major role in the development and implementation of new mental health legislation in 2016 and 2017 in the Australian state of Queensland. His chapter, co-authored with

Amber Manwaring, describes the introduction of safeguards and rules for the use of physical and mechanical restraint and discusses the comprehensive measures introduced to translate the new Queensland legislative scheme into practice. Allan and Manwaring describe significant implementation challenges, even in the context of considerable institutional support. They echo many of the issues identified earlier by Guy Cross in relation to English policy, such as a lack of suitable training programmes, difficulty identifying less restrictive approaches, the possibility that the scope and complexity of the mental health reforms meant the provisions relating to restraint could not be adequately communicated to staff, and inconsistent data collection and reporting.

The importance – and challenges – of reporting and monitoring restraint use are further explored by Grant Sara in Chapter 9. Sara describes the process of developing and using data to inform the reduction of restraint and seclusion, which includes defining the restrictive practice(s) of interest, operationalising the definition (including dealing with 'edge cases' that sit at the edge or boundary of the definition), defining indicators, collecting data, feedback and reporting of the data, and interpretation and action. Using the Australian example, Sara highlights the difficulties that can arise at one or more of these stages, many of which relate to challenges of defining different forms of restraint and operationalising those definitions. Chemical restraint has proved especially difficult to define and distinguish from medical treatment, because the intention of the actor is key and cannot be easily operationalised.

The last chapter in Part III flags other challenges in implementing regulatory change, in this case, restrictions on the use of several forms of restraint in German psychiatric hospitals following two decisions of Germany's Federal Constitutional Court. As Margret Osterfeld and Martin Zinkler explain in Chapter 10, a 2011 judgment that placed limitations on the use of forced medication led to an increase in the use of mechanical (known in Germany as 'physical') restraint. In 2018, the Court considered the question of whether the use of mechanical restraint constituted a deprivation of liberty and decided that more than short-term use of these measures did interfere with this constitutional right. This meant state legislatures around Germany were obliged to enact provisions requiring judicial authorisation for their use. The authors describe significant resistance to implementing these judicial decisions from both psychiatrists and health insurers (who provide mandatory cover for all citizens) and link this to a broader lack of societal concern with coercion and rights-based treatment in German psychiatric services. This again raises questions about the positive and negative influences of culture on restraint reduction and elimination efforts.

Challenging risk, fear and blame: the need for complementary culture and practice change

The role of culture and individual action in achieving (or stalling) change is the focus of Part IV. Concerns about risk of harm and occupational health and safety are commonly used to justify the use of restraint. In Chapter 11, Bernadette

McSherry queries the extent to which these rationales may mask other factors, especially poor organisational culture, that can lead to high rates of restraint use on people with mental health conditions, people with disabilities and older persons in aged care for convenience, punishment or other purposes. Even where occupational health and safety concerns (particularly the risk of harm to staff from a violent or aggressive service user) *are* cited by staff as the reason for restraint use in closed environments, these may be based on stigma, prejudice and discrimination towards 'risky' individuals. McSherry argues that organisational culture and risk-based decision-making reflect wider cultural processes of 'othering' service users, leading to an 'us and them' mentality that disregards users' human rights.

Lisa Brophy, Bridget Hamilton and Justine Fletcher argue that momentum for reducing and eliminating the use of restraint risks being lost if such cultural barriers to implementation are not addressed (Chapter 12). Using the example of mental health services in the Australian state of Victoria, they note that strong forces in favour of reducing the use of restraint have not led to consistent and widespread reform. Brophy, Fletcher and Hamilton argue that cultural changes such as greater tolerance of risk, as well as proper incorporation of human rights considerations and trauma-informed practice, are necessary to achieve change. These authors, like McSherry, suggest that effective senior leadership within care settings is a necessary first step in restraint reduction efforts. Drawing on qualitative research, they also flag the importance of lived experience and peer support roles in implementing such changes and providing support to service users and families.

The final chapters in Part IV examine the interplay of regulation, culture and practice in two particular senses. Juanita Breen (previously Westbury) (Chapter 13) discusses the continued high rates of psychotropic medication use in Australian aged care despite known adverse effects and concerns about the safety and autonomy of the older persons affected. This echoes the concerns raised in earlier chapters about the lack of evidence informing current restraint practices. Breen discusses her research on the drivers of psychotropic prescribing practices, noting that nursing and care staff were the most influential groups in requesting the use of psychotropic medications. Breen also examines international strategies for addressing this problem, including mandatory public reporting and safety warnings, as well as intervention projects aimed at reducing inappropriate psychotropic use. She ultimately argues for a multi-strategy, interdisciplinary programme that combines regulation to limit restraint use and facilitate monitoring with service-level interventions to change staff and clinicians approaches to requesting and providing prescriptions.

In Chapter 14, Nathan Gibson further examines the role of clinicians in reducing the use of restraint. Citing effective interventions introduced in the United Kingdom and France in the 1800s, Gibson highlights the long tradition of individual clinicians driving restraint reduction efforts and the startling similarities between these early efforts and contemporary strategies. He queries why widespread recognition among clinicians of the harms of restraint use has not led to sustained or generalised restraint reduction, identifying factors that might work against these outcomes including a lack of guidance in oaths, codes of ethics and other charters, as well as the multitude of personal and service-level factors that influence clinicians in situations that lead to restraint use. Echoing McSherry's discussion of organisational culture in Chapter 11, Gibson raises the possibility that a small number of staff who deviate from appropriate practice may influence poor practice throughout a service, which can be difficult to counteract. Again, the importance of leadership and engagement with clinicians, supported by multi-pronged and individualised interventions to change clinicians' behaviour, are proposed as necessary next steps.

In Chapter 15, we draw several conclusions about the role and limits of different forms of regulation, the potential for better implementation and monitoring and the significance of culture in multiple senses. We highlight regulatory measures and practices identified by the contributors to this volume as potential facilitators of restraint minimisation and elimination efforts and identify gaps in the research and opportunities for further inquiry.

References

Legislation and treaties

Convention on the Rights of Persons with Disabilities (CRPD) (2007) Opened for signature 30 March, 2515 UNTS 3 (entered into force 3 May 2008).

Disability Act 2006 (Vic).

Mental Health Act 2013 (Tas).

Mental Health Act 2014 (Vic).

National Disability Insurance Scheme (Restrictive Practices and Behaviour Support) Rules 2018 (Cth).

Books, journal articles and other texts

Bartlett, P. and Sandland, R. (2007) *Mental Health Law Policy and Practice*, 3rd edn, New York: Oxford University Press.

Bonner, G., Lowe, T., Rawcliffe, D. and Wellman, N. (2002) 'Trauma for All: A Pilot Study of the Subjective Experience of Physical Restraint for Mental Health Inpatients and Staff in the UK', *Journal of Psychiatric and Mental Health Nursing*, 9(4): 465–73.

Capezuti, E., Maislin, G., Strumpf, N. and Evans, L.K. (2002) 'Side Rail Use and Bed-Related Fall Outcomes Among Nursing Home Residents', *Journal of the American Geriatrics Society*, 50(1): 90–96.

Committee on the Rights of Persons with Disabilities (CRPD) (2015) *Guidelines on Article 14 of the Convention on the Rights of Persons with Disabilities.* Available https://tbinternet.ohchr.org/_layouts/15/treatybodyexternal/Download.aspx?symbolno=A/72/55&Lang=en (accessed 20 June 2020).

Daulima, N.H.C. (2018) 'Preventing *Pasung* by Mentally Ill Patients' Families', *Enfermeria Clinica*, 28(Supp 1): 256–59.

Department of Health (UK) (2014) *Positive and Proactive Care: Reducing the Need for Restrictive Interventions.* Available https://assets.publishing.service.gov.uk/

government/uploads/system/uploads/attachment_data/file/300293/JRA_DoH_Guidance_on_RP_web_accessible.pdf (accessed 13 April 2020).

Evans, D., Wood, J. and Lambert, L. (2003) 'Patient Injury and Physical Restraint Devices: A Systematic Review', *Journal of Advanced Nursing*, 41(3): 274–82.

Fish, R. and Culshaw, E. (2005) 'The Last Resort?: Staff and Client Perspectives on Physical Intervention', *Journal of Intellectual Disabilities*, 9(2): 93–107.

Foster, C., Bowers, L. and Nijman, H. (2007) 'Aggressive Behaviour on Acute Psychiatric Wards: Prevalence, Severity and Management', *Journal of Advanced Nursing*, 58: 140–49.

Foxlewin, B. (2012) *What Is Happening at the Seclusion Review That Makes a Difference?: A Consumer Led Research Study*, Canberra: ACT Mental Health Consumer Network. Available www.actmhcn.org.au/wp-content/uploads/2018/09/2012-06_REPORT_SRRM_RESEARCH_incl_Executive_Summary.pdf (accessed 20 June 2020).

Frueh, B.C., Knapp R.G., Cusack, K.J., Grubaugh, A.L., Sauvageot, J.A., Cousins, V.C., Yim, E., Robins, C.S., Monnier, J. and Hiers, T.G. (2005) 'Patients' Reports of Traumatic or Harmful Experiences Within the Psychiatric Setting', *Psychiatric Services*, 56(9): 1123–33.

Funk, M. and Drew, N. (2017) 'WHO QualityRights: Transforming Mental Health Services', *Lancet Psychiatry*, 4(11): 826–27.

Gooding, P., McSherry, B., Roper, C. and Grey, F. (2018) *Alternatives to Coercion in Mental Health Settings: A Literature Review*, Melbourne: Melbourne Social Equity Institute, University of Melbourne. Available https://socialequity.unimelb.edu.au/__data/assets/pdf_file/0012/2898525/Alternatives-to-Coercion-Literature-Review-Melbourne-Social-Equity-Institute.pdf (accessed 20 June 2020).

Grey, F. and O'Hagan, M. (2015) *The Effectiveness of Services Led or Run by Consumers in Mental Health: An Evidence Check Rapid Review Brokered by the Sax Institute for the Mental Health Commission of New South Wales*. Available https://nswmentalhealthcommission.com.au/resources/the-effectiveness-of-services-led-or-run-by-consumers-in-mental-health-rapid-review-of (accessed 20 June 2020).

Human Rights Council (2017) *Mental Health and Human Rights: Report of the United Nations High Commissioner for Human Rights*, 34th sess, UN Doc A/HRC/34/32.

Kumble, S. and McSherry, B. (2010) 'Seclusion and Restraint: Rethinking Regulation from a Human Rights Perspective', *Psychiatry, Psychology and Law*, 17(4): 551–61.

Maker, Y. and McSherry, B. (2019) 'Regulating Restraint Use in Mental Health and Aged Care Settings: Lessons from the Oakden Scandal', *Alternative Law Journal*, 44(1): 29–36.

Melbourne Social Equity Institute (2014) *Seclusion and Restraint Project Report: Prepared for the National Mental Health Commission*, Melbourne: University of Melbourne. Available https://socialequity.unimelb.edu.au/__data/assets/pdf_file/0017/2004722/Seclusion-and-Restraint-report.PDF (accessed 20 June 2020).

Mohr, W.K., Petti, T.A. and Mohr, B.D. (2003) 'Adverse Effects Associated with Physical Restraint', *The Canadian Journal of Psychiatry*, 48(5): 330–37.

Muir-Cochrane, E., Holmes, C. and Walton, J.A. (2002) 'Law and Policy in Relation to the Use of Seclusion in Psychiatric Hospitals in Australia and New Zealand', *Contemporary Nurse*, 13(2–3): 136–45.

National Association of State Mental Health Program Directors (2008) *Six Core Strategies to Reduce Seclusion and Restraint Use*. Available www.nasmhpd.org/content/six-core-strategies-reduce-seclusion-and-restraint-use (accessed 20 June 2020).

National Mental Health Consumer and Carer Forum (2009) *Ending Seclusion and Restraint in Australian Mental Health Services.* Available https://nmhccf.org.au/sites/default/files/docs/seclusion_restraint.pdf (accessed 20 June 2020).

National Technical Assistance Center for State Mental Health Planning (2005) *Six Core Strategies to Reduce the Use of Seclusion and Restraint Planning Tool*, Alexandria, VA: National Association of State Mental Health Program Directors. Available www.ot-innovations.com/wp-content/uploads/2014/09/2._six_core_sr20plan20template20with20cover207-05.pdf (accessed 18 August 2020).

New South Wales (NSW) Government (undated) *Restrictive Practices Guidance: Environmental Restraint.* Available www.facs.nsw.gov.au/__data/assets/pdf_file/0010/636949/Restrictive-Practices-Resources-environmental-restraint-guidance.pdf (accessed 20 June 2020).

Parker, K. and Miles, S.H. (1997) 'Deaths Caused by Bedrails', *Journal of the American Geriatrics Society*, 45(7): 797–802.

Riahi, S., Dawe, I.C., Stuckey, M.I. and Klassen, P.E. (2016) 'Implementation of the Six Core Strategies for Restraint Minimization in a Specialized Mental Health Organisation', *Journal of Psychosocial Nursing and Mental Health Services*, 54(10): 32–39.

Rose, D., Perry, E., Rae, S. and Good, N. (2017) 'Service User Perspectives on Coercion and Restraint in Mental Health', *BJPsych International*, 14(3): 59–61.

Strout, T.D. (2010) 'Perspectives on the Experience of Being Physically Restrained: An Integrative Review of the Qualitative Literature', *International Journal of Mental Health Nursing*, 19(6): 416–27.

Tinetti, M.E., Liu, W.L. and Ginter, S.F. (1992) 'Mechanical Restraint Use and Fall-Related Injuries Among Residents of Skilled Nursing Facilities', *Annals of Internal Medicine*, 116(5): 369–74.

United Nations General Assembly (2013) *Report of the Special Rapporteur on Torture and Other Cruel, Inhuman or Degrading Treatment or Punishment*, 22nd sess, UN Doc A/HRC/22/53.

United Nations General Assembly (2017) *Report of the Special Rapporteur on the Right of Everyone to the Enjoyment of the Highest Attainable Standard of Physical and Mental Health*, 35th sess, UN Doc A/HRC/35/21.

Voskes, R., Theunissen, J. and Widdershoven, G. (2011) *Best Practices Around Reducing Coercion in Mental Health Care* [*Best Practices rondom dwangreductie in de geestelijke gezondheidszorg*], Amsterdam: Vrije Universiteit Amsterdam. Available http://hic-psy.nl/wp-content/uploads/2012/09/Best-Practices-rondom-Dwangreductie-in-de-Geestelijke-Gezondheidszorg-2011.pdf (accessed 18 August 2020).

Wisdom, J.P., Wenger, D., Robertson, D., Van Bramer, J. and Sederer, L.I. (2015) 'The New York State Office of Mental Health Positive Alternatives to Restraint and Seclusion (PARS) Project', *Psychiatric Services*, 66(8): 851–56.

World Health Organisation (2012) *WHO QualityRights Tool Kit.* Available www.who.int/mental_health/publications/QualityRights_toolkit/en/ (accessed 20 June 2020).

World Health Organisation (2019) *Transforming Services and Promoting Human Rights–WHO QualityRights Training and Guidance: Mental Health and Social Services.* Available https://qualityrights.org/wp-content/uploads/FinalSPECIALISED_Transforming-services_Promoting-Rights2019.pdf (accessed 20 June 2020).

2 Ending restraint

An insider view

Cath Roper, Mary O'Hagan, Hamilton Kennedy and Helena Roennfeldt

Introduction

This chapter is written from the vantage point of people who have used mental health services in New Zealand and Australia. In it we expand the definition of restraint to mean anything that restricts a person's agency in the context of mental health care provision, and we call for the elimination of all forms of direct restraint. We discuss direct and indirect restraint. Direct restraint encompasses restrictions on bodily integrity, such as physical, mechanical and chemical restraint. These are the types of restraint most usually regulated by law and discussed in the literature. We discuss direct restraints on freedom of movement and freedom to make one's own decisions. We also introduce a discussion of indirect, hidden restraint, which refers to restrictions on people's sense of self arising from, and interconnecting with, experiences of direct restraint. These include the oppressive, ongoing and cumulative negative impacts on self-hood from restraints on meaning-making, self-expression, hope and trust in oneself. We position dominant societal beliefs as sites that give rise to discrimination and oppression but that could be sites of potential transformation and hope.

In 2009, the National Mental Health Consumer and Carer Forum (the Forum) published its position statement on ending the use of all involuntary seclusion and restraint in mental health services throughout Australia (National Mental Health Consumer & Carer Forum 2009). The Forum was established in 2002 and is funded through state, territory and federal government contributions. Its members represent mental health consumers' and carers' concerns at government and professional committees, forums and events. According to the position statement, the Forum views any instance of restrictive interventions, such as seclusion and restraint, as indicating a service failure. The position statement's authors stress that seclusion and restraint should be eradicated and point out that they are used at unacceptably high levels in mental health services, are associated with human rights abuse, are not therapeutic, are avoidable, cause short- and long-term emotional damage to consumers and preclude relationships of trust and respect between consumers, carers and clinical staff (National Mental Health Consumer & Carer Forum 2009: 7). While we agree fully with these points, we will present additional ideas about restraint and its harms that take us more deeply into the case for ending all forms of direct restraint.

This chapter has three aims: to present ideas about restraint from an insider perspective that go beyond how 'restraint' is typically defined, providing a theoretical model depicting how various forms of restraint may intersect; to outline the harms of restraint; and to argue the need for the elimination of restraint. We close by examining what is needed to support a shift in community/social attitudes and reforms to health and social policy and the repeal of mental health laws that permit restraint.

Situating ourselves

As authors, there is a deep and direct connection between our own experiences with mental health systems and a desire to contribute our analyses and knowledge to the collective 'lived experience' evidence base, whether through activism, education, research, policy or legal change. In this chapter, we invite readers to position service-user/survivor knowledge as particular, embodied and necessary, without which knowledge claims would be partial (Webb 2010: 108). As 'insiders' we aim to reframe conventional ways of thinking about restraint and engage in 'speaking back' to clinical power, law and the academy, as well as speaking across, to each other. Linda Tuhiwai Smith (1999: 39), writing in the context of de-colonisation practices, provides us with tools to understand our own project:

> [W]e constantly collide with dominant views while we are attempting to transform our lives on a larger scale than our own localised circumstances. This means struggling to make sense of our own world while also attempting to transform what counts as important in the world of the powerful.

Claire Spivakovsky and colleagues (2018) highlight the cruciality of assessing any claims about coercion from the perspective of those who have experienced it. In parallel, this chapter is founded on the principle that restraint must be considered from the perspective of people who have experienced and have been affected by restraint. While the authors acknowledge the variety of views about restraint from people who have experienced it in the context of mental health services, we take the view that any legal system operating only on the category of people labelled 'mentally ill' is inherently discriminatory. Our position is founded on the principle of 'equal recognition before the law' as expressed in the *Convention on the Rights of Persons with Disabilities* (CRPD) (2007: Article 12). We agree with Bonnie Burstow's description of the institution of psychiatry as 'traumatising' (2003: 1314) on the part of the state, towards people it should be caring for. Burstow (2003: 1307) observes:

> Psychiatry alienates people from their capacity to name, invalidates people's conceptualizations, imposes a stigmatized identity on them, places them on

> paths not of their own choosing, deprives them of liberty, and imposes harmful treatments on them.

We also adopt Linda Steele's (2017) concept of 'lawful violence' in thinking about restraint occurring within institutions. She argues that restrictive practices such as restraint are forms of violence facilitated by law, explaining that, '[w]hile absence of an individual's consent typically characterises unlawful violence against that individual, restrictive practices are lawful' (Steele 2017: 5). Under mental health laws, restraint on agency can occur both within and beyond institutions. Community treatment orders, also known as compulsory treatment orders or outpatient commitment, allow people to be treated involuntarily while living in the community (Brophy et al. 2018). In practice, this means a person must keep appointments and comply with mandated treatment or risk being readmitted to hospital.

We urge an end to calls for 'best practice' in the *reduction* of restrictive practices such as restraint and instead call for its *elimination*. We accordingly argue for practices that support people's self-agency, relationships and life opportunities, both within health and welfare services and within our communities, that would ultimately support the repeal of inherently discriminatory mental health laws legalising restraint practices.

Background

Australia's first national statement about safety improvement in mental health, endorsed in 2005, was the *National Safety Priorities in Mental Health: A National Plan For Reducing Harm.* This held (National Mental Health Working Group 2005: 17):

> [t]he goal of the Plan is to reduce the use of these interventions, and the adverse events that accompany them . . . . There is a close relationship between the use of restraint and seclusion and serious adverse events. The known adverse events associated with use of restraint and seclusion include dehydration, choking, circulatory and skin problems, loss of muscle strength and mobility, pressure sores, incontinence and injury from associated physical/mechanical restraint, injury from other patients, increased psychological distress and, in rare circumstances, death.

Although it has been mandatory for all Australian states and territories to report instances and duration of seclusion, it was only in 2017 that some form of data was required to be kept on restraint and only in some of these jurisdictions. However, due to significant differences between these jurisdictions on how restraint is defined, it is very difficult to compare data (Australian Institute of Health and Welfare (AIHW) 2018). The Australian Institute of Health and Welfare (2018) reported that there had been 13,321 physical restraint events (8.3 per 1,000 bed days) and 1,479 mechanical restraint events (0.9 per 1,000 bed days) in the 2016/17 period across Australia's mental health services.

Minority groups and restraint

Several studies have indicated that minority groups are over-represented in mental health, judicial and other health and welfare systems. A pernicious mix of racial stereotyping and staff fears is implicated (McKeown et al. 2019). A New Zealand Ministry of Health (2015) report found that Māori were three and a half times more likely to be subject to a community treatment order, and secluded almost four times more, than non-Māori. An audit of antipsychotic drug usage across Auckland indicated that Māori and Pacific people were prescribed higher doses of antipsychotic drugs than Europeans and were more likely to be on long acting antipsychotic regimes (Tapsell and Mellsop 2007). Similar statistics for Aboriginal Australians are not known, however, the rate of hospitalisations in Australia of Indigenous people for mental health-related conditions was twice the rate for non-Indigenous people (AIHW 2015).

Defining restraint

While there is variation in how different jurisdictions define 'restraint', mental health legislation makes lawful, usually as a 'last resort', restrictions to people's freedom of movement, bodily integrity and decision-making. In legislation, restraint is typically categorised into physical, mechanical and sometimes chemical restraint. In some cases, definitions include environmental (such as seclusion) and emotional/psychological restraint (see McSherry and Maker in Chapter 1 in this volume).

The New Zealand Health and Disability General Standard (2008a) defines restraint as 'the use of any intervention by a service provider that limits a consumer's freedom of movement' (2008a: 30), including personal restraint (the use of one's own body to intentionally limit the movement of a service user), physical restraint (the use of furniture, devices or equipment to limit movement; for example, belts on chairs) and environmental restraint (restricting access to the environment; for example, locked doors). The New Zealand Restraint Minimisation Standard (2008b) also includes chemical restraint (defined as various medicines used, to ensure compliance and to render the person incapable of resistance, rather than for therapeutic purposes). Unusually, the jurisdiction of Pennsylvania in the United States regulates 'psychological restraints' which are defined as including 'those therapeutic regimes or programs which involve the withholding of privileges and participation in activities' (Roper, McSherry and Brophy 2015: 299). This position aligns with the perspective of the authors in terms of the need to consider 'hidden' forms of restraint and underscores the necessity of including consumers' personal experiences of restraint in defining what it comprises, in order to gain the fullest possible picture.

In a 2014 research study commissioned by Australia's National Mental Health Commission and conducted by the Melbourne Social Equity Institute, separate focus groups were held with consumers and carers on their experiences and opinions about seclusion and restraint. This research resulted in a report

(Melbourne Social Equity Institute 2014), as well as several articles including one by Roper, McSherry and Brophy (2015). The following extract (Roper, McSherry and Brophy 2015: 300) demonstrates what is meant by emotional restraint and how it can be experienced as the exercising of seemingly omniscient and perhaps arbitrary power:

> so I think it is that, I think it's about a threat as well, I think it can be about just that threat, that knowledge, that you can have power taken from you. That's to me the essence of it, it's the power, the power differential that comes into play. It's something that you have no control over whatever it is and just the threat of it can screw you or it can coerce you to do things that you don't want or that . . . aren't going to be okay for you.

Table 2.1 sets out the types and examples of various forms of restraint that might be experienced by service users matched with examples of definitions of these practices found in Australian policies and legislation.

It is important to note that voluntary patients too, are impacted by the 'shadow of compulsion' engendered by the operation of mental health laws that allow others to make treatment decisions. As Fennell (2010: 24) explains:

> Detention, forcible treatment without consent, seclusion and restraint are the ultimate mechanisms of clinical power. A person may consent to treatment or to remain in hospital if they know that they will be compelled in the event of refusal. Compliance in the shadow of compulsion is an important feature of the psychiatric system.

All these forms of restraint are interventions permitted in mental health settings.

There is no evidence to demonstrate that they are effective in maintaining safety or controlling behaviour, despite being in common use (Said and Kautz 2013; Maker and McSherry 2019). It is well known that many instances of violence in acute mental health settings occur at the point of carrying out restrictive interventions. Increasingly, it is being recognised that seclusion is never therapeutic, but is a way of managing environments. The same discourse can be marshalled in support of practices aimed at eliminating restraint. This is a powerful platform from which to argue the need for change. New Zealand's guide on eliminating restraint states, '[t]his guidance is underpinned by the belief that the use of personal restraint is an adverse event in mental health inpatient settings' (Te Pou o Te Whakaaro Nui 2015: 4).

In the next section, we present a model that conceptualises restraint and associated harms from an insider perspective. While the model does incorporate forms of restraint already discussed, it adds additional forms, such as restraint on our minds, our decision-making and our freedom of movement and the impact of these on one's sense of self. The intention of the model is to allow consideration of cumulative impacts of restraint through an experiential lens.

Table 2.1 Examples of various forms of restraint defined in Australian law

Type	*Definition*	*Examples*
Physical restraint	'[B]odily force that controls a person's freedom of movement' (*Mental Health Act* 2013 (Tas): section 3)	Being held down ('take downs'); having hands placed on one's person. Use of suicide smocks, mittens so a person cannot scratch or remove treatment tubes, or 'spit hoods'.
Mechanical restraint	'[A] device that controls a person's freedom of movement' (*Mental Health Act* 2013 (Tas): section 3)	Straps, belts, harnesses, manacles, restraint vests or bedding being used to secure a person; being tied to a chair or gurney.
Environmental restraint	'[U]se of physical barriers, such as locks or padlocks, or enforceable limits or boundaries beyond normal community practices to limit a person's access to items, activities, or experiences, for the purpose of managing a risk or behaviour of concern' (New South Wales government undated)	Seclusion, when a person is deliberately confined alone in a room or area they cannot freely exit; when a staff member blocks a doorway; use of physical barriers; use of locks or padlocks; being in a locked ward with limited access to the outside world; enforceable limits or boundaries beyond normal community practices to limit a person's access to items, activities, or experiences for the purpose of managing a risk or behaviour of concern.
Chemical restraint	'[M]edication given primarily to control a person's behaviour, not to treat a mental illness or physical condition' (*Mental Health Act* 2013 (Tas): section 3)	Being given 'pro re nata' (as needed) medication instead of being offered an opportunity to talk or do an activity; being sedated prior to being secluded; being given medication when a person is upset, frustrated, overwhelmed; medication designed to sedate a person.
Emotional/ psychological restraint	'[T]he individual consumer is conditioned to such an extent that there is a loss of confidence in being able to express their views openly and honestly to clinical staff for fear of the consequences' (National Mental Health Consumer and Carer Forum 2009: 6)	Withholding privileges and participation in activities; being told one cannot go on leave unless one behaves in a particular way; threatening patients with seclusion as a way to control behavior; failing to give secluded patients access to toilets.

Intersectionality of restraint

This section presents a theoretical model depicting direct restraint and indirect restraint. Direct restraint refers to control and force on bodies, restraint on minds and restraints on other freedoms, such as freedom of movement and decision-making. Indirect restraint is more hidden and refers to restraints on self-hood including: forced acceptance of diagnosis; restraints to meaning-making, self-expression, hope and trust in oneself. The model positions the dominance of a Western biogenetic paradigm as (i) integral to the rationale for having mental health laws, with the potential for negative consequences on (ii) people's agency and (iii) sense of self. The top layer of Figure 2.1 depicts dominant societal beliefs which can either positively or negatively contribute to people's sense of self and actual opportunities in life.

The model depicts restraint from an insider perspective, enabling consideration of the 'intersectionality' of restraint – how various forms of restraint might interact and what the cumulative negative impacts might be. The upturned pyramid is intended to express the full weight of experienced restraint bearing down on bodies, which are depicted at the base of the diagram.

Direct restraint

Restraint on bodies and associated harms

Restraint on bodies includes restrictions in hospital settings such as 'take downs', 'code greys', use of belts or straps to secure people and putting 'hands on' people. Associated harms of such practices include pain, injury and death. The

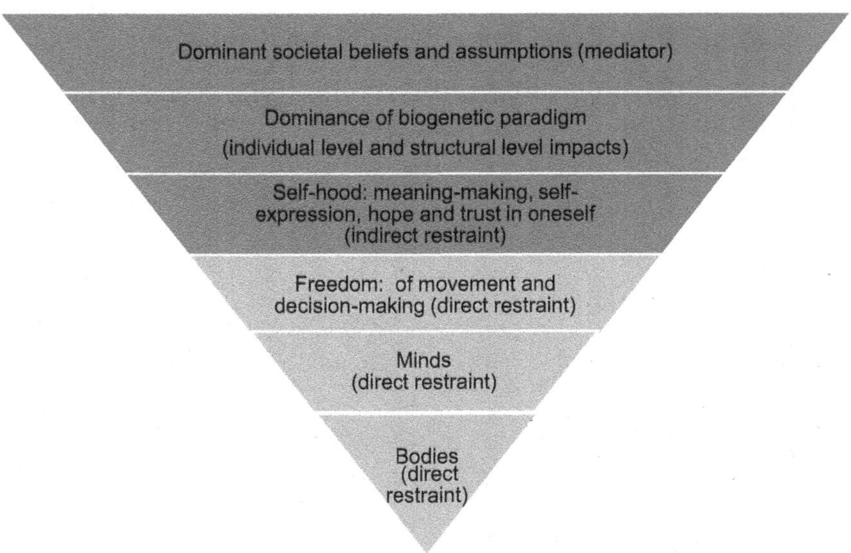

Figure 2.1 The intersectionality of restraint

experience of restraint can also result in feelings of powerlessness and shame. According to lived experience shared by 'Finley' (Anonymous Oral Communication to Authors 2019):

> Me and people I have worked for/with which has always been young people quite often talked about it being deeply embarrassing, disempowering and leaving a kind of psychic wound on them.

Violations of human dignity and autonomy are often linked to violations of bodily integrity which, in turn, have an impact on identity, voice and recognition (Oliver 2011: 99). In the following quote, taken from the Melbourne Social Equity Institute's 2014 study (Roper, McSherry and Brophy 2015: 299), the violation of the body described is also a vivid depiction of literal and symbolic loss of identity:

> A whole heap of people come around, I've got one on each arm, one behind here, one on this leg, get carried through the hall and then a big jab in the leg, and then when you wake up again suddenly all these people rush at you and it's another jab in the leg . . . some of these times I actually didn't even know who I was, I'd had this big amnesia of who, what my name was, where I was, what was going on.

The vividness of this experience is partly captured through its retelling in the present tense. The hearer is brought sharply into the process of being carried through the hall, the loss of consciousness and the disorientation upon waking up and 'suddenly all these people rush at you'. The phrase 'some of these times' points to this being just one occasion in many.

Re-traumatisation

Between 70 and 90 per cent of people who come to the attention of mental health services have already lived through multiple experiences of childhood and adult trauma (Varese et al. 2012; Mauritz et al. 2013). The use of seclusion and restraint with inpatients who have histories of childhood trauma may result in re-traumatisation. For example, it has been documented that many abuse survivors experienced being restrained, locked in cupboards, car trunks/boots and rooms (Hammer et al. 2011). It is shocking, then, to note that it is this group of people who are most vulnerable to the highest levels of seclusion and restraint during hospital stays (Bonner et al. 2002; Frueh et al. 2005; Hammer et al. 2011).

The term 'sanctuary trauma' has been coined to describe incidents within inpatient settings that meet the DSM-IV criteria for a traumatic event. In one study, 47 per cent of participants experienced sanctuary trauma whilst in hospital (Cusack et al. 2003). Those who had experienced previous trauma in their life reported higher levels of distress from the hospital experience and had more negative experiences during their admission when compared with those who had not. According to lived experience shared by 'Finley' (Anonymous Oral Communication to Authors 2019):

> My ongoing reoccurrences of madness place me back in environments where I am physically and chemically restrained. This is because I can be upset, confused or angry and restraint is considered the easiest way to work with me. I did not consent to these restrictions. There are other better ways of engaging with me.

'Sanctuary harm' refers to harms associated with an inpatient stay. Studies report a high proportion of inpatients witnessing aggressive incidents or traumatic events, whether these are interactions between staff and patients or inter-patient (Frueh et al. 2005; Robins et al. 2005; Grubaugh et al. 2007). The traumatic effects of restraint practices are long-standing and invariably psychologically damaging to patients and may also have negative impacts on staff (Bonner et al. 2002). Physical, mechanical and chemical restraint are experienced overwhelmingly as negative, associated with immediate worsening of distress and intense feelings such as despair, shame, terror and rage. Clearly alternatives to an environment where restraint occurs are necessary.

Restraint on minds and associated harms

Examples of restraints on our thinking include effects of medication, or on memory because of electro convulsive treatment, or the numbness of being 'acuphased', which is a practice where a fast-acting antipsychotic medication is administered (sometimes by force) as an intramuscular injection. The effect is often complete sedation. To be able to think freely is surely the most sacrosanct of all freedoms, and to interfere with this without a person's consent is both ethically and physically harmful. In the words of one former patient, as shared byRoper and Gooding (2018: 156):

> The drugs took away sensation, slowed thinking and caused internal alienation which was horrifying, like missing myself, watching myself die. Did they want part of me to die? Was it some form of eugenics?

People report being so groggy from medication that they are unable to work, study, look after their children, or get enjoyment from usual activities.

Restraint on freedoms and associated harms

Restraint on personal freedom includes restraint on freedom of movement, restraint on being able to make your own decisions and restraint on the freedom to act. Examples of losing freedom of movement include locked doors, seclusion and denial of leave. Other restraints on freedom include being divided from loved ones, having personal items scrutinised, loss of freedom to communicate through having electronic devices confiscated and obeisance to other freedom-limiting institutional rules. Loss of decision-making freedom under mental health laws includes being forbidden to make our own decisions and being unable to have refusals respected. The following quote from Roper, McSherry and Brophy's study (2015: 300) indicates the loss of agency of a person who has been trying to discontinue medication which was initiated without her consent:

> I just wanted to say something about medication too, you were talking about that's a form of restraint too when you get hospitalised. I was put on, because I was going through a psychotic episode, I was put on antipsychotics and I've remained on those since I've been hospitalised, and I haven't been able to get off them because of the side effects of trying to come off, and they've been too difficult for me to deal with, so I now feel restrained in my lifestyle because I'm taking this medication which I don't need any more but I can't get off them.

This person is 'restrained' in the way they want to live, their wishes thwarted in a catch-22 where efforts to cease medication are unsuccessful because of the medication withdrawal. It is not merely a single episode of interference with decision-making occurring within an institutional setting. Nor does it fit neatly into an example of interference with autonomy. Even though there is a sense that the person has the freedom legally to choose to discontinue medication, the person's freedom to live as they wish has been interfered with in ways that now seem permanent.

In the next section, the oppressive, ongoing and cumulative negative impacts on self-hood are discussed, from restraints on meaning-making, self-expression and hope to trust in oneself. We conceptualise these as 'indirect' restraints.

Indirect restraint and associated harms

Restraint and harms to self-hood

Harms to meaning-making – psychiatry enforcing its belief system

Restraint on sense of self includes forced acceptance of diagnosis, disqualification of our own ways of making meaning and loss of freedom to express individual opinions and emotions. This is significant within a mental health system where compliance and passivity seem to be preferred. Lisa Blackman (2007: 3) writes about the limited identities available to people:

> The non-compliant subject is not only the person who fails to take their psychotropic medication, but also the person who is unable or unwilling to take up a particular relationship to their mental health difficulties.

Whereas, Blackman (2007: 8) observes:

> The compliant subject is one who is able to declare themselves as suffering from a mental disorder. They are willing and able to position themselves as

> able to triumph over their affliction through the administering of drugs as both restoration and as a prophylactic.

Fleur Beaupert (2018) draws on the accounts of users/survivors of psychiatry to make the point that institutional psychiatry reorients people's own ways of making meaning and understanding their experiences. This leads on to the notion that institutional psychiatry and the worldview it adopts can radically alter someone's identity and even have a role in re-programming people's thoughts and opinions about themselves and their place in the world.

The constant scrutiny, monitoring, assessment and interference we are subjected to can affect our self-confidence and our sense of both self-efficacy and identity and prime us for accepting the institution's system of beliefs. Nikolas Rose (1989: 244) discusses the role of disclosure and surveillance which are primary activities in psychiatry and which may be considered as 'techniques' in the achievement of the 're-programming' to which Beaupert refers:

> In compelling, persuading and inciting subjects to disclose themselves, finer and more intimate regions of personal and interpersonal life come under surveillance and are opened up for expert judgment, and normative evaluation, for classification and correction.

Bonnie Burstow (2003: 1300) makes a similar point about the power of psychiatry to take away people's power to name their own experiences, and instead 'subject them to a naming controlled by a powerful international institution'.

Harms to self-expression

Harms to self-expression can occur via prolonged exposure to others making decisions for us, creating passivity through compliance (O'Hagan 2003), and can create a sense of not being entitled to, so not having or communicating, preferences. If our decision-making is consistently overridden, there is a risk of never experiencing 'full adult status and its expanded expectations of liberty' and thus a diminishment of belief in our power to take charge of our lives (O'Hagan 2003: 7). Inpatients who upon refusing treatment receive it involuntarily may develop particular identities marked by self-surveillance and mortification as they capitulate rather than resist in order to prevent further violence of forced administration of treatment (McKeown et al. 2019). People's self-confidence and independence can be restrained by paternalistic attitudes that place others' knowledge of what is wrong and what should be done above the person's insight (O'Hagan 2003).

Harms to sense of hope

Restraint to our sense of self extends to restraints on our citizenship occurring through loss of hope in our future, being discouraged to have aspirations and being told that we should not expect too much of ourselves, or that we will be on medication for the rest of our lives. As 'Finley' (Anonymous Oral Communication to Authors 2019) describes:

> My experiences of service use restriction are of profound disempowerment. Barely an adult and told that I was going to experience this 'illness' forever and that I would not recover. This is a kind of existential restriction, whereby I am not entitled to determine my own life and how it is. This, coupled with physical and mechanical restraint, rendered me useless. At that point I have been rendered both physically and psychologically useless.

Loss of hope can also be a consequence of being told you have a biological flaw (O'Hagan 2003), since there appears to be little that can be done to change one's destiny. Pat Deegan (1996: 92) calls such attitudes 'a prognosis of doom'.

Restraint on trust in oneself

Those of us who have been labelled as having 'mental illness' belong to a marginalised group, whose testimony is construed as fantasy rather than truth. As described by Maria Liegghio (2013: 126), individuals are '[r]endered incompetent, persons are disqualified as legitimate knowers and lose their epistemic agency, specifically losing their ability to speak on their own behalf and to be heard on their own terms and in their own styles'. To be given credence as a knower and teller is essential to human value, and when speakers are wronged in their capacity as knowers and tellers, it may interfere with their self-development, and they may be 'prevented from becoming who they are' (Fricker 2007: 5). We may be susceptible to doubting what we know, or even, *if* we know at all, as Roper (2018: 91) observes:

> once we have been psychiatrised, many of us internalise oppressive cultural ideologies, exposing us to an internal tyranny of 'sanity' in which the only allowable way to make meaning of our distress/Madness is medical, and the range of allowable behaviours shrink as we learn the exhausting arts of self-monitoring and censorship. Our sense of self crumbles, our way of being in the world, what we know, how we make meaning, is disparaged and wrong.

Although outside the scope of this chapter, we recognise there are myriad and interconnected cultural preferences, values, stereotypes, prejudices and discriminatory practices acting as restraints on the lives of individuals and groups. These attitudes and practices are created and recreated through the mechanism of othering people and reducing their human status (see also McSherry's discussion in Chapter 11 in this volume). However, we limit our discussion in the next section to the restraining impact of the biogenetic paradigm at individual and structural levels. As a social structure, the biogenetic paradigm functions as the rationale for mental health laws that engender forms of direct restraint and it is the dominant way of explaining and treating distress and unusual experiences. It is depicted as the second top layer of the restraint model presented in this chapter (see Figure 2.1) and has a bearing on all the other layers of restraint discussed so far.

Restraining impact of a biogenetic paradigm

The power of the biogenetic paradigm lies in its exclusivity as an interpretive frame, so that it appears to function as a 'natural truth'. In Western contexts, a biogenetic paradigm is the dominant way of explaining and treating people's distress and unusual experiences and these are viewed as 'health problems'. Mental health laws both emerge from this paradigm and legitimise it through the idea of 'necessary treatment' for 'illnesses' people may not realise they have due to lack of 'insight' (O'Hagan 2003). Regardless of whether or not a biogenetic explanation tallies with how we make sense of our experiences, we are nevertheless subjected to it, virtually to the exclusion of any alternative framework. On a practical level, this means that departure from biogenetic explanations for one's experiences of distress, either consciously or unconsciously, may incur suspicion, fear, outright hostility or alienation from others.

Individual level

The biogenetic paradigm acts as a form of restraint on individuals in that it limits available ways people have to understand their own experiences and may inspire shame in a person who does not share these beliefs. As Fleur Beaupert (2018: 2) writes, '[t]he processes by which psychiatry and the mental health paradigm push aside, diminish and nullify other understandings of experiences and interactions that are labelled as "mental illness", are increasingly recognised as involving symbolic violence'. We are not saying that medical explanations do not offer solace and self-direction for *individuals*, far from it, but we are pointing to ways in which unitary social beliefs can eclipse or even forbid other ways of being and knowing and can thus be experienced as deeply restraining.

As an example, Lisa Blackman (2007) discusses how under a biogenetic paradigm, available identities fall into victim/victor categories, where people are either pitied for their 'suffering' or lauded for 'overcoming' the odds (often known as 'inspiration porn'). When 'disease' discourses are the sole available way to understand experience, the holding of divergent views may push individuals into risky territory where their thoughts, experiences and testimony may be used against them in a catch-22 cycle as 'evidence' of 'lack of insight' and 'illness' (Hamilton and Roper 2006). As observed by Cath Roper and Piers Gooding (2018: 157–58):

> The State took away language, thieving meaning away and re-presenting it – in this case, as illness and malady. Between the State and the surrounding culture is a mutually agreed illness narrative concerning people like me. In that story, one's thinking is faulty, one's imagination is not to be trusted, one's feelings, unfathomable. One is *essentially* 'apart from' others.

Structural level

One consequence of the dominance of a biogenetic health paradigm is that it is difficult to foreground the human rights or ethical losses people experience when governed by mental health laws. This is because the paradigm is built on and reinforces social acceptance that mental health laws are needed to uphold people's 'right to health', displacing other concerns. Significantly, under a totalising biogenetic paradigm, the beliefs, traditions and healing concepts of minority and Indigenous cultures or indeed any alternative healing practices may not only be disqualified, but they may be interpreted as 'symptoms' of illness.

For instance, Indigenous world views and cultural practices may be 'colonised', misunderstood or marginalised within broader societal beliefs. As an example, in the cultures of many Indigenous groups, the spirits of the dead and living are real, and past and present are one (Spencer 1983 cited in Brown 2001: 31). An Indigenous person who hears or dreams the voices of their ancestors may be diagnosed and treated as a person with mental illness, which fails to recognise and respond to cultural norms and inhibits the gift of that person and their role within their community.

A biogenetic paradigm suggests people have individual maladies, without much reference to their spiritual, social, economic and political contexts. Again, taking Indigenous experiences as an example, there may be complex and ongoing consequences of griefs and losses due to factors such as dispossession, oppression, racism, environmental circumstances, economic factors, stress, trauma, grief, cultural genocide, psychological processes and ill-health which then impact on social and emotional wellbeing (Swan and Raphael 1995 cited in Brown 2001: 34). Staggeringly, in Australia, almost half (48 per cent) of Indigenous adults reported that either they or their relatives had been removed from their natural family (AIHW 2015). Clearly, to interpret such griefs and losses through a biogenetic lens, without consideration of a colonising context, would be a mistake. Paying attention to the spiritual, social, economic and political context of all people is vital to understanding their experience.

A potential, unfortunate consequence of a biogenetic lens is when processes of dehumanisation serve to legitimise restraint. Such processes involve the ongoing construction of a group of people as less than fully human. Dehumanisation involves viewing individuals through a particular lens, labelling them, othering and systematic exclusion, in which human beings are gradually rendered 'radically Other' (Oliver 2011: 89). Dehumanisation can be seen as a violation of two qualities that must be accorded all persons in order to perceive them as fully human: identity and community (Kelman 1973 in Oliver 2011: 87). To be dehumanised is to be excluded from the moral community, constructed as a particular kind of 'other' without moral responsibility, 'outside the scope of justice, and thus as a legitimate target for more active oppressions and exclusions' (Oliver 2011: 87).

Mental health laws are symbolic of dehumanisation because they create a legal space that is outside the scope of justice, where operations of human rights and ethics afforded other human beings are suspended. In turn, harm that befalls those outside the scope of justice 'does not prompt the concern, remorse, or outrage that occurs when those inside the scope of justice are harmed' (Opotow 1995: 347–48 in Oliver 2011: 87). These laws symbolically declare individuals governed by them to be 'morally irresponsible', and in the process, the laws are positioned as enabling the provision of benevolent and protective care. In the application of mental health laws, decisions about who gets to keep their human rights and who does not happen through someone else declaring whether or not we are capable of consenting to treatment. If deemed to lack capacity to consent, under mental health laws we are governed by this 'other' legal space, we are no longer part of the moral community, we are not moral, thinking persons, we have been legally defined as non-thinking, non-feeling. Perhaps the most important but challenging task of all (and for all), then, is to unmask and confront 'othering' attitudes towards people and groups with diverse ways of experiencing the world and expressing themselves.

Eliminating restraint

Why 'reducing' is not enough

Annual national seclusion and restraint forums have been held in Australia since 2006, during which time, the language of 'reducing' has sat alongside 'elimination'. The discourse of 'reducing' does not fundamentally challenge people's beliefs about what is possible in the real world. It instead still presumes the 'necessary evil' discourse, signalling a failure of imagination and leadership guaranteeing services will never fully eliminate such practices. Beneath the belief that restraint might be necessary in some cases lie fears and anxieties which in turn perpetuate an unsafe environment. We argue that 'reducing' is not the right path to humane and human rights informed service provision and will never address the multiple and cumulative harms engendered by experience of restraint. If communities want to ensure that services provide meaningful support that does not harm, then elimination of restraint is necessary.

Advocacy efforts, and policy and legal reform such as the influence of the CRPD, have resulted in increased recognition of the negative consequences of the use of restraint and its conceptualisation as an infringement on human rights (Maker and McSherry 2019: 31). Debates about eliminating restraint at least need to recalibrate to analysis of such practices as human rights breaches, rather than 'practices to ensure safety'. Restraints on bodily integrity and violations of other human rights and freedoms in the context of mental health service provision are considered in this chapter to be harmful, irrespective of questions of 'justification'. As an example, restraining a person's liberty through keeping them in an intensive care space, when it is not their wish, when it is feared they might otherwise leave and take their own life, would routinely be justified as life-saving. However, it is also a breach of their autonomy, human rights and freedom of movement and may be crushing to a person's sense of self, their dignity and self-respect. These losses cannot be brushed under the carpet. They are not cancelled out due to a particular outcome – the losses need to be counted, regretted and ameliorated.

Many legal scholars and consumer/survivor activists internationally are engaged in campaigns for the abolition of mental health laws on human rights and moral grounds (Minkowitz 2007, 2010). The United Nations High Commissioner for Human Rights (2017: 10) states that:

> Many practices within mental health institutions also contravene articles 15, 16 and 17 of the Convention on the Rights of Persons with Disabilities. Forced treatment and other harmful practices, such as solitary confinement, forced sterilization, the use of restraints, forced medication and overmedication (including medication administered under false pretences and without disclosure of risks) not only violate the right to free and informed consent, but constitute ill-treatment and may amount to torture. Accordingly, the Committee on the Rights of Persons with Disabilities has called for the abolition of all involuntary treatment and the adoption of measures to ensure that health services, including all mental health services, are based on the free and informed consent of the person concerned. The Committee has also urged the elimination of the use of seclusion and restraints, both physical and pharmacological.

Dyann Ross (2018) reflects that the current focus of risk discourse on the violence of service users rather than on interrogating what might be classed as state sanctioned torture, or inhuman and degrading treatment, serves to stymie the asking of hard questions like: who gains from the ongoing use of containment practices? We have argued the need to eliminate restraint on people's bodies and minds, on their freedom of movement and on their decision-making on grounds of cumulative negative impacts. These negative impacts include violations of people's human rights, de-humanisation, likelihood of re-traumatisation and further harms to self-hood.

What next?

We think there are steps that can be taken immediately to work towards the goal of elimination, such as: acknowledging the range of human rights breaches occurring under mental health legislation and ameliorating their negative consequences. Sophie Oliver (2011: 97) urges us to think of dignity as:

> embodied calls for a politics or ethics of witnessing that acknowledges and listens to the lived experience of those who have been excluded and dehumanized both past and present; it calls for us all, as bystanders and spectators of suffering, to attend to the concrete and individual humanity of the one who suffers and to reclaim, through recognition, their status as members of the human community.

The use of restraint is still debated as if it is acceptable within the 'Overton window'. The Overton window is the range of ideas which are acceptable in debates and discourse. Demanding/desiring elimination can bring us closer to it happening in reality even just by bringing it into discourse.

There are a number of consumer led or consumer endorsed crisis intervention programmes and initiatives that aim to not use restraint (Grey and O'Hagan 2015; Gooding et al. 2018). These provide important alternatives but also guidance for other services to learn from. However, we maintain that restraint practices cannot be eliminated while mental health laws are in existence, psychiatry dominates service provision, there is widespread community fear and prejudice and service users remain at the periphery of decision-making about solutions.

In terms of already – existing models, according to a recent study undertaken in the Australian state of Victoria, a pathway for reducing restrictive interventions can be found in Safewards, a model and a suite of interventions designed to improve ward safety for consumers and staff (Fletcher et al. 2019; see Brophy, Fletcher and Hamilton in Chapter 12 in this volume). Models such as this may help to eliminate restraint. Given the prevalence of trauma in the lives of people using mental health services, it is important that those services do not cause further harm to them. The sanctuary harm and sanctuary trauma frameworks (Frueh et al. 2000) designed to observe and measure traumatisation and re-traumatisation within hospitals could be used to assist in eliminating restraint practices. Many users of mental health services also look to the CRPD as a foundational advocacy document, articulating restrictive interventions as human rights breaches constituting acts of torture and inhumane treatment and articulating principles that could underpin the repeal of mental health legislation.

Fast forward to 2050: finally, the mad are free

Extract from the Australian and New Zealand Chronicle, 1 June 2050:

> *This year, we are celebrating a ground-breaking book chapter written 30 years ago by people with lived experience of mental distress that called for an end to restraint in mental health services. These authors expanded the definition of restraint beyond physical, environmental and chemical restraint to include restraint to self-hood imposed by dominant societal and psychiatric beliefs, such as restraint on meaning-making, self-expression, hope and trust in oneself. The establishment's response at the time ranged from patronising scepticism to angry derision. However, several forces were gathering for the end of restraint; it turns out these authors were on the right side of history. Our investigators take a historical look, to trace the momentum for coercion and restraint-free mental health services.*
>
> *The seeds of coercion and restraint-free mental health services were planted in the modern democratic principles of equality and freedom. Initially reserved for property-owning white men, these rights lay dormant for people with mental distress for over 200 years. They were eventually fertilised by a combination of social justice movements, system transformation, power shifts, more supportive communities and legal reforms.*
>
> *In New Zealand, the end of restraint was formalised by a suite of legislative changes dubbed as the 'care without coercion' laws that were passed by*

Parliament in 2040. Other jurisdictions have started to follow New Zealand's lead. In many countries, alongside the repeal of Mental Health Acts and insanity defence laws, new supported decision-making laws are being passed. These changes have been described as the biggest transformation in governments' responses to people who use mental health services in over 200 years, ensuring for the first time that they have equal rights to freedom as other citizens. Mental health services could no longer rely on special coercive powers to physically, mechanically, environmentally or chemically restrain people.

Key historical events leading to the abolition of all forms of restraint

In the 1970s the psychiatric survivor movement protested the use of force in mental health services. These protests seemingly went unheard until the Convention on the Rights of Persons with Disabilities (CRPD) was adopted by the United Nations General Assembly in 2006. The CRPD stated that persons with disabilities (including people with mental distress) were equal before the law and should not be deprived of their liberty because of their disability. Despite the clarity of the CRPD and the subsequent commentary on the issue of liberty, it took decades for countries that had ratified the treaty to achieve compliance.

Then in the 2020s people who had used mental health services, and their supporters, built international pressure for psychiatry to publicly acknowledge the harm it had done to people, often in non-consenting situations involving restraint. Finally, in 2037 the World Psychiatric Association issued a public acknowledgement of harm, with specific mention of Indigenous people, ethnic minorities and Rainbow people. Psychiatric associations around the world followed suit, often in association with their governments. These acknowledgements drew a line in the sand which signalled a genuine commitment for psychiatry to work towards a harm-free future.

Restraint and coercive interventions were used most on Indigenous peoples and ethnic minorities. In New Zealand, Māori made a series of claims in the 2020s that the high levels of restraint for Māori and other health related inequities were in breach of Te Tiriti o Waitangi. The Crown accepted these claims and responded by reducing restraint and coercive interventions through structural changes over the next decade, not just for Māori but for all New Zealanders.

During the last 30 years a major reorientation in services for people with mental distress has had a significant impact on reducing restraint. When the book chapter calling for the end to restraint was written, psychiatry was still the hub of the system, dominating discourse through a narrow biogenetic lens, managing risk on behalf of the community and using up most of the available resources. Today psychiatry is a 'bit player' as one of the spokes of the system, while multiple sectors and communities occupy the hub to share in the planning, funding and delivery of services. In 2020 the predominant response people using services had access to was psychiatric drugs. Now, people also have reliable access to talking therapies, peer support, cultural support, education and employment support, housing, income support and community crisis responses. Over the last 30 years, psychiatric hospital beds in Western countries such as Australia and New Zealand reduced by 90 per cent. This alone was responsible for a huge reduction in physical and environmental restraints. And psychiatry's soul searching over the harm it has done, as well as its loss of dominance in the system, have also reduced what the authors of the chapter written thirty years ago called 'restraint to self-hood'.

Alongside the reorientation of services, New Zealand started a programme in 1997 to reduce prejudice and discrimination against people with mental distress, which received a major funding boost in the early 2020s. By the 2030s this influential programme was adopted internationally in many countries. The effect was to gradually soften community prejudice, enabling an informed public discussion on human rights for people with mental distress. Community expectations that mental health services must be held accountable for the self-or-other harming actions by people with mental distress were replaced by an attitude that they are responsible actors who, like other citizens, may or may not be acting under mitigating circumstances.

Holistic services and more positive community attitudes also delivered better life and health outcomes. In countries that have implemented these changes over the last 30 years, unemployment rates of people with mental distress have dropped by as much as 50 per cent. Life expectancy is now only five years less than average, instead of 25 years less. Early attempts to reduce or end restraint inevitably failed because they focused on appealing to ethics, reason and evidence and on changing the practices of individuals and workforces without changing the larger settings they operated in. The experience of the last 30 years has taught us that the end of coercion and restraint required much more than good intentions and good practices – it required the reorientation of the whole system, an informed community and above all laws that don't allow it.

Conclusion

This chapter has relied on the vantage point of people who have used mental health services in New Zealand and Australia to expand the definition of restraint and to call for its elimination in all its forms. We have outlined some of the immediate steps that can be taken to eliminate restraint and set out a vision for 2050 which we trust is as inevitable as the abolition of slavery, the enfranchisement of women and gay marriage.

References

Legislation and treaties

Convention on the Rights of Persons with Disabilities (CRPD) (2007) Opened for signature 30 March, UN Doc A/61/611 (entered into force 3 May 2008).

Mental Health Act 2013 (Tas).

Books, journal articles and other texts

Australian Institute of Health and Welfare (AIHW) (2015) *The Health and Welfare of Australia's Aboriginal and Torres Strait Islander Peoples: 2015*, Canberra: AIHW. Available www.aihw.gov.au/reports/indigenous-health-welfare/indigenous-health-welfare-2015/contents/table-of-contents (accessed 20 June 2020).

Australian Institute of Health and Welfare (AIHW) (2018) *Mental Health Services–In Brief 2018*, Canberra: AIHW. Available www.aihw.gov.au/reports/mental-health-services/mental-health-services-in-australia-in-brief-2018/contents/table-of-contents (accessed 20 June 2020).

Beaupert, F. (2018) 'Freedom of Opinion and Expression: From the Perspective of Psychosocial Disability and Madness', *Laws*, 7(3): 1–26.

Blackman, L. (2007) 'Psychiatric Culture and Bodies of Resistance', *Body & Society*, 13(2): 1–23.

Bonner, G., Lowe, T., Rawcliffe, D. and Wellman, N. (2002) 'Trauma for All: A Pilot Study of the Subjective Experience of Physical Restraint for Mental Health Inpatients and Staff in the UK', *Journal of Psychiatric and Mental Health Nursing*, 9(4): 465–73.

Brophy, L., Edan, V., Gooding, P., McSherry, B., Burkett, T., Carey, S., Carroll, A., Callaghan, S., Finch, A., Hansford, M., Hanson, S., Kisely, S., Lawn, S., Light, E., Maher, S., Patel, G., Ryan, C.J., Saltmarsh, K., Stratford, A., Tellez, J.J., Toko, M. and Weller, P. (2018) 'Community Treatment Orders: Towards a New Research Agenda', *Australasian Psychiatry*, 26(3): 299–302.

Brown, R. (2001) 'Australian Indigenous Mental Health', *Australian and New Zealand Journal of Mental Health Nursing*, 10: 33–41.

Burstow, B. (2003) 'Toward a Radical Understanding of Trauma and Trauma Work', *Violence Against Women*, 9(11): 1293–317.

Cusack, K.J., Freuh, B.C., Hiers, T., Suffoletta-Maierle, S. and Bennett, S. (2003) 'Trauma Within the Psychiatric Setting: A Preliminary Empirical Report', *Administration and Policy in Mental Health*, 30(5): 453–60.

Deegan, P. (1996) 'Recovery as a Journey of the Heart', *Psychiatric Rehabilitation Journal*, 19(3): 91–97.

Fennell, P. (2010) 'Institutionalising the Community: The Codification of Clinical Authority and the Limits of Rights-based Approaches', in B. McSherry and P. Weller (eds) *Rethinking Rights-based Mental Health Laws*, Oxford: Hart Publishing, 13–46.

Finley (2019) 'Anonymous Oral Communication to Authors', March.

Fletcher, J., Buchanan-Hagen, S., Brophy, L., Kinner, S.A. and Hamilton, B. (2019) 'Consumer Perspectives of Safewards Impact in Acute Inpatient Mental Health Wards in Victoria, Australia', *Frontiers in Psychiatry*, 10(461): 1–11.

Fricker, M. (2007) *Epistemic Injustice: Power and the Ethics of Knowing*, New York: Oxford University Press.

Frueh, B.C., Dalton, M.E., Johnson, M.R., Hiers, T.J., Gold, P.B., Magruder, K.M. and Santos, A.B. (2000) 'Trauma Within the Psychiatric Setting: Conceptual Framework, Research Directions, and Policy Implications', *Administration and Policy in Mental Health*, 28(2): 147–54.

Frueh, B.C., Knapp, R.G., Cusack, K.J., Grubaugh, A.L., Sauvageot, J.A., Cousins, V.C., Yim, E., Robins, C.S., Monnier, J. and Hiers, T.G. (2005) 'Patients' Reports of Traumatic or Harmful Experiences Within the Psychiatric Setting', *Psychiatric Services*, 56(9): 1123–33.

Gooding, P., McSherry, B., Roper, C. and Grey, F. (2018) *Alternatives to Coercion in Mental Health Settings: A Literature Review*, Melbourne: Melbourne Social Equity Institute, University of Melbourne. Available https://socialequity.unimelb.edu.au/__data/assets/pdf_file/0012/2898525/Alternatives-to-Coercion-Literature-Review-Melbourne-Social-Equity-Institute.pdf (accessed 20 June 2020).

Grey, F. and O'Hagan, M. (2015) *The Effectiveness of Services Led or Run by Consumers in Mental Health: Rapid Review of Evidence for Recovery-Oriented Outcomes: An Evidence Check Rapid Review Brokered by the Sax Institute (www.saxinstitute.org.au) for the Mental Health Commission of New South Wales*. Available https://nswmentalhealthcommission.com.au/resources/the-effectiveness-of-services-led-or-run-by-consumers-in-mental-health-rapid-review-of (accessed 20 June 2020).

Grubaugh, A.L., Frueh, B.C., Zinzow, H.M., Cusack, K.J. and Wells, C. (2007) 'Patients' Perceptions of Care and Safety within Psychiatric Settings', *Psychological Services*, 4(3): 193–201.

Hamilton, B. and Roper, C. (2006) 'Troubling "Insight": Power and Possibilities in Mental Health Care', *Journal of Psychiatric and Mental Health Nursing*, 13(4): 416–22.

Hammer, J.H., Springer, J., Beck, N.C., Menditto, A. and Coleman, J. (2011) 'The Relationship Between Seclusion and Restraint Use and Childhood Abuse Among Psychiatric Inpatients', *Journal of Interpersonal Violence*, 26(3): 567–79.

Liegghio, M. (2013) 'A Denial of Being: Psychiatrisation as Epistemic Violence', in B.A. LeFrancois, R. Menzies and G. Reaume (eds) *Mad Matters: A Critical Reader in Canadian Mad Studies*, Toronto: Canadian Scholars' Press, 122–29.

Maker, Y. and McSherry, B. (2019) 'Regulating Restraint Use in Mental Health and Aged Care Settings: Lessons from the Oakden Scandal', *Alternative Law Journal*, 44(1): 29–36.

Mauritz, M., Goossens, P., Draijer, N. and van Achterberg, T. (2013) 'Prevalence of Interpersonal Trauma Exposure and Trauma-related Disorders in Severe Mental Illness', *European Journal of Psychotraumatology*, 4(19985): 1–15.

McKeown, M., Scholes, A., Jones, F. and Aindow, W. (2019) 'Coercive Practices in Mental Health Services: Stories of Recalcitrance, Resistance, and Legitimation', in A. Daley, L. Costa and P. Beresford (eds) *Madness, Violence and Power, A Critical Collection*, Toronto: University of Toronto Press, 263–85.

Melbourne Social Equity Institute (2014) *Seclusion and Restraint Project Report*, Melbourne: University of Melbourne. Available https://socialequity.unimelb.edu.au/__data/assets/pdf_file/0017/2004722/Seclusion-and-Restraint-report.PDF (accessed 20 June 2020).

Ministry of Health (NZ) (2015) *Office of the Director of Mental Health Annual Report 2014*. Wellington: Ministry of Health. Available www.health.govt.nz/publication/office-director-mental-health-annual-report-2014 (accessed 20 June 2020).

Minkowitz, T. (2007) 'The United Nations Convention on the Rights of Persons with Disabilities and the Right to be Free from Nonconsensual Psychiatric Interventions', *Syracuse Journal of International Law and Commerce*, 34(2): 405–28.

Minkowitz, T. (2010) 'Abolishing Mental Health Laws to Comply with the Convention on the Rights of Persons with Disabilities', in B. McSherry and P. Weller (eds) *Rethinking Rights-based Mental Health Laws*, Oxford: Hart Publishing, 151–77.

National Mental Health Consumer & Carer Forum (2009) *Ending Seclusion and Restraint in Australian Mental Health Services*. Available https://nmhccf.org.au/sites/default/files/docs/seclusion_restraint.pdf (accessed 20 June 2020).

National Mental Health Working Group (2005) *National Safety Priorities in Mental Health: A National Plan for Reducing Harm*, Canberra: Department of Health and Ageing, Commonwealth of Australia.

New South Wales (NSW) Government (undated) *Restrictive Practices Guidance Environmental Restraint*. Available www.facs.nsw.gov.au/__data/assets/pdf_file/0010/636949/Restrictive-Practices-Resources-environmental-restraint-guidance.pdf (accessed 20 June 2020).

O'Hagan, M. (2003) 'Force in Mental Health Services: International User/Survivor Perspectives', Keynote Address Presented at World Federation for Mental Health Biennial Congress, Melbourne, February. Available www.maryohagan.com/resources/Text_Files/Force%20Paper.pdf (accessed 20 June 2020).

Oliver, S. (2011) 'Dehumanization: Perceiving the Body as (In)human', in P. Kaufmann, H. Kuch, C. Neuhäuser and E. Webster (eds) *Humiliation, Degradation, Dehumanization, Human Dignity Violated*, London: Springer, 85–97.

Robins, C.S., Sauvageot, J.A., Cusac, K.J., Suffoletta-Maierle, S. and Freuh, B.C. (2005) 'Consumers' Perceptions of Negative Experiences and "Sanctuary Harm" in Psychiatric Settings', *Psychiatric Services*, 56(9): 1134–38.

Roper, C. (2018) 'Capacity Does Not Reside in Me', in C. Spivakovsky, K. Seear and A. Carter (eds) *Critical Perspectives on Coercive Interventions: Law, Medicine and Society*, Oxford: Routledge, 85–97.

Roper, C. and Gooding, P. (2018) 'This Is Not a Story: From Ethical Loneliness to Respect for Diverse Ways of Knowing, Thinking and Being', in E. Flynn, A. Arstein-Kerslake, C. de Bhailis and M. Laura Serra (eds) *Global Perspectives on Legal Capacity Reform: Our Voices, Our Stories*, London: Routledge, 154–64.

Roper, C., McSherry, B. and Brophy, L. (2015) 'Defining Seclusion and Restraint: Legal and Policy Definitions Versus Consumer and Carer Perspectives', *Journal of Law and Medicine*, 23(2): 297–302.

Rose, N. (1989) *Governing the Soul*, London: Free Association Books.

Ross, D. (2018) 'A Social Work Perspective on Seclusion and Restraint in Australia's Public Mental Health System', *Journal of Progressive Human Services*, 29(2): 130–48.

Said, A. and Kautz, D. (2013) 'Reducing Restraint Use for Older Adults in Acute Care', *Nursing*, 43(12): 59–61.

Smith, T.L. (1999) *Decolonizing Methodologies: Research and Indigenous Peoples*, London: Zed Books.

Spivakovsky, C., Seear, K. and Carter, A. (2018) 'Coercive Interventions in Law and Medicine: Setting the Scene' in C. Spivakovsky, K. Seear and A. Carter (eds) *Critical Perspectives on Coercive Interventions: Law, Medicine and Society*, Oxford: Routledge, 1–9.

Standards New Zealand (2008a) *Health and Disability Services (General) Standard*. Available www.standards.govt.nz/assets/Publication-files/NZS8134.0-2008.pdf (accessed 20 June 2020).

Standards New Zealand (2008b) *Health and Disability Services (Restraint Minimisation and Safe Practice) Standards*. Available www.standards.govt.nz/assets/Publication-files/NZS8134.2-2008.pdf (accessed 20 June 2020).

Steele, L. (2017) 'Lawful Institutional Violence Against Disabled People', *Precedent: Journal of the Australian Lawyers' Alliance*, 143: 4–8.

Tapsell, R. and Mellsop, G. (2007) 'The Contributions of Culture and Ethnicity to New Zealand Mental Health Research Findings', *International Journal of Social Psychiatry*, 53: 317–24.

Te Pou o Te Whakaaro Nui (2015) *Towards Restraint-free Mental Health Practice: Supporting the Reduction and Prevention of Personal Restraint in Mental Health Inpatient Settings.* Available www.tepou.co.nz/uploads/files/resource-assets/towards-restraint-free-mental-health-practice-may-15-web.pdf (accessed 20 June 2020).

United Nations High Commissioner for Human Rights (2017) *Annual Report, Promotion and Protection of All Human Rights, Civil, Political, Economic, Social and Cultural Rights, Including the Right to Development, Mental Health and Human Rights*, UN Doc A/HRC/34/32. Available www.un.org/disabilities/documents/reports/ohchr/a_hrc_34_32_mental_health_and_human_rights_2017.docx (accessed 20 June 2020).

Varese, F., Smeets, F., Drukker, M., Lieverse, R., Lataster, T., Viechtbauer, W., Read, J., van Os, J. and Bentall, R.P. (2012) 'Childhood Adversities Increase the Risk of Psychosis: A Meta-analysis of Patient-control, Prospective- and Cross-sectional Cohort Studies', *Schizophrenia Bulletin*, 38(4), 661–71.

Webb, D. (2010) *Thinking about Suicide: Contemplating and Comprehending the Urge to Die*, Ross-on-Wye: PCCS Books.

Part II

Designing legislation and policy to support change

Introduction to Part II

The use of restraint and other restrictive practices in mental health, disability and aged care sectors is regulated to varying degrees and via a range of mechanisms worldwide. The chapters in this part discuss the two primary forms of restraint regulation – legislation and policy – in two jurisdictions (Australia and England), as well as common law justifications and protections for the use of restrictive practices. The analyses herein suggest some common shortcomings of existing regulatory approaches in terms of promoting (human rights) goals of reducing or eliminating the use of restraint, and point to regulatory elements that might better support such aims in mental health, disability and/or aged care contexts.

Several common themes are apparent. First, while human rights considerations and obligations in relation to the use of restraint are frequently acknowledged in regulatory instruments, these instruments do not generally provide detailed guidance on what is required to realise these rights Nor do they create enforceable rights or redress mechanisms for breaches. For example, many of the NHS Trust policies on the use of rapid tranquillisation in the United Kingdom reviewed by Peter Bartlett and Stephanie Sampson in Chapter 3 mentioned human rights requirements in general terms, but policies predominantly framed decisions about the use of rapid tranquillisation to control behaviour as medical calculations to be made by clinicians. Kim Chandler in Chapter 4 describes human rights concerns raised by the use of restraint on people with intellectual or cognitive impairments in jurisdictions across Australia and the patchy regulatory frameworks currently surrounding these practices. She argues that, while stronger procedural safeguards to clarify procedures for authorising the use of restraint may go some way to addressing rights concerns, they are insufficient to guarantee the rights to liberty, security and equal recognition before the law for these service users.

The chapters in this part highlight other human rights and equality concerns that are inadequately addressed in regulation. For example, regulatory instruments do not acknowledge or address the disproportionate use and/or the differential impacts of the use of restraint on some service user groups, including women in Australia (Maker in Chapter 5) and people from black and minority ethnic communities, especially black men, in England (Bartlett and Sampson in Chapter 3).

A second theme is the overall lack of clear legal and practical guidance on avoiding and using alternatives to restraint in policy and legislation. For instance, in describing multiple tranches of policy change in England in recent years, Guy Cross in Chapter 6 criticises inconsistencies in the definitions of permissible and impermissible practices, a lack of guidance on safe alternatives and inadequate consideration of wider issues such as staff and bed numbers. He also notes some of the difficulties that arise when concepts or frameworks are imported to one sector from another. He provides the example of the concept of 'positive behaviour support', which is commonly used in policies relating to services for people with learning disabilities, being applied to mental health services. In regard to rapid tranquillisation use on elderly persons and persons with learning disabilities, Bartlett and Sampson suggest in Chapter 3 that the quantity and complexity of regulatory instruments, as well as inconsistencies between documents and a lack of clarity about their legal force and consequences, invites confusion and inconsistent application at the service level. In the Australian context, Yvette Maker in Chapter 5 observes the lack of 'gender awareness' in Australian legislation and policy relating to restraint use in mental health and disability services. This means considerations such as the need to avoid traumatising or retraumatising women service users, and the potential influence of gender stereotypes and discrimination in women's treatment, are not addressed.

The contributors to this part do point to some options for addressing the shortcomings of existing legislation and policy. Significantly, most highlight the need for further research and assessment of the operation of existing regulatory instruments, as well as the practices they prohibit or permit, in order to ensure that future reforms have a solid foundation. Bartlett and Sampson caution, however, that the human rights implications of any such research must be carefully considered.

Options for reform include the amendment of regulatory instruments to protect the rights of those subject to restraint and/or to mandate the minimisation or avoidance of restraint use altogether. Such changes must, of course, be supported by clear and practical guidance on alternatives, along with adequate staffing and other resources. Contributors also note the importance of culture change in ensuring that reforms on paper are translated into action. These themes are developed further in Parts III and IV in this volume. Maker in Chapter 5 makes a similar point to that made by Cath Roper and colleagues in Chapter 2, namely, that identifying, consulting and incorporating the views and requirements of the full diversity of service users – with the leadership of service users themselves – is an essential precursor to any reform process. This is also more likely to ensure that factors including, but not limited to, 'race', ethnicity, gender, sexuality and sexual identity are meaningfully addressed in regulation. Cross, in Chapter 6, suggests that service providers and pressure groups must also be involved in these processes in order to ensure that good practice can be identified and reform efforts understood and supported by all concerned.

3 Human rights and rapid tranquillisation

Peter Bartlett and Stephanie Sampson

Introduction

The use and overuse of sedation and tranquillisation for the management of behaviour raises serious human rights concerns. In the last decade, questions have been raised in the United Kingdom about the overuse of psychotropic medication in the elderly and among people with learning disabilities (Banerjee 2009), with a finding by Public Health England in 2015 that 13 per cent of people with learning disability – approximately 23,800 people – were receiving antipsychotics in the absence of a psychotic illness. The same report found that roughly 10 per cent of people with learning disabilities – 19,500 people – were receiving antidepressants without having an affective condition. Allowing for some people receiving both, the report estimated that 30,000 to 35,000 people were receiving one or the other, in the absence of the conditions for which they are administered (Public Health England 2015). In its most recent visit to the United Kingdom, the European Committee for the Prevention of Torture criticised the overuse of rapid tranquillisation in the adult psychiatric facility it visited (Committee for the Prevention of Torture 2017: 118).

Following the death of Seni Lewis on a psychiatric ward in 2010, restrained by 11 police officers, a bill was introduced which became the *Mental Health Units (Use of Force) Act 2018*. This requires hospitals providing inpatient psychiatric care to publish a policy on the use of force, to appoint a person responsible at each site to oversee the use of force, to require staff training in the use of force, and to improve and standardise the recording of the use of force. As regards the requirement that policies be created, it did little to change the status quo. The Mental Health Act Commission and its successor body, the Care Quality Commission – public bodies charged with the inspection and oversight of psychiatric detentions and, with the creation of the Care Quality Commission, of hospitals and care homes more generally – had long required that policies be in place for the use of restraint in psychiatric settings. Such policies were also common in other hospital contexts as well, such as accident and emergency units, geriatric wards and in facilities caring for children. In 2005 the National Institute of Health and Clinical Excellence (NICE), a public body operationally independent of government charged with providing guidance on best professional practice in health and social care settings, issued guidance on the short-term management of disturbed or violent behaviour by adults within inpatient psychiatric settings and emergency departments. That guidance expected policies to be created for the overall management of such behaviour, relevant staff training, and engagement with and observation of service users, and for rapid tranquillisation specifically (NICE 2005: paras 8.1.2.1, 8.1.3.1, 8.1.7.1, and for rapid tranquillisation specifically para 8.1.8.4.2). This was replaced in 2015 by guidance that included adolescents and young people and people with learning disability, and extended to all health settings (both hospital and community) (NICE 2015). The Code of Practice to the Mental Health Act – statutory guidance from the Department of Health on the scope of the *Mental Health Act 1983* and best practice for its implementation, to which all practitioners must 'have regard' – also contains a full chapter on 'Safe and therapeutic responses to disturbed behaviour' that requires the creation of institutional policies governing interventions (Department of Health 2015: ch 26, esp para 26.7; see the detailed discussion by Cross in Chapter 6 in this volume).

In late 2016, the second author of this chapter, through a Freedom of Information request, gathered the policies on rapid tranquillisation from all English Healthcare Trusts – the bodies that provide secondary and tertiary health care services in England. The present chapter analyses those policies from the perspective of human rights law. That is taken here in part to include the specifics of human rights instruments and jurisprudence. Of particular relevance are the requirements of the *European Convention on Human Rights* (ECHR), which is directly enforceable in English law through the *Human Rights Act 1998*, and the United Nations *Convention on the Rights of Persons with Disabilities* (CRPD), which came into force in 2008. The interpretation of the CRPD, particularly as it relates to mental disability law, remains a matter of considerable dispute (see e.g. Schulze 2010; Bartlett 2012; Flynn and Arstein-Kerslake 2014; Dawson 2015; Gooding 2015; McSherry and Wilson 2015; Degener 2016). While those are important arguments, their detail need not concern us here. For present purposes, we adopt a generalist and uncontroversial reading of the treaty. That is, the CRPD rejuvenates the requirement that full and effective rights be accorded to people with disabilities (including people with mental health difficulties/psychosocial disabilities and people with cognitive difficulties), that respect for the will and preferences of people with disabilities must be central to policies affecting them, and that they and their representative organisations must be directly involved in all stages of policy design and implementation. In addition to the specific human rights instruments, this chapter also looks to broader principles of human rights. Human rights law of course demands appropriate domestic law governing the exercise of human rights, so this chapter also explores the interaction between domestic law in England and Wales (most notably the *Mental Health Act 1983* (the Mental Health Act) and the *Mental Capacity Act 2005* (the Mental Capacity Act), both as amended) and relevant policies.

The following discussion comes with a caveat. The chapter is based on institutional policies. That is not necessarily a helpful guide to what is actually happening on wards. As a question of law and employment conditions, staff on a psychiatric ward will be expected to know the relevant statutory law. This most notably includes the Mental Capacity Act with its near-incomprehensible Deprivation of Liberty Safeguards, and the Mental Health Act, the relevant Codes of Practice (running to 300 pages for the Mental Capacity Act, 125 pages for the Deprivation of Liberty Safeguards and 464 pages for the Mental Health Act), regulations from professional bodies, NICE and the Care Quality Commission, and the content of literally dozens of other hospital policies, usually running to considerable length. It would be miraculous if staff were able to retain the detail of this vast panoply of regulation, even before questions are asked about how regulation interacts with the realities of working on understaffed and busy wards. What actually happens on the wards and in direct patient care, and how patients experience life on the wards, are questions of vital importance, but they are not questions the present chapter can answer. The policies should instead be understood as an indication of how health managers within Trusts perceive the appropriate threshold for care. Whether those thresholds are achieved is outside the scope of this chapter.

Consistent with that, the rapid tranquillisation policies often referred to a wide array of other policies that provided context for specific elements of the policy – for example policies on consent in general, or the Mental Capacity Act, or the use of compulsory treatment in psychiatric settings (i.e., for the treatment of the disorder, rather than the controlling of behaviour). Sometimes, the rapid tranquillisation policy would refer to quite a large number of these additional policies. These additional policies were not requested for this project, and the Trusts in general did not send them. Analysis of these additional policies would, in any event, have made the present project unmanageable in scale. It nonetheless does place a limit on the present analysis.

The data set

Between October and December 2016, Freedom of Information requests were sent to all 243 National Health Service (NHS) Foundation Trusts in England. Requests were made (in writing) for a copy of Trusts' most recent rapid tranquillisation or chemical restraint policies, and then sent in the form of an email directly to individual Trusts. A total of 201 Trusts (83 per cent) responded to the original requests. Of the 243 Trusts, 111 (46 per cent) replied with a copy of their policy attached; six (2 per cent) stated that they had no such policy but consulted relevant NICE guidelines when required; and three (1 per cent) provided an algorithm or 'holding policy' as opposed to a developed rapid tranquillisation policy. Of the total 120 policies provided by these Trusts, 107 were specific to rapid tranquillisation.

No policies were provided for 123 Trusts. Eighty-one Trusts (35 per cent) stated that they had no such policy, with seven of these stating that a specific rapid tranquillisation policy was under development at the time of the Freedom of Information request. Finally, 14 Trusts (6 per cent) acknowledged receipt of the request only, with no further correspondence, and 28 (12 per cent) did not reply at all. The reasons are not clear why 81 Trusts did not have a specific policy and we did not have sufficient time to qualitatively investigate, but reasons for non-return of policies may include: not offering those relevant restraint services, not having a specific rapid tranquillisation policy but a generic 'restraint' policy, definitional differences (one Trust requested a clarification of the meaning of 'rapid tranquillisation'), or failure to develop a policy through oversight or other conflicting time priorities.

The publication dates of policies obtained ranged from September 2011 to September 2016, with length of the policy documents ranging from a single page (usually an algorithm) to 70 pages. We were interested in obtaining polices that provided guidance for practitioners in the administration of fast-acting sedative medication resulting in 'rapid tranquillisation' for the purposes of behavioural control and restraint. Therefore we excluded policies that did not specifically provide guidance in the administration of rapid tranquillisation, for example where policies (i) provided guidance for clinical sedation as part of broad health policy; (ii) related to prevention and management of violence and aggression in the workplace; (iii) related to Deprivation of Liberty Safeguards, unless those policies referred in addition to the use of tranquillisation; (iv) provided general mental health guidelines or Trust medicines policy; or (v) provided guidance on rapid anesthesia to allow for physical health care treatment (i.e. not for control or restraint purposes). Policies that included significant discussion of the practice of rapid tranquillisation within broader policies (for example, policies on restraint in general that included significant guidance on rapid tranquillisation as part of that larger package) were included in the analysis.

We have not identified individual Trusts in the discussion that follows. That is in part in compliance with the terms on which some Trusts provided their policies. It is also consistent with the ethos of this paper. Our interest is in understanding and exploring overall practice in what we view as a difficult area, not in singling out particular Trusts for criticism.

The overall structure of the policies

The policies are generally the creations of pharmaceutical or medicines committees of the Trust. A significant element of the policies is the drugs to be used and the dosages to be administered, so there is an obvious logic to this choice of authorship, but as will be noted later, it does affect the characterisation of the subject. Membership on these committees is not generally listed on the policy, so it is not possible to know the prevalence and range of backgrounds that went into the development of the policies (although given the apparent remit of these committees, it is certainly fair to assume a significant medical and pharmaceutical involvement). In particular, it is not possible to know whether people with mental disabilities were involved in the development of the policies. Such involvement would be consistent with the requirements of the CRPD (see for example Article 4(3)) and in a policy of such direct impact on the rights of patients would be particularly important.

The considerable bulk of the policies relate specifically to rapid tranquillisation. While these policies differ in some detail and focus, they tend to share specific elements:

- A statement of context at the beginning. This is generally a statement of purpose, or aims and objectives. These generally refer to the need to ensure both a safe environment on the ward, and that the tranquillisation occurs in a safe and appropriate fashion. Very frequently, the statement of aims or purposes will make the point that the intervention is not to induce sleep or unconsciousness, but rather to promote a calmer state so that the individual can participate in further assessment or treatment.
- A statement that rapid tranquillisation must be used only as a last resort, when other attempts to de-escalate the situation have failed, and that it must be administered consistently with law and human rights. Often, there is a statement that the policy concerns the control of dangerous behaviour, rather than treatment of an underlying condition.
- Determining the medication that is to be used for rapid tranquillisation. This tends to be a fairly specific determination, with particular drugs and dosages stated in the policy, including variation for children and young people or the elderly, if the policy covers those groups.
- Processes that occur prior to the intervention. These include screening the patient to determine his or her dangerousness, determining drug allergies and obtaining the views of the patient as to how emergency situations should preferably be dealt with.
- Processes directly connected to the intervention. These include immediate monitoring of vital signs such as blood pressure, pulse and respiratory rate. Monitoring following the procedure is also usually included. Oral medication is to be preferred, if accepted by the patient; otherwise intramuscular injection, with intravenous injection as a last resort. Often, the policies provide advice regarding further medication if the desired suppression of the aggressive state is not achieved. There is often some discussion of patient consent at the time of the intervention.
- A list of the required emergency equipment that must be available prior to the intervention is generally included. This normally includes a defibrillator, a bag valve mask, oxygen, cannulas, fluids, pulse oximeter, suction and first-line resuscitation medications.
- Definitions of the roles of various people. Usually it will be a doctor or experienced nurse who will be in charge of administering the medication. If the latter, a doctor will be required to be available if needed, and to review the procedure with reasonable promptness.
- A statement of training needs is generally included. Sometimes these are quite specific; often, they are much more general.
- Processes following the intervention. These include an indication of where the incident is to be recorded. Usually, the policy would require the patient to be debriefed; sometimes, the patient will be able to provide a response to

> the intervention in the notes. The tranquillisation is to be reviewed at regular intervals and discontinued when it ceases to be necessary. Monitoring is to continue until that time. Sometimes, ward staff are required to review and reflect on the overall use of tranquillisation on the ward on a periodic basis (for example quarterly).

Much of the preceding appears to flow directly from the NICE guidance, which is cited directly by 63 of the Trusts. Of these, 18 Trusts refer only to the 2005 guidance. In most of these cases, the policies in question had been drafted prior to the 2015 guidance and had not come up for triennial review prior to this project. However, three Trusts had revised their policies well after the 2015 guidance was issued, and still referred only to the 2005 version.

Policies that are not specific to rapid tranquillisation generally place it in the context of broader restraint. The result is usually not entirely convincing. A good deal of the specific material relating to rapid tranquillisation is often lost. Occasionally, however, these combined policies do provide additional insights as to how rapid tranquillisation fits in with the range of approaches to restraint, and how restraint as a whole is to be understood in terms of overall patient experience on wards.

Overall objectives and context

The statements of purposes, or aims and objectives appearing in these policies present a range of not entirely consistent values and objectives. Sometimes the policy purports in part to be about patient dignity, for example:

> Purpose: To ensure a consistently safe and effective approach to the use of rapid tranquillisation for the short-term management of violence and aggression, ensuring that service users are informed at each stage of the process and if treatment is necessary ensures that individuals are treated with dignity and respect.

Sometimes, the policy is stated to be about ensuring that rapid tranquillisation is conducted consistently with the law.

Generally, however, the purpose of the policies refers to the reduction of violence on the ward. This creates an initial tension in the policies. Certainly, as a matter of their human rights, patients have a right to a certain level of safety on the wards (see *Osman v United Kingdom* (2000) and the jurisprudence flowing therefrom) and there are indications that a suitable standard is not met in this regard. For example in 2008, 12 per cent of psychiatric inpatients experienced a physical assault on the ward (Healthcare Commission 2008: 35). There is also frequently a sense that the policy is about occupational health and safety for staff. Indeed, in response to the request for information, one Trust did not send a policy related to rapid tranquillisation specifically, but its policy on 'zero tolerance of aggression in the workplace' – a policy clearly motivated by concerns of staff safety. Staff safety is also a perfectly appropriate concern, but it does lay bare a tension. Are these policies about the safety of staff, or are they about the rights of patients not to be subjected to a very intrusive intervention?

Perhaps in part because the policies are usually drafted by medicines or pharmaceutical committees with the Trusts, the policies tend to be cast within a medical model. One Trust, for example, spends more than two pages discussing the nature of behavioural change and its possible causes; all are biomedical and none environmental or social. This is in direct contrast to the NICE guidelines and the Mental Health Act Code of Practice, which also discuss environmental factors, staff attitudes, the individual's personal situation and the effects of institutionalisation as additional factors relevant to the rise of violent incidents.

The exclusively medical focus is though not universal. Twenty-two Trusts do acknowledge non-biomedical causes of disruptive behaviour. These most commonly included noise (18 Trusts), over-crowding (9 Trusts), lack of privacy (9 Trusts), boredom (6 Trusts), staff shortages (5 Trusts) and lack of activities on the ward (5 Trusts). Ward physical environments were also mentioned occasionally, including lack of pleasant surroundings, appropriate natural light and fresh air. Poor clinical leadership is identified as a factor in six policies. Poor staff attitudes more generally are mentioned only a few times, even though they are identified as a factor in the 2005 NICE guidance. Pain, fear or anxiety, thirst or hunger, and confusion brought on by loss of memory or waking up in unknown surroundings are mentioned in a very few policies. Other personal factors, such as dysfunctional relationships with family members, poverty, or histories of abuse are almost entirely outside the frame of reference, as are social causes such as poverty.

Even in the minority of polices that do mention these environmental or social causes of disruptive behaviour, the focus of the policies remains almost invariably biomedical. As acknowledged in the 2005 NICE guidance, disruptive or violent behaviour is likely to be the result of a complex combination of social factors, issues related to disability or illness, and personal factors. The focus of the policies is largely on the biomedical elements and responses. This does seem a place where the social model of disability, which frames disability as flowing from social factors rather than inherent failings or impairments within individuals, ought to be of considerable relevance. Too frequently, social and environmental causes of disruptive behaviour do not seem to penetrate these policies. That is of particular note, since the social model is at the core of the CRPD, which the United Kingdom has signed and ratified.

This raises questions about how far human rights are actually a driving force in the policies. The policies of 94 Trusts reference human rights or equality directly, and many more allude to values or principles consistent with a human rights approach, but it is fair to question the level of understanding of the authors of these policies. Often, the reference takes the form of a general expression of intent near the beginning of the policy, perhaps a clause inserted in many policies as a matter of routine. The Public Sector Equality Duty, introduced by section 149 of the *Equality Act 2010*, took effect on 5 April 2011, and since that time Trusts have been required to consider the consistency of their policies with equalities legislation – legislation that protects individuals from discrimination based on prohibited criteria such as race, gender, sexual orientation or disability. Seventy of the Trusts included an express statement that they had done so. Very few indeed identified potential problems with their policies. Thirty Trusts attached copies of their equality impact assessments. Only three of these identified that there may be issues regarding overuse or perceived overuse of rapid tranquillisation among black service users, even though the criticism of the use of restraint on black people (black men in particular) had been a matter of particular concern in the development of the 2005 NICE guidance (NICE 2005: sections 6.4.2, 7.8.4.2, 7.8.7). This flowed from criticism following the death of David ('Rocky') Bennett in a psychiatric hospital in 1998 (see Department of Health 2005). The 2015 NICE guidance makes no reference to issues of race or ethnicity, beyond general advice not to make unwarranted assumptions based on culture (NICE 2015: para 1.2.9). This is somewhat surprising, as concerns about the application of compulsory powers in black and minority ethnic communities certainly have not gone away. Indeed, overuse of the compulsion provisions in the Mental Health Act among black and minority communities was an express justification for the establishment of the Wessely Committee on the reform of the *Mental Health Act* in 2017 (Department of Health 2018).

When issues of race were identified in the policies, the response tended to be that information needed to be available in a variety of languages (4 Trusts) – a factor that was also raised occasionally regarding disability discrimination – or that monitoring needed to take place to ensure that the rapid tranquillisation was not overused in these groups (2 Trusts). Almost invariably, the impact assessments did not note the need to understand the concrete cultural meaning of compulsion and its likely effect on the individual, although one impact assessment does note that people in seclusion should be permitted to keep items of cultural or religious significance with them. This same Trust also noted that some drugs metabolise differently depending on ethnicity. Given the overall medical focus of the policies, it is interesting that other Trusts did not raise that as an issue, although one did note that the increasing physical frailty in advancing age meant that particular care should be taken in cuffing the hands of elderly patients as over-tightening could result in bone injury.

As noted, the policies themselves often contained overarching statements of commitment to human rights and equality; but there was generally very little to connect those noble statements to the actual understanding of and responses to individual patients. Indeed, several of the equalities impact statements took the express view that the policies positively advanced equality rights, for example on the basis that the policy's establishment of clear guidance would reduce the use of compulsion, or that the policy is 'highly likely to promote equality of opportunity and good relations as the policy promotes good practice that can be applied by all staff, for all individuals/patients'. Whether the policies in fact reduce the use of compulsion or promote good relations is an empirical question outside the scope of this chapter. As will be discussed later, however, the policies generally offer little concrete advice about how staff and service users should interact, or indeed in any specific sense when rapid tranquillisation should be used. On that basis, it is difficult to see that the policies in themselves beneficially affect non-discrimination and equality.

The equality impact assessments return us to the overall contextualisation of the policies. Frequently, the impact assessments describe the objective of the policy as the provision of rapid tranquillisation in a safe manner. If that is understood in a medical context, it is a small step for the logic to become about safe and appropriate dosages, rather than asking cultural questions about the appropriateness of rapid tranquillisation as a response to the situation. When the discussion is located in a largely technical biomedical realm, questions of human rights and equality are perceived as less relevant. Thus, while the policies seem to say at various points that human rights are at their core, it is difficult to see how in fact that plays out in the policies themselves.

Procedural issues

Rapid tranquillisation and care planning

The policies generally require the assessment of the patient early in his or her admission. This in part is to identify purely medical issues, such as drug allergies and intolerances, but also includes a risk assessment – whether the individual is likely to engage in disturbed or violent behaviour. The care plan of the individual is meant to include a proposed response in the event that such behaviour occurs, and the patient is meant to have a role in the formulation of that plan. In particular, both statements of wishes and advance statements to refuse treatment are to be included.

In one sense, it is hard to criticise the hospitals for developing these procedures. If the patient does engage in behaviour such that intervention is required to restore a safe environment on the ward for staff and other patients, it is obviously desirable that a response will have been thought through in advance, rather than coercion being determined 'on the fly'. This is most clearly the case regarding drug allergies and intolerances. As a number of the policies note, some of the drugs can produce very unpleasant and indeed sometimes fatal reactions. Equally, the policy allows for the involvement of the patient in the process, a clear benefit if a Trust is to view care as a co-operative exercise with the patient. All of that is unquestionably laudable.

At the same time, the approach places the individual immediately into a place in a hierarchy of dangerousness – they become, to a greater or lesser degree, a risky person. Few of the policies on rapid tranquillisation specifically address how the risk assessment is to be conducted in detail, but many of the policies cross-reference separate policies on risk assessment. It would seem that these assessments tend to use actuarial risk assessment tools, such as the Violence Risk Appraisal Guide (VRAG) (Quinsey et al. 1998) or the Historical, Clinical, Risk-20 Item (HCR-20) (Webster et al. 1997). Elements of the individual's life that he or she find distressing and may warrant empathy are recast as 'trigger factors' for violence. It is difficult to imagine that this does not affect both the view of that individual by professional staff and indeed the individual's own view of himself or herself. Insofar as this is a dehumanising or objectifying process, it is hard to see that it is consistent with the ethos of the CRPD.

Implementing rapid tranquillisation

The policies consistently refer to rapid tranquillisation as a response to 'severe agitation', 'disturbed behaviour', 'aggression', 'violence' or the like. These terms are rarely if ever further defined. It would seem instead that they are understood to be sufficiently clear on their own terms. Occasionally the policies will require an 'urgent' need for the intervention, or address an 'immediate threat'. Eight policies expressly reinforce that the intervention is not to be used to punish, inflict pain, suffering or humiliation, or to establish dominance, and, in one case, enjoin staff to whistle-blow if the procedure is being used to these ends. Nonetheless, the absence of further elaboration leaves a void in the policies. It is difficult to escape the conclusion that the determination of when the process is to be used is a matter left to largely professional judgment, taken generally by a senior nurse or a doctor. As this is a highly intrusive procedure, the absence of further definition of its permitted scope is notable.

The policies do generally convey a sense that rapid tranquillisation is a serious intervention, not to be undertaken lightly. Many make clear that there are serious potential adverse effects from the procedure. These tend to be phrased in terms of biomedical effects, with the policies rarely referring to the human or psychological costs of compulsory intervention. The policies universally reinforce that rapid tranquillisation is a last resort, to be used only if other techniques of de-escalation have failed. With only a small number of exceptions, however, few of the policies provide much by way of concrete guidance as to what de-escalation techniques are likely to be successful at removing the need for tranquillisation. Certainly, a small number of policies offer a few concrete suggestions – such as moving the patient to a less crowded or private space, spending time listening to the patient's concerns and the like – but detail is limited, particularly when compared for example with the detailed indications of medications to be used if tranquillisation is necessary.

The discussion of implementation is complicated by ambiguities in the policies as to how far rapid tranquillisation is to be understood as a response to an immediate and quite possibly unanticipated event, how much part of a planned strategy of care and treatment and how rapid tranquillisation is distinguished from ongoing treatment. Certainly, the policies often make it clear that the objective of rapid tranquillisation is the control of behaviour, rather than the treatment of the underlying condition. However, as a number of the policies makes clear, ongoing medication is also prescribed for this purpose, and the medications prescribed – generally psychotropics – may well be the same in each context. These medications may be prescribed on a 'PRN' (pro re nata – as needed) basis as part of the treatment plan, and the use of these medications in that way is expressly viewed by a number of the policies as an appropriate part of a de-escalation strategy, as distinct from their use as rapid tranquillisation as defined by the policy. The policies appear to view this as part of general treatment rather than restraint.

The line between the two can become even more blurred. A number of the policies include the following provision, or something similar to it:

> Oral p.r.n. psychotropics should always be tried or offered prior to [intramuscular rapid tranquillisation]. The patient must be informed that medication is going to be given and must be given the opportunity at any stage to accept oral medication voluntarily. Patients should be given the opportunity to make an informed choice where at all possible.

If the medication is 'going to be given', it is fair to wonder how 'voluntary' the patient's consent will be in the circumstances. Whatever the ethics or practical realities, this does not appear to be a legal problem in the English domestic law (see *Freeman v Home Office (No 2)* [1984]). It may however be an issue in the context of Article 8 of the ECHR (see *YF v Turkey* (2004): para 34). Some policies note further that where the patient lacks capacity, the PRN medication may be administered in his or her best interests, citing the Mental Capacity Act. As studies have noted, it seems that notwithstanding the language of that Act, determinations of capacity may be influenced by whether the patient's decision is considered by the capacity assessor to be within acceptable bounds (see e.g.Willner et al. 2013; Williams et al. 2012; Emmett et al. 2013). While the matter does not appear to have been studied regarding tranquillisation, it is reasonable to wonder whether those concerns apply with force to decisions to refuse sedating medication of patients where violence or seriously disruptive behaviour is anticipated. Insofar as that is the case, again, there are questions as to the borderline between tranquillisation as treatment and as restraint.

The distinction matters for a number of reasons. As will be discussed later, the legal justifications for treatment and for restraint are different, and it is appropriate to insist on a reasonable degree of clarity as to what the legal authorisation for the intervention is. The provision of PRN medication is not necessarily recorded as restraint (indeed, in some policies staff are expressly directed not to record it so, although the policies as a whole do not have a consistent line on this), so that it may not be scrutinised in the same way as treatment classified as rapid tranquillisation. That in turn raises human rights concerns, as the person on the receiving end of the medication may well view himself or herself as subject to compulsion and control, whether the institution classifies the intervention as treatment or as restraint by rapid tranquillisation. It is therefore at least arguable that human rights protections ought equally to apply in both cases.

The policies do little to assist staff with this distinction. Some policies refer to consent as a particular indicator. For the reasons noted earlier, that is problematic. Others focus on the levels of disturbed behaviour and apparent imminence of the risk of violence. Others draw the distinction as whether the intervention is largely proactive (treatment) or reactive (rapid tranquillisation). Others distinguish between whether the medication is part of a larger strategy of de-escalation (treatment), or used on its own regarding a specific episode of aggression (rapid tranquillisation). All of these are problematic, since they imply that the event giving rise to the rapid tranquillisation is a discrete event outside the planning process, where the rest of the policy seems to be designed to ensure that rapid tranquillisation is anticipated and planned for. The policies also in general make it clear that de-escalation techniques are to continue while the rapid tranquillisation is occurring, so the inclusion of medication as part of a larger strategy seems also to be a false distinction. It is difficult to see that the policies assist much here.

Fourteen of the policies refer to the provision of advocacy either generally, as part of the planning process, or when the decision is being taken to implement rapid tranquillisation, particularly when the patient is considered to lack mental capacity. If this functions effectively, it is presumably a desirable and appropriate way to promote the involvement of the patient. At the same time, it does reinforce that the decision to introduce rapid tranquillisation is not necessarily to be understood as taken in haste. Advocacy services take time to respond. One of the policies notes that the turnaround time for an initial response by the hospital advocacy service was 24 hours. It therefore makes sense to think of it as part of a process of ongoing planning, rather than as an immediate response to a crisis event.

Procedures following rapid tranquillisation

The policies universally require staff to document the use of rapid tranquillisation, to monitor the patient until the medications have ceased to have effect and to re-visit the plan for rapid tranquillisation in light of the event. Many require a more reflective analysis of how the incident developed, and how it was responded to. Some require a periodic systematic review of these records by ward staff, with a view to enhancing good practice and minimising the need for such interventions. These appear to be highly desirable provisions in human rights terms, although here as elsewhere, it is not possible from the policies themselves to know how effectively these reviews actually change practice.

Most of the policies include an expectation that the patient will be debriefed after the procedure, with the provision of information about what was done and why. Many expressly allow the patient to add his or her comments, views or reflections about what occurred to the clinical record. There does seem to be an expectation that the patient will be supported in doing this, with 12 policies specifically providing for the provision of advocacy at this point, again primarily for those with problems of mental capacity. The difficulty with these provisions is that there is rarely any indication what use the institution is to make of the reflections. Presumably, they are meant to feed back into the care plan to be taken into account in any future incidents. Insofar as that occurs, there is an obvious overlap with the expectation of the CRPD that the will and preferences of a person with disabilities ought to be at the centre of programmes involving them. Again, it is not possible from the policies themselves to know how effectively this occurs.

The medications

The Mental Health Act Code of Practice (2015) (the Code of Practice) recognises that restrictive interventions may be required in health and social care settings as part of a broader therapeutic programme, but when they are required they should be planned, evidence-based, lawful, in the patient's best interests, proportionate and dignified (Department of Health 2015: para 26.7). The Code of Practice further provides that rapid tranquillisation 'should be prescribed in accordance with evidence-based practice guidelines such as those published by NICE . . . [and] must be in line with legal requirements' (Department of Health 2015: para 26.95). It is widely recognised in systematic review and evidence-based practice guidelines, however, that interventions given in coercive circumstances lack an empirical, randomised evidence-base on which health care practitioners are required to rely as per the Code of Practice, creating somewhat of a catch-22 situation (Sailas and Fenton 2000; NICE 2015). Current NICE guidelines recommend the use of intramuscular lorazepam on its own, or intramuscular haloperidol combined with promethazine for rapid tranquillisation in adults, where oral medication is 'not possible or appropriate and urgent sedation with medication is needed' (taking into account patient preferences or advanced decisions; other pre-existing health conditions; intoxication; previous recorded response to medications; potential interactions with other medication; and total daily dose prescribed and administered) (NICE 2015). Though there are many other drugs used for the purposes of rapid tranquillisation (as we see from obtained policies), the NICE guidelines advocate the use of these three very different compounds due to the fact there is at least some existing evidence from (albeit very few) randomised controlled trials as to their potential benefits and harms. The NICE guidelines however promote the first-line use of intramuscular lorazepam, and suggest the haloperidol promethazine mix in the event of no response. This purports with the assumption that rapid tranquillisation is only delivered via a needle (indeed, only two Trust policies included oral administration in their definition of rapid tranquillisation). However there are oral formulations that, although would have the same desired effect, may presumably be a less physically intrusive route of administration. NICE guidelines also state that rapid tranquillisation may be delivered in exceptional circumstances intravenously (that is, through the vein), however the guidelines do not go into specifics on how to deliver this more risky and precise route of administration in a situation that could involve physical force and greater risk of injury.

Route of administration and rapid tranquillisation drugs

The vast majority of policies took a 'tiered' approach to medication, including (i) oral dosages, when needed in an 'escalating' situation in which violence or aggression was perceived as imminent; (ii) intramuscular dosages, when a situation was considered 'urgent'; and (iii) intravenous dosages, when needed for 'immediate' sedation. This largely reflects the categorical oral > intramuscular > intravenous hierarchy imposed by the NICE clinical guidelines (NICE 2015). The majority of policies (70 per cent) provide for intramuscular administration of lorazepam on its own or combined with an antipsychotic, with the haloperidol plus promethazine mix also included (28 per cent of policies). The remaining 22 per cent of policies recommend a varied selection of antipsychotic/ benzodiazepine drugs not recommended specifically under the current NICE guidelines, including aripiprazole, olanzapine or midazolam. A particular drug of interest was intramuscular zuclopenthixol acetate – a longer-acting antipsychotic with effects lasting for two to three days; not a drug recommended for use in rapid tranquillisation by NICE – a sentiment reflected in around 25 per cent of the obtained policies. None of the included policies identified this drug as a first-line treatment in rapid tranquillisation, however there seemed to be a devised rule amongst a few Trusts (7 per cent) that intramuscular zuclopenthixol acetate should only be administered 'to patients that are detained under a section of the Mental Health Act', with the justification that 'informal patients have the right to leave the hospital at any time and the adverse reactions such as extra pyramidal side effects (EPSE) or hypotension may not peak until 24 hours after giving the injection'. This suggests that this compound is not particularly rapid for a start. This is an example of an arbitrary clinical decision potentially impacting on the liberty of patients, or the denying of a potentially beneficial antipsychotic drug, not resting on any existing evidence on which to base practice.

With less guidance provided particularly for intravenous formulations, policies seemingly go off-piste from the recommendations leading to wide variations between Trusts. Few Trusts discouraged the use entirely of particular rapid tranquilisation compounds specifically in intramuscular form. For example, diazepam was discouraged by some policies for its erratic pattern of absorption, while midazolam was discouraged for 'insufficient evidence', while other Trusts provide recommended dosages of these same drugs via the much more potent intravenous route – directly into the bloodstream. Even though the NICE guidelines recommend the use of intravenous in very 'exceptional circumstances' (which is not defined), around 7 per cent of Trust policies stated that intravenous administration is not recommended for rapid tranquillisation, and provided no guidance as to practice.

Where policies do not adhere to the choices of rapid tranquillisation drugs as recommended by NICE clinical guidelines, it is not clear the evidence on which alternative choices are based. Indeed, only 23 per cent of policies acknowledged the lack of evidence on which their recommendations were based. A recent national UK survey of drugs used in specialist mental health Trusts for the purposes of rapid tranquillisation in practice showed that intramuscular lorazepam is most commonly used in rapid tranquilisation (in 99 per cent of cases), as per NICE recommendations. However, the haloperidol plus promethazine mix was barely used, and a vast array of alternative compounds were found to be in use contrary to what is currently recommended (Paton et al. 2019). Although evidence-based guidelines are available on which to base policy, both policy and actual treatment on the ground still varies widely.

Evidence-based practice, rapid tranquillisation and human rights

Though the concern as to which drug is most 'suited' or 'acceptable' to induce rapid tranquillisation rests as a clinical question, there are human rights concerns interwoven. Issues relating to human rights abound in psychiatric health care, and with greater calls for psychiatrists to justify treatment practice and choice through research evidence, it seems sensible to expect that the most intrusive, and coercive of drug interventions rests on a good bulk of evidence. This has not historically been, and is still not, the case. Indeed, the entirety of existing research evidence up to now has been undertaken in countries outside the United Kingdom, with the practical choices of which drugs to randomise having far-reaching effects on policy, but not necessarily practice (Innes and Sethi 2013). For example, NICE guidelines recommend the use of the haloperidol plus promethazine mix if there is no response to the first-line lorazepam. This is based on the evidence from one trial with 200 participants conducted in India, the TREC-India trial (Alexander et al. 2004). In this trial, the two drugs lorazepam and haloperidol plus promethazine mix, used routinely and with similar costs, were randomised to compare efficacy. Both drugs demonstrated equal effectiveness for 'controlling violent/agitated behaviour', with the haloperidol plus promethazine favoured for 'speed of sedation' (Alexander et al. 2004). The pragmatic design of this study (i.e. testing drugs used in routine practice) strengthened its internal validity, with existing patients randomised to either drug as and when they became unwell, without their consent (indeed, as in real-world practice). Consent to treatment was sought by a 'responsible relative if patients refused or lacked capacity to consent to treatment' (Alexander et al. 2004). It is unclear however whether participants were given the opportunity to withdraw their data after the intervention. Based on this model of trial to gather more evidence, we can see the potential of human rights violations in not only arguably being coerced to receive rapid tranquillisation, but also being coerced to participate in research.

Randomised controlled trials in rapid tranquillisation exist that required obtaining consent from participants before administration of the drug. This, however, also raises questions relating to consent as well as applicability of the results. How far can the consent be valid in this coercive situation? And how far can the results of a trial in which participants were well enough to provide consent before rapid tranquillisation be generalisable to a more acutely unwell, 'violent or agitated' patient population?

It is unclear precisely why the combined haloperidol plus promethazine mix is barely, if at all, used in practice (Paton et al. 2019) when fairly pragmatic evidence suggests that it is as safe and effective as lorazepam. It is unclear how often this combination was used before the results of the TREC-India trial made their way into NICE clinical guidelines. The study was undertaken in a single psychiatric emergency services unit in Vellore, India, with 200 participants given a rapid tranquillisation drug over a five-month period. This represents a large amount of people being sedated in one setting over a short space of time. The Prescribing Obsevatory for Mental Health (POMH-UK) survey of 58 specialist mental health Trusts in the United Kingdom found that intramuscular rapid tranquillisation was used on 936 patients, also over a five-month period, which is an average of 16 events per Trust over five months (Paton et al. 2019). This may well imply a difference in treatment culture, or the desired 'endpoint' for rapid tranquillisation, but it raises questions regarding the applicability of the evidence that is being promoted in policy and guidelines, the human rights of the research participants, as well as the human rights of patients on the receiving end of policy and practice.

Would the existence of more high-quality research evidence relating to rapid tranquillisation, resulting in a change in so-called evidence-based practice, actually help to promote human rights? Further evidence would undoubtedly help give clinicians greater confidence in treatment choices regarding risks and benefits, but it is unclear the extent to which the human rights of patients will be impinged in garnering the evidence in the first instance.

Legal contexts

Roughly two-thirds of the policies discuss law explicitly. This is almost universally domestic law – the common law relating to restraint, the *Mental Health Act 1983* and the *Mental Capacity Act 2005.*

The ECHR and the *Human Rights Act 1998* (the Human Rights Act), which incorporates the Convention into English law, are mentioned in 33 policies, not including policies mentioning the ECHR or Human Rights Act only in the pro forma elements of the equality assessment instruments previously discussed. As noted previously, many of the mentions in these 33 policies appear to be standard wordings, probably contained in all policies of those Trusts. A few of the policies do go so far as to mention specific articles of the ECHR – generally Articles 2 (right to life), 3 (right to be free from inhuman or degrading treatment), 5 (right to liberty) and 8 (right to privacy and family life). However, apart from very occasional discussions of when deprivations of liberty arise under Article 5, no policies contain any meaningful elaboration on the scope of the articles or their application in the context of rapid tranquillisation. Staff are told they must comply, but with no indication as to what that actually means.

That is the format of much of the policies' approach to legal authority, with the policies providing little to enlighten staff on what are very murky areas of law. As noted earlier, the distinction between restraint through tranquillisation and treatment is not straightforward. Yet the preponderance of policies do make clear that the point of rapid tranquillisation is the control of behaviour, rather than the treatment of an underlying medical or psychiatric condition. In legal terms, the policies are therefore about chemical restraint.

The policies that include psychiatric wards tend to advise that the Mental Health Act be relied upon to justify rapid tranquillisation. The view would appear widely to be that the general compulsory treatment provisions of that Act are broad enough to include rapid tranquillisation. Thus rapid tranquillisation would be able to be given to detained patients for up to three months without the patient's consent and simply on the direction of the patient's responsible clinician, and after that time with the provision of a second opinion by an independent psychiatrist (known as a 'Second Opinion Appointed Doctor', or SOAD).[1] These provisions cover detained patients only, and for this reason the policies tend to encourage practitioners to consider whether detention under the Act is appropriate, if a patient requires rapid tranquillisation. While the policies do usually make clear that the need for rapid tranquillisation is insufficient on its own to warrant such detention, they tend to suggest that people needing tranquillisation may well meet the detention criteria.

This approach is at best doubtful. The relevant statutory provisions concern 'any medical treatment given to him for the mental disorder from which he is suffering' (*Mental Health Act 1983*: section 36). While this does extend to interventions which 'alleviate, or prevent a worsening of, the disorder or one or more of its symptoms or manifestations' (*Mental Health Act 1983*: section 145(4)), it stretches language to the breaking point to say the provisions cover drugs given expressly not for the purpose of treating the disorder, but instead to control behaviour, particularly when the behaviour may or may not have any causal relationship to the underlying medical condition.

The Second Opinion Appointed Doctor requirement raises a different set of difficulties. Second Opinion Appointed Doctors are appointed and dispatched centrally by the Care Quality Commission. With the best will in the world, it may well take at least days for the Second Opinion Appointed Doctor to visit the hospital, consider the case and express a view. If the Second Opinion Appointed Doctor is approving the plan for intervention developed when the patient is initially admitted, this may be workable. However, if an intervention is required which is not anticipated in the plan, as in a case of real and unanticipated urgency, it is difficult to see that the Second Opinion Appointed Doctor will be able to respond sufficiently quickly to make the Mental Health Act justification practical.

Notwithstanding the approach of the policies, it is therefore difficult to see that the standard treatment provisions of the Mental Health Act apply to these situations.

Only 33 of the policies mention section 62 of the Mental Health Act. This section allows for treatment to be given which '(not being irreversible or hazardous) is immediately necessary and represents the minimum interference necessary to prevent the patient from behaving violently or being a danger to himself or others'. There does not appear to be a requirement in this section that the treatment be for the patient's mental disorder.[2] While not entirely unproblematic – a

1 This is the combined effect of sections 58 and 63 of the Mental Health Act. The adequacy of these provisions, which essentially collapse the processes for compulsory admission with those for compulsory treatment (at least for the first three months) are probably not consistent with the ECHR: see *X v Finland* (2012) and the Wessely Report (Department of Health 2018: 73).

2 The section of the Mental Health Act refers to 'treatment' rather than 'medical treatment'. While the latter is a defined term in the Act and refers specifically to treatment for the mental disorder (see *Mental Health Act 1983*: section 145), the former is not a statutorily defined term.

number of the policies quite properly stress the serious adverse effects that can flow from rapid tranquillisation, raising an interesting question as to what the word 'hazardous' means – this is by some margin the most convincing legal justification in the Act for the use of rapid tranquillisation. It is not at all clear why the policies tend to focus on the general treatment provisions of the Act, which are unconvincing regarding this intervention, rather than section 62.

All of these Mental Health Act justifications cover only people who are detained – in this context meaning progressed through the detention process. Informal patients and those for whom the detention application is in process are not within its remit. Also, of course, patients who may become violent in places such as accident and emergency wards, where psychiatric detention is not possible, are outside the realm of the Act. If these people do not lack capacity, the policies look to the common law to justify rapid tranquillisation.

Roughly one-third of the policies refer to common law as a justification for tranquillisation. Once again, the policies tend to adopt a simplistic reading of the law, if they offer any explanation at all. For example, they may state that such treatment including rapid tranquillisation is permitted 'in an emergency situation, for the safety and protection of themselves and others', or that when a patient

> is in the acute stages of illness causing them to act in [a] way which may cause harm to others, staff may, under the common law, take appropriate and necessary action to restrain or remove the person, in order to prevent harm, both to the person concerned and to anyone else.

The references to common law in the policies are problematic. Most do not refer expressly to the branch of common law upon which they rely; those that do, tend to refer to 'necessity'. It has been established since 1989 that this defence does allow medical treatment in the best interests of people who lack capacity (*F v West Berkshire Health Authority* [1989]), but that is not the issue here, as people lacking capacity are likely instead to be dealt with through the restraint provision of the Mental Capacity Act, noted later. At issue in the present context is the tranquillisation of people with capacity, and the 'necessity' in question thus must be taken to refer to a broader tort doctrine that allows individuals 'to prevent . . . any breach of the peace occurring in his presence or some other form of violent disorder or disturbance and itself necessarily involves a criminal offence' (*R (Laporte) v Chief Constable of Gloucestershire Constabulary* [2007]: para 29). In the current context, there are at least two difficulties with this doctrine however.

The first is that it must involve a breach of the peace, violent disorder and criminal behaviour. This is likely to be the case for violence directed at other people or at property, a potentially relevant point since the Mental Health Act and Mental Capacity Act provisions appear only to cover harm to the individual, not harm to others or damage to property. On the flip side, it is not obvious that behaviour that is purely self-harm constitutes a breach of the peace, violent disorder or criminal behaviour. Tranquillisation of people only self-harming would accordingly need to be justified under other law – and for patients not sectioned under the Mental Health Act and not lacking capacity, it is not clear what that law would be. After *Rabone v Pennine Care NHS Foundation Trust* (2012) it may be that there is a duty under both negligence law and the ECHR to detain informal psychiatric patients in need of intervention, but it is not obvious that this solves the immediate problem. As noted earlier, the Mental Health Act provisions apply only once the civil commitment process is complete, and that will at the least be some hours. It is not obvious what Trusts would be meant to do in the meantime.

Second, the case law in this area does seem to stress a certain immediacy and certainty to the crime about to be committed (see e.g. *R (DPP) v Stratford Magistrates' Court* [2018]: paras 15–25). That suggests that tranquillisation will be possible under the necessity defence only if matters really have come to a head. As discussed earlier in this chapter, that fits with some of the discussion of process; but other parts of the policies would appear to favour earlier interventions, presumably, to keep optimal control of the ward environment, to ensure that the medications can be introduced in the least fraught manner possible and to minimise the amounts of medication that may be necessary. However desirable these objectives may be, it is not obvious that the law of necessity allows for them.

It is notable that the case law regarding necessity is almost all in circumstances far removed from disruptive behaviour in hospitals. How much, for example, does the disruption of a trade fair promoting the sale of weapons of war (*R (DPP) v Stratford Magistrates' Court*) tell us about the scope of hospital powers to impose rapid tranquillisation? No English case law would appear to explore the use of tranquillisation or sedation in hospitals or similar environments in the context of the common law justification. How far that is significant is an open question. Involuntary tranquillisation relates to assault in a criminal context, and battery in tort, and the necessity defense does arise in other battery and assault cases. Does the fact that the issue here is a battery using a syringe rather than a fist make a difference? In pure law, the answer may well be no, on the basis that a battery is a battery. The context does appear different, however. Would the law, for example, be content to countenance rapid tranquillisation on prison wards, or by the police in the arrest of difficult suspects or in police cells? If the answer is no, are we restricting the rights of people in hospital in ways that we would not restrict the rights of others? At the core of the CRPD is a concern that discrimination against people with disabilities is unacceptable in the provision of rights. Is this therefore precisely the sort of result the CRPD would preclude? This is not, after all, about treating people for their disorders; this is about controlling their behaviour, whether or not that behaviour is even caused by the mental disorder. Why would it be acceptable to drug disruptive people in health care environments, but not elsewhere?

Somewhat surprisingly, the policies in general do not cite the common law of self-defence. This allows individuals to use reasonable force to protect themselves and those at risk immediately around them from attacks or imminent attacks by a violent person. Self-defence has a much more developed jurisprudential base than necessity, with at least some case law that feels more directly relevant. Thus police using tasers to restrain people actually engaged in brawling behaviour that puts others at risk have been provided with a defence to battery (*McCarthy v Chief Constable of Merseyside Police* [2016]). This is perhaps a good parallel with tranquillisation, as tasers like the tranquillising medication do have serious risks (the plaintiff in the instant case suffered a heart attack, for example), but are perceived (rightly or wrongly) as less intrusive than the other interventions that would be possible in the circumstances. That said, self-defence raises many of the same issues as necessity – proportionality of response and imminence of the event, and the unavailability of the defence if, for example, the sole person at risk is the violent person himself or herself.

The policies generally provide very little guidance on the scope of the common law as it relates to rapid tranquillisation (while, at the same time, enjoining staff that absent other justification they need to make sure they comply with it). Those that do provide more detail are hit and miss in their advice. Thus the following statement in a Trust policy is almost certainly reliable:

> Staff have the right, through both common law and statute, to defend themselves and/or others including healthcare staff from physical attack using reasonable force. Where required, either Security Staff and/or the Police are to be contacted to support them in dealing with a violent or aggressive incident.

For the reasons just outlined, the following is probably not:

> Common Law provision may apply in order to save life, relieve serious suffering, prevent deterioration in an urgent setting, or if it represents the minimum interference necessary to prevent a service user from behaving violently or from posing a risk to themselves.

For patients lacking capacity, the policies looked to the *Mental Capacity Act* as authority for rapid tranquillisation. The scope of this Act is helpful in the context of some of the policies. It does not distinguish between medical treatment and other forms of intervention (although it does allow for advanced decisions to refuse treatment), and it applies to all people lacking capacity, whether on a psychiatric ward, another hospital ward, or anywhere else. Unlike the common law power and section 62 of the Mental Health Act, there is no flavour of urgency in the Mental Capacity Act provisions, so long as they are in the best interests of the person concerned.

The Mental Capacity Act does have concrete substantive content, however, and little explanation of this is provided, with policies generally noting merely that if a person lacks capacity (with no further explanation), he or she may be treated in his or her best interests (again, with no further explanation). The policies do generally refer to other bespoke policies based on the Mental Capacity Act, which exist in all or nearly all Trusts, and these matters should be covered in general in those policies. It seems unlikely however that these general policies will discuss the scope of permitted restraint in detail, let alone the application of the Act to rapid tranquillisation in particular. For even in those rapid tranquillisation policies that do discuss some of the detail of the Mental Capacity Act, little detail is provided as to the nuances of the Act as it applies to rapid tranquillisation.

Section 6 of the Mental Capacity Act is specifically devoted to restraint, defined as the use or threatened use of force to secure the doing of an act which the individual resists, or restricting the individual's liberty of movement whether or not the individual resists. Restraint is allowed under the Act only if it is necessary to prevent harm to the individual to be restrained, and if the restraint is proportionate to the seriousness and likelihood of the harm to be prevented (*Mental Capacity Act 2005*: section 6(2)–(4)). This provision is rarely mentioned specifically in the policies regarding rapid tranquillisation, and while a more general need for proportionality is sometimes identified, the policies do not all include this as an express requirement.

The Mental Capacity Act was amended in 2007 to take into account the decision of the European Court of Human Rights in *HL v United Kingdom* (2005). That case required that appropriate procedural and substantive safeguards be provided for people who were deprived of liberty and lacked capacity to consent to the conditions of their accommodation. In response, the 2007 legislation introduced the so-called Deprivation of Liberty Safeguards (often referred to as the DoLS).[3] For present purposes, the DoLS become relevant where the intervention was sufficiently intrusive that it resulted in a deprivation of liberty under Article 5 of the ECHR. The definition of deprivation of liberty was much disputed in the years after the European Court of Human Rights' *HL* decision, but was clarified by the UK Supreme Court in *P v Cheshire West* ([2014]: para 49), where it was said that the 'acid test' was whether an individual was under constant supervision and control and not free to leave his or her accommodation. The criteria for the interventions which deprive the individual of liberty are substantively similar to those contained in section 6 of the Mental Capacity Act, for restraint generally, but they do introduce additional procedures, most notably the requirement that two independent assessors ensure the ongoing appropriateness of the intervention.

Roughly 40 of the policies refer to the DoLS, generally with the advice that it should be considered whether the tranquillisation was sufficiently intrusive as to constitute a deprivation of liberty. None refer to the *Cheshire West* decision specifically, and few provide meaningful guidance on when tranquillisation would become a deprivation of liberty, although almost certainly this would be covered under other Trust policies related to the Deprivation of Liberty Safeguards,

3 The 2007 scheme, in effect at the time the policies were drafted, was roundly criticised (see e.g. House of Lords: 139). Legislation replacing the 2007 amendments, the *Mental Capacity (Amendment) Act 2019* has not come into effect when this chapter went to press. An initial perusal suggests that the new legislation will raise comparable problems to the 2007 scheme as regards rapid tranquillisation, but as this legislation is not reflected in the policies examined, this is not the place for extended consideration of this question.

referred to in many of the tranquillisation policies. To be fair to the Trusts, this is an area where legally correct advice would not make a great deal of sense. The ECHR jurisprudence holds that deprivations of liberty may be for very short periods of time – in *Gillan and Quinton v United Kingdom* a detention of less than 30 minutes sufficed (2010: para 57). The policies require that the patient be monitored either constantly or on 15-minute observations until the effects of the medication have worn off – almost certainly well more than an hour – and this would certainly be within the scope of 'constant supervision and control' and not free to leave as held by the Supreme Court in *Cheshire West* ([2014]: para 49). That in turn raises the possibility that virtually all rapid tranquillisation of people lacking capacity will result in deprivations of liberty, and require the use of the DoLS process. Even in the optimistic legislative world of the DoLS requirements, though, it is accepted that it may well take up to a week for the two assessors to complete their function. By this time, the individual may well no longer be affected by the tranquillisation. It is difficult to see how it is sensible to ask Trusts to complete voluminous administrative applications to approve the ongoing approval of an intervention which is likely to be over before the relevant assessors have any prospect of arriving. At the same time, the failure to provide a meaningful process here leaves some of the most vulnerable without formal safeguards.

A related DoLS problem concerns the individual who is already subject to a DoLS order, and subsequently needs rapid tranquillisation. This is an issue of some concern, since it is arguable that many – perhaps almost all – people with mental disabilities in hospitals and similar institutions are deprived of liberty (Eldergill 2019). It is not obvious what, if any, additional safeguards are to arise in this situation. The individual is already deprived of liberty, and the traditional approach of the European Court of Human Rights is that Article 5 of the ECHR does not consider degrees of deprivation of liberty or questions of 'residual' liberty. If that were the case, assuming the original DoLS were well-founded, it is not clear that any further requirements for process would arise, at least under Article 5. Insofar as this is correct, it seems to raise considerable human rights issues as, once again, people who may be exceptionally vulnerable are left without formal human rights protections. It may be that the conventional wisdom about Article 5 and residual liberty is now open to question (*Schneiter c La Suisse* (2005)), but it is notable that the Court declined in 2012 to apply Article 5 to the segregation of an individual already detained in a psychiatric hospital (*Munjaz v United Kingdom* [2012]). The obligation to provide some protections might perhaps arise under Article 3 (freedom from inhuman or degrading treatment) of the ECHR, but at least in the past, the Court has tended to be generous to clinicians in matters of restraint: see, for example, *Herczegfalvy v Austria* (1992). More recently, there have been indications of a more robust approach by the Court to Article 3, at least in matters of physical restraint: see e.g., *Bureš v the Czech Republic* (2013) and *MS v Croatia (No 2)* (2015), but it remains to be seen how this will develop. The policies do not engage with any of these issues in detail.

There are further complications with reliance on the Mental Capacity Act as a justification of rapid tranquillisation. The first limitation is that it applies only to harm to the individual who is about to be restrained; it does not apply to restraint for the protection of others. When the issue is the protection of other people, the common law justification and, for detained patients, the Mental Health Act will remain available if they apply, as discussed previously. None of the Trust policies make this distinction.

It is also unclear how the issues surrounding rapid tranquillisation play out in the framework of the broader Mental Capacity Act. Consistent with NICE guidance and as discussed previously, the policies tend to encourage clinical staff to obtain the views of the individual regarding restraint as part of a planning process. Little guidance is provided as to how this information is to be used. That is not necessarily a legal problem as the Mental Capacity Act requires that the decision-maker only 'consider' statements of wishes and feelings as part of the best interests determination, but they are not determinative (*Mental Capacity Act 2005*: section 4(6)). That provides the flexibility for staff to respond to specific situations, which will have advantages from some perspectives. It also of course allows the individual's views to be overridden based on factors such as objective best interests in situations where the individual would not want their views overridden, which raises human rights concerns.

The situation becomes more complex when the views are expressed as an advance decision to refuse treatment. In that event, the refusal has the same effect when treatment is to be given as if the individual had capacity and was refusing the treatment (*Mental Capacity Act 2005*: section 26). If the refusal refers to one specific medication, this is not necessarily a practical problem, as most policies contain alternative medications which the refusal may not cover and which may therefore be used. If the refusal is of all tranquillising medication, however, the Mental Capacity Act would not provide legal authority to use those medications.

That would not necessarily preclude resort to other legal justifications. The Mental Capacity Act is designed to provide a mechanism for people lacking capacity which serves the same role as consent (or in this case, refusal) does for people who have capacity. Consistent with this, the compulsory provisions of the Mental Health Act continue to apply, so patients detained under that Act could be restrained if the provisions of section 62 of the Mental Health Act are met. The common law justification would also presumably continue to apply, although here the lack of definition of that mechanism comes back to bite. Would the common law allow (and are we comfortable with the common law allowing) the use of medication in this situation, when the individual to be medicated has considered the situation in advance, and indicated that he or she does not want to be medicated in these circumstances? Is the answer different if the refusal is of a specific medication rather than a refusal of all tranquillising medications, with the effect that clinical staff could simply override the refusal, even in circumstances where other drugs were available, where for example the clinician has a preference for one drug over another? The human rights issues regarding these outcomes are obvious, and the current case law provides no answer as to how the current law would deal with them.

Thirty-two of the Trusts refer to such advance decisions to refuse treatment in their rapid tranquillisation policies, and a number actively encourage patients to make such advance decisions as part of the planning process. None reflect the complexities that these advance decisions raise.

A comparable problem arises if the individual has signed a lasting power of attorney for personal care or where, much less frequently, a deputy for personal decision-making has been appointed for the individual by a court. In that event, the clinical staff can do nothing that conflicts with the decision of the attorney or deputy (*Mental Capacity Act 2005*: section 6(6)). Seven policies refer to lasting powers of attorney as part of the rapid tranquillisation process. Almost invariably they state that such holders of lasting powers of attorney should be 'consulted' or, occasionally, can 'provide consent'. None consider how to respond if the holder of the lasting power of attorney refuses the tranquillisation. In the event of a refusal, the same questions arise regarding the availability of the common law justification as were discussed regarding advance decisions to refuse treatment, with the same uncertain answers. Again, there is no discussion of these difficulties in the policies.

The treatment of the Mental Capacity Act is thus problematic. Even appreciating that it will often allow the use of chemical restraint, the policies neither identify nor provide guidance that would meaningfully assist staff in meeting its terms. Only part of that can be explained away by the existence of parallel policies relating to the Act specifically.

Conclusion

As the policies recognise, rapid tranquillisation is a serious intervention. Some elements of the policies are encouraging. The emphasis on the involvement of the patient himself or herself in planning responses does suggest a movement towards patient-centred care and, perhaps, the enhanced subjective status favoured by the CRPD. At the same time, the overall tenor of the policies sees tranquillisation as something done to the patient, reinforcing a medical approach. There is little evidence in the policies that legal complexities are understood, and the influence of human rights law is negligible.

To some degree, this will not come as a surprise. The policies are written by clinicians, for clinicians. It is therefore unsurprising that they have a clinical focus. There is nonetheless an implied challenge for human rights. Rapid tranquillisation raises profound human rights concerns; how can these be addressed if the relevant policies are written from a clinical reference point? And do we end up with chemical restraints allowed in clinical settings when they would not be elsewhere – arguably precisely the sort of discrimination that the CRPD is concerned about.

The caveat raised at the beginning of this chapter is perhaps the final concern, as it is not obvious that the policies themselves are any guide to what is happening on the ground. If it is accepted that what needs to be explored (and quite possibly to change) is the professional culture, it is not obvious that policy changes will have much of an effect. The *Mental Health Units (Use of Force) Act 2018* will require Trusts to collect data on the use of restraint, which will allow some meaningful systematic assessment as to whether the frequency of restraint is changing. It is less obvious how we use that information to reduce the use of rapid tranquillisation to control behaviour in health facilities, either through different staff intervention methods, environmental change, or non-coercive responses to patient needs. Those issues remain largely untouched by the policies; and in human rights terms, they are issues of serious concern.

References

Cases

Bureš v the Czech Republic, Application no. 37679/08, judgment of 18 January 2013.
F v West Berkshire Health Authority [1989] 2 All ER 545 (HL).
Freeman v Home Office (No 2) [1984] 1 QB 524 (CA).
Gillan and Quinton v United Kingdom (2010) 50 EHRR 45.
Herczegfalvy v Austria, 24 September 1992, § 82, Series A no. 244.
HL v United Kingdom (2005) 40 EHRR 32.
McCarthy v Chief Constable of Merseyside Police [2016] EWCA Civ 1257.
MS v Croatia (No 2), Application no. 75450/12, judgment of 19 May 2015.
Munjaz v United Kingdom [2012] MHLR 351.
Osman v United Kingdom (2000) 29 EHRR 245.
P v Cheshire West [2014] UKSC 19.
R (DPP) v Stratford Magistrates' Court [2018] 4 WLR 47.
R (Laporte) v Chief Constable of Gloucestershire Constabulary [2007] 2 AC 105.
Rabone v Pennine Care NHS Foundation Trust [2012] 2 AC 72.
Schneiter c La Suisse, Application no. 63062/00, judgment of 31 March 2005.
X v Finland [2012] ECHR 1371.
YF v Turkey, Application no 24209/94, judgment of 22 July 2003, (2004) 39 EHRR 34.

Books, journal articles and other texts

Alexander, J., Tharyan, P., Adams, C., John, T., Mol, C. and Philip, J. (2004) 'Rapid Tranquillisation of Violent or Agitated Patients in a Psychiatric Emergency Setting: Pragmatic Randomised Trial of Intramuscular Lorazepam v. Haloperidol Plus Promethazine', *The British Journal of Psychiatry*, 185(1): 63–69.
Banerjee, S. (2009) *The Use of Antipsychotic Medication for People with Dementia: Time for Action–A Report for the Minister of State for Care Services (UK)*. Available www.jcpmh.info/wp-content/uploads/time-for-action.pdf (accessed 20 June 2020).
Bartlett, P. (2012) 'The United Nations Convention on the Rights of Persons with Disabilities and Mental Health Law', *Modern Law Review*, 75(5): 752–78.
Committee for the Prevention of Torture (2017) *Report to the Government of the United Kingdom on the visit to the United Kingdom carried out by the European Committee for the Prevention of Torture and Inhuman or Degrading Treatment or*

Punishment (CPT) from 30 March to 12 April 2016, CPT/Inf (2017) 9. Available https://rm.coe.int/168070a773 (accessed 20 June 2020).

Dawson, J. (2015) 'A Realistic Approach to Assessing Mental Health Laws' Compliance with the UNCRPD', *International Journal of Law and Psychiatry*, 40: 70–79.

Degener, T. (2016) 'Disability in a Human Rights Context', *Laws*, 5: 35.

Department of Health (UK) (2005) *Delivering Race Equality in Mental Health Care: An Action Plan for Reform Inside and Outside Services and the Government's Response to the Independent Inquiry into the Death of David Bennett*. Available http://research.bmh.manchester.ac.uk/ReACH/resources/keypaper4.pdf (accessed 20 June 2020).

Department of Health (UK) (2015) *Mental Health Act 1983: Code of Practice*, London: The Stationery Office. Available https://assets.publishing.service.gov.uk/government/uploads/system/uploads/attachment_data/file/435512/MHA_Code_of_Practice.PDF (accessed 20 June 2020).

Department of Health (UK) (2018) *Modernising the Mental Health Act: Increasing Choice, Reducing Compulsion. Final Report of the Independent Review of the Mental Health Act 1983* (The Wessely Report). Available https://assets.publishing.service.gov.uk/government/uploads/system/uploads/attachment_data/file/778897/Modernising_the_Mental_Health_Act_-_increasing_choice__reducing_compulsion.pdf (accessed 20 June 2020).

Eldergill, A. (2019) 'Are All Incapacitated People Confined in a Hospital, Care Home or Their Own Home Deprived of Liberty?', *ERA Forum*, 19(4): 551–35.

Emmett, C., Pøole, M., Bond, J. and Hughes, J. (2013) 'Homeward Bound or Bound for a Home? Assessing the Capacity of Dementia Patients to Make Decisions About Hospital Discharge: Comparing Practice with Legal Standards', *International Journal of Law and Psychiatry*, 36: 73–82.

Flynn, E., and Arstein-Kerslake, A. (2014) 'Legislating Personhood: Realising the Right to Support in Exercising Legal Capacity', *International Journal of Law in Context*, 10: 81–104.

Gooding, P. (2015) 'Navigating the "Flashing Amber Lights" of the Right to Legal Capacity in the United Nations Convention on the Rights of Persons with Disabilities: Responding to Major Concerns', *Human Rights Law Review*, 15(1): 45–71.

Healthcare Commission (UK) (2008) *Count Me in 2008: Results of the 2008 National Census of Inpatients in Mental Health and Learning Disability Services in England and Wales*, London: Commission for Healthcare Audit and Inspection.

House of Lords Select Committee on the Mental Capacity Act 2005 (2014–14) *Mental Capacity Act 2005: Post-Legislative Scrutiny*, London: The Stationary Office. Available https://publications.parliament.uk/pa/ld201314/ldselect/ldmentalcap/139/139.pdf (accessed 20 June 2020).

Innes, J., and Sethi, F. (2013) 'Current Rapid Tranquillisation Documents in the UK: A Review of the Drugs Recommended, Their Routes of Administration and Clinical Parameters Influencing Their Use', *Journal of Psychiatric Intensive Care*, 9(2): 110–18.

McSherry, B. and Wilson, K. (2015) 'The Concept of Capacity in Australian Mental Health Law Reform: Going in the Wrong Direction?', *International Journal of Law and Psychiatry*, 40: 60–69.

National Institute of Health and Clinical Excellence (NICE) (2005) *Violence and Aggression: Short-term Management in Mental Health, Health and Community Settings*, NICE Guideline 10. Available www.nice.org.uk/guidance/ng10 (accessed 20 June 2020).

National Institute of Health and Clinical Excellence (NICE) (2015) *Violence: The Short-term Management of Disturbed/Violent Behaviour in In-patient Psychiatric Settings and Emergency Departments*, NICE Guidelines 25. Available www.ncbi.nlm.nih.gov/books/NBK55521/ (accessed 20 June 2020).

Paton, C., Adams, C.E., Dye, S., Fagan, E., Okocha, C. and Barnes, T.R. (2019) 'The Pharmacological Management of Acute Behavioural Disturbance: Data from a Clinical Audit Conducted in UK Mental Health Services', *Journal of Psychopharmacology*, 33(4): 472–81.

Public Health England (2015) *Prescribing of Psychotropic Drugs to People with Learning Disabilities and/or Autism by General Practitioners in England*, London: The Stationary Office. Available www.bl.uk/collection-items/prescribing-of-psychotropic-drugs-to-people-with-learning-disabilities-andor-autism-by-general-practitioners-in-england (accessed 20 June 2020).

Quinsey, V.L., Harris, G.T., Rice, M.E. and Cornier, C.A. (1998) *Violent Offenders: Appraising and Managing Risk*, Washington, DC: American Psychological Association.

Sailas, E. and Fenton, M. (2000) 'Seclusion and Restraint for People with Serious Mental Illness', *Cochrane Database of Systematic Reviews*, 1: CD001163.

Schulze, M. (2010) *Understanding the UN Convention on the Rights of Persons with Disabilities*, 2nd edn, New York: Handicap International. Available www.hiproweb.org/uploads/tx_hidrtdocs/HICRPDManual2010.pdf (accessed 20 June 2020).

Webster, C.D., Douglas, K.S., Eaves, D. and Hart, S.D. (1997) *HCR-20: Assessing Risk for Violence*, 2nd ver, Burnaby: Simon Fraser University, Mental Health, Law and Policy Institute.

Williams, V., Boyle, G., Jepson, M., Swift, P., Williamson, T. and Heslop, P. (2012) *Making Best Interests Decisions: People and Processes*, London: Mental Health Foundation.

Willner, P., Bridle, J., Price, V., Dymond, S. and Lewis, G. (2013) 'What Do NHS Staff Learn from Training on the Mental Capacity Act (2005)?', *Legal and Criminological Psychology*, 18: 83–101.

4 The regulation of restrictive practices on people with intellectual impairment

The challenges and opportunities posed by a rights-based approach

Kim Chandler

Introduction

Persons with intellectual and cognitive impairments – including people diagnosed with intellectual disability (sometimes also called learning disability) and/or cognitive impairment (which may be expressed in conditions such as Alzheimer's disease, dementia, autism and autism spectrum disorders, multiple sclerosis and acquired brain injury) – may be subject to restrictive practices in a range of facilities, including aged care facilities, disability support services, hospitals and other health facilities (Carter 2006; Victorian Law Reform Commission 2003, 2012; Australian Law Reform Commission 2014: paras 8.11–8.16). In real terms this means, for example, being detained in facilities so that free exit is prevented; being secluded in locked rooms; the use of ties and straps to physically restrain; and the use of psychotropic medication to control behaviour. These practices are used in response to behaviours that may put the person with disability, or the people that provide them support and care, at risk of harm.

There is a growing recognition and concern about the use of restrictive practices in relation to people with intellectual impairment in Australian society. The often unregulated use of restrictive practices has been observed by the Australian Law Reform Commission and state-level law reform commissions (Victorian Law Reform Commission 2012: 318). In its *Final Report on Equality, Capacity and Disability in Commonwealth Laws*, for example, the Australian Law Reform Commission (2014: 247) noted that the use of such practices may contravene the United Nations' *Convention on the Rights of Persons with Disabilities* (CRPD) (2007) and the *Convention Against Torture* and Other Cruel, Inhuman or Degrading Treatment or Punishment (1985). In the concluding observations on Australia's initial report under the CPRD, the United Nations Committee on the Rights of Persons with Disabilities recommended that Australia 'take immediate steps to end such practices, including by establishing an independent national preventative mechanism to monitor places of detention' (Australian Law Reform Commission 2014: 247).

The aim of this chapter is twofold: to explore the most common legal bases relied upon to authorise restrictive practices on persons with intellectual and cognitive impairments in Australia (and thus the gaps and inconsistencies in approaches) and to explore the challenges and opportunities of developing a rights-based approach to regulating restrictive practices in the future. This chapter focuses primarily on the regulation of the use of restrictive practices in disability services and aged care settings.

An important starting point to the regulation of restrictive practices, consistent with the rule of law and the principles of justice and equality, should be clear authorisation for the use of restrictive practices, incorporating appropriate procedural safeguards. Yet, as this chapter discusses, Australia falls well short in this regard, with the regulation of restrictive practices on people with intellectual and cognitive impairments characterised by a disparate and inconsistent approach with many gaps. While this issue must be addressed, I argue that authorisation in itself is insufficient to both truly realise the human rights of persons with disabilities and lead to the reduction and elimination of the use of restrictive practices. Adopting a rights-based approach to equality in designing a regulatory approach is necessary to achieve these goals. This moves beyond purely 'procedural' approaches to the rule of law (or what some commentators would label as 'legalism') and provides the opportunity to address the fundamental structural inequalities that have led to the lack of regulation and overuse of restrictive practices. Such an approach to regulation means the 'problem' for the law of how to authorise restrictive practices can be reframed. It can be less about positive authorisation, which requires the elaboration of extensive criteria (based on potentially discriminatory factors such as disability, impairment and risk of harm) and more about the positive obligations on those who seek to use these practices. This provides an opportunity to refocus the energies of policymakers and lawmakers and even our regulatory institutions towards addressing deficits in support and environments for persons with intellectual and cognitive impairments.

Background

The use of restrictive practices to respond to behavioural issues

Some persons with intellectual and cognitive impairment express what are known as *challenging behaviours* or *behaviours of concern*. The latter term is preferred by some commentators because it emphasises the environmental context of such behaviours, including for example the lack of appropriate supports and assistance, and does not stigmatise individuals (Chan et al. 2012: 36). In practical terms, such behaviours may involve aggressive behaviours towards others including physical assault and inappropriate sexual behaviours, as well as causing extensive property damage. It may also involve self-injurious behaviours including head-banging, self-biting, self-scratching and over-eating, including compulsive eating of indigestible objects (Association of Professional Behavior Analysts 2010).

Restrictive practices (sometimes known as restrictive interventions) may be utilised to control and prevent such behaviour. These practices commonly include detention; seclusion; and chemical, physical and mechanical restraint (see Chapters 1, 2 and 5 in this volume for discussion of the definitions of these terms in the Australian context). Persons with intellectual and cognitive impairments may live in a variety of circumstances that involve the use of one or more restrictive practices, as illustrated in the following three hypothetical scenarios.

Scenario one

Alfred, aged 75 years, lives in an aged care facility. He has early stage dementia. He would prefer to live at home, but he lives on his own and following a number of admissions to hospital both his family and the hospital social worker thought it best he lived somewhere he could have 24 hours a day care and support. Some days he becomes distressed and asks to go home, but he eventually calms down. There is a keypad entrance to the facility and Alfred does not know the combination so he cannot exit or enter without the supervision of staff. Staff are concerned that he would wander off and become lost or be hit by a car if he was allowed to come and go as he pleased. On occasion, medication that has a sedative effect is administered when Alfred becomes distressed.

Scenario two

Mary, aged 26 years, has an intellectual disability and lives in a house she shares with three other people who also have intellectual disabilities. Mary and her housemates always have at least one paid support person in the house with them. On most days, Mary is allowed to go on outings, usually with a support person accompanying her and one or two other house mates. Mary has occasionally visited the local shops on her own but must return promptly to the house. Mary sometimes gets upset and annoyed, particularly if another housemate takes something from her room, or has an item like an iPad that Mary wants. Sometimes she has hit a housemate or support worker. On these occasions, the support worker places her in a room (the 'time-out' room) on her own until she calms down.

Scenario three

John, aged 34 years, has an acquired brain injury as a result of a serious illness when he was a child. He was placed in state care at the age of 15 when he began exhibiting violent behaviours. Since that time he has lived in a variety of secure facilities. As he became older his violent outbursts became more severe. He now lives in a purpose-built residential facility where he is confined most days to one room. His food and other necessities are passed to him by staff through a slot in the door. Staff supervise him via a Perspex window. He is occasionally taken on outings to a park, but this happens rarely because it requires three or more support workers to accompany him.

Regardless of whether these conditions are in place for the safety and well-being of the person with intellectual impairment, or for the safety of the support workers, other residents, or the general community, all scenarios involve an impact on the person's right to liberty and security. These are important human rights and common law rights that belong to all persons regardless of whether or not they have intellectual or cognitive impairments. For this reason, the use of restrictive practices must be regulated.

Why the use of restrictive practices must be regulated

Restrictive practices have implications for individuals' liberty and security

Personal liberty has been described in Australian case law as the most basic freedom (*South Australia v Totani* (2010): 423; *Al Kateb v Godwin* (2004): 577) and one of the most fundamental of all rights (*Minister for Immigration v Al Masri* (2003): para 86; *Minister for Immigration v VFAD* (2002): paras 108–112). The common law has developed remedies for restrictions on personal liberty and security and there are equivalent criminal sanctions that punish the use of detention and restraint unless authorised by law. The common law right to liberty is secured by the imposition of limits on the exercise of powers of arrest, detention and deprivation of liberty unless authorised by law. These interests are manifested in the writ of habeas corpus (*Antunovic v Dawson* [2010]), the tort of false imprisonment (*Watson v Marshall* [1971]) and criminal law prohibitions on deprivation of liberty (see *Criminal Code Act 1899* (Qld): section 355; *Criminal Code Act 1913* (WA): section 333; *Criminal Code Act 1983* (NT): section 196; *Crimes Act 1958* (Vic): section 31). Invasions of bodily security or integrity represented by physical or mechanical restraint of a person are, at civil law, protected by the tort of trespass, in particular battery (*Collins v Wilcock* [1984]), while the use of physical restraint may amount to an assault at criminal law (*Criminal Code Act 1899* (Qld): section 335; *Criminal Code Act 1913* (WA): section 333; *Criminal Code Act 1983* (NT): section 188; *Crimes Act 1900* (NSW): section 61; *Crimes Act 1958* (Vic): section 31; *Criminal Law Consolidation Act 1935* (SA): section 20).

These protections also apply to persons with intellectual or cognitive impairments, by virtue of the rule of law. At a foundational level, the rule of law requires 'the consistent application of the ordinary law to every person'. In this sense, as Allan (1993: 23) has said, ensuring equality in the fundamental sense is also vitally important to those vulnerable to abuses of power, because it means political rulers 'cannot single out particular persons for special treatment'. According to Bingham (2010: 4), in so far as the rule of law safeguards and promotes justice for the vulnerable, it is essential. He points out that laws and legal processes are most needed for 'minorities, particular unpopular minorities'.

Liberty and security are also important human rights

In international human rights instruments, liberty and security are characterised as civil and political rights, and are enunciated in Article 3 of the *Universal Declaration of Human Rights* (1948) as the right to 'life, liberty and security' and Article 9 of the *International Covenant on Civil and Political Rights* (ICCPR)

(1966), which recognises that 'everyone has the right to liberty and security of the person'. United Nations bodies have asserted that the protection of liberty as a human right is not confined to imprisonment or police custody, but includes a wide range of circumstances in which a person may be deprived of their liberty including, for example, by involuntary hospitalisation (Human Rights Committee 2014: para 5). Expressions of this right impose prohibitions on arbitrary arrest and detention.

Deprivation of liberty other than in accordance with procedures established by law is also prohibited (Human Rights Committee 2014: para 11). As a human right, the right to security of the person entails 'freedom from injury to the body and the mind, or bodily and mental integrity' (Human Rights Committee 2014: para 3). The right to freedom from torture and cruel, inhuman or degrading treatment and punishment in Article 7 of the ICCPR also overlaps with the right to liberty and security and may be relevant to the use of restrictive practices (Human Rights Committee 2014: para 56). Australia is bound by these international human rights obligations, although they do not form part of Australian law unless they are incorporated by Parliament into domestic law (McSherry and Wilson 2015: 61).

As Bartlett and Sampson discuss in Chapter 3 in this volume, there has been significant consideration of the human right to liberty and security with respect to people with disability in environments such as hospitals, residential facilities and other health facilities in the United Kingdom courts, where statutory provisions in the *Human Rights Act 1998* (UK) prohibit deprivations of liberty (Law Commission (UK) 2017). This culminated in the 'acid test' set out by Lady Hale in the Supreme Court judgment *P v Cheshire West* [2014], which provides that the objective elements of a deprivation of liberty are satisfied if a person is (i) under continuous supervision and control and (ii) not free to leave. Lady Hale also held that factors such as the person's compliance or lack of objection, the relative normality of the placement and the reason or purpose behind the placement were irrelevant.

Some, but not all, Australian states or territories have a Human Rights Act or Charter (*Human Rights Act 2004* (ACT); *Charter of Human Rights and Responsibilities Act 2006* (Vic); *Human Rights Act 2018* (Qld)), and the instruments that do exist are not equivalent to the United Kingdom's *Human Rights Act 1998*. Nevertheless, similar factors have been considered by Australian courts in relation to the concrete living conditions of people with intellectual impairment when considering whether there has been false imprisonment, or a deprivation of liberty sufficient for the issue of a writ of habeas corpus at common law. With respect to false imprisonment, while the rule is that the imprisonment must amount to a total restraint (Balkin and Davis 2009; *R v Bournewood and Community and Mental Health NHS Trust; Ex parte L* [1999]), the concept of restraint or imprisonment is broader than what would normally be understood as imprisonment (*Collins v Wilcock* [1984]), with the focus being on a person's freedom of movement (*Meering v Grahame-White Aviation Co Ltd* [1919]; *Myer Stores Ltd v Soo* [1991]).

Darcy (bht Diane Aldridge) v New South Wales [2011] is a case in point. Joanne Darcy, a woman with an intellectual disability and borderline personality disorder, who had shown violent behaviour towards others, was 19 years old when she was sent to the Kanangra Centre, a residential service operated by the Department of Community Services in New South Wales. During her stay she was moved between different residential units, some of which were locked and some of which afforded her the ability to move freely between various parts of the facility. She also accessed the community. Justice Whealy concluded that she was 'detained in the sense that this is expressed in the tort of false imprisonment', placing emphasis on the fact that while Ms Darcy could leave the centre, she could not leave without permission and when permission was granted, she had to return at the end of her 'sojourn' (*Darcy (bht Diane Aldridge) v NSW* [2011]: para 153). Justice Whealy accepted counsel for Ms Darcy's argument that the critical test was that if she had attempted to leave, she would have been prevented from doing so (para 151). While, after reviewing judicial precedent, Justice Whealy acknowledged that the tort required that a 'total restraint' is placed on the plaintiff, he found 'that restraint, however, need bear no similarity to what would normally be described as imprisonment' (para 145; see also *South Australia v Lampard-Trevorrow* [2010]). Ultimately the Court found that Ms Darcy's detention was lawful because consent had been provided by the Public Guardian.

A writ of habeas corpus was issued in respect of a resident of a nursing home in *Skyllas v Retirement Care Australia (Preston) Pty Ltd* [2006]. The nursing home confirmed that Mrs Skyllas had expressed a wish to return home but the Director of Nursing was of the opinion that this was not practicable given her high level of care due to her physical and medical issues. Justice Byrne stated that 'as a matter of law the nursing home cannot detain a patient against her wishes' (para 9).

Deprivation of liberty must be authorised, excused or justified by law

Given the protection of the rights to liberty and security, any deprivation of these rights will be unlawful unless otherwise authorised, justified or excused by law. But consistent with the significance of these common law principles and their protection in both the civil and criminal law, the circumstances in which this interference will be excused or justified are generally tightly restricted. Broadly, defences such as self-defence, medical emergency and necessity (as it is usually applied) will only provide for the lawfulness of detention or restraint in very limited circumstances, usually in the case of an absolute emergency (Chandler, White and Willmott 2016). For example, if a support worker or health professional was in immediate danger of being harmed or was under attack, there would potentially be a defence to battery if they physically restrained the person or used other physical actions in their own defence. After the immediate danger had passed, however, and the support worker or health professional's safety was assured, further acts of restraint or confinement would not be covered by the defence (*McClelland v Symons* [1951]).

The common law doctrine of necessity has been applied to provide authorisation for long-term detention and restraint of people with intellectual and cognitive impairments in the United Kingdom (see Bartlett and Sampson in Chapter 3 in this volume). While there has been speculation about whether the doctrine of necessity may provide some authorisation for restrictive practices in Australia (*R v Bournewood and Community and Mental Health NHS Trust; Ex parte L* [1999]; *QNN* [2013]; Devereux 1998; Allen and Tulich 2015), Australian courts have largely not followed developments in the United Kingdom (Chandler, White and Willmott 2016). Consequently, while common law defences may provide protection from criminal and/or civil liability for the very short-term use of detention and restraint in situations akin to emergencies, they will not provide protection for longer-term restraint and detention of people in residential disability services, hospitals, health facilities and aged care facilities. The ongoing use of restrictive practices in Australian disability services, aged care services and other health care facilities therefore necessitates another form of legal authorisation.

The current regulatory approach in Australia

Current sources of authorisation for restrictive practices

In Australia, the use of restrictive practices in hospitals, health care facilities, disability services and aged care facilities occurs in the context of a disparate, inconsistent and complex legislative and regulatory framework (Chandler, Willmott and White 2014). In broad terms there are three levels of regulation. First, in a minority of cases, restrictive practices are explicitly regulated and authorised under specific regulatory regimes. Secondly, many jurisdictions rely on the authorisation or consent for such practices by guardians and other substitute decision-makers under each state and territory's legislative frameworks on guardianship. Lastly, there are numerous policies and regulatory frameworks that apply to the standards of care in residential aged care services, disability services and other health facilities.

Regulatory schemes

At the time of writing, only some states and territories had legislative frameworks governing the use of restrictive practices on people with intellectual and cognitive impairments in certain settings. Queensland, Victoria, the Northern Territory, the Australian Capital Territory and Tasmania have regulatory frameworks for the authorisation of restrictive practices (see *Disability Services Act 2006* (Qld); *Guardianship and Administration Act 2000* (Qld); *Disability Act 2006* (Vic); *Disability Services Act 1993* (NT); *Senior Practitioner Act 2018* (ACT); *Disability Services Act 2011* (Tas)). These are, however, restricted to regulating practices in government-funded disability services (Chandler, Willmott and White 2014). That is, they do not regulate the use of restrictive practices in aged care services, hospitals, rehabilitation services and other health facilities. The Australian Capital Territory regulatory scheme also extends to education and the care and protection of children (*Senior Practitioner Act 2018* (ACT)). In Western Australia, South Australia and New South Wales, legislative regulation of restrictive practices is confined to services governed by mental health legislation (*Mental Health Act 2014* (WA); *Mental Health Act 2009* (SA); *Mental Health Act 2007* (NSW)). The Commonwealth also does not specifically regulate the use of restrictive practices in aged care services.

Guardianship

All Australian states and territories now have regulatory frameworks for substitute decision-making for people with impaired decision-making capacity. For example, guardianship regimes in one or more parts of Australia allow for guardians to be appointed by tribunals to make decisions about personal matters (see *Guardianship and Administration Act 2019* (Vic): section 30) and for non-tribunal appointed decision-makers to make decisions about health care or medical treatment (see statutory health attorneys under the *Powers of Attorney Act 1998* (Qld): section 62). Only in a minority of cases however are guardians (or guardianship tribunals) granted specific statutory powers to make decisions about restrictive practices, this being restricted to Queensland and Tasmania's statutory regimes (*Guardianship and Administration Act 2000* (Qld): Chapter 5B; *Disability Services Act 2011* (Tas): Part 6). Tribunals may appoint guardians to consent to restrictive practices under the guise of authority to make decisions about health care or medical treatment (*MLI* [2006]; *Re WCM* [2006]); or even under guardians' broad plenary powers (*JP* [2008]; *OMF* [2008]; *SDF* [2013]). Some statutory regimes provide for guardians to authorise 'coercive powers' – that is, guardianship tribunals may authorise the use of force to ensure guardians' consent to medical treatment and other decisions about a person's day-to-day care are carried out despite the person's objections (see *Guardianship and Administration Act 1993* (SA): section 32(1)(e).

An examination of the authorisation of restrictive practices under guardianship regimes by Chandler, White and Willmott (2017) found that, unless the relevant statute was explicit in allowing guardians to exercise restrictive practice functions, there was a lack of certainty about whether and on what basis guardians could consent to restrictive practices (see Allen and Tulich 2015: 10; O'Neil and Peisah 2018). This has led to inconsistency in decision-making across and even within jurisdictions. In their reviews of their respective state guardianship legislation, the Victorian Law Reform Commission (2012: 336), the Queensland Law Reform Commission (2010: 362) and the New South Wales Law Reform Commission (2018) have all noted the continuing gaps in the regulation of restrictive practices.

Regulating standards of care

The most common approach to the regulation of restrictive practices in aged care and disability services is reliance on broad policy or position statements, codes of practice or standards of care (see Maker in Chapter 5 in this volume). South Australia and New South Wales have policy frameworks that apply to the use of restrictive practices in disability services (Department for Communities and Social Inclusion (SA) 2017; Department of Family and Community Services (NSW) 2018). Western Australia has a code of practice (Department of Communities (WA) 2019). In the context of residential aged care, the Commonwealth government also takes this approach. For example, restrictive practices are addressed in a 'Decision-Making Tool' to assist care workers to promote a restraint free environment (Department of Health and Ageing 2012), as well as accreditation standards (*Quality of Care Principles 2014* (Cth): Part 4A; see Breen in Chapter 13 in this volume).

Australia has now moved towards a national approach to the funding of disability services with the National Disability Insurance Scheme (NDIS), which is enacted under Commonwealth legislation. Yet, the Commonwealth government has only gone part way to creating a national approach to regulating restrictive practices. The *National Disability Insurance Act 2013* (Cth) (*NDIS Act*) provides for an NDIS Quality and Safeguards Commissioner (the Commissioner), one of whose functions is 'behavioural support'. The Commissioner's role also involves providing leadership in relation to the reduction and elimination of restrictive practices, as well as monitoring and practice improvement (*NDIS Act 2013*: section 181H). The role of the Commissioner only extends to the use of restrictive practices in NDIS-funded disability services. Furthermore, actual authorisation of the use of restrictive practices will continue to be dealt with at the state and territory level (Department of Social Services 2016).

Does legalism offer the best way to address regulatory gaps?

An alternative approach to regulation from the mental health sector

The complex and inconsistent situation in relation to the regulation of restrictive practices in disability and aged care services is in stark contrast to the regulation of involuntary treatment, detention and restrictive practices in mental health services. All Australian states and territories have statutes that regulate the involuntary care and support of people with mental illness, including the use of seclusion and restraint (Kumble and McSherry 2010; Freckelton 2018). In comparison to disability services legislation, these regimes impose fairly uniform requirements which offer more extensive procedural safeguards including professional assessments, regular reviews of involuntary treatment and detention by independent tribunals and access to appeal to a higher court (Freckelton 2018). By and large, states' and territories' legislation for the regulation of involuntary treatment of mental illness, including detention and restraint, provides for clear authorisation of deprivation of liberty; clear criteria; opportunities for review (consistent with a procedural approach to the rule of law and a lack of arbitrariness); and usually a requirement to use the least restrictive approach (embodying the human rights requirement for proportionality).

This approach, which Fennell (2010) has defined as 'legalism', and Unsworth (1993: 501) as 'juridicism', is consistent with the procedural approach to the rule of law focused on adequate procedural safeguards. As such it embraces what Carney (2010: 257) has called 'a cultural endorsement of liberal values of personal autonomy', or what Unsworth (1993: 501) describes as central to the Enlightenment discourse of natural rights and abstract liberties.

At the time it emerged, this approach was innovative and reformist (Unsworth 1993: 498) and arguably today, as Carney (2010: 257) has said, the benefits of this approach (reflected in Australia's mental health laws) largely outweigh its weaknesses. It protects against unlawful and arbitrary detention and provides some transparency and oversight of involuntary treatment and restraint. It reflects a departure from a paternalistic and protectionist approach with absolute discretion placed with the medical and allied health professions.

The question that remains, however, is whether adopting a similar approach would be successful in reducing or eliminating the use of restrictive practices on people with intellectual and cognitive impairments. Many commentators have criticised the application of this approach (broadly described as legalism) to the regulation of involuntary treatment for mental illness on the basis that it fails to realise the human rights of those subject to it (Unsworth 1993; Fennell 2010). Carney (2010: 260) has acknowledged that the approach is limited and requires serious renovation. Fennell (2010) argues that legalism simply codifies clinical authority to deprive people of their liberty; while Lewis contends that people with psychosocial disabilities have suffered from a 'compliance gap', that is, a gap between 'lofty declaration and rights reality' (Lewis 2010: 97). With respect to people with intellectual and cognitive impairments, as disability theorists have argued (Fennell 1986: 36; Nussbaum 2007: 90; Carlson and Kittay 2010: 8; Goodey 2016: 327), people with disabilities, in particular people with intellectual and cognitive impairments, have been marginalised by theories of justice and equality. While they may have had a claim to formal equality with respect to civil and political rights, in reality such a claim has not guaranteed the equal realisation of these rights in practice.

The limits of legalism and persons with disability

The limitations of legalism arguably arise from its liberal foundations, which while important to the protection of fundamental rights and the rule of law, also have serious shortcomings when it comes to the rights of people with disabilities. Understanding these limitations and their origins is a necessary precursor to devising an approach to transcend them (see Fennell 1986; Carlson and Kittay 2010; Chandler, White and Willmott 2018).

First, born as they were of the Enlightenment emphasis on the individual, the Kantian belief in the moral worth inherent in human beings, and the idea of the 'free, equal and independent' human being, liberal theories of rights and justice have historically grounded such entitlements in the actual possession of reason and rationality (Fennell 1986: 41; Nussbaum 2007: 19, 2011: 29). As Carlson and Kittay (2010: 1) have pointed out, the ability to reason is generally taken to be the foundation for human dignity and the special moral status that we accord human beings. Dignity is also a foundational value of modern human rights. Article 1 of the Universal Declaration of Human Rights (1948), reflecting the Kantian belief in the inherent moral worth of human beings, declares that '[a]ll human beings are born free and equal in dignity and rights. They are endowed with reason and conscience and should act towards one another in a spirit of brotherhood'. Hence, argues Finegan (2012: 186), 'human rights inhere in human nature, a nature which is characterised by reason and conscience'.

While this Enlightenment philosophy gave birth to the modern conception of the principles of justice, equality and human rights, it also posed a particular problem for people with intellectual and cognitive impairments who were not attributed with reason or rationality. In turn, this raised philosophical questions about their entitlement to the same human rights and to justice. John Rawls' (1971) theory of justice draws on this substantive liberal tradition that emphasises distributive justice, reflects the Kantian focus on human dignity and is a modern version of traditional social contract theories (such as that of John Loch). As Wong (2010: 130) says, for Rawls, 'human beings count as free and equal persons when they have the moral powers necessary to engage in social cooperation'.

The lack of entitlement to protections offered by justice in this formulation, according to Carson and Kittay (2010: 8), leaves people with disability 'at the mercy of another's charity' and hence more likely to 'suffer poverty, neglect, and abuse'. At best, people with cognitive and intellectual impairments have been subject to a 'soft law' or welfare approach, with most of the early developments in realising the rights of people with disability still tending towards a medical/welfare model as expressed in security and welfare legislation, health law or guardianship (Kayess and French 2008: 14).

A further limitation is that the primary focus of this approach is on civil and political rights, and protection from interference with these 'negative' rights. This is of little assistance to persons with disabilities who may face serious barriers to exercising those rights, including in applying for administrative or judicial review of decisions about their treatment, detention and restraint. Related to this is the fact that, while regulatory frameworks may include principle-based statements about the 'least restrictive' approach, they offer little in the way of positive obligations to provide services, supports or environmental conditions that would reduce the need to use restrictive practices. Fundamentally, a legalistic approach ignores the fact that equal enjoyment of certain rights is dependent upon other structural adjustments and conditions. The principle that 'like should be treated as like' is one of the most common expressions of equality and is the foundation for the approach to non-discrimination known as formal equality (Fredman 2016: 716). Like the procedural or formal approach to the rule of law, formal equality is an important starting point. However, it fails to address the underlying disadvantage of those for whom equal treatment may in fact result in their disadvantage being entrenched (Fredman 2016: 718). It likewise fails to recognise that unequal treatment may be needed to achieve equality and, further, that genuine equality may only be achieved if certain pre-conditions are met, or accommodations made.

A rights-based approach to safeguarding the rights to liberty and security

A rights-based approach to equality: moving beyond 'legalism'

Implementing the procedural safeguards that are largely absent in existing regulation of restraint use on people with intellectual and cognitive impairments, while an important starting point, will not be sufficient to guarantee people with intellectual and cognitive impairments rights to liberty and security on an equal basis to others. Truly challenging the discriminatory attribution of rights to people with intellectual and cognitive impairments requires an approach to equality that is not dependent on a certain physical, intellectual or cognitive status; that recognises that people with disability are holders of rights, not subjects of a welfare or protectionist approach; that recognises that people start from certain points of structural disadvantage; and that recognises that the primary responsibility for ensuring people with disability realise their human rights rests on the state.

Such an approach – which I have termed 'a rights-based approach to equality' – is reflected in the CRPD. That paradigm-shifting instrument, while based on the same liberal tradition of justice and human rights as the international human rights instruments discussed previously, provides an historic opportunity to transcend some of the limitations of traditional rights-based and justice oriented approaches that have fallen short in securing the rights of persons with disabilities. A rights-based approach to equality, which draws influence from a variety of approaches, including the capabilities approach and other disability theories of social inclusion, can meet these demands. At the heart of this approach is a focus on the concrete opportunities people with disability need to realise their rights. It has particular relevance to the use of restrictive practices like restraint and seclusion which are often used in lieu of appropriate models of support and assistance.

The interdependence of justice and capabilities or enabling conditions

While many disability theorists and ethicists have critiqued traditional approaches to justice and rights and their tendency to exclude or marginalise persons with disabilities, views differ as to whether traditional theories of justice can accommodate persons with intellectual or cognitive disabilities. Nussbaum (2010: 77) for example argues that theories of justice cannot accommodate persons with disabilities, because such theories do not adopt the position that human beings should be treated as an end in themselves regardless of their level of cognitive functioning. Wong (2010: 131) alternatively claims that people with disability are not necessarily excluded from theories of justice if – rather than relying on persons who hold actual moral powers (that is, actual rationality and reasonableness) – moral powers are understood as potential. This potentiality brings the claims of justice into play for people with disability.

Regardless of the underlying critique of the theory of justice and rights, the corrective action required to ensure that persons with disabilities can enjoy their rights on an equal basis with others is similar. A common factor is the requirement for what Nussbaum would call 'capabilities' or Wong would call 'enabling conditions'. That is, adherents to many of these approaches would argue that resources must be devoted to people with intellectual and cognitive impairments in order to meet certain conditions necessary for a person to have a flourishing life on an equal basis with others (Kittay and Carlson 2010: 9). For Nussbaum (2010: 78), who draws on the capabilities approach of Amartya Sen, this does not require equalising capabilities for everyone, or allocating equal financial resources, but rather the realisation that there is a certain 'threshold' for each basic entitlement necessary for a good life (such as education) that must be met so that a person can live with dignity. Wong's enabling conditions are those (such as socialising and developing relationships) that will assist persons with disabilities to develop the necessary moral powers. Wong (2010: 143) argues that the conditions of support that many persons with disabilities live in (lack of privacy, little assistance to help with communication, few opportunities for choices) impede the development of these moral powers. The state, Wong (2010: 143) asserts, has a responsibility to provide the environment, resources and support services (the enabling conditions) necessary for people to become fully cooperative members of society.

Rather than emphasising the so-called limitations of persons with disabilities, a capabilities approach places an obligation on society to provide the 'enabling conditions' or 'capabilities' so that all persons can live a life with dignity, which includes access to justice. As Carlson and Kittay (2010: 9) express it, this recognises that questions of justice and resources are intimately bound up with one another. They are more than complementary – 'each can be viewed as functional for the other'.

Complementary to the capabilities approach is a rights-based approach to equality. This, too, goes beyond ideas of formal equality and equal treatment and emphasises the need for structural adjustments or enabling conditions, including positive obligations on the state to ensure people with disability can realise their human rights on an equal basis with others. It also eschews divisions between civil and political rights and social, economic and cultural rights. It recognises with respect to the use of restrictive practices that there is an interdependency between justice and resources and between civil and political rights and social, economic and cultural rights, between the right to liberty and security and the right to social support, habilitation, appropriate accommodation, integration into the community and education for example.

The human rights model in the CRPD

Importantly this approach to equality is also reflected in the CPRD (Degener 2016: 35). While originating from the same liberal tradition as other modern human rights instruments, the CPRD represents a significant paradigm change (Kayess and French 2008: 3), one that must be integrated into any liberal theory of justice aimed at ensuring equality for people with disability. First, the CRPD challenges the medical idea of disability, namely, that disability is defined by a person's impairment, including mental impairment. It is based on an alternative approach known as the social model of disability. The social model locates a person's disadvantage or discrimination in the social environment, rather than the person's impairment (Kayess and French 2008: 6). The definition of disability in Article 1 of that instrument emphasises interaction between impairment and social and structural barriers to equality (Fredman 2016: 279).

The CPRD approach to disability is, by definition, founded in a human rights model that recognises the inherent and intrinsic dignity of human beings regardless of differences, including impairments. Article 3 refers to 'respect for the inherent dignity of persons' alongside the 'respect for difference and respect of human diversity and humanity'. Article 5 prohibits discrimination on the basis of disability. The CPRD extends the definition of discrimination beyond those found in other human rights instruments to encompass not only direct and indirect discrimination but also the denial of 'reasonable accommodation' (Article 2). 'Reasonable accommodation' is defined (in Article 2) as:

> necessary and appropriate modifications and adjustments not imposing a disproportionate or undue burden, where needed in a particular case, to ensure to persons with disabilities the enjoyment or exercise on an equal basis with others of all human rights and fundamental freedoms.

That is, obligations are placed on States Parties to ensure human rights of people with disability are respected, protected and fulfilled (Harnacke 2013: 774). Degener (2016: 19) argues that this goes beyond a substantive model of equality, providing a more comprehensive road map for change – it 'strives to overcome structural, institutional, as well as direct and indirect discrimination by introducing positive duties to transform society'.

Crucially, this recognition of people with disability as bearers of human rights, not objects of welfare, extends to all people, including people with intellectual and cognitive impairments. This, in large part, is owed to Article 12, which is titled '[e]qual recognition before the law'. Its second paragraph recognises that legal capacity (and thus the rights and duties that accompany it) is an inherent right and belongs to the person with disability, including a person with intellectual impairment. The United Nations Committee on the Rights of Persons with Disabilities (2014: para 12) has clarified that legal capacity differs from mental capacity. Paragraph three of the CRPD's Article 12 goes further, placing an obligation on States Parties to support people with disability to exercise their legal capacity.

The obligation to make reasonable accommodations in regard to liberty and security is specifically addressed in Article 14 of the CRPD. It holds that States Parties must ensure that people with disability enjoy liberty and security on the same basis as others. It also states that in no case should having a disability be a justification for being deprived of liberty or security.

The Office of the High Commissioner for Human Rights (2014: para 1) has interpreted Article 14 as meaning that laws permitting the involuntary detention of persons with disabilities are incompatible with the right to liberty. However, some states, including Australia, have interpreted Article 14 as meaning that while persons with a disabilities cannot be involuntarily detained 'solely' because of their disability, a deprivation of liberty can be justified if there is a risk of harm to self or others (McSherry and Wilson 2015).

At the very least, read with States' overarching responsibility for non-discrimination, and the obligation to provide reasonable accommodation, Article 14 means that persons with disabilities should have optimal access to the conditions and supports necessary to reduce or eliminate the need to resort to restraints and detention in aged care facilities and disability services. There is a growing body of work that highlights that restrictive practices are often used in lieu of appropriate supports and emphasises the importance of working to understand the causes and triggers of such behaviours so that the response can be a preventative one, with a focus on changing services, systems and environments (Hayes and Hannold 2007; Royal College of Psychiatrists, British Psychological Society and Royal College of Speech and Language Therapists 2007; Disability Rights Now 2012: 91–101; Chan et al. 2012).

Applying a rights-based approach to equality in the regulation of restrictive practices

A rights-based approach to equality in the regulation of restrictive practices requires both clear authorisation and procedural safeguards (associated with the rule of law and traditional approaches characterised as 'legalism'), as well as mechanisms to enforce the state's obligations to provide 'enabling conditions' and support (characterised earlier as a rights-based approach). I next briefly outline what this might mean in practice in terms of a regulatory framework for restrictive practices.

Clear authorisation and procedural safeguards

As I described in the first part of this chapter, the use of practices like detention and restraint affect two fundamental rights – the right to liberty and the right to security. Except where these practices are excused, justified or otherwise authorised by law they are unlawful and may attract one or more remedies (civil or criminal). Yet the regulation of restrictive practices in Australia is characterised by significant gaps, and where it does exist there are significant inconsistencies across jurisdictions. It overwhelmingly relies on 'soft law' approaches such as standards, codes of practice and guardianship law.

To ensure that rights to liberty and security are protected, restrictive practices should not be used, other than in emergencies, unless they are authorised as part of a regulatory approach that provides specific statutory authority along with appropriate procedural safeguards consistent with the rule of law and the principles of justice and human rights. There must be clear authority in explicit statutory provisions and approval or authorisation by an authority independent to the service that seeks to use them. Clear criteria are necessary so that their use and authorisation are transparent and open to judicial oversight and review. There must be access to regular review, or review of decisions to detain and restraint people as of right. Independent monitoring is also important.

Human rights jurisprudence incorporates the procedural demands of the rule of law. Article 9 of the ICCPR demands that deprivation of liberty be 'on such grounds and in accordance with such procedures as are established by law' (see Nowak 2005). Article 9 of the ICCPR also prohibits arbitrary detention, that is, detention under law that has 'elements of inappropriateness, injustice, lacking of predictability and the due process of the law' (Human Rights Committee 2014: para 12). Therefore, not only should any deprivation of liberty be clearly authorised under law, any such law should also define precisely the terms on which a deprivation is permitted and define the procedures to be applied. In this way independent judicial oversight is capable of determining what is a lawful and what is an unlawful deprivation of liberty (Nowak 2005: 212). Rather than being based on vague or subjective criteria of 'best interests', criteria for detention should be 'defined with sufficient precision to avoid overly broad or arbitrary interpretation or application' (Human Rights Committee 2014: para 22). There should also be a right to seek a review of the lawfulness of your detention before an independent court or tribunal (Human Rights Committee 2014: para 15).

Further, while it is recognised that rights such as liberty and security are not absolute, and there may be circumstances where the state may seek to curtail or limit the human rights of people with intellectual impairment for legitimate purposes, such as the safety of the person or others (Alexy 2017: 34), any limitation must also be proportionate (*European Convention on Human Rights* 1950: Article 5(1); Nowak 2005; European Court of Human Rights 2019). As recognised by Justice Bell in *Kracke v Mental Health Review Board* (2009: para 111), the proportionality test is a foundational concept in international human rights jurisprudence, applied 'universally across the various jurisdictions in determining whether limitations on human rights are justified'.

While there are four basic components of the principle of proportionality (proper purpose, rational connection, least restrictive means and appropriate balance), at its essence is *the requirement of necessity*, or in other words the *least restrictive means* (Barak 2012: 317). That is, the law must limit the right to the smallest degree possible. With respect to detention and other restrictive practices, this means the law should apply such practices only as a last resort. If held to be necessary, they should be used for the shortest time possible and continually re-evaluated as to their continuing necessity (Human Rights Committee 2014: para 19). If there are other hypothetical means that could achieve the same purpose but impose less of a limitation on the person's liberty and security, then those means should be chosen. For example, if appropriate supports, including behavioural therapy and ensuring the person is living in an appropriate residential environment, would reduce the need to use restrictive practices but are not provided, then the use of detention, physical and chemical restraints would not be proportionate. Finally, monitoring and independent oversight would also be an important safeguard.

Enforcing obligations to provide 'enabling conditions'

The obligations on the state do not end here. Rather than simply providing for the lawful authority of restrictive practices and procedural safeguards when they are used, the obligation on the state arises much earlier. In repositioning people with intellectual and cognitive impairments as rights-bearers, rather than as objects of protection, the CPRD does not allow disability to be a used as a justification for violation of the rights to liberty or security (Article 14). Read with the overarching responsibility of non-discrimination, or the obligation to make reasonable accommodations in Article 5, the state is under a positive obligation to redress the structural disadvantages faced by people with intellectual and cognitive impairments by providing access to appropriate supports and conditions necessary to reduce the need to resort to restraints and detention.

It is this component of the regulatory framework that should arguably be the focus of any regulation of restrictive practices. In Australia, it is also the component that needs the most development. The extensive literature on this subject recognises that there are a large number of well-understood factors that can contribute to 'behaviours of concern' that lead to the use of restrictive practices such as the person's environment (including their physical accommodation and other residents); the behaviour of support staff; lack of professional expertise amongst support staff; resource constraints; reactive/crisis responses as opposed to preventative and positive strategies; undiagnosed and untreated mental and physical health issues; and communication difficulties, to name but a few (Carter 2006; McVilly 2009).

The exact strategies that should be mandated by legislation would depend on the context in which restrictive practices will be used – aged care facilities, disability services or other health or rehabilitation services. It would also require expert knowledge and should be informed by multi-disciplinary cross-collaborations between lawyers, people with disability and professionals with experience and expertise in working with people with intellectual and cognitive impairments (Brophy et al. 2016; McSherry et al. 2017).

It is here, with prescribing proactive strategies, that existing statutory frameworks for restrictive practices have the potential to be radically enhanced. Such requirements should be more than principle-based statements such as strategies that will ensure 'the adult's quality of life will be improved in the long-term' (see *Guardianship and Administration Act 2000* (Qld): section 80V(2)(f)(ii)); and more than soft approaches to regulation contained in broad principles and codes of practice. They must impose actual obligations, adherence to which can be objectively determined during review by a court or tribunal, that must be fulfilled before restrictive practices can be utilised. Overall there should be a prohibitive rather than an authoritative approach to the use of restrictive practices. Strong justification should be provided for their continued use. Anything less would be inconsistent with the CRPD's stipulation that disability should in no case be a justification for the deprivation of liberty or security (Article 14).

As Amita Dhanda (2007: 459) has expressed, the CPRD assists in refocusing the energies and attentions of policy and law-makers. It also means that the approach taken will necessarily be context specific. This will require a departure from existing approaches to regulation. Ultimately, it means less energy going into threshold criteria that are potentially discriminatory such as 'disability' and 'impaired capacity'. It also requires a refocusing of the role of key regulatory institutions. Carney (2010: 259), for example, has discussed how tribunals – the institutions associated with traditional procedural safeguards in the regulation of involuntary treatment for mental illness – can play a role beyond enforcing civil and political rights to engage in other domains.

Ultimately a rights-based equality approach to the regulation of restrictive practices is about addressing discrimination and providing equality under the law. Addressing environmental and social support deficits will mean that people with intellectual and cognitive impairments will have a greater opportunity to realise their civil and political rights to liberty and security and the benefits that the rule of law offers to others in Australian society.

Conclusion

Given that the regulation of restrictive practices in Australia under the new NDIS, in aged care facilities, and in other health facilities is a relatively 'greenfields site', Australia can seize an opportunity to move beyond approaches that have historically marginalised and excluded people with intellectual and cognitive impairments.

The use of restrictive practices on people with intellectual and cognitive impairments requires clear authorisation, but authorisation (even with appropriate procedural safeguards usually associated with principles of justice and rights) is not necessarily sufficient to realise the rights to liberty and security of persons with disabilities on an equal basis with others.

According to a rights-based approach to equality, any approach to regulation that does not impose positive obligations to address structural disadvantages and inequities is discriminatory. This approach requires that a person with disability should not be lawfully deprived of their liberty or security simply on the basis of their disability; instead, environmental, support and other deficits that prevent them from exercising their rights and living a life with dignity must be addressed.

Taking a rights-based approach to regulation to its logical conclusion, there is a strong argument for a prohibition on the use of restrictive practices, even under specific statutory frameworks (other than in absolute emergencies), unless environmental and support deficits are addressed first. Regulation should impose real obligations, not simply reflect broad principles of least restrictive alternatives. In this way, the 'problem' for the law of how to authorise restrictive practices can begin to be reframed and refocused. It can be less about how to provide authorisation for their use, or protection from civil and criminal liability for those who use them, and become more about what positive obligations should be imposed on the state to reduce and eliminate the need to use restrictive practices.

References

Cases

Al Kateb v Godwin (2004) 219 CLR 562.
Antunovic v Dawson (2010) 30 VR 355.
Collins v Wilcock [1984] 1 WLR 1172.
Darcy (bht Diane Aldridge) v New South Wales [2011] NSWCA 413.
JP [2008] WASAT 3.
Kracke v Mental Health Review Board [2009] VCAT 646.
McClelland v Symons [1951] VLR 157.
Meering v Grahame-White Aviation Co Ltd (1919) 122 LT Rep 44.
Minister for Immigration and Multicultural and Indigenous Affairs v Al Masri (2003) 126 FCR 54.
Minister for Immigration and Multicultural and Indigenous Affairs v VFAD (2002) 125 FCR 249.
MLI [2006] QGAAT 31.
Myer Stores Ltd v Soo [1991] 2 VR 597.
OMF [2008] NSWGT 5.
P v Cheshire West [2014] UKSC 19.
QNN [2013] NSWGT 25.
R v Bournewood and Community and Mental Health NHS Trust; Ex parte L [1999] 1 AC 458.
Re WCM [2006] QGAAT 26.
SDF [2013] NSWGT 1.
Skyllas v Retirement Care Australia (Preston) Pty Ltd [2006] VSC 409.
South Australia v Lampard-Trevorrow (2010) 106 SASR 331.
South Australia v Totani (2010) 242 CLR 1.
Watson v Marshall (1971) 124 CLR 621.

Legislation and international instruments

Charter of Human Rights and Responsibilities Act 2006 (Vic).
Convention Against Torture and Other Cruel, Inhuman or Degrading Treatment or Punishment (1985) Opened for signature 4 February, 1465 UNTS 85 (entered into force 26 June 1987).
Convention on the Rights of Persons with Disabilities (2007) Opened for signature 13 December, 2515 UNTS 3 (entered into force 3 May 2008).
Crimes Act 1900 (NSW).
Crimes Act 1958 (Vic).
Criminal Code Act 1899 (Qld).
Criminal Code Act 1913 (WA).
Criminal Code Act 1983 (NT).

Criminal Law Consolidation Act 1935 (SA).
Disability Services Act 1993 (NT).
Disability Services Act 2006 (Qld).
Disability Act 2006 (Vic).
Disability Services Act 2011 (Tas).
European Convention for the Protection of Human Rights and Fundamental Freedoms, as amended by Protocols Nos. 11 and 14 (European Convention on Human Rights) (1950) Opened for signature 4 November, ETS 5 (entered into force 3 September 1953).
Guardianship and Administration Act 1993 (SA).
Guardianship and Administration Act 2000 (Qld).
Guardianship and Administration Act 2019 (Vic).
Human Rights Act 1998 (UK).
Human Rights Act 2004 (ACT).
Human Rights Act 2018 (Qld).
International Covenant on Civil and Political Rights (1966) Opened for signature 16 December, 999 UNTS 171 (entered into force 23 March 1976).
National Disability Insurance Scheme Act 2013 (Cth).
Powers of Attorney Act 1998 (Qld).
Quality of Care Principles 2014 (Cth).
Senior Practitioner Act 2018 (ACT).
Universal Declaration of Human Rights (1948) GA Res 217A(III), 3rd sess, 183rd plen mtg, UN Doc A/810.

Books, journal articles and other texts

Alexy, R. (2017) 'The Absolute and the Relative Dimensions of Constitutional Rights', *Journal of Legal Studies*, 37(1): 31–47.
Allan, T.R.S. (1993) *Law, Liberty and Justice: The Legal Foundations of British Constitutionalism*, Oxford: Clarendon Press.
Allen, J. and Tulich, T. (2015) 'I Want to Go Home Now: Restraint Decisions for Dementia Patients in Western Australia', *Law in Context*, 33(2): 1–23.
Association of Professional Behavior Analysts (2010) *Statement on Restraint and Seclusion.* Available www.abainternational.org/about-us/policies-and-positions/restraint-and-seclusion,-2010.aspx (accessed 20 June 2020).
Australian Law Reform Commission (2014) *Equality, Capacity and Disability in Commonwealth Laws.* Available https://www.alrc.gov.au/publication/equality-capacity-and-disability-in-commonwealth-laws-alrc-report-124/ (accessed 18 August 2020).
Balkin, R.P. and Davis, J.L.R. (2009) *Law of Torts*, 4th edn, Chatswood, NSW: LexisNexis Butterworths.
Barak, A. (2012) *Proportionality*, Cambridge: Cambridge University Press.
Bingham, T. (2010) *The Rule of Law*, London: Penguin.
Brophy, L., Roper, C., Hamilton, B., Tellez, J.J. and McSherry, B. (2016) 'Consumers and Their Supporters' Perspectives on Poor Practice and the Use of Seclusion and Restraint in Mental Health Settings: Results from an Australian Focus Group', *International Journal of Mental Health Systems*, 10(6): 1–10.
Carlson, L. and Kittay, E.F. (2010) 'Introduction: Rethinking Philosophical Presumptions in Light of Cognitive Disability', in L. Carlson and E.F. Kittay (eds) *Cognitive Disability and Its Challenge to Moral Philosophy*, Chichester: Wiley-Blackwell, 1–26.

Carney, T. (2010) 'Involuntary Mental Health Treatment Laws: The "Rights" and Wrongs of Competing Models?', in B. McSherry and P. Weller (eds) *Rethinking Rights-based Mental Health Laws*, Oxford: Hart Publishing, 257–74.

Carter, W. (2006) *Challenging Behaviour and Disability: A Targeted Response.* Available www.communities.qld.gov.au/resources/dcdss/disability/service-providers/centre-excellence/carter-report-full.pdf (accessed 20 June 2020).

Chan, J., Arnold, S., Webber, L., Rihes, V., Parmenter T. and Stancliffe, R. (2012) 'Is It Time to Drop the Term "Challenging Behaviour"?', *Learning Disability Practice*, 15(5): 36–38.

Chandler, K., Willmott, L. and White, B. (2014) 'Rethinking Restrictive Practices: A Comparative Analysis', *QUT Law Review*, 14(2): 90–122.

Chandler, K., White, B. and Willmott, L. (2016) 'The Doctrine of Necessity and the Detention and Restraint of People with Intellectual Impairment: Is There Any Justification?', *Psychology, Psychiatry and the Law*, 23(3): 361–87.

Chandler, K., White, B. and Willmott, L. (2017) 'What Role for Adult Guardianship in Authorising Restrictive Practices', *Monash University Law Review*, 43(2): 492–529.

Chandler, K., White, B. and Willmott, L. (2018) 'Safeguarding Rights to Liberty and Security Where People with Disability Are Subject to Detention and Restraint–A Rights-based Approach (Part One)', *Psychology, Psychiatry and the Law*, 25(3): 465–84.

Committee on the Rights of Persons with Disabilities (2014) *General Comment No. 1 Article 12 – Equal Recognition before the Law.* 11th sess, UN Doc CRPD/C/GC/1.

Degener, T. (2016) 'Disability in a Human Rights Context', *Laws*, 5(3): 35.

Department for Communities and Social Inclusion (SA) (2017) *Safeguarding People with Disability–Restrictive Practices Policy.*

Department of Communities (WA) (2019) *Code of Practice: A Guide for the Elimination of Restrictive Practices.* Available www.disability.wa.gov.au/Global/Publications/For%20disability%20service%20providers/Guidelines%20and%20policies/Behaviour%20Support/Code-of-Practice-for-the-Elimination-of-Restrictive-Practices%202019.docx (accessed 20 June 2020).

Department of Family and Community Services (NSW) (2018) *Restrictive Practices Authorisation Procedural Guide.* Available www.facs.nsw.gov.au/download?file=593319 (accessed 20 June 2020).

Department of Health and Ageing (2012) *Decision-Making Tool: Supporting a Restraint Free Environment in Residential Aged Care.* Available www.aph.gov.au/DocumentStore.ashx?id=624bd679-6023-41e6-a3b9-0de367517bac (accessed 20 June 2020).

Department of Social Services (2016) *NDIS Quality and Safeguarding Framework.* Available www.dss.gov.au/disability-and-carers/programs-services/for-people-with-disability/ndis-quality-and-safeguarding-framework (accessed 20 June 2020).

Devereux, J. (1998) 'Medical Law Reporter: R v Bournewood and Mental Health NHS Trust, Ex Parte L', *Journal of Law and Medicine*, 6(1): 22–23.

Dhanda, A. (2007) 'Legal Capacity in the Disability Rights Convention: Stranglehold of the Past or Lodestar for the Future?', *Syracuse Journal of International Law and Commerce*, 34(2): 429–62.

Disability Rights Now (2012) *Civil Society Report to the United Nations Committee on the Rights of Persons with Disabilities.* Available https://pwd.org.au/wp-content/uploads/2019/06/CRPD_Civil_Society_Report_Word.pdf (accessed 20 June 2020).

European Court of Human Rights (2019) *Guide on Article 5 of the European Convention on Human Rights–Right to Liberty and Security*. Available www.echr.coe.int/Documents/Guide_Art_5_ENG.pdf (accessed 20 June 2020).

Fennell, P. (1986) 'Law and Psychiatry: The Legal Constitution of the Psychiatric System', *Journal of Law and Society*, 13(1): 35–65.

Fennell, P. (2010) 'Institutionalising the Community: The Codification of Clinical Authority and the Limits of Rights-based Approaches', in B. McSherry and P. Weller (eds) *Rethinking Rights-based Mental Health Laws*, Oxford: Hart Publishing, 13–46.

Finegan, T. (2012) 'Conceptual Foundations of the Universal Declaration of Human Rights: Human Rights, Human Dignity and Personhood', *Australian Journal of Legal Philosophy* 37: 182–218.

Freckelton, I. (2018) 'Mental Health Law', in B. White, F. McDonald and L. Willmott (eds) *Health Law in Australia*, 3rd edn, Prymont: Lawbook Co., 729–72.

Fredman, S. (2016) 'Substantive Equality Revisited', *International Journal of Constitutional Law*, 14(3): 712–38.

Goodey, C.F. (2016) *A History of Intelligence and 'Intellectual Disability': The Shaping of Modern Psychology in Early Modern Europe*, Farnham: Ashgate.

Harnacke, C. (2013) 'Disability and Capability: Exploring the Usefulness of Martha Nussbaum's Capabilities Approach for the UN Disability Rights Convention', *Journal of Law, Medicine and Ethics*, 41: 768–80.

Hayes, K. and Hannold, E. (2007) 'The Road to Empowerment: A Historical Perspective on the Medicalisation of Disability', *Journal of Health and Human Services Administration*, 30(3): 352–72.

Human Rights Committee (2014) *General Comment No. 35 – Article 9 (Liberty and Security of Person)*. 112th sess, UN Doc CCPR/C/GC/35.

Kayess, R. and French, P. (2008) 'Out of the Darkness into Light? Introducing the Convention on the Rights of Persons with Disabilities', *Human Rights Law Review*, 8(1): 1–34.

Kumble, S. and McSherry, B. (2010) 'Seclusion and Restraint: Rethinking Regulation from a Human Rights Perspective', *Psychology, Psychiatry and the Law*, 17(4): 551–61.

Law Commission (UK) (2017) *Mental Capacity and Deprivation of Liberty–Report*. Available www.lawcom.gov.uk/project/mental-capacity-and-deprivation-of-liberty/ (accessed 20 June 2020).

Lewis, O. (2010) 'The Expressive, Educational and Proactive Role of Human Rights: An Analysis of the Convention on the Rights of Persons with Disabilities', in B. McSherry and P. Weller (eds) *Rethinking Rights-based Mental Health Laws*, Oxford: Hart Publishing, 97–128.

McSherry, B., Brophy, L., Roper, C., Tellez, J.J. and Hamilton, B. (2017) 'Reducing Seclusion and Restraint: Hearing from Consumers and Their Supporters', *Health Advocate*, 41: 34–35.

McSherry, B. and Wilson, K. (2015) 'The Concept of Capacity in Australian Mental Health Law Reform: Going in the Wrong Direction?', *International Journal of Law and Psychiatry*, 40: 60–69.

McVilly, K. (2009) *Physical Restraint in Disability Services: Current Practices, Contemporary Concerns and Future Directions*. Available https://webarchive.nla.gov.au/awa/20091126035653/http://pandora.nla.gov.au/pan/110928/20091126-1045/osp_rmit_physcial_restraint_review_300309.pdf (accessed 20 June 2020).

New South Wales Law Reform Commission (2018) *Review of the Guardianship Act 1987 – Report*. Available www.lawreform.justice.nsw.gov.au/Pages/lrc/lrc_current_projects/Guardianship/Report-145.aspx (accessed 20 June 2020).

Nowak, M. (2005) *United Nations Covenant on Civil and Political Rights–CCPR: Commentary*, Kehl: NP Engel.

Nussbaum, M.C. (2007) *Frontiers of Justice: Disability, Nationality, Species Membership*, Cambridge, MA: Harvard University Press.

Nussbaum, M.C. (2010) 'The Capabilities of People with Cognitive Disabilities', in L. Carlson and E.F. Kittay (eds) *Cognitive Disability and Its Challenge to Moral Philosophy*, Chichester: Wiley-Blackwell, 75–96.

Nussbaum, M.C. (2011) 'Capabilities, Entitlements, Rights: Supplementation and Critique', *Journal of Human Development and Capabilities*, 12(1): 23–37.

O'Neil N. and Peisah, C. (2018) *Capacity and the Law*. Available http://austlii.community/wiki/Books/CapacityAndTheLaw/ (accessed 20 June 2020).

Queensland Law Reform Commission (2010) *A Review of Queensland's Guardianship Laws–Report: Volume 3*. Available www.qlrc.qld.gov.au/__data/assets/pdf_file/0010/588241/qlrc-report-67-vol-3-web-with-cover.pdf (accessed 20 June 2020).

Rawls, J. (1971) *A Theory of Justice*, Cambridge, MA: Harvard University Press.

Royal College of Psychiatrists, British Psychological Society and Royal College of Speech and Language Therapists (2007) *Challenging Behaviour: A Targeted Response*. Available www.rcpsych.ac.uk/docs/default-source/improving-care/better-mh-policy/college-reports/college-report-cr144.pdf?sfvrsn=73e437e8_2 (accessed 20 June 2020).

Unsworth, C. (1993) 'Law and Lunacy in Psychiatry's "Golden Age"', *Oxford Journal of Legal Studies*, 13(4): 479–507.

Victorian Law Reform Commission (2003) *People with Intellectual Disabilities at Risk: A Legal Framework for Compulsory Care*. Available www.lawreform.vic.gov.au/sites/default/files/Report_People_with_intellectual_disabilities_at_risk.pdf (accessed 20 June 2020).

Victorian Law Reform Commission (2012) *Guardianship: Final Report*. Available www.lawreform.vic.gov.au/projects/guardianship/guardianship-final-report (accessed 20 June 2020).

Wong, S.I. (2010) 'Duties to Citizens with Cognitive Disabilities', in L. Carlson and E.F. Kittay (eds) *Cognitive Disability and Its Challenge to Moral Philosophy*. Chichester: Wiley-Blackwell, 127–46.

5 Beyond restraint

Gender-sensitive regulation of the control of women's behaviour in Australian mental health and disability services

Yvette Maker

Introduction

Around Australia, legislation and policy permit the use of one or more forms of restraint to control service users' behaviour in mental health and disability services. These practices are generally permitted for specific 'emergency' or urgent purposes, such as preventing self-harm or harm to others (*Mental Health Act 2016* (Qld): section 272(3); Department of Communities 2019 (WA)); preventing damage to property where it also involves a risk of harm to the person (*Mental Health and Related Services Act 1998* (NT): section 61; *Disability Act 2006* (Vic): section 140); and preventing absconding (*Mental Health Act 2015* (ACT): section 65(2)(ii)). While terminology and definitions vary, legislation and policy in most Australian states and territories address one or more of three forms of restraint: physical restraint (bodily restriction, such as holding someone's arms or holding them on the ground); mechanical restraint (the use of devices like straps, belts and jackets); and chemical restraint (the administration of medication, usually for sedation) (Sashidharan and Saraceno 2017; see McSherry and Maker in Chapter 1 in this volume).

In recent years, United Nations bodies have criticised the legal use of restraint in many parts of the world, characterising it as a clear and unacceptable violation of individuals' human rights and calling for its elimination on this basis (Human Rights Council 2013: para 63, 2017: para 33; Committee on the Rights of Persons with Disabilities 2015: para 12). Law reform bodies, parliamentary committees, advocacy groups and advisory bodies around Australia have expressed concern about the high rates of restraint use in mental health and disability services, as well as the lack of clear and consistent regulation. Many have proposed the goals of minimisation and elimination and have developed statements, guidelines, or other documents to promote these goals (for example, Australian Law Reform Commission 2014; Department of Social Services 2014; Senate Community Affairs References Committee 2014; Restrictive Practice Working Group 2016; see Roper et al. in Chapter 2 in this volume).

One driver of this shift in perspective has been the insistent voices of people who have been subject to restraint describing the practice as dehumanising, traumatising, painful and contrary to their rights, wellbeing and recovery (World Network of Users and Survivors of Psychiatry 2001; Strout 2010; European Network of (Ex-) Users and Survivors of Psychiatry 2016; Kinner et al. 2016; Rose et al. 2017; Victorian Mental Illness Awareness Council (VMIAC) 2018). The specific experiences, perspectives and needs of women who are subject to restraint have been highlighted by advocacy organisations and in a small body of scholarly research, mostly from England and North America. This research indicates that women's experiences of restraint are 'profoundly different to men's' in many respects (Fish and Hatton 2017: 804). It also suggests that any changes to the regulation of restraint and other forms of behaviour control must be gender-sensitive, especially in regard to women's experiences of trauma and gender-based discrimination and disadvantage (and how this intersects with other dimensions of identity and inequality), women's emotional expression and relational security, and women's sense of respect, dignity and empowerment.

In this chapter, I first review the existing research on women's gendered experiences of restraint and the conditions that are necessary to create a gender-sensitive, intersectional approach to restraint and other means of controlling behaviour. I then discuss the limited extent to which legislation, policies and guidelines in Australia's nine disability services jurisdictions and eight mental health jurisdictions currently address these matters. In the final section, I highlight elements of existing regulation that could provide the scaffolding for a nationally consistent approach to regulating restraint and/or behaviour control that addresses women's needs and experiences. I then identify additional features of legislation and policy that are necessary to create a truly gender-sensitive framework. Many of the proposed changes are also likely to benefit service users who are men, who have also reported feelings of pain, powerlessness, fear and trauma when subject to restraint (see for example Johnson 1998; Bonner et al. 2002; Knowles, Hearne and Smith 2015).

A note on terminology

Most of the literature and regulation in this field uses the term 'gender' to refer to binary categories of 'female' and 'male' or 'women' and 'men'. Discussions of 'gender sensitivity' and 'gender awareness' usually focus on the exclusion of women's perspectives, or perspectives other than men's, in law, policy and practice. Gender diverse and intersex people have not been well-served in this field, as in many others, although this is slowly changing (see for example Commonwealth of Australia 2019). In this chapter, I intend to address the experiences and needs of all people who identify as women, although it is important to note that most of the existing research has not explicitly included non-cisgender women. I have also endeavoured to note where the perspectives and needs of trans, gender diverse and intersex people can and should be included in improved regulation of the use of restraint and other means of controlling behaviour.

The terminology used to identify and describe women who might be subject to restraint also varies across the literature and regulatory documents. When citing or quoting a particular study, I follow the language used in that study. Otherwise, I use the terms 'mental health services user' and 'disability services user', on the basis that these terms highlight the (range of) settings in which women are subject to restraint rather than individual women's diagnoses or actual or perceived impairment(s).

Research on the gendered dimensions of restraint

There has been little published research on women's experiences of restraint, or their perspectives and needs relating to the use of restraint and other restrictive practices to control behaviour in mental health and disability services contexts. The small amount of research that does exist indicates that women have different needs and experiences to men regarding the use of restraint, and these needs are not met via conventional service provision (Agenda 2017; Fish and Hatton 2017). While mental health services and disability services are different, and serve different (although potentially overlapping) groups, two main problems common to users of both service types are identified. The first is that services are not 'gender aware' – gender is not considered to be a relevant factor in service provision, including in the use of restraint, despite women having gendered experiences and needs, and being subject to discrimination and other gender-based disadvantage. The second is that women's experiences of trauma and retraumatisation are gendered and require a response that avoids restraint and other potentially traumatising practices. These two problems are explored in turn.

Services ignore the relevance of gender to women's needs and experiences

Consumer advocacy groups and researchers have been critical of the prevailing gender-neutral approach to mental health policy in Australia on the basis that it fails to recognise that women have different experiences and service needs to men (Judd, Armstrong and Kulkarni 2009; Duggan 2016). A range of negative consequences of this failure to apply a 'gender lens' have been identified, including insufficient responses to the social causes of women's mental ill health (such as social inequalities, gender discrimination, and gendered social roles and cultural expectations); inadequate processes for avoiding and addressing sexual assault and sexual harassment; and a lack of coordinated, woman-centred services that are based on evidence of women's experiences and needs (Victorian Women and Mental Health Network (VWMHN) 2009; Women's Centre for Health Matters (WCHM) 2009; Kulkarni 2012; Duggan 2016; Mental Health Complaints Commissioner (Vic) 2018; Watson et al. 2020).

While a lack of 'gender awareness' (Aitken and Noble 2001) or 'gender sensitivity' (Newbigging 2017) regarding the use of restraint has not been a major focus of critiques in Australia, research from the UK has highlighted some potential shortcomings of gender-neutral service provision in this regard. These issues have been raised in relation to both mental health and disability services. First, some studies suggest that the ways in which staff interact with service users, including decisions about the use of restraint, are implicitly or explicitly influenced by gendered expectations and stereotypes, leading to inequitable and counter-therapeutic treatment. Beliefs that women with intellectual disability and women with certain mental health diagnoses are manipulative and attention-seeking, and how these beliefs inform staff decisions about the use of restraint, have been highlighted and problematised in several studies. In an unpublished study cited by Jennie Williams, Sara Scott and Sue Waterhouse, Scott interviewed staff in a variety of roles in secure mental health settings and found that women were associated with dimensions such as 'difficult', 'demanding', 'emotional', 'needy' and 'manipulative', whereas men were characterised as 'self-contained, 'straightforward', 'uncommunicative' and 'accept the rules' (Williams, Scott and Waterhouse 2001: 99).

Rebecca Fish and Chris Hatton interviewed 16 women with intellectual disabilities who had been physically restrained while living in a forensic locked unit in England, and ten staff members who worked with them. Staff in that study characterised women's behaviour as 'relational aggression', which the authors explain 'was considered to be more difficult to deal with than the type of aggression shown by male service users', and often justified the use of physical restraint (Fish and Hatton 2017: 796). Esther Wilcox, WM Finlay and Jane Edmonds earlier explored the discourses surrounding the 'challenging behaviour' of women and men with a learning disability in England via interviews with ten paid carers. Most of the women discussed in the study were constructed by the paid carers as 'either manipulative or attention-seeking' (Wilcox, Finlay and Edmonds 2006: 209). These constructions of women's behaviour as a consequence of 'flawed character' led to responses to 'outbursts' that emphasised control over the service user (Wilcox, Finlay and Edmonds 2006: 210).

Ruth Bankey (2001: 38) notes that the pathologisation of women 'as unstable, deceitful, naturally inferior and irrational . . . is a recurring theme within traditional Western medical culture and practice' and is also apparent in the long-standing characterisation of women as hysterical or otherwise deviant and unstable in psychiatric contexts. Feminist scholars such as Elaine Showalter (1987) have argued that the psychiatric diagnosis and (forced) treatment of women have been used to manage those who are deemed 'difficult' or who behave in socially unacceptable ways. This has been characterised as the application of an individualistic, medicalised interpretation to behaviour and distress that is actually a complex product of gendered power dynamics and gender-based oppression (Shaw and Proctor 2005). As Jane Ussher (2013: 66) puts it, 'women's emotions are deemed a sign of pathology, whereas men's are understandable'.

A failure to recognise the relevance of gender has been characterised as problematic for a related reason, namely, it leads to approaches that downplay relationships and emotions and instead focus on 'technological' solutions such as medication or treatment programmes (Clements, Clare and Ezelle 1995: 429). This means staff are taught techniques of control – such as restraint – rather than knowledge and skills for developing good relationships. Mental health researchers have identified this 'asocial' (Clements, Clare and Ezelle 1995) or non-relational approach to service delivery and managing aggression or challenging behaviour as particularly problematic for women. For instance, Jennie Williams, Sara Scott and Sue Waterhouse (2001) cited Georgie Parry-Cooke's (2000) report on the experiences of women in secure units, which indicated that women were commonly dissatisfied by a 'lack of attention and understanding' from staff, or their being too busy or otherwise unavailable. Ruth Gallop and her colleagues (1999) interviewed ten women who were subject to restraint while hospitalised in a psychiatric setting in Ontario, Canada. They concluded that 'the experience of restraint' for women in their study 'represent[ed] an extreme example of the sense of not being heard'; participants reported, for example, that staff were 'more into paperwork' and 'not . . . involved with patients' and that '[t]hey would talk to me as if I wasn't there and they seemed hostile' (Gallop et al. 1999: 412, 414). The participants identified engagement and responsiveness as key to avoiding behaviour escalation and the use of restraint.

A further criticism of approaches that fail to recognise the relevance of service users' gender is that the gender of staff, including those involved in restraint, is not considered to be relevant to the planning or delivery of services. This ignores the discomfort or concerns that both service users and staff may have about men's involvement in restraining women (Fish and Hatton 2017: 798–99; Watson et al. 2020), and the reality that men are more likely than women to commit sexual assault or other abuse on women (Clements, Clare and Ezelle 1995: 433; McGuire 2014; Woodlock, Western and Bailey 2014).

Gender, trauma and restraint are interrelated

Researchers, advocates and health bodies in Australia and elsewhere have discussed the link between women's mental health and their experiences of violence and abuse (for example Kulkarni 2012; Agenda 2017). The prevalence of trauma among mental health service users is well-known, and it is accepted that trauma in childhood and/or adulthood is a key social determinant of women's mental health (Mental Health Complaints Commissioner (Vic) 2018: 45). Penelope Weller (2016) suggests that the ongoing use of restraint is one indicator and consequence of the failure of Australia's mental health system to acknowledge and address the effects of such trauma, particularly as they affect women.

Research and public inquiries have highlighted that women with disabilities are also more likely than non-disabled women in Australia (and elsewhere) to experience trauma and violence (Cottis 2009: 1, 4; Senate Community Affairs References Committee 2015). The risk of violence may be higher again for Aboriginal and Torres Strait Islander women with disabilities; women with disabilities from culturally and linguistically diverse communities; and gay, lesbian, bisexual and trans women, among others (Dowse et al. 2016: 341; Ortoleva and Lewis 2012: 228; French, Dardel and Price-Kelly 2009: 158).

Service users are also at considerable risk of experiencing or witnessing violence or abuse, including at the hands of staff, in psychiatric inpatient settings and disability service settings (Frueh et al. 2005; Judd, Armstrong and Kulkarni 2009; Cambridge et al. 2011; Thiara, Hague and Mullender 2011; Parliament of Victoria Family and Community Development Committee 2016). Restraint is not defined as a form of violence in the Australian legislation, policies and guidelines that permit and regulate its use, although Linda Steele (2014) has argued that it should be characterised as a form of 'lawful violence' (see also Roper et al. in Chapter 2 in this volume). Women who have been subject to restraint have described feeling pain, fear, humiliation and powerlessness during the experience. For example, Heather Sequiera and Simon Halstead (2001) interviewed five women who were subject to one or more 'emergency interventions' in an independent psychiatric hospital in England. They identified several prominent themes in women's descriptions of their experience, such as physical pain or discomfort, anxiety and mental distress (including fear and sadness), and feelings of anger and aggressiveness during seclusion, restraint or tranquilisation. Participants in that study said, '[i]t really hurts', '[i]t's awful, when they restrain you it's awful' and '[i]t had taken everything out of me. I was going to hang [myself] so I could come back and haunt them' (Sequiera and Halstead 2001: 467–68). Indeed, staff may be trained in the use of 'pain compliance' – the deliberate infliction of pain to control behaviour – during physical or mechanical restraint (Hawkins, Allen and Jenkins 2005; Paterson 2005; Wright et al. 2005; see also Cross in Chapter 6 in this volume).

Most of the women in Fish and Hatton's (2017) study who had been restrained also said that restraint was painful. Some said that they were not warned about the behaviours that might precipitate the use of restraint, meaning they did not know when it was coming or what had triggered it: 'Helen, a woman detained in the unit, said: "They don't tell you they're going to restrain you, you just know that if you do an act they're going to respond in that way"' (Fish and Hatton: 798; see also Mind and National Survivor User Network 2015).

This and several other studies have indicated that women's experiences of restraint do not accord with the purposes for which restraint is officially sanctioned – for instance, to protect them (or others) from harm or to control aggression. Rather, they have reported experiencing restraint as a form of punishment and control (Johnson 1998; Mohr, Mahon and Noone 1998; Sequiera and Halstead 2001; see also Griffith, Hutchinson and Hastings 2013). These and other 'physical security measures' in secure settings have been criticised for removing women's responsibility and reinforcing their powerlessness and dependency on mental health workers to offer solutions. On this basis, Gill Aitken and Kate Noble (2001: 77) characterise the use of physical restraint as a breach of 'relational security'. They argue that 'the use of medication and control and restraint procedures privilege a separation between (unacceptable to the system) feelings and behaviour and [serve] to undermine a woman's sense of control over her own body' (Aitken and Noble 2001: 76). After interviewing five women and five men about their experiences of mechanical restraint in psychiatric services in Illinois in the United States, Mary Johnson (1998: 200–201) reported that 'the worst part of being restrained [for most participants] was the taking away of all power and control', and further led some people to feel dehumanised.

Some of the literature has focused on the potential for the use of restraint to re-traumatise women who have previously been subject to violence or abuse because it reproduces earlier experiences, and/or the feelings associated with them. All the women in Ruth Gallop and colleagues' (1999) study had a history of sexual abuse, including child sexual abuse. The authors reported that restraint (which variously entailed physical restraint, mechanical restraint and/or 'forced medication') did not make any of the participants feel safe; all of them felt that it was unnecessary and, even years later, did not view it as therapeutic. The women who participated in this study recounted harrowing stories of their experiences (Gallop et al. 1999: 411):

> When I was tied to the chair . . . it seemed to me like I was back in my childhood . . . and being terrified that it was going to happen to me again.
>
> It brought it all back. I felt–I actually physically felt like I was being raped that whole night long.

The authors concluded that 'the experience of restraint engenders traumatic emotional reactions, such as fear, anxiety, and rage', as well as feelings of humiliation, degradation and powerlessness (Gallop et al. 1999: 414). One participant described it as 'the most terrifying experience', and another said she was 'scared to death' (Gallop et al. 1999: 410). In relation to their past experiences of abuse, participants reported that restraint brought about nightmares, flashbacks and other experiences of retraumatisation. This can be doubly damaging for women whose 'symptoms' that led to psychiatric diagnosis originated in traumatic experiences (Shaw and Proctor 2005: 486). Some of the women in Fish and Hatton's study (2017: 798) also said that being restrained made them recall 'bad experiences in their past'. Some women living in a medium secure learning disability service in north-west England interviewed by Rebecca Fish and Eloise Culshaw (2005) similarly reported that restraint brought back traumatic memories, such as memories of sexual assault. Mary Johnson (who interviewed both women and men) observed (1998: 201) that several participants in her study of mechanical restraint in a psychiatric setting 'felt frightened and vulnerable to harm' when mechanically restrained, especially if they did not know or trust the staff members involved. She also found the experience of restraint 'stayed with' some participants, and 'for the most part, they remembered this experience as unpleasant' (Johnson 1998: 203).

Experiences of powerlessness and trauma can be exacerbated by gendered power asymmetries. The power dynamic when male staff are involved in restraint has been highlighted in the research literature. In several studies involving interviews with women with intellectual disabilities, participants have expressed feelings of fear, humiliation or powerlessness when being restrained by men, including during instances where their clothes were ripped or disturbed during the restraint (Fish and Culshaw 2005; Fish and Hatton 2017). Gwen Bonner and colleagues (2002: 468) interviewed service users and staff in the aftermath of physical restraint in psychiatric inpatient units in the UK, and observed that '[t]wo female participants reported being upset by the presence of male nurses during incidents', with one participant saying she was '[d]isgusted that a male nurse was present . . . it was bad enough having the injection without the embarrassment of having a male nurse present'. The mental health service users interviewed by Gallop and her colleagues (1999: 410) mentioned the role of male staff in restraining them, commenting for example that they were 'so huge' and 'all bigger than I was' (see also Potier 1993). When asked '[d]o you feel safe here?', a woman interviewed by Fish and Hatton (2017: 798) said, '[n]o, I have been in one particular restraint by a male and a female where they've ripped my top and I've had no clothes on the top half, where there've been males restraining me'.Juliet Watson and colleagues (2020) interviewed women in the Australian state of Victoria who had experienced gender-based violence during or as a result of a stay in an inpatient mental health unit; some interviewees described highly distressing experiences of restraint and seclusion involving male staff. One interviewee, Elizabeth, reported having 'flashbacks of [the restraint] and the removing of my underwear', while another, Amanda, described being restrained as 'repeating the trauma' she had experienced in the past (Watson et al. 2020: 37).

Structural or cultural explanations for the use of restraint appear to be influential in the ongoing use of restraint despite its negative consequences for women. For example, Gill Aitken and Kate Noble (2001: 76) highlight the attitude of preventing self-harm 'at all cost' and argue that it problematically ignores the implications of physical restraint, and its symbolic or actual recreation of past abuse; in other words, the short-term goal of preventing harm is considered more important than longer-term recovery goals. Jennie Williams, Sara Scott and Sue Waterhouse (2001: 100) point to the 'huge asymmetry of power between service user and service provider', which is not generally acknowledged and perpetuates an environment where actions perceived by users as abusive is the norm (see also Potier 1993). This can also contribute to an environment that fosters and tolerates abuse or violence against women.

Essential elements of gender-sensitive, trauma-informed practice

While the research literature indicates a range of problems with prevailing approaches to restraint from the perspective of women service users, it also provides guidance on the necessary elements of more gender-sensitive, trauma-informed practice.

Enhance gender awareness and challenge stereotypes

A more 'gender-aware' or 'gender-sensitive' approach to mental health and disability service provision generally requires the recognition and treatment of service users as 'gendered, sexual people with a history', rather than assuming that standard services are appropriate for all (Clements, Clare and Ezelle 1995: 428). In other words, service users' gender, in both an individual and a structural sense, must be recognised as a relevant feature of their experiences and a factor in the services and support they require and access (WCHM 2009).

Gender awareness necessitates a detailed knowledge and incorporation of 'gendered perspectives' (Aitken and Noble 2001: 78) on a range of issues, including behaviour control and the use of restraint and other restrictive practices. Especially in light of the lack of Australian research on these matters, the meaningful involvement – and ideally leadership – of women service users and their representative organisations in all elements of services, including the regulation and monitoring of restraint, would be necessary to achieve this (Clark et al. 2005; Long, Fulton and Hollin 2008; see also Roper et al. in Chapter 2 in this volume). Such consultation must ensure that the individual and cultural experiences and needs of all women are contemplated, recognised and addressed. Such an intersectional approach requires an awareness that women's experiences, including their experiences of inequality and oppression, are multidimensional (for instance, on the basis of gender, gender identity, sexuality, class, 'race', ethnicity and/or religion) and that services must be responsive to difference along these multiple dimensions (see Weller 2016).

The avoidance of inequitable or counter-therapeutic outcomes for women also requires recognition and challenging of gender stereotypes and attitudes – especially assumptions that women are difficult, manipulative or attention-seeking – that may influence staff decisions about the use of restraint and other counter-therapeutic responses to behaviour (Fish and Hatton 2017: 804).

Focus on relationships

The most common suggestion for addressing women's needs in relation to restraint is to introduce services that prioritise positive interactions and strong therapeutic relationships between staff and service users (see Department of Health (UK) 1999; Aitken and Noble 2001; VWMHN 2009; Long et al. 2012; Fish and Hatton 2017). These features of service provision are the most commonly identified measures to support the avoidance of restraint, although the extent to which this approach meets the needs of all women, including women of all cultural backgrounds, lesbian and bisexual women, trans women and intersex people, requires further inquiry.

The ten women in Gallop and colleagues' study (1999) said talking with and being heard by 'people who really care to listen' would improve their overall experience and potentially avoid the use of restraint or forced medication. They emphasised capacity for empathy and responsiveness to needs – which in practice meant understanding what was driving a woman's behaviour and offering responses that promoted safety and empowerment – as important qualities for staff (Gallop et al. 1999: 412; see also Williams, Scott and Waterhouse 2001; Lunksy and Gracey 2009; Archer, Lau and Sethi 2016). Such an approach should create space for women to express and explain their emotions, including anger, and develop coping strategies (Fish and Hatton 2017: 804). This has also been proposed as a means to redress power imbalances between service users and staff, promoting more equitable interactions (Aitken and Noble 2001; Sequiera and Halstead 2001; see also Knowles, Hearne and Smith 2015). Alternative strategies can enable service users to express themselves and feel comfortable, while also preventing escalation that might lead to restraint (Gallop et al. 1999: 412). A focus on de-escalation, in the context of a safe and settled environment, was valued by women in one study of UK low and medium secure settings (Long, Fulton and Hollin 2008: 573). The women with intellectual disabilities in Fish and Hatton's (2017) study similarly suggested that they would prefer staff to talk to them when they were distressed and find out what was bothering them.

These requirements are sometimes characterised as a means of prioritising greater 'relational security' for women (Aitken and Noble 2001; Long et al. 2012). Relational security generally refers to well-staffed services that emphasise good relationships (characterised by high levels of trust and plenty of time spent with service users), recognition and management of women's distress, a 'balance between intrusiveness and openness' and knowledge and understanding of the service user and the environment (Parry-Crooke and Stafford 2009: 42; see also Archer, Lau and Sethi 2016: 270). The Safewards programme in the Australian state of Victoria is focused on improving relationships and promoting positive interactions between staff and mental health service users and may offer a model for increasing relational security and better meeting women's needs in the context of restraint across jurisdictions and sectors (Bowers 2014; see also Brophy, Fletcher and Hamilton in Chapter 12 in this volume).

Recognise trauma and avoid perpetuating it

A 'trauma-informed' approach to services has been proposed by scholars, activists, peak bodies and other stakeholders as an essential response to many women's experiences of violence and abuse, including their experiences of restraint. Trauma-informed care 'inquires sensitively about trauma in order to understand a person's life circumstances and to provide services sensitive to trauma and associated vulnerabilities' (Fernbacher 2012: 422). As discussed earlier, the prevalence of violence against women with disabilities, and the use of restraint and other 'lawful violence' (Steele 2014) in disability services, indicates that trauma-informed practice is necessary for, and relevant to, women across both sectors.

Most fundamentally in relation to the use of restraint, trauma-informed practice necessitates the avoidance of further trauma or otherwise causing injury or distress to mental health and disability service users. This means avoiding and eliminating the use of restraint (among other 'potentially harmful practices'), on the basis that such practices often cause new trauma or recreate elements of past trauma, as well as feelings of powerlessness, humiliation and pain (Mueser et al. 2010; Kezelman and Stavropoulos 2012: 91–92; Mental Health Coordinating Council 2013; Watson et al. 2020). This must be accompanied by training and adequate resources for staff to implement alternatives (Williams, Scott and Waterhouse 2001). Key to these approaches is a recognition that the way in which people present, including 'challenging' behaviour, anger, aggression and self-harm, may be a consequence of past or present trauma and a 'strategy for coping' with stressful or threatening situations, and that women may experience services themselves as 'unsafe, disempowering and/or invalidating' (Sequiera and Halstead 2001: 473 and citing Whittington and Mason 1995; see also Stafford 1999; Dowse 2017).

For as long as restraint is still in use, changes to staffing during restraint – ensuring that only female staff are involved in the restraint of women, or that service users are consulted about their preferences in terms of the gender of staff involved in different tasks and interventions – as well as training on restraint practices to minimise pain and maximise 'respect and empowerment', may minimise the negative consequences of restraint (Sequiera and Halstead 2001: 475; see also Parry-Crooke, Oliver and Newton 2000; Byrt et al. 2001: 48; Williams, Scott and Waterhouse 2001; Fish and Hatton 2017: 798–99; Watson et al. 2020: 48). It is unclear, however, from existing research whether such measures are effective from the perspective of women service users themselves.

A service-wide recognition of the link between women's mental health, trauma and violence or abuse is also essential for trauma-informed practice and can be empowering for service users, as well as being necessary for staff to understand clients and avoid retraumatisation (VWMHN 2009; Agenda 2017; Azeem et al. 2011). This must include universal awareness of and sensitivity to:

- the high prevalence of trauma, especially sexual trauma, among women;
- the relevance of '[c]ultural, historical and gender contexts', including the particularly high prevalence of trauma among women with intellectual disability, Aboriginal and Torres Strait Islander women, women from migrant and refugee backgrounds and people who identify as LGBTI, and the potentially compounding impacts of 'racism, ableism, sexism, homophobia or ageism';
- the potential impacts of trauma on service users in terms of their behaviours and needs; and
- appropriate ways to inquire about and respond to disclosures of trauma, including trauma in service settings (Mental Health Complains Commissioner (Vic) 2018: 50–51).

A trauma-informed approach further entails recognising and responding to individuals' experiences while also acknowledging and addressing the structures that permit and normalise violence against women (Williams, Scott and Waterhouse 2001: 100).

Individualised service and safety planning, mentioned earlier as an important element of relationally secure services for women, has been highlighted in the literature as a crucial element of trauma-informed practice. In order to recognise and address trauma, this planning must include routine, regular and sensitive inquiry about service users' experiences of trauma, proceeding on the assumption that all service users may have been subject to trauma in the past (Kezelman and Stavropoulos 2012; Weller 2016; Watson et al. 2020). Previous experiences of restraint and other forms of coercion must be treated as potential sources of trauma in themselves and recorded accordingly (Clark et al. 2005). The discussion and identification of anything that might trigger aggression, self-harm or 'challenging behaviours' is also important here; it is a precursor to adopting strategies that 'reduce loss of control and manage dangerous and at-risk behaviors' in a manner that does not lead to the need for, or use of, restraint (Gallop et al. 1999: 414). The involvement of peer workers and other supporters and advocates in planning has also been flagged as an important element of such trauma-informed practice (Azeem et al. 2011).

Does existing Australian regulation promote gender-sensitive, trauma-informed services?

The use of one or more forms of restraint in mental health and disability services is addressed in legislation and/or policy and guidelines in all Australian states and territories. The gender-related needs and experiences of women using mental health or disability services generally, and more specific needs relating to the use and/or avoidance of restraint, are not dealt with comprehensively in any jurisdiction, although some regulatory documents touch on one or two of the issues raised in the literature. As Peter Bartlett and Stephanie Sampson note in Chapter 3 in this volume, an analysis of policy or other regulatory documents cannot provide insight into current practice at the service or ward level, and I discuss the need for further inquiry and research on the latter at the end of this chapter.

Gender needs and gender-sensitivity in legislative principles

The objects or principles sections of mental health and disability services legislation in many Australian jurisdictions refer to 'gender' or 'sex' as relevant considerations in the provision of services and oblige service providers to recognise and address gender-related matters in one or more respects. While some only require the promotion of 'equality between men and women' (for example, *Disability Services Act 2011* (Tas); see also Department of Social Services 2013: 9), others highlight some of the elements of gender-sensitive or gender-aware services identified in the literature. Some legislation is quite general, asserting service users' right to 'respect' in regard to a range of characteristics, including gender, age, 'cultural or linguistic diversity' and sexual orientation (see *Disability Inclusion Act 2014* (NSW): section 4(6); *Disability Inclusion Act 2018* (SA): section 9(1)(h); see also *Mental Health Act 2009* (SA): section 7(ca)(ii), although this section arguably conflates – or at least does not clearly delineate – gender and sexuality). Other statutes include principles stating that services should meet the gender-related circumstances and needs of service users, although they do not specify what those needs might be, or how services might ascertain them. For example, the *Disability Services Act 1993* (WA) requires disability programmes and services 'to be designed and administered so as to be sensitive and responsive to the individual and diverse needs of all people with disability taking into account their age, gender, religion, Aboriginality, cultural or linguistically diverse backgrounds or geographic location' (schedule 2, item 5). Along similar lines, section 6(f)(i) of the *Mental Health Act 2015* (ACT) states that

> a person with a mental disorder or mental illness has the right to be able to access services that . . . are sensitive and responsive to the person's individual needs, including in relation to age, gender, culture, language, religion, sexuality, trauma and other life experiences.

(See also *Mental Health and Related Services Act 1998* (NT); *Mental Health Act 2007* (NSW); *Disability Inclusion Act 2014* (NSW); *Mental Health Act 2016* (Qld); *Disability Inclusion Act 2018* (SA)). Similar principles are found in the Tasmanian, Victorian, Western Australian, New South Wales, Queensland and Northern Territory mental health statutes, although 'trauma' is only mentioned in the ACT statute (*Mental Health and Related Services Act 1998* (NT): section 9(f); *Mental Health Act 2007* (NSW): section 68(g); *Mental Health Act 2013* (Tas): schedule 1 item 1(d); *Mental Health Act 2014* (Vic): section 11(1)(g); *Mental Health Act 2014* (WA): schedule 1, item 6; *Mental Health Act 2016* (Qld): section 5(f)).

The principles in some disability services statutes allude to gender *inequality* and the gender-related disadvantages that women may face in service provision; some refer to the 'double disadvantage' (*Disability Services Act 1993* (NT): schedule 3(e)), 'potential increased disadvantage' (*Disability Act 2006* (Vic): section 5(3)(o)), 'additional disadvantage' (*Disability Services Act 1991* (ACT): schedule 2, item 5) or 'additional barriers' (*Disability Services Act 2006* (Qld): section 25) associated with sex or gender, while others recognise 'that women with disability may face multiple disadvantage and are potentially more vulnerable to risk of abuse or exploitation' (*Disability Inclusion Act 2014* (NSW): section 5(4)). This approach has the advantage of highlighting the structural inequalities that affect women service users, rather than focusing on individual women's circumstances and experiences in isolation.

Principles set out in the *Disability Inclusion Act 2014* (NSW) and *Disability Inclusion Act 2018* (SA) do contain provisions that could support the identification of gender issues in service provision. The New South Wales legislation states that '[s]upports and services provided to women with disability are to be provided in a way that . . . is informed by consultation with women with disability' (section 9(2)). The South Australian legislation makes a similar call for services to be 'informed by working in partnership with women with disability to enhance their lives' (section 5(4)).

None of the Australian mental health or disability services statutes mention gender (or gender-related consultation) as a relevant consideration specifically in regard to the use of restraint. Legislation only imposes gender-related requirements or targets in the conduct of personal searches involving the removal of clothing (which must be conducted by or in the presence of someone of the same gender) and regarding the composition of oversight and review bodies such as community panels and tribunals (for example, *Disability Services Act 1993* (NT):

section 26(2A); *Mental Health Act 2013* (Tas): section 111; *Mental Health Act 2016* (Qld): sections 399(2), 400(2)). The relegation of gender issues to statements of principle in most statutes creates the risk that such issues will not be meaningfully addressed; the principles are not enforceable, and their generality stands in stark contrast to the numerous specific and enforceable provisions in the substantive parts of the same legislation (Weller 2016).

A notable gap in the legislative principles is the lack of discussion of intersectionality. As already mentioned, legislation in multiple jurisdictions refers to a range of dimensions of identity and potential disadvantage or discrimination, including gender, religion, cultural or spiritual beliefs and practices, sexuality, age, family and disability. Disability services legislation in some jurisdictions acknowledges the need for programmes to address interrelated dimensions of disadvantage, but only on two dimensions. For instance, the *Disability Services Act 1991* (ACT) specifies a set of '[r]equirements to be complied with in relation to the design and implementation of programs and services relating to people with disabilities', including that '[p]rograms and services should be designed and administered to meet the needs of people with disabilities who may experience additional disadvantage because of their sex, sexuality, ethnic origin, physical isolation or Aboriginality' (schedule 2, item 5). The Northern Territory's *Disability Services Act 1993* also states, as one of the 'objectives for providers and researchers', that programmes or services 'should be designed and administered to meet the needs of people with disabilities who experience a double disadvantage as a result of their gender, ethnic origin or Aboriginality' (schedule 3(e); see also *Disability Services Act 2006* (Qld): section 25). The *Disability Act 2006* (Vic) also refers to 'any potential increased disadvantage which may be experienced by persons with a disability as a result of their gender, language, cultural or indigenous background or location' (section 5(3)(o)). The possibility that service users' experiences and needs will vary depending on a combination of a range of these (or other) dimensions of identity and/or marginalisation is not explicitly addressed.

Restraint-specific gender considerations in legislation, policies and guidelines

In many Australian jurisdictions, policies and guidelines for mental health and disability services provide more detailed guidance on the use of restraint than does legislation. Most of these documents are, however, also silent on any matters relating to gender awareness. No publicly available documents address issues such as the impacts of gender stereotypes, gender discrimination and other structural issues on the use and experience of restraint, the need to consider intersectionality in designing and delivering services or deploying restrictive practices or the benefits of relational security and strong relationships. Some briefly mention gender as a relevant consideration in the use of restraint, and a small number explicitly address gender-sensitivity and trauma-informed practice as it pertains to the use of restrictive practices.

Gender as a general consideration

New South Wales policy flags gender as a general consideration during the use of restraint. It cites the Mental Health Standing Committee's (2009) 'key principles of restraint and seclusion', including a principle that, '[d]uring restraint and seclusion, the individual needs of the consumer are recognised, including sensitivity to cultural, spiritual, language and gender concerns' (NSW Health 2012a). Concepts like 'gender', 'gender-sensitivity' and 'gender concerns' are not defined in this or other documents. One exception is the Western Australian guideline on minimising disturbed behaviour in psychiatric settings, which provides a very brief, theoretical definition of gender, describing '[t]hose characteristics of women and men that are socially determined, as opposed to "sex" which is biologically determined' (Department of Health (WA) 2006: 43). Only the Victorian government offers detailed guidance on implementing gender-sensitive practice in mental health services, including in regard to gay, lesbian, bisexual, trans and intersex people, via a 'Service Guideline for Gender Sensitivity and Safety' (Department of Health (Vic) 2011). That document does not mention restraint, even in the context of detailed discussions of trauma and gender-sensitivity.

Specific gender-related considerations: measurement, gender-sensitivity and trauma

Three Chief Psychiatrists' guidelines and one state government's reference guide for disability services delve into gender issues in more detail. Section 3 of the *Restrictive Practices Reference Guide for the South Australian Disability Service* sets a requirement that could develop further awareness of gender issues relating to restraint, namely, that gender should be recorded when reporting on the demographics of a person subject to restraint (Department for Communities and Social Inclusion (SA) 2017: 21).

The Victorian Chief Psychiatrist's guideline on Restrictive Interventions in Designated Mental Health Services and the two equivalent Tasmanian Chief Civil Psychiatrist's guidelines on the use of mechanical and physical restraint and the use of chemical restraint, respectively, provide substantially more detail on gender-relevant issues in short sections dedicated to '[g]ender safety and sensitivity' (Department of Health (Vic) 2014; Department of Health and Human Services (DHHS) (Tas) 2017a, 2017b). They suggest '[s]ensitivity to gender-specific needs is crucial' (Department of Health (Vic) 2014: 7), focusing on a range of matters such as clothing, searches, toileting, review and the possibility of pregnancy (Department of Health (Vic) 2014: 15; DHHS (Tas) 2017a: 7, 2017b: 8). The provision of 'gender-specific toilets, washing facilities and sleeping accommodation' is similarly identified as an essential aspect of providing a 'gender-sensitive' environment in the Western Australian guidelines on managing disturbed or violent behaviour in inpatient psychiatric settings. These guidelines similarly urge 'gender sensitivity' in relation to providing an appropriate environment for consumers (Department of Health (WA) 2006: 2, 4).

The Victorian and Tasmanian guidelines also identify women's experiences of trauma as a key issue in delivering gender-sensitive services, addressing some of the key aspects of trauma-informed practice identified in the literature and discussed previously. For example, the Victorian guideline states that 'a key component of providing gender sensitive care is to understand trauma and how it manifests in people when they are in acute distress' (Department of Health (Vic) 2014: 15). The Tasmanian and Victorian guidelines mention the role of restraint in potentially triggering 'extreme' responses in those with a history of trauma. The Tasmanian guidelines suggest that 'as a universal precaution, it should be presumed that every person in a treatment setting has been exposed to trauma' (DHHS (Tas) 2017a: 7, 2017b: 7). These guidelines touch on one of the issues raised by women in the international research literature, proposing that 'services should ensure that staff demonstrate sensitivity to individual patient's [sic] needs and wellbeing in carrying out such interventions, particularly with regard to gender' in light of the impact of both past trauma and restraint (DHHS (Tas) 2017a: 7, 2017b: 8). They explain that:

> restraint may be experienced by the patient as particularly traumatic or humiliating where nursing and security staff are predominantly male or female. As such, different patients may have different preferences about the gender of staff involved in the intervention. Where possible, the patient's preferences should be sought and responded to.

The Victorian guidelines also note that service users might have 'different preferences about the gender of staff involved in prevention and early intervention' and state that these preferences 'should be sought and responded to' (Department of Health (Vic) 2014: 15). Several other guidelines on the use of restraint in mental health settings mention the 'gender mix of staff' prior to and during restraint. For example, the New South Wales policy on Aggression, Seclusion and Restraint in Mental Health Facilities proposes 'a gender mix of staff during the intervention' both to 'protect staff from allegations of abuse and to promote a feeling of safety for consumers' (NSW Health 2012a: 14). The Australian Capital Territory's guidelines on the restraint of adults obliges staff to consider 'the presence of gender appropriate staff and application of gender diverse practices, (for example, a female staff member may need to be present even if not involved in the actual restraint)' (ACT Health 2016: 8). The Western Australian guidelines state that staff should receive training on 'interventions used for the management of disturbed/violent behaviour' that 'highlights awareness of racial, cultural, social and religious/spiritual needs, age and gender differences, along with other special concerns', on the basis that this 'also mitigates against disturbed/violent behaviour' (Department of Health (WA) 2006: 9). While such provisions flag the gender of staff as a relevant consideration, they are not specific about what is actually required or preferable.

Gaps in policy and guidelines: gender stereotypes, relational security, pain and intersectionality

Existing regulatory documents do not encourage or require services and staff to consider the relevance of gender stereotypes and assumptions to staff decisions about behaviour management. Nor do they prioritise approaches to service provision that advance relational security, de-escalation and restraint avoidance. Many policies and guidelines express the need for the use of restrictive interventions to be reduced and highlight the potential harms of these practices, although this is more pronounced in the mental health documents than in the disability services documents (for example, NSW Health 2012a; Department of Health (Vic) 2014; ACT Health 2016; cf Disability and Community Services (Tas) 2014). Nevertheless, at least some forms of restraint are contemplated, described and permitted in every jurisdiction. Only one, the New South Wales Health guideline on Aggression, Seclusion and Restraint in Mental Health Facilities–Guideline Focused on Older People suggests the avoidance of coercive practices as a response to the prevalence and impacts of trauma (NSW Health 2012b). This document, which is a supplement to the general policy directive on the use of restraint, also suggests respectful collaboration between consumers and people close to them, and (when restraint or seclusion is being used) remaining as calm as possible, explaining why restraint is being used, what is happening, and how to stop it (NSW Health 2012b: 2).

Policies and guidelines indicate little recognition of the implications of restraint use for women, including feelings of pain, fear and powerlessness and retraumatisation. While the Tasmanian and Victorian Chief Psychiatrists' guidelines note the severe impacts that trauma can have on women's mental health and their experiences of restraint, the guidelines are nevertheless set within a wider system that permits and assumes the use of multiple forms of restraint.

Some policies on restraint use make some (usually sweeping) references to gender-related 'cultural' difference. For instance, the Office of the Chief Psychiatrist policy on restraint in South Australian mental health services (SA Health 2015: 18–19) mentions specific considerations for Aboriginal and Torres Strait Islander people, identifying '[n]ot interacting with the opposite sex' as one behaviour 'that may have some cultural basis'. It also states that, 'where ever [sic] possible' using 'the same gender of staff to the individual' is a 'consideration' in relation to 'Culturally and Linguistically Diverse' people. The Tasmanian Chief Civil Psychiatrist guideline on the use of mechanical and physical restraint discussed earlier also addresses 'Communication with Patients from Culturally and Linguistically Diverse Backgrounds', stating that '[e]very effort should be made to understand and respond to cultural sensitivities by, for example, providing language services and by taking into account the gender of direct care staff' (DHHS (Tas) 2017a: 9). Existing policies and guidelines are clearly far from comprehensive in regard to intersectional issues that might affect women service users, and fail to define or address intersectionality in a manner that is likely to meaningfully inform practice.

Sketching a comprehensive approach to regulation

Many of the legislative principles and policy provisions outlined earlier touch on some element of gender-aware service provision and restraint use, but none comprehensively address the gender-related experiences, needs and treatment of women subject to restraint in Australian mental health or disability services. The analysis presented in this chapter is limited by the lack of qualitative research on women's experiences and on the extent to which the gender considerations I have identified are implemented in practice (as opposed to being prescribed on paper) in Australian services. The analysis nevertheless suggests that there is considerable scope for strengthening regulation to support better experiences for women who use mental health and/or disability services and who may be subject to restraint or other forms of behaviour control. To be effective, any changes to regulation must be accompanied by appropriate planning and resourcing for implementation.

Beneficial regulatory changes might entail some or all of the following.

Legislation

The principles or objects sections of relevant legislation should clearly state the importance of gender-sensitivity and meeting gender-related needs, including specific issues of trauma, gendered power dynamics and gender-based and intersectional inequality. Linking these principles with human rights obligations would emphasise their gravity and encourage service provision that emphasises the dignity and rights of all women who use mental health or disability services (Weller 2016). The legislative inclusion of such principles would be insufficient on its own but could form the symbolic backdrop to better recognition of women's needs and perspectives in mental health and disability services provision, including those relating to the use (and avoidance) of restraint. Existing statutes, outlined previously, offer some guidance in this regard.

Substantive legislative provisions that ban the use of restraint altogether would ensure that trauma and retraumatisation from restraint is avoided. Such an approach would not be acceptable or feasible without a range of supporting mechanisms for minimising and ultimately eliminating the use of restraint in a manner that preserves safety for all and promotes therapeutic outcomes. Restraint minimisation is addressed to some degree in existing policies and guidelines on restraint use, but the avoidance of restraint and uptake of alternatives could be made enforceable through inclusion in legislation. For example, legislation could create an obligation on services to implement evidence-based restraint avoidance techniques (such as de-escalation techniques and individualised planning, discussed further later). It could also impose a related obligation – along the lines of the principles sections of the New South Wales and South Australian disability services statutes discussed earlier – to consult with women with disabilities, mental health consumers, and their representative organisations, in formulating policies and practices, including those regarding restraint avoidance (Sequiera and Halstead 2001; Clark et al. 2005). Such consultation should be broad-ranging and should include the identification and consultation of the full range of identity groups and communities of women who might be affected, to ensure that intersectional needs and issues are addressed (Weller 2016; see Roper and colleagues in Chapter 2 in this volume).

Individualised planning mechanisms that currently exist in legislation could be adapted or replaced to prioritise discussion and recording of issues relating to service users' experiences of trauma and other gender-related requirements, including those associated with behaviours that might lead to the use of restraint (Soininen et al. 2013). In some jurisdictions, the use of restraint in disability service settings must be discussed in a service user's 'behaviour support plan', which sets out matters such as service users' history of problematic or undesirable behaviour, possible triggers and strategies for 'managing' such behaviour (including restraint) (for example, *Disability Services Act 1993* (NT): Part 4; *Disability Services Act 2006* (Qld): Part 6). In some mental health legislation, advance statements, advance health directives or advance consent directions give service users the option to set out their preferences about their treatment (for example, *Mental Health Act 2014* (Vic): section 19; *Mental Health Act 2014* (WA): section 8; *Mental Health Act 2015* (ACT): sections 24–32; *Mental Health Act 2016* (Qld): section 222). These mechanisms – while subject to criticism on a number of fronts (see Ouliaris and Kealy-Bateman 2017; Maylea et al. 2018) – may offer a starting point for better planning about behaviour control and restraint avoidance.

Legislation could also include measures for monitoring and evaluating progress, including collecting and publishing statistics disaggregated according to gender and other demographic characteristics (National Technical Assistance Center for State Mental Health Planning (NTACSMHP) 2005). It could also enact obligations in terms of staffing ratios that facilitate positive relationship building and relational security and adequate resources for implementing restraint avoidance (Fish and Hatton 2017).

If the lawful use of restraint is preserved in legislation for circumstances of last resort, these restraint-avoidance requirements might nevertheless lead to a reduction in rates of restraint and improved experiences for women who are subject to the practice. A range of other changes would also be necessary, including an obligation to consult service users about the preferred gender of staff involved in restraint. This may address some of the gender-related risks of abuse and trauma identified in the literature. This could be similar to existing legislative provisions on the gender of staff involved in personal searches (for example, *Mental Health Act 2014* (WA): section 163; *Mental Health Act 2016* (Qld): section 399). Existing obligations to report on the use of restraint could be amended to include an obligation to report on the gender of service users (as per South Australian guidelines) and a range of other demographic characteristics, and an obligation to report the circumstances leading to the use of restraint (see for example *Disability Services Act 2006* (Qld): section 199; *Mental Health Act 2014* (WA): section 533(2)(f); *Mental Health Act 2016* (Qld): section 307); Department for Communities and Social Inclusion (SA) 2017: 21).

Policies and guidelines

While existing mental health and disability services legislation could accommodate a greater level of detail on restraint and restraint avoidance, policies and guidelines are an important complement. A statutory obligation on Chief

Psychiatrists, Chief Practitioners and other relevant authorities to produce and publish policies and guidelines currently exists in some jurisdictions (for example, *Disability Services Act 2011* (Tas): section 35; *Mental Health Act 2016* (Qld): section 273). These could be augmented with a further obligation for the documents to prioritise restraint avoidance, trauma-informed care and (intersectional) gender considerations.

Policies and guidelines on the use and/or avoidance of restraint should include detailed information on a range of matters, including:

- The meaning and relevance of gender to women's experiences and needs in mental health and disability services (and how this varies for women depending on a range of characteristics);
- Gender stereotypes and gender discrimination, their impacts on how staff respond to women's behaviour, and how to challenge them;
- The meaning of trauma-informed practice and how it can be implemented; and
- Restraint avoidance techniques that focus on respect for, and empowerment of, women service users in the wider context of good relationships and high relational security (Williams, Scott and Waterhouse 2001; Fish and Hatton 2017).

These issues must be framed as part of a change to culture and practice, particularly by characterising the minimisation and elimination of restraint, in the context of trauma-informed practice, as a serious and achievable goal for services. The Victorian and Tasmanian Chief Psychiatrist's guidelines on the use of restraint offer a partial template for these details.

If restraint continues to be permitted and used, policies and guidelines should also set out review and de-brief processes to support women who have been subject to restraint, as well as staff involved in the application of restraint, to express themselves, process strong emotions and potentially traumatic experiences, and identify ways to avoid future incidents (Sequiera and Halstead 2001; see NTACSMHP 2005). Mandatory training of staff (at all levels) and medical practitioners on the matters contained in legislation, policies and guidelines will be essential for their effective implementation and should also be outlined in these documents (Clements, Clare and Ezelle 1995; Stafford 1999; see Allan and Manwaring in Chapter 8 in this volume for a discussion of the challenges of implementation).

Conclusion

International research indicates that women's experiences and needs relating to the use (and avoidance) of restraint are not adequately addressed in conventional disability and mental health service provision. I have argued in this chapter that gender-aware service provision requires, first, recognition of the relevance of gender (as one of multiple intersecting dimensions of difference) to women's experiences and service needs. It also necessitates services that support strong relationships and relational security that promote, among other things, listening, empathy, relationship-building, de-escalation and safety. Finally, gender-aware services must take a trauma-informed approach that acknowledges the potential impacts of trauma on women's mental health and behaviour, offers safe and supportive responses and avoids re-traumatisation.

While there is little information about the extent to which these matters are currently considered in practice in Australian services, the preceding analysis of Australian legislation, policies and guidelines on the use of restraint in these contexts suggest that current regulatory frameworks are ill-equipped to support practices that meet these requirements. Existing documents make only general statements about identifying and meeting women's gender-related needs, and there is little detailed discussion of the steps that must be taken to recognise and address these issues. The instruments applying to disability services address gender-related matters much less comprehensively than those applying to mental health services, which is consistent with the tendency for women (and men) with intellectual disabilities to be perceived and treated as non-gendered and non-sexual. Some important matters, notably intersectionality, are hardly addressed in existing instruments at all.

The growing efforts to minimise and/or eliminate the use of restraint in Australia are unlikely to be successful unless these matters are dealt with in regulation and practice. A range of changes to legislation, policy and guidelines are arguably necessary in this regard. These include legislative reforms to establish the significance of gender considerations in relation to trauma, power and gender-based and intersectional inequalities, to require the avoidance of restraint and the development and implementation of alternatives in consultation with service users and to ensure that gender considerations are captured in monitoring and reporting. Policies and guidelines can complement legislation, providing greater guidance on the relevance of gender-related considerations and the role of different actors in addressing them.

There is a clear need for further research to inform any changes to regulation and practice. There is little existing research investigating Australian women's experiences of restraint and other restrictive or coercive practices, or their needs regarding gender-sensitive and trauma-informed treatment and services more generally (VMIAC 2013). Research to address this gap must include all women who are potentially subject to restraint, including women with disability; Aboriginal and Torres Strait Islander women; lesbian, bisexual and trans women; women from all cultural and religious backgrounds; and other women who experience gender-based and/or intersectional oppression (Weller 2016). There is also a need for research that examines the gendered dimensions of emotional expression that typically leads to the use of restraint (including anger, aggression and 'challenging behaviour'), the gendered responses of staff to these behaviours, including differences in the use of restraint, and the consequences of restraint use for both service users and staff (Sequiera and Halstead 2001; Clark et al. 2005; VWMHN 2009). Finally, gender-sensitive analyses of alternatives to restraint are needed to ensure that efforts to minimise and eliminate the use of restraint will be effective for all service users (Fish and Hatton 2017).

References

Legislation and legislative instruments

Disability Act 2006 (Vic).
Disability Inclusion Act 2014 (NSW).
Disability Inclusion Act 2018 (SA).
Disability Services Act 1991 (ACT).
Disability Services Act 1993 (NT).
Disability Services Act 1993 (WA).
Disability Services Act 2006 (Qld).
Disability Services Act 2011 (Tas).
Mental Health Act 2007 (NSW).
Mental Health Act 2009 (SA).
Mental Health Act 2013 (Tas).
Mental Health Act 2014 (Vic).
Mental Health Act 2014 (WA).
Mental Health Act 2015 (ACT).
Mental Health Act 2016 (Qld).
Mental Health and Related Services Act 1998 (NT).

Policies and guidelines

ACT Health (2016) *Restraint of a Person–Adults Only*, Canberra: ACT Government.

Department for Communities and Social Inclusion (SA) (2017) *Restrictive Practices Reference Guide for the South Australian Disability Service Sector*, Adelaide: Government of South Australia.

Department of Communities (WA) (2019) *Code of Practice: A Guide for the Elimination of Restrictive Practices*, 3rd edn, Perth: Government of Western Australia.

Department of Health and Human Services (Tas) (DHHS) (2017a) *Mechanical and Physical Restraint: Chief Civil Psychiatrist Clinical Guideline 10A*, Hobart: Tasmanian Government.

Department of Health and Human Services (Tas) (DHHS) (2017b) *Chemical Restraint: Chief Civil Psychiatrist Clinical Guideline 10*, Hobart: Tasmanian Government.

Department of Health (Vic) (2011) *Service Guideline on Gender Sensitivity and Safety: Promoting a Holistic Approach to Wellbeing*, Melbourne: Victorian Government.

Department of Health (Vic) (2014) *Restrictive Interventions in Designated Mental Health Services*, Melbourne: Victorian Government.

Department of Health (WA) (2006) *Guidelines: The Management of Disturbed/Violent Behaviour in Inpatient Psychiatric Settings*, Perth: Government of Western Australia.

Department of Social Services (2013) *National Standards for Disability Services*, Canberra: Australian Government.

Disability and Community Services (Tas) (2014) *Restrictive Interventions in Services for People with Disability Policy*, Hobart: Tasmanian Government.

Mental Health Standing Committee (2009) *National Documentation Relating to Seclusion and Restraint Reduction*, Canberra: National Mental Health Seclusion and Restraint Project.

New South Wales (NSW) Health (2012a) *Aggression, Seclusion and Restraint in Mental Health Facilities in New South Wales*, Sydney: NSW Government.

New South Wales (NSW) Health (2012b) *Aggression, Seclusion and Restraint in Mental Health Facilities–Guideline Focused upon Older People*, Sydney: NSW Government.

South Australia (SA) Health (2015) *Restraint and Seclusion in Mental Health Services Policy Guideline*, Adelaide: Government of South Australia.

Books, journal articles and other texts

Agenda Alliance for Women and Girls at Risk (Agenda) (2017) *Agenda Briefing on the Use of Restraint Against Women and Girls.* Available https://weareagenda.org/wp-content/uploads/2017/03/Restraint-FOI-research-briefing-FINAL1.pdf (accessed 20 June 2020).

Aitken, G. and Noble, K. (2001) 'Violence and Violation: Women and Secure Settings', *Feminist Review*, 68: 68–88.

Archer, M., Lau, Y. and Sethi, F. (2016) 'Women in Acute Psychiatric Units, Their Characteristics and Needs: A Review', *BJPsych Bulletin*, 40(5): 266–72.

Australian Law Reform Commission (2014) *Equality, Capacity and Disability in Commonwealth Laws.* Available www.alrc.gov.au/publication/equality-capacity-and-disability-in-commonwealth-laws-alrc-report-124/ (accessed 20 June 2020).

Azeem, M.W., Augla, A., Rammerth, M., Binsfeld, G. and Jones, R.B. (2011) 'Effectiveness of Six Core Strategies Based on Trauma Informed Care in Reducing Seclusions and Restraints at a Child and Adolescent Psychiatric Hospital', *Journal of Child and Adolescent Psychiatric Nursing*, 24(1): 11–15.

Bankey, R. (2001) 'La Donna é Mobile: Constructing the Irrational Woman', *Gender, Place & Culture*, 8(1): 37–54.

Bonner, G. Lowe, T., Rawcliffe, D. and Wellman, N. (2002) 'Trauma for All: A Pilot Study of the Subjective Experience of Physical Restraint for Mental Health Inpatients and Staff in the UK', *Journal of Psychiatric and Mental Health Nursing*, 9(4): 465–73.

Bowers, L. (2014) 'Safewards: A New Model of Conflict Containment on Psychiatric Wards', *Journal of Psychiatric and Mental Health Nursing*, 21(6): 499–508.

Byrt, R., Lomas, C., Gardiner, G. and Lewis, D. (2001) 'Working with Women in Secure Environments', *Journal of Psychosocial Nursing and Mental Health Services*, 39(9): 42–50.

Cambridge, P., Mansell, J., Beadle-Brown, J., Milne, A. and Whelton, B. (2011) 'A Study of Adult Protection Referrals in Two Local Authorities: An Overview of Findings for Managers and Practitioners', *The Journal of Adult Protection*, 13(5): 238–50.

Clark, C., Becker, M., Giard, J., Mazelis, R., Savage A. and Vogel, W. (2005) 'The Role of Coercion in the Treatment of Women with Co-occurring Disorders and Histories of Abuse', *The Journal of Behavioral Health Services & Research*, 32(2): 167–81.

Clements, J., Clare, I. and Ezelle, L.A. (1995) 'Real Men, Real Women, Real Lives? Gender Issues in Learning Disabilities and Challenging Behaviour', *Disability & Society*, 10(4): 425–36.

Committee on the Rights of Persons with Disabilities (CRPD) (2015) *Guidelines on Article 14 of the Convention on the Rights of Persons with Disabilities.* Available https://tbinternet.ohchr.org/_layouts/15/treatybodyexternal/Download.aspx?symbolno=A/72/55&Lang=en (accessed 20 June 2020).

Commonwealth of Australia (2019) *Actions to Support Lesbian, Gay, Bisexual, Trans and Gender Diverse and Intersex Elders: A Guide for Aged Care Providers*. Available www.health.gov.au/resources/publications/actions-to-support-lgbti-elders-a-guide-for-aged-care-providers (accessed 20 June 2020).

Cottis, T. (2009) 'Introduction', in T. Cottis (ed.) *Intellectual Disability, Trauma and Psychotherapy*, East Sussex: Routledge, 1–8.

Department of Health (UK) (1999) *Secure Futures for Women: Making a Difference*, London: Department of Health.

Department of Social Services (2014) *National Framework for Reducing and Eliminating the Use of Restrictive Practices in the Disability Service Sector*. Available www.dss.gov.au/sites/default/files/documents/04_2014/national_fraemwork_restricitive_practices_0.pdf (accessed 20 June 2020).

Dowse, L. (2017) 'Disruptive, Dangerous and Disturbing: The "Challenge" of Behaviour in the Construction of Normalcy and Vulnerability', *Continuum*, 31(3): 447–57.

Dowse, L., Soldatic, K., Spangaro, J. and van Toorn, G. (2016) 'Mind the Gap: The Extent of Violence against Women with Disabilities in Australia', *Australian Journal of Social Issues*, 51(3): 341–359.

Duggan, M. (2016) *Investing in Women's Mental Health: Strengthening the Foundations for Women, Families and the Australian Economy*. Available www.vu.edu.au/sites/default/files/AHPC/pdfs/investing-in-womens-mental-health.pdf (accessed 20 June 2020).

European Network of (Ex-) Users and Survivors of Psychiatry (2016) *Forced Psychiatric Interventions Constitute a Violation of Human Rights and Disable Care*. Available www.absoluteprohibition.org/enusp-forced-psychiatric-interventions-constitute-a-violation-of-rights-and-disable-care/ (accessed 20 June 2020).

Fernbacher, S. (2012) 'Interpersonal Trauma and Mental Health Care: Making the Connections', in G. Meadows, J. Farhall, E. Fossey, M. Grigg, F. McDermott and B. Singh (eds) *Mental Health in Australia: Collaborative Community Practice*, 3rd edn, South Melbourne: Oxford University Press, 422–26.

Fish, R. and Culshaw, E. (2005) 'The Last Resort?: Staff and Client Perspectives on Physical Intervention', *Journal of Intellectual Disabilities*, 9(2): 93–107.

Fish, R. and Hatton, C. (2017) 'Gendered Experiences of Physical Restraint on Locked Wards for Women', *Disability & Society*, 32(6): 790–809.

French, P., Dardel, J. and Price-Kelly, S. (2009) *Rights Denied: Towards a National Policy Agenda about Abuse, Neglect & Exploitation of Persons with Cognitive Impairment*. Available https://pwd.org.au/wp-content/uploads/2019/05/RightsDenied2010.doc (accessed 18 August 2020).

Frueh, B.C., Knapp, R.G., Cusack, K.J., Grubaugh, A.L., Sauvageot, J.A., Cousins, V.C., Yim, E., Robins, C.S., Monnier, J. and Hiers, T.G. (2005) 'Patients' Reports of Traumatic or Harmful Experiences within the Psychiatric Setting', *Psychiatric Services*, 56(9): 1123–33.

Gallop, R., McCay E., Guha, M. and Khan, P. (1999) 'The Experience of Hospitalization and Restraint of Women Who Have a History of Childhood Sexual Abuse', *Health Care for Women International*, 20(4): 401–16.

Griffith, G.M., Hutchinson, L. and Hastings, R.P. (2013) '"I'm Not a Patient, I'm a Person": The Experiences of Individuals with Intellectual Disabilities and Challenging Behavior–A Thematic Synthesis of Qualitative Studies', *Clinical Psychology: Science and Practice*, 20(4): 469–88.

Hawkins, S., Allen, A. and Jenkins, R. (2005) 'The Use of Physical Interventions with People with Intellectual Disabilities and Challenging Behaviour – The Experiences of Service Users and Staff Members', *Journal of Applied Research in Intellectual Disabilities*, 18(1): 19–34.

Human Rights Council (2013) *Report of the Special Rapporteur on Torture and Other Cruel, Inhuman or Degrading Treatment or Punishment, Juan E Mendez*. 22nd sess, UN Doc A/HRC/22/53.

Human Rights Council (2017) *Mental Health and Human Rights: Report of the United Nations High Commissioner for Human Rights*. 34th sess, UN Doc A/HRC/34/32.

Johnson, M.E. (1998) 'Being Restrained: A Study of Power and Powerlessness', *Issues in Mental Health Nursing*, 19(3): 191–206.

Judd, F., Armstrong, S. and Kulkarni, J. (2009) 'Gender-sensitive Mental Health Care', *Australasian Psychiatry*, 17(2): 105–11.

Kezelman, C. and Stavropoulos, P. (2012) *Practice Guidelines for Treatment of Complex Trauma and Trauma Informed Care and Service Delivery–Blue Knot Foundation*. Available www.blueknot.org.au/Resources/Publications/Practice-Guidelines/Practice-Guidelines-2012 (accessed 20 June 2020).

Kinner, S., Harvey, C., Hamilton, B., Brophy, L., Roper, C., McSherry, B. and Young, J. (2016) 'Attitudes towards Seclusion and Restraint in Mental Health Settings: Findings from a Large, Community-based Survey of Consumers, Carers and Mental Health Professionals', *Epidemiology and Psychiatric Sciences*, 26(5): 1–10.

Knowles, S.F., Hearne, J. and Smith, I. (2015) 'Physical Restraint and the Therapeutic Relationship', *Journal of Forensic Psychiatry & Psychology*, 26(4): 461–75.

Kulkarni, J. (2012) *Women and Mental Health–Australian Women's Health Network Position Paper*. Available https://awhn.org.au/wp-content/uploads/2015/03/100_AWHNWomenMentalHealthPositionPaper2012.pdf (accessed 20 June 2020).

Long, C.G., Fulton, B. and Hollin, C. (2008) 'The Development of a "Best Practice" Service for Women in a Medium-Secure Psychiatric Setting: Treatment Components and Evaluation', *Clinical Psychology and Psychotherapy*, 15(5): 304–19.

Long, C.G., Knight, C., Bradley, L. and Thomas, M. (2012) 'Effective Therapeutic Milieus in Secure Services for Women: The Service User Perspective', *Journal of Mental Health*, 21(6): 567–78.

Lunsky, Y. and Gracey, C. (2009) 'The Reported Experience of Four Women with Intellectual Disabilities Receiving Emergency Psychiatric Services in Canada: A Qualitative Study', *Journal of Intellectual Disabilities*, 13(2): 87–98.

Maylea, C., Jorgensen, A., Matta, S., Ogilvie, K. and Wallin, P. (2018) 'Consumers' Experiences of Mental Health Advance Statements', *Laws*, 7(22): 1–16.

McGuire, M. (2014) *Voices Against Violence Paper Four: A Review of the Office of the Public Advocate's Records on Violence against Women with Disabilities*. Available www.wdv.org.au/wp-content/uploads/2018/10/Voices-Against-Violence-Paper-Four-A-Review-of-the-Public-Advocates-Records-on-Violence-Against-Women-with-Disabilities-PDF-1.1MB-1.pdf (accessed 20 June 2020).

Mental Health Complaints Commissioner (Vic) (2018) *The Right to Be Safe–Ensuring Sexual Safety in Acute Mental Health Inpatient Units: Sexual Safety Project Report*. Available www.mhcc.vic.gov.au/Api/downloadmedia/%7B76BF660A-3A27-4B20-A30C-448376D319C0%7D (accessed 20 June 2020).

Mental Health Coordinating Council (MHCC) (2013) *Trauma Informed Care and Practice: Towards a Cultural Shift in Policy Reform across Mental Health and Human Services in Australia – A National Strategic Direction*. Available www.

mhcc.org.au/wp-content/uploads/2018/05/ticp_awg_position_paper__v_44_final___07_11_13-1.pdf (accessed 20 June 2020).

Mind and National Survivor User Network (2015) *Restraint in Mental Health Services: What the Guidance Says.* Available https://restraintreductionnetwork.org/wp-content/uploads/2016/11/restraintguidanceweb.pdf (accessed 20 June 2020).

Mohr, W.K., Mahon, M.M. and Noone, M.J. (1998) 'A Restraint on Restraints: The Need to Reconsider Restrictive Interventions', *Archives of Psychiatric Nursing*, 12(2): 95–106.

Mueser, K.T., Lu, W., Rosenberg, S.D. and Wolfe, R. (2010) 'The Trauma of Psychosis: Posttraumatic Stress Disorder and Recent Onset Psychosis', *Schizophrenia Research*, 116(2–3): 217–27.

National Technical Assistance Center for State Mental Health Planning (NTACSMHP) (2005) *Six Core Strategies to Reduce the Use of Seclusion and Restraint: Planning Tool.* Available www.ot-innovations.com/wp-content/uploads/2014/09/2._six_core_sr20plan20template20with20cover207-05.pdf (accessed 20 June 2020).

Newbigging, K. (2017) 'Mainstreaming Gender Equality to Improve Women's Mental Health in England', in M.P. Sanchez-Lopez and R.M. Liminana-Gras (eds) *The Psychology of Gender and Health: Conceptual and Applied Global Concerns*, Amsterdam: Elsevier, 343–61.

Ortoleva, S. and Lewis, H. (2012) *Forgotten Sisters: A Report on Violence against Women with Disabilities: An Overview of Its Nature, Scope, Causes and Consequences.* Available https://repository.library.northeastern.edu/files/neu:332599/fulltext.pdf (accessed 18 August 2020).

Ouliaris, C. and Kealy-Bateman, W. (2017) 'Psychiatric Advance Directives in Australian Mental-Health Legislation', *Australasian Psychiatry*, 25(6): 574–77.

Parliament of Victoria Family and Community Development Committee (2016) *Inquiry into Abuse in Disability Services: Final Report.* Available www.parliament.vic.gov.au/fcdc/article/1851 (accessed 20 June 2020).

Parry-Crooke, G. (2000) *The Gender Training Initiative: Training Needs Analysis*, Liverpool: University of Liverpool.

Parry-Crooke, G. and Stafford, P. (2009) *My Life: In Safe Hands–Dedicated Women's Medium Secure Services in England.* Available www.ohrn.nhs.uk/resource/policy/WMSSEvaluationFinalReport.pdf (accessed 20 June 2020).

Parry-Crooke, G., Oliver, C. and Newton, J. (2000) *Good Girls: Surviving the Secure System.* Available www.womenatwish.org.uk/wp-content/uploads/2010/03/GoodGirls_SurvivingtheSecureSystem.pdf (accessed 20 June 2020).

Paterson, B. (2005) 'Thinking the Unthinkable: A Role for Pain Compliance and Mechanical Restraint in the Management of Violence?', *Mental Health Practice*, 8(7): 18–23.

Potier, M.A. (1993) 'Giving Evidence: Women's Lives in Ashworth Maximum Security Psychiatric Hospital', *Feminism and Psychology*, 3(3): 335–47.

Restrictive Practice Working Group (2016) *National Principles to Support the Goal of Eliminating Mechanical and Physical Restraint in Mental Health Services.* Available www.apha.org.au/wp-content/uploads/2017/05/Att-A-Nat-Principles-mechanical_physical-_restraint-2.pdf (accessed 20 June 2020).

Rose, D., Perry, E., Rae, S. and Good, N. (2017) 'Service User Perspectives on Coercion and Restraint in Mental Health', *BJPsych International*, 14(3): 59–61.

Sashidharan, S.P. and Saraceno, B. (2017) 'Is Psychiatry Becoming More Coercive?', *BMJ*, 357: j2904.

Senate Community Affairs References Committee (Australia) (2014) *Care and Management of Younger and Older Australians Living with Dementia and Behavioural and Psychiatric Symptoms of Dementia (BPSD)*. Available www.aph.gov.au/Parliamentary_Business/Committees/Senate/Community_Affairs/Dementia/Report/index (accessed 20 June 2020).

Senate Community Affairs References Committee (Australia) (2015) *Violence, Abuse and Neglect against People with Disability in Institutional and Residential Settings, Including the Gender and Age Related Dimensions, and the Particular Situation of Aboriginal and Torres Strait Islander People with Disability, and Culturally and Linguistically Diverse People with Disability*. Available www.aph.gov.au/Parliamentary_Business/Committees/Senate/Community_Affairs/Violence_abuse_neglect/Report (accessed 20 June 2020).

Sequiera, H. and Halstead, S. (2001) '"Is It Meant to Hurt, Is It?": Management of Violence in Women with Developmental Disabilities', *Violence Against Women*, 7(4): 462–76.

Shaw, C. and Proctor, G. (2005) 'I. Women at the Margins: A Critique of the Diagnosis of Borderline Personality Disorder', *Feminism & Psychology*, 15(4): 483–90.

Showalter, E. (1987) *The Female Malady Women, Madness, and English Culture, 1830–1980*, London: Virago.

Soininen, P., Välimäki, M., Noda, T., Puuka, P., Korkeila, J., Joffe, G. and Putkonen, H. (2013) 'Secluded and Restrained Patients' Perceptions of Their Treatment', *International Journal of Mental Health Nursing*, 22(1): 47–55.

Stafford, P. (1999) *Defining Gender Issues... Redefining Women's Services: Report from Women In Secure Hospitals (WISH)*. Available www.womenatwish.org.uk/wp-content/uploads/2010/03/Defining_Gender_Issues.pdf (accessed 20 June 2020).

Steele, L. (2014) 'Disability, Abnormality and Criminal Law: Sterilisation as Lawful and "Good" Violence', *Griffith Law Review*, 22(3): 467–97.

Strout, T.D. (2010) 'Perspectives on the Experience of Being Physically Restrained: An Integrative Review of the Qualitative Literature', *International Journal of Mental Health Nursing*, 19(6): 416–27.

Thiara, R.K., Hague, G. and Mullender, A. (2011) 'Losing Out on Both Counts: Disabled Women and Domestic Violence', *Disability & Society*, 26(7): 757–71.

Ussher, J.M. (2013) 'Diagnosing Difficult Women and Pathologising Femininity: Gender Bias in Psychiatric Nosology', *Feminism & Psychology*, 23(1): 63–69.

Victorian Mental Illness Awareness Council (VMIAC) (2013) *Zero Tolerance for Sexual Assault: A Safe Admission for Women*. Available www.abc.net.au/reslib/201305/r1115028_13591277.pdf (accessed 20 June 2020).

Victorian Mental Illness Awareness Council (VMIAC) (2018) *Election Platform: By and For Consumers and Survivors of Mental Health Services*. Available www.vmiac.org.au/wp-content/uploads/VMIAC-Election-Platform_VIC_2018-1.pdf (accessed 20 June 2020).

Victorian Women and Mental Health Network (VWMHN) (2009) *Increasing Safety and Gender Sensitivity in Mixed Sex Psychiatric Units: Gathering Information About Clinical Mental Health Service Initiatives*. Available http://wwda.org.au/wp-content/uploads/2013/12/vwmhn1.pdf (accessed 20 June 2020).

Watson, J., Maylea, C., Roberts, R., Hill, N. and McCallum, S. (2020) *Preventing Gender-based Violence in Mental Health Inpatient Units*. Available https://d2rn9gno7zhxqg.cloudfront.net/wp-content/uploads/2020/01/20215312/ANROWS-Watson-RR-VAW_MH_Units.pdf (accessed 20 June 2020).

Weller, P. (2016) 'The Contradictions of Gender: Women, Men and Violence in Mental Health Research-Policy, Law and Human Rights', *Griffith Law Review*, 25(1): 87–103.

Whittington, R. and Mason, T. (1995) 'A New Look at Seclusion: Stress, Coping and the Perception of Threat', *The Journal of Forensic Psychiatry*, 6(2): 285–304.

Wilcox, E., Finlay, W.M. and Edmonds, J. (2006) 'His Brain Is Totally Different: An Analysis of Care-Staff Explanations of Aggressive Challenging Behaviour and the Impact of Gendered Discourses', *British Journal of Social Psychology*, 45(1): 197–216.

Williams, J., Scott, S. and Waterhouse, S. (2001) 'Mental Health Services for "Difficult" Women: Reflections on Some Recent Developments', *Feminist Review*, 68(1): 89–104.

Women's Centre for Health Matters (WCHM) (2009) *WCHM Position Paper on Gender Sensitive Health Service Delivery*. Available www.wchm.org.au/wp-content/uploads/2015/02/WCHM-position-paper-on-gender-sensitive-health-service-delivery.pdf (accessed 20 June 2020).

Woodlock, D., Western, D. and Bailey, P. (2014) *Voices against Violence–Paper Six: Raising Our Voices–Hearing from Women with Disabilities*. Available www.wdv.org.au/documents/Voices%20Against%20Violence%20Paper%20Six%20Hearing%20from%20Women%20with%20Disabilities%20(PDF%201.2MB).pdf (accessed 20 June 2020).

World Network of Users and Survivors of Psychiatry (2001) *Human Rights Position Paper of the World Network of Users and Survivors of Psychiatry*. Available www.wnusp.net/index.php/human-rights-position-paper-of-the-world-network-of-users-and-survivors-of-psychiatry.html (accessed 20 June 2020).

Wright, S., Sayer, J., Parr, A., Gray, R., Southern, D. and Gournay, K. (2005) 'Breakaway and Physical Restraint Techniques in Acute Psychiatric Nursing: Results from a National Survey of Training and Practice', *Journal of Forensic Psychiatry & Psychology*, 16(2): 380–98.

6 Attempts to reduce the use of restrictive interventions in England between 2014 and 2019

Guy Cross

Introduction

This chapter explores the complexity of restraint reduction by considering two tranches of policy initiatives taken in England since 2014. It also considers what further steps may be useful for future action in this area. I am neither a clinician, nor an academic or lawyer, but was the civil servant tasked with leading the work of England's then Department of Health in reducing the use of restrictive practice. In this role I led the implementation of *Positive and Proactive Care* (Department of Health 2014) – the policy guidance for health and social care providers aimed at reducing the use of restrictive practice. I also jointly wrote chapter 26 of the Mental Health Act Code of Practice 2015, which is statutory guidance for organisations and individuals relying on or subject to the *Mental Health Act 1983*.

I am now the Care Quality Commission's lead officer responsible for working with other national organisations to develop and implement all aspects of a second tranche of initiatives to reduce the use of restrictive interventions. I am writing in a personal capacity, but with the knowledge and support of the Care Quality Commission and would like to acknowledge the advice and expertise offered by clinicians and colleagues.

In England over the time period discussed in this chapter, the National Health Service (NHS) had a commissioner/provider split. All services, including mental health, learning disability and autism, are commissioned by one arm of the NHS. Commissioning can be summarised as setting standards, reviewing the quality of care and paying for services. The services are then provided by the other arm of the NHS and independent organisations such as private and third sector providers. The policy context is set by England's Department of Health and Social Care, previously known as the Department of Health. The Care Quality Commission is the independent regulator of health and social care. Its role encompasses oversight and power to take action about the misuse of restrictive interventions by providers of mental health, learning disability and autism services.

Context

Several past incidents including the deaths of two patients and abuse of inpatients with learning disabilities and/or autism have led to growing concerns about the use of restrictive interventions in the UK. Restrictive interventions are defined by the NHS (Department of Health 2014: 14; NHS Data Dictionary 2019) as:

> deliberate acts on the part of other person(s) that restrict an individual's movement, liberty and/or freedom to act independently in order to: take immediate control of a dangerous situation where there is a real possibility of harm to the person or others if no action is undertaken; and end or reduce significantly the danger to the person or others; and contain or limit the person's freedom.

In 1998 David 'Rocky' Bennett died after being restrained by nursing staff at the Norvic secure psychiatric unit in Norwich (Sallah et al. 2003). Then in 2010, Olaseni Lewis died after being restrained by police officers called to assist health care staff at Bethlem Hospital, South London (INQUEST 2017). According to Freedom of Information data received from 48 of England's 56 NHS Mental Health Trusts, 3,652 patients suffered an injury through being restrained during 2016/17 and 2,600 staff were injured while using restraint (Greenwood 2017). Physical restraint is defined as 'any direct physical contact where the intervener's intention is to prevent, restrict, or subdue movement of the body (or part of the body) of another' (Department of Health 2015: 295). The last data collected by NHS Protect, covering 2015/16, indicated that there were over 46,000 assaults on NHS mental health and learning disability staff (NHS Protect 2016). NHS Protect was until 2017 the organisation responsible for addressing fraud, violence, corruption and other criminal activity in relation to the NHS.

Campaigning organisations have raised concerns about the psychological impact of restraint, particularly its potential to traumatise or re-traumatise (Mind 2013; Agenda 2017; see Maker in Chapter 5 and Brophy, Fletcher and Hamilton in Chapter 12 in this volume). There are also concerns about the abuse of human rights that occurs during restraint, including absolute rights such as the right to life and the right not to be subject to cruel and degrading treatment. The human rights concerns also encompass rights that can be restricted within the legal framework such as the right to liberty and the right to have a private and family life.

It is noteworthy that in 2011, only a year after the latest death attributed to restraint (Olaseni Lewis), the government strategy for Mental Health in England, *No Health Without Mental Health*, did not mention restraint or restrictive practice (HM Government 2011). It took a 2011 BBC documentary to prompt Her Majesty's (HM) government to take action about the perceived overuse of restrictive practice. The documentary investigated abuse of people with learning disabilities at the private hospital Winterbourne View (Scally et al. 2012: 1), revealing that patients had been subject to slapping, deliberate provocation to justify restraint and the use of chairs to prevent movement. In its June 2012 Interim Review of Events at Winterbourne View, the Department of Health committed to working with the Department for Education, who had policy responsibility for children's services, to promote the use of Positive Behaviour Support and ensure that restraint was only ever used as a last resort (Department of Health 2012: 32). The regulator of health and social care in England, the Care Quality Commission, reviewed 150 learning disability services. Its report was published at the same time as the interim review; it reported that whilst there was no evidence of similar abuse elsewhere, there was evidence of an over-reliance on restraint (Care Quality Commission 2012).

Whilst the government was considering its policy response to events at Winterbourne View, the mental health charity Mind submitted Freedom of Information requests to all the English NHS mental health providers about their use of restraint. Mind's report, *Mental Health Crisis Care: Physical Restraint in Crisis* was published in June 2013 (Mind 2013). It showed that the rates of restraint and prone restraint (where the patient is held face down) varied greatly between providers. It should be noted that Mind did not attempt to distinguish between the size of provider or take account of the different services each provider was commissioned to provide. Mind's definition of restraint was also broad, with incidents ranging from the use of a guiding hand, staff sitting with a patient and preventing him or her from harming themselves, and more forceful action by multiple staff all recorded as single incidents of restraint. In addition, not all providers had systems that enabled them to distinguish the use of prone restraint from other forms of restraint.

More recently two further events illustrate the ongoing concern about inappropriate use of restrictive interventions. In October 2018, BBC Radio Four's flagship morning news programme 'Today' included a piece about the increase in the use of restraint in inpatient settings for people with learning disabilities and/or autism (BBC 2018). Later in the same year, the Secretary of State for Health and Social Care, Matt Hancock MP asked the Care Quality Commission to undertake a detailed review of the use of restraint, prolonged seclusion and segregation in services for people who are autistic, have a learning disability or mental health condition (Care Quality Commission 2020).

The policy initiatives and their impact

Positive and Proactive Care

Positive and Proactive Care: Reducing the Need for Restrictive Interventions (Positive and Proactive Care) was published in April 2014 (Department of Health 2014). The policy covered health and social care services for adults. There was an expectation that together with the Department for Education, the Department of Health would quickly develop corresponding guidance for children and young people's services across health, education and social care. After much delay that guidance, *Reducing the Need for Restraint and Restrictive Interventions* (Department for Education and Department of Health and Social Care 2019) was eventually published in 2019.

Positive and Proactive Care promoted a focus on developing therapeutic relationships between staff and patients; understanding behaviour, particularly promoting the use of Positive Behaviour Support (often termed PBS); working only within the prescribed legal and ethical framework; and most importantly only ever using restraint as a last resort. Positive Behaviour Support is a framework for developing an understanding of behaviour that challenges based on the physical, social and individual circumstances in which the behaviour occurs. This information is used to develop approaches that prevent the challenging behaviour occurring and the likelihood of restrictive interventions being considered (PBS Academy 2015). Positive and Proactive Care also included the prohibition of the planned or intentional use of prone restraint and physical techniques or breakaways that caused pain, with the exception of life-threatening situations.

The guidance set out requirements relating to improving care, leadership assurance and governance, transparency, monitoring and oversight. This approach mirrors the six core strategies recommended by Kevin Ann Huckshorn at the National Technical Assistance Center for State Mental Health Planning (2005) in the United States, which form the basis of some of the more successful attempts by providers in England to reduce the use of restrictive practice (Advancing Quality Alliance 2017; Mersey Care NHS Foundation Trust 2019; see McSherry and Maker in Chapter 1 in this volume).

Significantly, Positive and Proactive Care treated reducing restrictive practice as a stand-alone issue and took no account of system wide pressures including the shortage of staff, the reduced number of inpatient beds and pressure on community services that were subsequently identified in NHS England's *Five Year Forward View for Mental Health* report (Independent Mental Health Taskforce 2016).

Assessing the impact of Positive and Proactive Care is complex and, to date, there has been no academic analysis of the policy's implementation. In my role, I became aware of concerns from clinicians about their safety in managing violent incidents and the absence of guidance and resources to implement alternatives to prone restraint and use of pain.

The prohibition of prone restraint and staff concerns

The hopes for improving care were based on the prohibitions mentioned previously and on the requirements for providers to develop individualised personal support plans and involve patients' carers and advocates in all aspects of care. Looking first at the prohibition of prone restraint, it is noticeable that alternative approved techniques were not put forward nor were the risks of other techniques acknowledged. Some clinical staff and academics questioned the focus on prone restraint (Paterson, Bennet and Bradley 2014), suggesting that more injuries are associated with prone restraint because it is the most often-taught technique, rather than being more dangerous than the alternatives. They argue that prone restraint is safe if it is performed correctly. There was also an appreciation that supine restraint (where the patient is held on their back), the most obvious alternative to prone restraint, is potentially more dangerous for staff as a resisting patient could more easily kick out. Supine restraint could also risk retraumatising patients who have suffered physical and sexual abuse. In 2018 a group of academics and clinicians looked at the risks involved in all manual restraint techniques. Having considered the limited evidence available and the obvious problems involved with randomised controlled trials, the authors suggested that there was insufficient evidence to support a ban on any position (Sethi et al. 2018).

Criticism of the guidance's apparent prohibition of pain compliance (the use of pain to make a patient do what staff ask) did not indicate a desire for staff to be able to inflict pain more often, but rather a concern about the level set for its use. Training courses typically included breakaway techniques, some of which cause pain. Setting the bar at a threat to life failed to acknowledge the NHS Protect data that suggested staff members are often the victims of assault. It had the effect of penalising all staff for the abuse by rogue individuals at Winterbourne View. Some of the most challenging interviews and conversations that I personally experienced in my 20-year civil service career were with clinicians visibly angry, distressed and concerned about their own safety, who asked, 'What are we allowed or supposed to do when faced with violence?'

Concern about what the police role should be in relation to assisting health care staff manage violent incidents in inpatient settings resulted in the National Police Chiefs' Council establishing a working group. The group included police, academic, service user, health care and government representatives. It took some time, but a memorandum of understanding between the National Police Chiefs' Council, the Royal College of Nursing, the Royal College of Psychiatrists and Mind was published in January 2017 (College of Policing 2017).

Positive changes in practice

Turning to the positive changes in practice, these were well received by clinical staff. Positive and Proactive Care called for individualised support plans which include Positive Behaviour Support plans for all patients who may display behaviour that challenges. These plans should include primary, secondary and tertiary interventions to prevent, mitigate and eventually respond to behaviour that challenges. Primary interventions call for clinical staff to put plans in place that would prevent incidents from occurring. These could include nursing care being provided by staff members of the same gender, providing meaningful activity to prevent boredom and generally getting to know the patient's preferences, interests, triggers, personality and background. Secondary interventions are strategies to reduce or mitigate challenging behaviour before it escalates to a position where restrictive interventions may be required. Such interventions include distraction, diversion, de-escalation and contact with friends and family. Finally, tertiary interventions are those that are taken when the behaviour has reached a point where an intervention is required to keep the patient, other patients and staff safe. They include both physical and nonphysical interventions. Some providers were already using these techniques and this part of the guidance was seen as promoting existing positive practice rather than suggesting a new approach.

However, Positive and Proactive Care's championing of Positive Behaviour Support was more controversial. Positive Behaviour Support has its roots in

American children's services (Carr et al. 2002). In the UK, it is widely used in adult learning disability services (Gore et al. 2013; PBS Academy 2015). When Positive and Proactive Care was published in 2014, though, it was not a recognised and evidence-based approach in mental health services.

Positive and Proactive Care also required someone at board level to be responsible for the organisation's Restrictive Intervention Reduction Programme. The Care Quality Commission agreed to include the existence of behaviour support plans and Restrictive Intervention Reduction Programmes within its inspection model but there was no accepted structure or content for either plan. To date, little is known about the content or effectiveness of these programmes.

Workforce development to support Positive and Proactive Care

The provider organisation's board or equivalent was also to be responsible for the quality of the training given to staff. *A Positive and Proactive Workforce* (Skills for Care and Skills for Health 2014) was published at the same time as Positive and Proactive Care, with the UK government earmarking £2 million to support training in England. Unfortunately, there were disagreements about how the investment should be used. On the one hand, there were calls for investment in Positive Behaviour Support training that focused on preventing the need for restraint. On the other hand, there was a long held concern about the content of training courses and the competence of instructors to deliver it in regard to the safety of restraint practice. This concern led to calls for the development of standards and accreditation of trainers. Frustration about the absence of training standards was heightened by the knowledge that standards had been suggested and indeed developed (although not published) by the National Institute for Mental Health in England as far back as 2004 as part of the policy response to the death of David 'Rocky' Bennett. Those who favoured investment in Positive Behaviour Support were not opposed to training standards to improve the safety of restraint practice but there was disagreement about the role of pain compliance and prone restraint.

Some progress was made in both the training to reduce the need for restraint and in improving the safety of practice. The three high secure hospitals in England worked together to develop a positive and safe training manual for their staff (West London NHS Trust 2019). Their approach was subsequently accredited by the National Institute for Health and Care Excellence (NICE). The British Institute of Learning Disability had provided a voluntary accreditation scheme for learning disability services since 2002. They were commissioned to test the same approach in a mental health service.

As for Positive Behaviour Support, a significant proportion of the funding for workforce development was used to provide training for staff teams. Concerns about how to train teams and the efficacy of Positive Behaviour Support training nevertheless remained. Firstly, some training providers were using the terminology of Positive Behaviour Support while still delivering training based on reactive approaches rather than focusing on understanding the meaning of a patient's behaviour and looking for adaptations in their care plan that would mitigate the need for restrictive practice. There were unsuccessful calls from the Positive Behaviour Support Academy (a group of UK academics and clinicians formed to promote the use of Positive Behaviour Support) for an accreditation system (PBS Academy 2015). Furthermore, even where the content of the training (which ranged from e-learning to doctorates) was appropriate, there was no consensus about how to train a staff team to support an individual. The debate about how to identify good Positive Behaviour Support training and how to train a staff team continues to this day.

Data collection and its limitations

The data available when Positive and Proactive Care was published in 2014 was patchy at best. Despite a statutory requirement to return data for the Mental Health Minimum Data Set, many providers either did not submit any data, or the data they did submit was not credible when compared with the 2013 Mind report. The Department of Health commissioned the NHS benchmarking network to collect data from all NHS providers, and on a voluntary basis, independent (non-NHS) sector providers. This data however raised as many questions as it answered. The second iteration provided data that was comparable at a service level, such as a psychiatric intensive care unit or older people service rather than at a provider level. Even so, the data for manual restraint still used the broad definition set out in the *Mental Capacity Act 2005* and covered such a wide area of practice that it was impossible to identify the most restrictive services. Even for prone restraint, where the definition is clear, there were debates about what should be recorded as prone restraint. For example, should an incident be recorded if the patient put themselves or fell into a prone position during an incident and was then restrained once in that position? There was also a suggestion that prone restraint for a given time period before turning the patient into a supine position should not count. Accordingly, a seemingly simple measure was interpreted in different ways by different providers meaning that valid comparisons were not possible (see Sara in Chapter 9 in this volume for further discussion of the challenges of construct definition and data collection).

In my discussions with providers, several reasons were put forward to explain the apparently higher use of restraint in some services compared to others. For example, some providers pointed to particular individuals who were very unwell skewing their overall figures. Similarly, due to the shortage of appropriate beds, some patients were cared for in a service that was not used to or resourced for their level of need. There were also suggestions that some services would not accept patients with the most challenging behaviour, meaning that those services appeared to be less restrictive than others. It was also apparent that services with a greater reliance on agency staff faced additional problems, in that the staff did not have the same knowledge and understanding of the patient and may have been trained to use different techniques.

How should we assess the impact of Positive and Proactive Care? It certainly raised the profile of reducing restrictive practices and its influence can be seen in the *Mental Health Units (Use of Force) Act 2018* and the initiatives led by NHS England, discussed later in the chapter.

The call for a governance structure and policies around the use of restrictive interventions resulted in providers reviewing existing plans and in many cases appointing specialist nurses to lead the organisation's attempts to reduce restrictive practice. Many of these posts are still in place today. This work was complemented by the Department of Health setting up a Reducing Restrictive Practice Champions Network which enabled organisations to learn from each other. By the time the Department of Health stopped funding work related to Positive and Proactive Care in 2016 there were almost 300 people involved in the network. There was also some evidence that providers were learning from each other and adapting their practice.

However, the guidance also appeared to alienate some staff. The input needed from other national organisations such as NHS Digital and NHS England was not sufficiently forthcoming and the infrastructure required to take full advantage of Positive and Proactive Care's recommendations are, as we will see later, only now being put in place. The paucity of the data made it impossible to identify whether there was a reduction in the use of restrictive interventions. Data released by NHS Digital over recent years demonstrates that Positive and Proactive Care certainly did not eliminate the use of prone restraint (NHS Digital 2018).

Mental Health Act Code of Practice 2015

Chronologically, the next policy initiative involving restrictive practice was the 2015 Mental Health Act Code of Practice (the 2015 Code) (Department of Health 2015). The 2015 Code provides statutory guidance rather than primary legislation, but staff who deviate from it would be expected to show good reason for doing so.

The previous iteration of the code, published in 2008 (the 2008 Code) (Department of Health 2008), listed issues that may contribute to what it termed 'disturbed behaviour', which in turn may lead to restrictive interventions being required. These included boredom, excessive stimulation, difficulties in communication, an unsuitable mix of patients, antagonism, aggression or provocation on the part of others and the influence of alcohol or drugs. The 2008 Code dedicated only 19 pages (66 paragraphs) to this subject (Department of Health 2008: 112–30). Reflecting the increased importance and priority of attempts to manage behaviour that challenges, the 2015 Code dedicates 34 pages (179 paragraphs) to the same matter (Department of Health 2015: 281–314).

Chapter 26 of the 2015 Code, 'Safe and Therapeutic Responses to Disturbed Behaviour', mirrors Positive and Proactive Care with its emphasis on reducing restrictive practice. There is also more detail on process and recording. However, perhaps the most notable addition is the introduction of reference to primary, secondary and tertiary interventions into statutory guidance.

The cogency approach to the use of pain and prone restraint

The 2015 Code says that prone restraint and pain compliance must not be used unless there are cogent reasons for doing so. The Code suggests that a threat to life would be a cogent reason for using pain but does not provide any cogent reasons for using prone restraint. Describing the weight that should be given to the Code of Practice in his judgment in *R (Munjaz) v Mersey Care NHS Trust* [2006]: para 21, Lord Bingham said:

> It is not instruction, but it is much more than mere advice which an addressee is free to follow or not as it chooses. It is guidance which any hospital should consider with great care, and from which it should depart only if it has cogent reasons for doing so . . . . In reviewing any challenge to a departure from the Code, the court should scrutinise the reasons given by the hospital for departure with the intensity which the importance and sensitivity of the subject matter requires.

The introduction of 'cogent reasons' for using either prone restraint or pain compliance therefore reiterates that the expectation is that prone restraint and pain compliance should not be used and that there must be sound reasons for using either technique.

I was recently asked whether the Care Quality Commission had done or intended to do any work about cogent reasons for using prone restraint. In my view, listing situations where it would be appropriate to use prone restraint would be simplistic and misses the point. Incidents of violence and aggression are fluid and unpredictable with staff facing a difficult, potentially dangerous situation. The guidance from the 2008 Code, through to Positive and Proactive Care and then the 2015 Code is clear: staff should attempt to de-escalate and use the least restrictive approach. Furthermore, steps should have been put in place to prevent incidents happening in the first place. When a decision to intervene physically is taken, the staff do not know how long the incident will last or what level of hold will be necessary but the requirement for them to use the least restrictive approach (one of the principles that applies throughout the 2015 Code) remains. The staff team therefore needs to conduct dynamic risk assessments of what is happening and potentially adapt their approach rather than consider whether the situation they are faced with falls within a category where pain compliance or prone restraint may be used.

I would suggest that in many incidents where a staff team eventually decided to use prone restraint and rapid tranquillisation, different approaches could have been taken earlier in the incident, or events that led up to the incident could have been managed differently (Taxis 2002; Lewis and Parks 2009; Kontio et al. 2010). That is not to say that staff acted incorrectly or used more force than was necessary, nor that there was not a cogent reason for the action they took. It is to acknowledge that situations are fluid and unpredictable.

The 2015 Code also recognises the importance of well trained and consistent staff by including the requirement for staff to only use restraint techniques in which they have been trained and the need for a staff team to be able to work together in managing incidents.

Overall, my view is that the 2015 Code helped to ameliorate some of the concern amongst clinicians about Positive and Proactive Care, without giving ground on the importance of prevention and de-escalation.

National Institute for Health and Care Excellence guidance

The National Institute for Health and Care Excellence (NICE) published its guideline NG10 *Violence and Aggression: Short-term Management in Mental Health, Health and Community Settings* in May 2015 (the NICE Guideline) (NICE 2015). This guideline is notable in relation to two matters – time limits on restraint and post-incident reviews.

The time limit on restraint

The NICE Guideline's position on prone restraint had been awaited with some interest but, far from clarifying matters, it added another consideration. It calls for staff to avoid taking patients to the ground but recommends that when restraint on the ground is used, supine restraint – where a person is held on their back – should be used. If prone restraint is necessary, it should be used for the shortest time possible. The guideline goes on to say that any manual restraint should not be used for more than ten minutes. The guideline is clear that any manual restraint can be dangerous and cautions staff to avoid interfering with a patient's airway, breathing or circulation. In suggesting that supine restraint is preferable to prone restraint, there is an assumption that the supine position is less dangerous. However, what research there is (Sethi et al. 2018) suggests that there is not sufficient evidence to support this position. In addition, there does not seem to be any evidence to suggest that ten minutes is a safe duration for any restraint position.

Post-incident reviews

The other significant contribution from the NICE Guideline was its focus on post-incident reviews. The inclusion of guidance about post-incident reviews was not new. But the NICE quality standards methodology, working with clinicians to identify the most important elements of the NICE Guideline and then focusing on developing metrics for achievable standards that can be used to drive quality improvement, has the potential to improve practice. Looking back with a clear head on a restrictive intervention gives an opportunity for reflection and for lessons to be learnt that could mitigate against recurrence. Talking to the patient after the incident has the potential to reduce any adverse effect on the therapeutic relationship (Taxis 2002: 164; Ling, Cleverley and Perivolaris 2015). There is also an opportunity for the multidisciplinary team to think about the antecedents to the incident and how effective the agreed primary, secondary and nonphysical tertiary interventions listed in the care plan had been used (Riahi et al. 2016: 35).

The second tranche of initiatives

Care Quality Commission concerns about safety on mental health wards

Despite the emphasis on reducing the use of restrictive interventions since 2014, concern about organisational responsibility, variation in practice and recording persisted in the following years. In 2017 the Care Quality Commission published *The State of Care in Mental Health Services 2014–2017* based on its inspections. This assessment raised several concerns about safety on mental health wards, including the variation in the amount of restrictive interventions used by providers as a response to challenging behaviour (Care Quality Commission 2017a: 32).

The Care Quality Commission noted differences in interpretation of guidance by providers, the poor quality (or in some cases absence) of national data returns and differences in the content and quality of Prevention and Management of Violence and Aggression training. Given the continued absence of national standards for the content of training and the competence of trainers, it is not surprising that each provider and in some cases different services within an organisation had continued to make their own decisions about the content, duration and delivery of training for their staff.

The differences in the interpretation of data definitions are a more complex matter. Guidance accompanying the Mental Health Services Dataset since 2015 made it clear that any time a patient spends in prone restraint, regardless of how they arrived in that position, should be recorded as prone restraint (NHS Digital 2017). Yet discussions with providers revealed that arbitrary decisions about duration, intent and policy (for example, whether they teach prone restraint) resulted in incidents not being recorded. It is hard to avoid the conclusion that the controversy surrounding the 2013 Mind report and the singling out of prone restraint in Positive and Proactive Care contributed to decisions about how incidents would be recorded.

In December 2017, as part of its work to encourage quality improvement, the Care Quality Commission published examples of providers who have been successful in reducing their use of restrictive interventions. The approaches taken included a focus on providing better and individualised care, quality improvement, implementing the Safewards programme (see Brophy, Fletcher and Hamilton in Chapter 12 in this volume) and trialling the use of alternative injection sites such as the shoulder or thigh rather than the buttock for rapid tranquillisation, thereby avoiding the need for prone restraint (Care Quality Commission 2017b).

The Mental Health Units (Use of Force) Act 2018

Unrelated to the Care Quality Commission's report and inspired by the death of Olaseni Lewis in 2010, the *Mental Health Units (Use of Force) Act 2018* (the Act) (described in more detail by Peter Bartlett and Stephanie Sampson in Chapter 3 in this volume) sets legal requirements for providers of NHS-funded mental health and learning disability services to report their use of force and reduce their use of restrictive interventions (which under the Act are considered force). Section 12 of the Act also requires the police to use body worn cameras when they are called to assist staff in the management of disturbed behaviour.

A joint work programme to reduce the use of restrictive interventions

The requirements of the Act, the Care Quality Commission's concerns and pressure to reduce the use of restrictive interventions in nationally commissioned learning disability services all created an impetus for the national organisations (NHS England, NHS Improvement, Health Education England, NHS Digital, the Care Quality Commission and the now Department of Health and Social Care) to work together. The joint work programme established by these national organisations identified three priorities.

Firstly, there was clearly a need to improve the available data to facilitate a better understanding of practice and enable meaningful comparisons of services. The report of the Royal College of Psychiatrists' Faculty of the Psychiatry of Intellectual Disability summarises the inadequacies of the currently available data (Royal College of Psychiatrists 2018: 23–40). From April 2019 the Mental Health Services Dataset required providers to submit data about the position and duration of restraint. The data return records the start and finish times of restraints in standing, seated, kneeling, supine, side and prone positions. This change to the data collection also includes a requirement for providers to report on injuries sustained by patients, staff and others immediately before and during restraint, and whether post-incident reviews took place.

There has already been some concern from providers about their ability to accurately record the duration of each part of an incident. For example, how long a patient was held in a standing position before the incident moved to a seated position or restraint on the ground. It will be interesting to see how quickly providers adapt and how effectively the system is able to share the good practice of those organisations who already record incidents in this way.

Secondly, Health Education England commissioned the Restraint Reduction Network, a coalition of organisations committed to reducing restraint, to develop standards for providers of physical interventions training (Restraint Reduction Network 2019). Health Education England also worked with the United Kingdom Accreditation Service to develop a process for certifying training that adheres to the Restraint Reduction Network standards (Restraint Reduction Network 2019). From April 2020 all providers of NHS-funded mental health and learning disability services were contractually required to develop plans for their organisation to use certified training providers from April 2021.

Certified training is undoubtedly a key step in improving practice. The standards set expectations about understanding human rights and the legal framework for the use of restraint. They also require training attendees to demonstrate their competence in preventative practice as well as in physical interventions. However, the absence of a single agreed curriculum means that it will still be the case that staff in one provider will be trained to use a range of different holds and techniques to those taught in neighbouring organisations. This leaves open the possibility of confusion when staff are managing dangerous situations. Agency staff present an additional problem. The standards suggest that service providers ensure agency staff receive certified training. However, it is not clear how providers will ensure that this happens.

Thirdly, NHS Improvement commissioned the National Collaborating Centre for Mental Health, part of the Royal College of Psychiatrists, to provide quality improvement support for 42 NHS mental health or learning disability wards.

A summary of the projects and their results was delivered at the Restraint Reduction Network conference in 2019.

The *Mental Health Units (Use of Force) Act 2018* and the work being undertaken by the national organisations are clearly building on the initiatives announced in Positive and Proactive Care, adding legal force and coordinated effort to drive change.

Should any restrictive interventions be prohibited?

The evidence suggests that any manual restraint can be dangerous and that prolonged restraint is more dangerous (NICE 2015; Sethi et al. 2018). The most obvious risks come about from pressure on the airway or the circulatory system. There are additional risks associated with existing health conditions, frailty, or – in the case of children and young people – their stage of development. Restraint also risks traumatising or re-traumatising people of all ages. However much staff teams and organisations work to prevent the need for physical restraint, there will always be situations when not using restraint would be more dangerous than doing so. It would therefore be sensible to have a clear and consistent policy position focused on ensuring that the time spent in restraint is minimised.

Earlier in this chapter I considered the implications of the cogency test for the use of prone restraint in the Mental Health Act Code of Practice 2015 and concluded that where any form of physical restraint is used the situation could result in a restraint on the ground. More work is needed to clarify whether one form of restraint on the ground is safer than another. Until there is incontrovertible evidence about safe duration and position, perhaps the focus should be on minimising the number of incidents where patients are restrained on the ground or other surface.

Mechanical restraint, that is, the use of belts, cuffs or other instruments to prevent movement, is not commonly used in UK care settings. Where it is used, there is a requirement that there is sign off by the executive team or equivalent and that clinicians not involved in the care of the individual in question have considered whether there is a less restrictive alternative to mechanical restraint. The Care Quality Commission (2016) recognises that mechanical restraint can sometimes be the least restrictive approach. A clearer statement of national policy would help to ensure that mechanical restraint remains the exception.

Chemical restraint is more complex to consider. As discussed elsewhere in this volume by Peter Bartlett and Stephanie Sampson (Chapter 3) and Juanita Breen (Chapter 13), there are risks involved in the use of any medication, such as known side effects and atypical reactions. For rapid tranquillisation there is additional risk associated with the accuracy of its use, with some studies suggesting that a proportion of injections are not administered into a muscle and are therefore ineffective (Soliman et al. 2018). The 2015 Code also requires observation of the patient after the use of rapid tranquilisation. Combinations of different medications present a different risk, as does the use of psychotropic and antipsychotic medication to subdue individuals and prevent challenging behaviour developing.

There is much to be done in this area in the UK to determine which practices are the most dangerous and where additional safeguards may be required.

Reducing restrictive practice is not a stand-alone issue

A confident and consistent workforce is a key component in implementing the initiatives considered in this chapter. However, mental health and learning disability services face the same challenges identified in a 2018 report on the health care workforce (Health Foundation, Kings Fund and Nuffield Trust 2018), namely, increasing numbers of vacancies and falling numbers of students entering nurse training. In its manifesto to influence political parties ahead of the 2019 UK general election, the Royal College of Nursing called for increased investment to support retention of staff and improved support for nursing students (Royal College of Nursing 2019).

Furthermore, between 1998 and 2012 the number of mental health beds fell by 39 per cent (Independent Mental Health Taskforce 2016: 9). The reduction in inpatient beds has led to out of area placements, where patients are treated some distance from their homes, families and friends because there are no beds available locally. It is also not unknown for patients who have been given leave as part of their journey to recovery to have to move to another hospital because their bed has been used for another patient. Distance from support networks and enforced changes in location can both increase a patient's sense of isolation, which is a known antecedent of aggression. There is also an argument that pressure on beds results in earlier discharges from hospital and a higher barrier for access to inpatient services.

Implementing NHS England's *Five-Year Forward View for Mental Health* (Independent Mental Health Taskforce 2016) and the NHS long-term plan announced in January 2019 (NHS England 2019) could provide the investment and focus to address both the preceding issues. Failing to do so would make reducing restrictive practices more difficult.

Additional actions and approaches

It may also be helpful to mandate approaches that have been shown to be successful in reducing restrictive practice. The effectiveness of Safewards in particular is supported by a wealth of academic evidence (Bowers et al. 2015; Fletcher et al. 2017; Stensgaard et al. 2018; Baumgardt et al. 2019; see Brophy, Fletcher and Hamilton in Chapter 12 in this volume). Safewards was developed by Len Bowers and his team at the Institute of Psychiatry, Psychology and Neuroscience at King's College London, who noticed that even neighbouring wards with the same ethos had markedly different rates of the use of restrictive interventions. They identified 100 simple and inexpensive modifications in practice that influenced the need for restraint, seclusion and other interventions. Some are as straightforward as using soft words; staff saying something positive about a patient when shifts change rather than focusing on their negative experience with the individual; having a range of sensory items available to assist in de-escalation; and having a noticeboard with information about staff such as musical preferences and favourite sporting teams. Most organisations who say they have implemented Safewards have focused on thoroughly implementing ten changes, but more of the 100 interventions could be used. Safewards was initially developed for adult mental health services but has been successfully modified and implemented in learning disability services, forensic settings and services for all ages. It has also been implemented and shown to be successful in numerous other countries, such as Australia (Fletcher et al. 2017), Denmark (Stensgaard et al. 2018) and Germany (Baumgardt et al. 2019).

Similarly, NICE identified the importance of post-incident reviews as a marker of a quality service. The Mental Health Minimum Data Set now records whether reviews take place but is there a further step to be taken by insisting, either contractually or otherwise, that they do take place? Another example is the use of audit. Reflecting on a single incident is undoubtedly helpful, but considering all incidents on a ward over a month or year could reveal times of the day when incidents are more likely to happen and areas where further focus or additional training would be helpful.

The requirement for providers to publish data and the work done to improve data quality and relevance, described earlier, will provide a much-improved understanding of practice from which national organisations could set requirements for review of incidents (see Sara in Chapter 9 in this volume). For example, any restraint on the floor for more than a set time could trigger a requirement for a provider-level review. Repetition or a longer period of restraint could trigger a review by commissioners and/or regulators.

With its focus on potential improvements across different organisational levels, linked to the implementation of the *Mental Health Units (Use of Force) Act* 2018, the evidence-based guidance *Towards Safer Services* (Restraint Reduction Network 2020) should lead to more consistency in the content of Restrictive Intervention Reduction Programmes. Research and collaboration across the sector will also be necessary to understand what works in different services. It will also be important that providers, academics and pressure groups have an established process for coming together to share ideas and good practice. To this end, the Positive and Safe Champions Network, now supported by the Restraint Reduction Network, has reconvened and has events planned through to 2021.

De-escalation is often heralded as an alternative to restraint. The evidence suggests that a rapport with the patient, experienced staff, a calm tone and positive body language are all important elements (Price and Baker 2012). More work is required to train staff effectively in this area but ongoing investment and the time required for training would be time and money well spent. There are also examples of providers taking a truly proactive stance in their work to anticipate aggression and violence. Many use the concept of safety huddles, where the multidisciplinary team comes together at least once per shift to discuss their interactions with patients and the likelihood of incidents developing (Health Foundation 2019). Where concerns are identified one or more of the team will be given agreed actions for working with the individual in question to mitigate the identified risk.

The requirement under the *Mental Health Units (Use of Force) Act 2018* for the police to wear body worn cameras will provide an accurate record of their involvement in an incident. There may be scope for wider use of similar technology. Staff at Northampton Healthcare NHS Foundation Trust have been piloting the use of body worn cameras and other providers are now trialling the same approach (Summers 2017). Some commentators have raised concerns about patient consent and privacy, but in Northampton patients were consulted and welcomed the use of cameras. What evidence there is suggests that both patients and staff like them. There is a suggestion that their use has prevented some incidents from escalating and it gives an objective way to look at complaints from patients. Most of all, the cameras provide an invaluable asset for staff training and identifying poor practice. Similarly, and for the same reasons, many providers now use CCTV (closed-circuit television) cameras in communal areas and corridors. There is debate about the appropriateness of their use in a patient's bedroom and in seclusion rooms and en suite facilities, with obvious concerns about privacy and dignity (and see Osterfeld and Zinkler's discussion of camera use in German settings in Chapter 10 in this volume). These concerns are surely not insurmountable and a national policy about the use of body worn cameras and CCTV could be another step towards safer services.

Finally, there is much more to be done around training. Firstly, the national organisations should review the impact of the Restraint Reduction Network's training standards. Secondly, programmes of work and research to develop a single approved modular curriculum for Prevention and Management of Violence and Aggression training is required. Thirdly, work to understand how to implement training for staff teams in using Positive Behaviour Support focused on an individual is long overdue. Fourthly, continued support for the development of our understanding and training in de-escalation is essential.

Conclusion

In 1998 a Canadian psychiatrist acknowledged that 'restraint is not itself harmless' and went on to say 'some proportion of those who are restrained may die. We do not know what this proportion is, or how many others will come near death and be revived' (Milliken 1998). More work is required to be certain about the number of deaths directly attributable to restraint. The *Mental Health Units (Use of Force) Act 2018* puts a duty on the Department of Health and Social Care to report on deaths caused by restraint, but the process for coroners to record a cause of death will make timely reporting challenging.

Efforts to reduce the psychological harm and injuries sustained by patients and staff during incidents must continue. Governments or their agents have a responsibility to monitor practice effectively, support efforts to reduce the use of restrictive interventions and set standards for the quality of care. This in turn requires a commitment to fund ongoing research and ensure that there is sufficient capacity (including appropriately trained staff) for the standards to be achievable.

References

Advancing Quality Alliance (2017) *REsTRAIN YOURSELF Toolkit*. Available www.aquanw.nhs.uk/resources/restrain-yourself-toolkit/20917 (accessed 20 June 2020).

Agenda Alliance for Women and Girls at Risk (Agenda) (2017) *Agenda Briefing on the Use of Restraint Against Women and Girls*. Available https://weareagenda.org/wp-content/uploads/2017/03/Restraint-FOI-research-briefing-FINAL1.pdf (accessed 20 June 2020).

Baumgardt, J., Jäckel, D., Helber-Böhlen, H., Stiehm, N., Morgenstern, K., Voigt, A., Schöppe, E., McCutcheon, A., Velasquez Lecca, E.E., Löhr, M., Schulz, M., Bechdolf, A. and Weinmann, S. (2019) 'Preventing and Reducing Coercive Measures–An Evaluation of the Safewards Model in Two Locked Wards in Germany', *Frontiers in Psychiatry*, 10(340): 1–10.

Bowers, L., James, K., Quirk, A., Simpson, A., Stewart, D. and Hodsoll, J. (2015) 'Reducing Conflict and Containment Rates on Acute Psychiatric Wards: The Safewards Cluster Randomised Controlled Trial', *International Journal of Nursing Studies*, 52(9): 1412–22.

British Broadcasting Corporation (BBC) (2018) *My Daughter's Been in a Seclusion Cell for Almost Two Years*. Available www.bbc.co.uk/programmes/p06vgbnb (accessed 20 June 2019).

Care Quality Commission (2012) *Learning Disability Services Inspection Programme: National Overview*. Available www.cqc.org.uk/sites/default/files/documents/cqc_ld_review_national_overview.pdf (accessed 26 June 2020).

Care Quality Commission (2016) *Brief Guide: Restraint (Physical and Mechanical)*. Available https://cqc.org.uk/sites/default/files/20160422_briefguide-Restraint_physical_mechanical.pdf.pdf (accessed 20 June 2020).

Care Quality Commission (2017a) *The State of Care in Mental Health Services 2014 to 2017: Findings from CQC's Programme of Comprehensive Inspections of Specialist Mental Health Services*. Available www.cqc.org.uk/publications/major-report/state-care-mental-health-services-2014-2017 (accessed 20 June 2020).

Care Quality Commission (2017b) *Mental Health Act–A Focus on Restrictive Intervention Reduction Programmes in Inpatient Mental Health Services*. Available www.cqc.org.uk/publications/themed-work/mental-health-act-restrictive-intervention-reduction-programmes (accessed 20 June 2020).

Care Quality Commission (2020) *Our Review of Restraint, Seclusion and Segregation*. Available www.cqc.org.uk/publications/themes-care/our-review-restraint-seclusion-segregation (accessed 20 June 2020).

Carr, E.G., Dunlap, G., Horner, R.H., Koegel, R.L., Turnbull, A.P, Sailor, W., Anderson, J.L., Albin, R.W., Koegel, L.K. and Fox, L. (2002) 'Positive Behaviour Support: Evolution of an Applied Science', *Journal of Positive Behavior Interventions*, 4(1): 4–16.

College of Policing (2017) *Use of Restraint in Mental Health Settings*. Available www.college.police.uk/News/College-news/Pages/Mental_health_restraint_MoU.aspx (accessed 20 June 2020).

Department for Education and Department of Health and Social Care (2019) *Reducing the Need for Restraint and Restrictive Intervention*. Available www.gov.uk/government/publications/reducing-the-need-for-restraint-and-restrictive-intervention (accessed 20 June 2020).

Department of Health (2008) *Code of Practice: Mental Health Act 1983*. Available https://webarchive.nationalarchives.gov.uk/20130124042632/www.dh.gov.uk/

prod_consum_dh/groups/dh_digitalassets/@dh/@en/documents/digitalasset/dh_087073.pdf (accessed 20 June 2020).

Department of Health (2012) *Department of Health Review: Winterbourne View Hospital Interim Report.* Available https://assets.publishing.service.gov.uk/government/uploads/system/uploads/attachment_data/file/141591/Department-of-Health-Review-Winterbourne-View-Hospital-Interim-Report1.pdf (accessed 20 June 2020).

Department of Health (2014) *Positive and Proactive Care: Reducing the Need for Restrictive Interventions.* Available https://assets.publishing.service.gov.uk/government/uploads/system/uploads/attachment_data/file/300293/JRA_DoH_Guidance_on_RP_web_accessible.pdf (accessed 20 June 2020).

Department of Health (2015) *Mental Health Act 1983: Code of Practice.* Available https://assets.publishing.service.gov.uk/government/uploads/system/uploads/attachment_data/file/435512/MHA_Code_of_Practice.PDF (accessed 20 June 2020).

Fletcher, J., Spittal, M., Brophy, L., Tibble, H., Kinner, S., Elsom, S. and Hamilton, B. (2017) 'Outcomes of the Victorian Safewards Trial in 13 Wards: Impact on Seclusion Rates and Fidelity Measurement', *International Journal of Mental Health Nursing*, 26(5): 461–71.

Gore, N.J., McGill, P., Toogood, S., Allen, D., Hughes, J.C., Baker, P., Hastings, R.P., Noone, S.J. and Denne, L.D. (2013) 'Definition and Scope for Positive Behavioural Support', *International Journal of Positive Behavioural Support*, 3(2): 14–23.

Greenwood, G. (2017) 'Mental Health Trusts Restrain Patients "Every 10 Minutes" ', *BBC News*, 16 November. Available www.bbc.com/news/uk-england-41914555 (accessed 20 June 2020).

Health Foundation (2019) *Huddling Up for Safer Healthcare (HUSH).* Available www.health.org.uk/improvement-projects/scaling-up-patient-safety-huddles-to-enhance-patient-safety-and-safety-culture (accessed 20 June 2020).

Health Foundation, Kings Fund and Nuffield Trust (2018) *The Health Care Workforce in England: Make or Break?* Available www.kingsfund.org.uk/sites/default/files/2018-11/The%20health%20care%20workforce%20in%20England.pdf (accessed 20 June 2020).

Her Majesty's (HM) Government (2011) *No Health Without Mental Health: A Cross-Government Mental Health Outcomes Strategy for People of All Ages.* Available https://assets.publishing.service.gov.uk/government/uploads/system/uploads/attachment_data/file/213761/dh_124058.pdf (accessed 20 June 2020).

Independent Mental Health Taskforce (2016) *The Five Year Forward View for Mental Health – A Report from the Independent Mental Health Taskforce to the NHS in England.* Available www.england.nhs.uk/wp-content/uploads/2016/02/Mental-Health-Taskforce-FYFV-final.pdf (accessed 20 June 2020).

INQUEST (2017) *Inquest Opens into the Death of Olaseni Lewis Following Police Restraint at Bethlem Royal Hospital in August 2010.* Available www.inquest.org.uk/olaseni-lewis-inquest-opening (accessed 20 June 2020).

Kontio, R., Välimäki, M., Putkonen, H., Kuosmanen, L., Scott, A. and Joffe, G. (2010) 'Patient Restrictions: Are There Ethical Alternatives to Seclusion and Restraint?', *Nursing Ethics*, 17(1): 65–76.

Lewis, M. and Parks, J. (2009) 'Crisis Prevention Management: A Program to Reduce the Use of Seclusion and Restraint in an Inpatient Mental Health Setting', *Issues in Mental Health Nursing*, 30(3): 159–64.

Ling, S., Cleverley, K. and Perivolaris, A. (2015) 'Understanding Mental Health User Experiences of Restraint Through Debriefing: A Qualitative Analysis', *Canadian Journal of Psychiatry*, 60(9): 386–92.

Mental Health Units (Use of Force) Act 2018.

Mersey Care NHS Foundation Trust (2019) *No Force First.* Available www.merseycare.nhs.uk/about-us/striving-for-perfect-care/no-force-first/ (accessed 20 June 2020).

Milliken, D. (1998) 'Death by Restraint', *Canadian Medical Association Journal*, 158(12): 1611–12.

Mind (2013) *Mental Health Crisis Care: Physical Restraint in Crisis–A Report on Physical Restraint in Hospital Settings in England.* Available https://www.mind.org.uk/media-a/4378/physical_restraint_final_web_version.pdf (accessed 20 June 2020).

National Institute for Health and Care Excellence (NICE) (2015) *Violence and Aggression: Short-Term Management in Mental Health, Health and Community Settings*, NICE Guideline NG10. Available www.nice.org.uk/guidance/NG10 (accessed 20 June 2020).

National Technical Assistance Center for State Mental Health Planning (2005) *Six Core Strategies to Reduce the Use of Seclusion and Restraint Planning Tool*, Alexandria, VA: National Association of State Mental Health Program Directors. Available www.nasmhpd.org/content/six-core-strategies-reduce-seclusion-and-restraint-use (accessed 20 June 2020).

NHS Data Dictionary (2019) *Restrictive Intervention.* Available www.datadictionary.nhs.uk/data_dictionary/nhs_business_definitions/r/restrictive_intervention_de.asp (accessed 20 June 2020).

NHS Digital (2017) *Mental Health Services Data Set v3.0.* Available https://digital.nhs.uk/data-and-information/data-collections-and-data-sets/data-sets/mental-health-services-data-set/tools-and-guidance/mental-health-services-data-set-archived-specification (accessed 20 June 2020).

NHS Digital (2018) *LDA – Restraints, Assaults and Self-harm Data 2016–2018.* Available https://digital.nhs.uk/data-and-information/find-data-and-publications/supplementary-information/2018-supplementary-information-files/lda—restraints-assaults-and-self-harm-data-2016-2018 (accessed 26 June 2020).

NHS Protect (2016) *Reported Physical Assaults on NHS Staff Figures (2015–16).* Available https://webarchive.nationalarchives.gov.uk/20170726163554tf_/www.nhsbsa.nhs.uk/crime-prevention/nhs-protect-statistics (accessed 20 June 2020).

Paterson, B., Bennet, L. and Bradley, P.J. (2014) 'Positive and Proactive Care: Could New Guidance Lead to More Problems', *British Journal of Nursing*, 23(17): 939–41.

Positive Behaviour Support (PBS) Academy (2015) *PBS Academy.* Available http://pbsacademy.org.uk/ (accessed 20 June 2020).

Price, O. and Baker, J. (2012) 'Key Components of De-Escalation Techniques: A Thematic Synthesis', *International Journal of Mental Health Nursing*, 21(4): 310–19.

R (Munjaz) v Mersey Care NHS Trust [2006] 2 AC 148.

Restraint Reduction Network (2019) *Restraint Reduction Network Training Standards 2019 – Materials to Download.* Available https://restraintreductionnetwork.org/about/rrnstandardsdownloads/ (accessed 20 June 2020).

Restraint Reduction Network (2020) *Towards Safer Services: National Minimum Standards Organisational Restraint Reduction Plans.* Available https://restraintreductionnetwork.org/wp-content/uploads/2020/03/Towards_Safer_Services_final_report.pdf (accessed 20 June 2020).

Riahi, S., Dawe, I.C., Stuckey, M.I. and Klassen, P.E. (2016) 'Implementation of the Six Core Strategies for Restraint Minimization in a Specialized Mental Health Organisation', *Journal of Psychosocial Nursing and Mental Health Services*, 54(10): 32–39.

Royal College of Nursing (2019) *The RCN Manifesto: UK Government General Election 2019.* Available www.rcn.org.uk/-/media/royal-college-of-nursing/documents/publications/2019/november/007-943.pdf?la=en (accessed 20 June 2020).

Royal College of Psychiatrists (2018) *Restrictive Interventions in In-Patient Intellectual Disability Services: How to Record, Monitor and Regulate*, College Report CR220. Available www.rcpsych.ac.uk/improving-care/campaigning-for-better-mental-health-policy/college-reports/2018-college-reports/cr220 (accessed 20 June 2020).

Sallah, D., Sashidharan, S., Stone, R., Stuthers, J. and Blofeld, J. (2003) *Report of the Independent Inquiry into the Death of David Bennett.* Available http://image.guardian.co.uk/sys-files/Society/documents/2004/02/12/Bennett.pdf (accessed 20 June 2020).

Scally, G., Chalmers, J., Fallon-Williams, R. and Sly, P. (2012) *Report of the NHS Review of Commissioning of Care Treatment at Winterbourne View.* Available https://webarchive.nationalarchives.gov.uk/20121127132959/www.southofengland.nhs.uk/wp-content/uploads/2012/03/Final-Report-for-publication-Report-of-the-NHS-Review-of-Commissioning-of-Care-and-Treatment-at-Winterbourne-View-30-July-2012.pdf (accessed 20 June 2020).

Sethi, F., Parkes, J., Baskind, E., Paterson, B. and O'Brien, A. (2018) 'Restraint in Mental Health Settings: Is it Time to Declare a Position?', *British Journal of Psychiatry*, 212(3): 137–41.

Skills for Care and Skills for Health (2014) *A Positive and Proactive Workforce: A Guide to Workforce Development for Commissioners and Employers Seeking to Minimise the Use of Restrictive Practices in Social Care and Health.* Available www.skillsforcare.org.uk/Document-library/Skills/Restrictive-practices/A-positive-and-proactive-workforce-WEB.pdf (accessed 20 June 2020).

Soliman, E., Ranjan, S., Xu, T., Gee, C., Harker, A., Barrera, A. and Geddes, J. (2018) 'A Narrative Review of the Success of Intramuscular Gluteal Injections and Its Impact in Psychiatry', *Bio-Design and Manufacturing*, 1(3): 161–70.

Stensgaard, L., Andersen, M.K., Nordentoft, M. and Hjorthøj, C. (2018) 'Implementation of the Safewards Model to Reduce the Use of Coercive Measures in Adult Psychiatric Inpatient Units: An Interrupted Time-Series Analysis', *Journal of Psychiatric Research*, 105: 147–52.

Summers, N. (2017) 'UK Trials Body Cameras for Staff in Mental Health Wards: The Technology Could Calm Patients and Reduce Instances of Physical Restraint', *Engadget*, 5 May. Available www.engadget.com/2017/05/05/nhs-body-cameras-mental-health-patients/ (accessed 20 June 2020).

Taxis, J.C. (2002) 'Ethics and Praxis: Alternative Strategies to Physical Restraint and Seclusion in a Psychiatric Setting', *Issues in Mental Health Nursing*, 23(2): 157–70.

West London NHS Trust (2019) *Violence Reduction and Management Manual.* Available www.westlondon.nhs.uk/pmva-manual/ (accessed 20 June 2020).

Part III

Implementing and monitoring reform

Introduction to Part III

This part explores the implementation and monitoring of regulatory frameworks and measures aimed at reducing or eliminating the use of restraint. The predominant focus is on mental health and psychiatric settings. The authors identify features of effective implementation and monitoring, and considerable challenges to progress, in several Australian jurisdictions as well as in the Netherlands and Germany. They discuss implementation and monitoring mechanisms built into regulatory frameworks (such as the formal statements of law and policy discussed in Part II) and measures that are not specified in regulation but are also necessary to realise change.

A common theme across the chapters is the importance of adequate resources to facilitate effective monitoring of current practices and effective implementation and monitoring of reforms designed to minimise and/or eliminate the use of restraint. These include resources for changing service environments and processes; ensuring adequate staffing levels and training and supporting clinicians, nurses and other staff. The importance of leadership to guide culture change is also highlighted. For example, John Allan and Amber Manwaring in Chapter 8 discuss the implementation of the *Mental Health Act 2016* in the Australian state of Queensland. They describe the importance of a clear and common understanding of the purpose and goals of reform, as well as the provision of adequate information and ongoing support for staff to understand changes and implement alternatives to restraint, as key prerequisites for effective change. Several contributors also observe the importance of service user leadership and involvement in these processes.

The value of good quality data in monitoring existing practices and guiding reform efforts, and the challenges in defining and gathering this data, is another key theme of Part III. Grant Sara in Chapter 9 for example, emphasises the need for clear and consistent definitions and processes to permit the collection of data. He notes that these must be accompanied by improved data literacy and sharing. The challenges associated with defining and measuring some forms of restraint, especially chemical restraint, and the limited insights into motivations and impacts of restraint that traditional data collection can offer, suggest that multiple complementary measures are required before data collection and utility can improve. Privacy and data protection concerns, discussed by Lisa Waddington in Chapter 7, can add further layers of difficulty in gathering and utilising data. Waddington also observes that data collection will have limited effectiveness unless it is used effectively to inform local practice.

Other authors describe further significant implementation challenges. For example, Margret Osterfeld and Martin Zinkler in Chapter 10 discuss the considerable institutional and cultural resistance to the implementation of two recent Federal Constitutional Court decisions restricting the use of some forms of restraint in Germany. These authors point to the potential of inspectorates and other visiting or supervising bodies – such as National Preventive Mechanisms created under the *Optional Protocol to the Convention Against Torture and Other Cruel, Inhuman or Degrading Treatment or Punishment* – to support the implementation of law reform and accompanying cultural change in institutions.

Even where there are resources, leadership and goodwill, Allan and Manwaring point out in Chapter 8 that change may be impeded by difficulties associated with communicating and monitoring the roll-out of comprehensive and complex change to diverse, dispersed and ever-changing workforces. A theme that arose earlier in this volume recurs here, with authors arguing that clear guidance on alternatives to restraint is essential, but often missing, from regulatory reform efforts. This raises the potential for retrogressive consequences such as an increase in the use of alternative forms of restrictive or coercive measures when another form is prohibited. This in turn invites questions about the extent to which isolated, as opposed to systemic, changes can achieve the broader goals of restraint minimisation and elimination.

7 Legal regulation and policy on the use of restraint and coercive measures in health care institutions in the Netherlands

Lisa Waddington

Overview

Dutch psychiatric hospitals have been engaged in a range of projects to reduce the use of seclusion and others forms of coercive treatment since 1998. Between 2006 and 2012, this goal was supported by Dutch government funding of 35 million euros and involved a nationwide approach coordinated by GGZ Nederland (translated as the Dutch Association of Mental Health and Addiction Care), the country's mental health umbrella organisation (Voskes 2015: 34; Noorthoorn et al. 2016: 1321). There was a particular focus on reducing the use of seclusion, because seclusion rates in the Netherlands were above average compared to similar countries, both in terms of number and duration. In contrast, as noted by Voskes (2015: 52), in most European countries chemical restraint (or involuntary or forced medication) is 'the primary coercive measure of choice'. Subsequent evaluations have revealed that the rate of seclusion has reduced somewhat in the Netherlands, although this has been partially accompanied by an increase in the use of involuntary medication. A key factor in allowing for such longitudinal evaluations was mandatory registration of all individual uses of restraint and coercive treatment in all psychiatric institutions. This registration allowed for benchmarking but has also proved problematic from the perspective of protecting the privacy of individuals subject to coercive measures.

This chapter begins by briefly setting out relevant background information about the Dutch (mental) health care system and introducing key terms. The chapter then examines the legal framework in the Netherlands which regulates the use of restraint and coercive measures in psychiatric institutions, as well as institutions housing people with intellectual disabilities and people with psychogeriatric conditions. That legal framework has recently been subject to significant change, with the previous legislation, the *Psychiatric Hospitals (Committals) Act* (also translated into English as the *Compulsory Admissions Act* or the *Special Admission to Psychiatric Hospitals Act*) ceasing to have effect from 1 January 2020, and replaced on that date by two new statutes: the *Compulsory Mental Health Care Act* and the *Care and Compulsion Act*, which are intended to be more client-centred. The chapter also examines the registration system, which was designed to record each use of restraint, coercion and involuntary treatment in Dutch psychiatric institutions, and the controversies surrounding the system related to patient privacy. Lastly, on the basis of desk research, the chapter identifies factors which seem to have influenced the (reduced) use of coercive measures, and particularly seclusion, in psychiatric institutions in the Netherlands.

Introduction to the Dutch (mental) health care system and terminology

This section provides relevant background information, including relating to terminology.

The (mental) health care system in the Netherlands

The Netherlands has a population of approximately 17 million people and, in 2017, spent 10.1 per cent of its gross domestic product on health care (Organisation for Economic Co-operation and Development (OECD) 2019). In comparison, in the same year, Australia spent 9.1 per cent, the United Kingdom spent 9.6 per cent and the United States spent 17.2 per cent of their gross domestic products on health care (OECD 2019). The Dutch health care system is regulated through four main statutes: the *Health Insurance Act*, the *Long-term Care Act*, the *Social Support Act* and the *Youth Act*. Treatment and care related to the first two statutes account for the vast majority of the health care budget (Netherlands Ministry of Health, Welfare and Sport [Ministrie van Volksgezondheid, Welzijn en Sport] 2016: 3). Under the *Health Insurance Act* every resident of the Netherlands is obliged to take out insurance covering health care (Netherlands Ministry of Health, Welfare and Sport 2016: 7). The minimum health insurance coverage, which is fairly broad, is determined by the government (Netherlands Ministry of Health, Welfare and Sport 2016). Insurance providers on the market are obliged to accept all individuals, irrespective of their state of health; and the premium charged cannot be based on an individual's state of health or anticipated health needs (Netherlands Ministry of Health, Welfare and Sport 2016: 7). Most insurance providers are cooperative non-profit making organisations (Netherlands Ministry of Health, Welfare and Sport 2016). The minimum package includes extramural mental health care (Netherlands Ministry of Health, Welfare and Sport 2016: 8) and long-term care (up to three years) provided in a mental health institution (Netherlands National Health Care Institute [Zorginstituut Nederland] 2019).

The average cost of such insurance for individuals was 1200 euros in 2016. In addition, individuals must cover the first 385 euros (as of 2016) of the cost of health care themselves per year, although this does not apply to general practitioner consultations and some other forms of treatment (Netherlands Ministry of Health, Welfare and Sport 2016: 10). Individuals who receive mental health care without their consent are also obliged to pay this sum (GGZ Centraal 2019). Lastly, employers must make an income related contribution to the health insurance of each employee. At a macro level, this contribution is similar to the annual premium paid by individuals (GGZ Centraal 2019). All individuals also have the option to take out insurance to cover additional risks, although pre-selection or additional conditions are allowed in such cases. About 90 per cent of insured individuals take out this additional risk cover, which includes for example, (partial) reimbursement of the costs of dental treatment, physiotherapy, glasses and contact lenses (Netherlands Ministry of Health, Welfare and Sport 2016: 10). The government covers the cost of insuring children under the age of 18, and people on low incomes receive financial support to help cover the cost of health insurance (Netherlands Ministry of Health, Welfare and Sport 2016: 10).

This approach aims to realise a 'demand driven' system, whereby health insurers contribute to improvements in the health care system, such as shorter waiting lists, less bureaucracy and more attention to quality. Health insurers can also influence the price charged for health care, and its quality, by negotiating contracts with selected providers (Netherlands Ministry of Health, Welfare and Sport 2016: 4).

The *Long-term Care Act* is also relevant in the context of certain kinds of mental health care and disability-related care. However, it should be noted that there are complex rules regarding which statute, and therefore which organisation, is responsible for funding mental health care (Netherlands National Health Care Institute 2017). The *Long-term Care Act* establishes a mandatory collective health insurance which covers risks which cannot be insured on an individual basis. The Act is based on the principle of solidarity and covers health care needs of people who are regarded as particularly 'vulnerable', including people with chronic mental health problems or an intellectual disability (Netherlands Ministry of Health, Welfare and Sport 2016: 3). The cost of this care is covered from general taxation, although individuals are required to pay a contribution to the cost of their treatment based on their income (Netherlands Ministry of Health, Welfare and Sport 2016: 15). The cost of long-term care provided in a psychiatric or disability-care institution is covered under the *Long-term Care Act*, where the stay exceeds three years. Stays of shorter duration are covered by the *Health Insurance Act* (Netherlands National Health Care Institute 2019). However, if an individual has received an official 'indication' (a finding of entitlement to a particular form of treatment) that they require long-term mental health care in an institutionalised setting, the cost of the care is covered by the *Long-term Care Act* before the three-year period has passed.

In terms of mental health care, the Netherlands has a relatively high number of psychiatric hospital beds, with 139 beds per 100,000 members of the population (World Health Organisation 2019).

Terminology

This chapter refers to different forms of treatment and interventions. The term 'involuntary treatment' is used to refer to any kind of treatment or intervention, such as placing an individual in a seclusion room, which takes places without the individual's consent. Consent can be withheld in a number of ways, including by refusing to sign a consent form, but also by displaying physical resistance or refusing to agree to an intervention verbally or non-verbally. Under Dutch law, involuntary treatment is treatment which takes place without the consent of the individual and involves treatment which is not foreseen in the individual's care plan. Such treatment may only take place in institutions which have been registered with the Ministry of Health, Welfare and Sport (discussed further later).

The term 'coercion' covers not only involuntary treatment, as defined earlier, but also the situation where a person is pressured to accept a treatment or intervention which they do not wish to receive. This may occur, for example, where an individual is told that they will be physically restrained if they do not accept certain medication, or vice versa, leading them to agree to the intervention which they regard as least bad in the circumstances. However, true consent is not given in such a situation, and such treatment can also be regarded as involuntary (Janssen 2012: Chapter 1). Since coercive treatment may involve elements which give the appearance of consent, such as the signing of a consent form or acceptance of treatment without demonstrating physical resistance, it may not be classified as involuntary by health care providers in situations where they are obliged to record all incidents of involuntary treatment. This form of coercion, resulting from placing individuals under pressure to make a certain choice, is not regulated under Dutch law.

'Freedom restricting' measures are interventions which impair an individual's ability to move freely or behave as they would wish to. This term can also be interpreted more strictly only to mean an intervention that restricts a person's freedom to act as they would wish. In that context, freedom restricting measures are a form of coercion. However, if freedom restricting measures are seen as also including measures which restrict a person's freedom to move, they could result either from coercion or a request from an individual. For example, a request from an individual to be placed in a secluded environment which they cannot leave for some time restricts their freedom but is done with their consent. The term seemed to be understood in this broad way in the Argus register (discussed later), since freedom restricting interventions made at the request of the patient also had to be reported to the register.

The term 'restraint' covers any intervention which is used to control a person's actions against their will. It includes the administration of medication primarily intended to control an individual's behaviour rather than to treat a medical condition; the use of mechanical restraint, such as a strap or belt or other device, to control a person's freedom of movement; and the use of physical restraint, involving bodily force to control a person's freedom of movement. For the purposes of this chapter, it also covers 'environmental restraint' which involves controlling or restricting a person's freedom to move outside the immediate area in which they are detained. This occurs, for example, where a person is placed in an isolation or seclusion room against their will. Seclusion and restraint, as described by Janssen (2012: Chapter 1, 5), concern 'interventions with the highest level of force and limitations in which the patient no longer has a choice'.

In the Netherlands, the focus of legislative protection is on involuntary treatment although, as seen from the preceding definitions, there is a broad overlap between involuntary treatment and restraint measures.

The legal framework regulating the use of involuntary treatment, coercion and restraint in Dutch health care institutions

The Psychiatric Hospitals (Committals) Act *(Bopz)*

The *Psychiatric Hospitals (Committals) Act* (1992) (acronym in Dutch: Bopz), which came into force in 1994, and which was repealed in 2019, regulated forced admissions to psychiatric hospitals. Unlike some countries, in the Netherlands a hospital committal does not automatically mean that a patient can also be subject to involuntary medical or coercive treatment, such as restraint (Pols 2002: 322). The Bopz therefore also regulated the conditions which had to be met for each individual case of involuntary medical treatment or restraint to be lawful. The Act only applied in cases where an individual had been committed (Bopz: Chapter III), meaning that individuals who were being treated on a voluntary basis had in principle less rights when it came to the use of coercion (Arends 2004: 826f; Arends 2010: 95; Arends 2015: 222). The Bopz also only applied to closed institutions, which had to be licensed by the Ministry of Health, Welfare and Sport. The use of restraint in other settings, such as within the community, is not regulated to the same degree (Arends 2004: 828), although coercive treatment outside of psychiatric institutions is addressed in the *Medical Treatment Agreements Act* (acronym in Dutch: WGBO). This allows for compulsory treatment of 'incompetent' patients to prevent serious damage to health.

In spite of its name, the Bopz also regulated committals and involuntary medical or coercive treatment in institutions housing people with intellectual disabilities and people with dementia and similar conditions. However, this broad scope was not regarded as unproblematic, with the second evaluation of the Bopz finding that the legislation, which was originally designed to address the situation of psychiatric patients, provided little protection for patients in psychogeriatric settings or for patients with an intellectual disability and did not provide an appropriate legal framework (Arends 2004: 821; Arends 2010: 95; Frederiks and Blankman 2013: 346; Frederiks 2015: 226). Furthermore, the third evaluation of the Bopz found that the law was too complicated and no longer reflected current views on admission policies in mental health care (Arends 2010: 95; Broer, Koetsier and Mulder 2014: 247; Arends 2015; Ploem and Gevers 2015: 206).

As of 1 January 2020, the Bopz has been replaced by two separate acts covering the mental health sector, and treatment of people with an intellectual disability or a psychogeriatric condition respectively, although arguments have also been made in favour of a single law regulating the use of coercion in both sectors (Arends 2010: 103; Frederiks 2015: 230; Ploem and Gevers 2015: 210–11). The two new statutes that came into effect in 2020, the *Compulsory Mental Health Care Act* (acronym in Dutch: Wvggz) and the *Care and Compulsion (Psychogeriatric and Intellectually Disabled Patients) Act* (acronym in Dutch: Wzd) are intended to be more patient- or client-centred than the Bopz and, while the Bopz was regarded as an 'admissions' or 'committal' law, the new laws are regarded as 'care' or 'treatment' laws (Broer, Koetsier and Mulder 2014: 240; Frederiks and Steen 2018: 157). However, the new laws continue to allow the use of involuntary treatment and restraint in certain situations and, unlike the Bopz, are intended to also regulate some forms of compulsory treatment in the community (Frederiks and Steen 2018).

Under the Bopz, involuntary treatment or restraint was only allowed in order to prevent a situation of danger, or where the involuntary treatment was the only means of treating an individual's condition within a reasonable period of time (Bopz: Article 38c(1) (a) and (b)). There must have been no other less intrusive measure available, with the Act referring to the treatment being 'absolutely necessary' (Bopz: Article 38c(1) (b); Verlinde et al. 2014: 644–45). The Bopz defined danger both from the perspective of the individual (the patient) and from the perspective of others. Danger existed for the individual if there was a risk of suicide or harm to oneself; harm to the individual's environment, for example, serious disturbances in the community; serious neglect to oneself; or causing so much annoyance to others that there was a risk that this would lead others to respond aggressively (Bopz: Articles 1(f), 1(a–d)). Danger existed for others if there was a risk that the individual would cause serious harm or kill someone else; if the individual posed a risk to the mental health of others; or if the individual seriously neglected another person who was dependent on his/her care (Bopz: Articles 1(f), 2(a-c)). A last form of danger listed in the former Act related to a general threat to the safety of other people or property (Bopz: Article 1(f)3). In all cases the danger was required to be related to the individuals' psychiatric, intellectual or memory 'disorder'.

The Bopz distinguished between two forms of involuntary treatment: 'means and measures' and other forms of coercive treatment. Means and measures (*middelen en maatregelen*) were forms of coercive treatment, including restraint, which could be used in an emergency situation, where the situation leading to the use of the coercive treatment was not addressed in the patient's treatment plan (Bopz: Article 39; *Bopz Decision Means and Measures*). They could only be used if no less intrusive measures were available to prevent danger, and for a maximum of seven days, as per the delegated legislation *Bopz Decision Means and Measures* (Article 3) issued by the Minister of Justice. These 'means and measures' could also never be used as a form of punishment. In addition to allowing the forced administration of fluids or food (*Bopz Decision Means and Measures*: Article 2(e)), this delegated legislation identified four forms of interventions (Article 2(a–d)) which could be used on a short-term basis in an emergency situation:

- Isolation (*afzondering*), whereby the patient was placed in a room which was specially designed for isolation. The door was locked.
- Seclusion (*separatie*), whereby the patient was placed in a room which was specially designed for seclusion. The room was required to be officially approved by the Ministry of Health, Welfare and Sport for the use of seclusion, and was more sober (had less facilities) than the room used for isolation. Seclusion was only allowed in psychiatric hospitals, and not in the elderly or disabled care sector.

- Mechanical or physical restraint (*fixatie*), whereby the patient's ability to move was restricted.
- Medication, whereby the patient was given medicine. This related to medication given without the consent of the patient.

If the health care provider believed that the 'means and measures' were still needed after seven days, because a situation of danger was ongoing, the measures were required to be incorporated in the patient's treatment or care plan and needed to be discussed with the patient and/or their representative as far as possible. Coercive treatment included within a treatment plan must have been intended to have a therapeutic effect. For example, in the case of psychiatric patients, coercive treatment (such as the forcible administration of medication) must have been the only available means of removing the danger resulting from the psychiatric condition within a reasonable period of time (Bopz: Article 38c(1)(a)). In such cases, the maximum duration of the treatment was three months, although this period could be extended under certain conditions and was subject to regular review (Bopz: Article 38c(2)).

Some of the measures identified above could also be foreseen in a patient's treatment plan, which the patient had consented to. If the treatment was foreseen in the plan in specific circumstances, and only administered in those circumstances, the treatment was not regarded as involuntary, unless the patient withdrew consent. The Bopz also allowed for a patient who was committed to draw up a self-binding declaration, whereby he or she gave a health care provider permission to carry out treatment in the future, even if at the moment the treatment was given the patient objected (Bopz: Articles 34a–34p). This was regarded as offering patients the possibility to participate in decision-making and allowed for the patient's wishes to be respected. However, it seems that this tool was hardly ever used (Blankman and Vermariën 2015: 32). A patient could also choose to enter a special care unit/room, which is a unit which is more comfortably furnished than an isolation or seclusion room and which the patient could request to leave at any time. This too did not amount to restraint.

Where the patient was classified as 'mentally incompetent' (*wilsonbekwaam*), the health care provider was required to consult the patient's representative, such as a close family member, when deciding whether to apply involuntary treatment. If the representative consented, but the patient did not, this also amounted to involuntary treatment, and the conditions set out in the Bopz were still required to be met.

A number of controls or restrictions were imposed on the use of coercive treatment under the Bopz. As noted earlier, involuntary treatment, including restraint, was only allowed on the basis of the Bopz in institutions which had been licensed to carry out such measures by the Dutch Ministry of Health, Welfare and Sport, and which were registered as such. Under the Bopz coercive treatment could only be used in the case of patients who had been admitted to a health care institution against their will. This occured either through a detention order (*inbewaringstelling*) or court order (*rechterlijke machtiging*) or through being admitted under Article 60 of the Bopz, meaning that they were admitted without their consent, but also without showing any sign of resistance (Arends 2004: 823). This last procedure was reserved for psychogeriatric patients and people with an intellectual disability. The number of detention orders and, in particular, court orders leading to involuntary admission under the Bopz increased significantly between 2003 and 2013. The total number of committals in 2003 was 14,294, while in 2013 this had risen to 22,866. Broer, Koetsier and Mulder (2014: 242–43) have identified a number of reasons for this increase.

The use of involuntary treatment had to cease once the goal has been achieved – namely the removal of the danger or the improvement in the patient's health. All institutions which provide coercive treatment must have a protocol identifying the kind of treatment which can be provided and implement appropriate ongoing training for staff (Dutch Association of Psychiatry 2008). However, the Bopz did not explicitly identify the party which was competent to administer coercive treatment, although certain forms of treatment, such as administering an injection, could only be provided by registered health care professionals. The use of coercive measures had to be evaluated after the fact and patients had to be able to complain to a complaints committee about their treatment.

The Dutch Health Care Inspectorate had the task of monitoring institutions registered under the Bopz, including with regard to their use of involuntary medical treatment and restraint. The use of involuntary treatment, including its termination, was required to be reported to the Health Care Inspectorate (Bopz: Article 38c(5)), along with a number of other measures, such as the refusal to grant a patient's request for a transfer to another institution (Bopz: Article 43(3)), or the discharge from the institution of a patient who was committed (Bopz: Article 58(3)). The patient could complain about (involuntary) treatment, coercion and restraint to the board of the institution providing the treatment, which then had to appoint a commission to consider the complaint (Bopz: Article 41). It was also possible for the patient to ask the Health Care Inspectorate to take legal action (Bopz: Article 41(a)) or initiate legal action him or herself (Bopz: Article 41(a)5; Steinert, Noorthoorn and Mulder 2014: 2).

In spite of these safeguards under the Bopz, a 2015 report (Blankman and Vermariën 2015) which examined *inter alia* the compatibility of the Bopz with the United Nations (UN) Convention on the Rights of Persons with Disabilities (CRPD) (2007), found that the law lacked a provision requiring respect for the will and preferences of the patient, did not regulate who was competent to establish that a patient was 'mentally incompetent', or the criteria to be used in making this assessment. This was particularly significant because only patients regarded as 'mentally incompetent' (*wilsonbekwaamheid*) could be subject to coercive treatment and restraint (Blankman and Vermariën 2015: 32).

As noted earlier, as of 1 January 2020 the Bopz was replaced by the *Compulsory Mental Health Care Act* (Wvggz) and the *Care and Compulsion (Psychogeriatric and Intellectually Disabled Patients) Act* (Wzd). These are examined further in the following sections.

The Compulsory Mental Health Care Act *(Wvggz)*

Under the Wvggz, patients have a right to indicate what care and treatment they prefer. However, unlike the Bopz, the Wvggz does not actually refer to 'patients', but rather 'the person concerned', or *betrokkene*. Article 2(1) of the Wvggz identifies the starting points of the law, which includes the wishes and preferences of the concerned individual. Article 5(5) allows for the individual, with or without family members, to draw up their own care plan, and Article 5(12)(4) refers to the need to take account of the wishes and preferences of the individual in drawing up a plan (*zorgkaart*).

Under the Wvggz, unlike the Bopz, the will and preferences of the patient are of central importance (Blankman and Vermariën 2015: 33). Involuntary treatment and restraint will only be allowed in extreme situations and as a last resort (Broer, Koetsier and Mulder 2014: 241). However, such measures can be applied if a patient's behaviour is the result of a psychiatric condition, leads to a serious disadvantage (*ernstig nadeel*) for the individual or others, and the involuntary treatment or restraint is the only way to remove the serious disadvantage. The latter requirement means that consensual treatment must not be possible, no less intrusive treatment is possible and the treatment is proportionate and effective (Wvggz: Articles 2:1(2) and (3)). The new term 'serious disadvantage' (Wvggz: Article 1:1(2)) has largely the same meaning as 'danger' under the Bopz and is not intended to allow for coercion in a broader range of situations (Ploem and Gevers 2015: 205). However Broer, Koetsier and Mulder (2014: 245) have argued that the requirement, as set out in the law when it was at draft stage, is possibly 'lighter' (as in easier to satisfy) than the 'danger' criterion under the Bopz. Psychiatric care providers which provide involuntary treatment under the Wvggz must also be licensed, as was the case under the Bopz.

The Wvggz allows for more possibilities for involuntary treatment and restraint than the Bopz. Possible involuntary treatment and coercive measures include restrictions on movement, seclusion, observation, checking for the presence of behaviour influencing substances, requiring the patient to do or not do something, restricting the patient's use of communication tools, administration of involuntary medication or involuntary therapeutic treatment (Wvggz: Article 3:2). The Wvggz foresees a number of procedures for authorising involuntary treatment and restraint, the most important of which are a court-issued care authorisation or a short-term crisis measure, which is approved by the local mayor (Wvggz: Article 3:1). If there is not a crisis which presents a risk of immediate danger, involuntary treatment can only take place if it has been provided for via a care authorisation order approved by a judge (Wvggz: Chapter 6). In an emergency situation, where there is no time to apply and wait for a court issued care authorisation, the local mayor can allow crisis measures to be taken (Wvggz: Chapter 7). This procedure also existed under the Bopz, when it was known as a detention order. However, the crisis measure under the Wvggz is broader than the detention order, because it can regulate all forms of involuntary treatment and restraint, and not only a forced admission or committal. During the procedure, which has an imposed maximum time of 18 hours (Wvggz: Article 7(3)(2)), involuntary treatment can be administered. Unlike the Bopz, the

Wvggz will also apply to some elements of ambulant care provided in the community (Wvggz: Article 5:14).

A study has concluded that the Wvggz complies with the requirements of the CRPD to a greater extent than the Bopz, although there remain some issues of concern (Blankman and Vermariën 2015). Blankman and Vermariën (2015: 33), in their study on the conformity of relevant Dutch law with the CRPD, did not find that Article 12 of the CRPD required States Parties to abolish all forms of adult guardianship that partially or wholly affect the legal capacity of a person with a disability. They recognised that the UN Committee on the Rights of Persons with Disabilities took this position on the meaning of Article 12 in its General Comment No. 1, but noted 'convincing evidence supporting the correctness of this view could not be found'. Instead Blankman and Vermariën (2015: 33) found a need for a general provision that 'should apply in all care situations, where there may be a person with a handicap lacking the mental capacity to decide for himself and where a supporting person or representative may be needed'.

The Netherlands has submitted a number of declarations when ratifying the CRPD which, in essence, declare that the Dutch approach to regulating and using coercion in psychiatric settings are compatible with Articles 12 and 14 of the CRPD (Welie and Widdershoven 2018: 8). The Dutch Declaration on Article 14 states

> the Kingdom of the Netherlands declares its understanding that the Convention allows for compulsory care or treatment of persons, including measures to treat mental illnesses, when circumstances render treatment of this kind necessary as a last resort, and the treatment is subject to legal safeguards.

However, some authors have argued that Dutch regulations, set out in both the Bopz and its replacements Wvggz and Wzd, are not in line with the 'UN's view' of Articles 12 and 14 of the CRPD (Welie and Widdershoven 2018: 9–11).

As noted earlier, the will and preferences of the patient are of central importance under the Wvggz. In addition, the law defines the concept of 'mental incompetence' (*wilsonbekwaamheid*) and, except in the case of a court authorisation, a patient's representative can only take decisions once this has been legally established (Blankman and Vermariën 2015: 33). However, the Wvggz (Article 1(3)(7)) does not provide for clear criteria according to which the representative should act, only indicating that they should act in good conscience and must involve the 'incompetent' person in decisions as far as possible. Specific issues regarding involuntary treatment, coercion or restraint were not identified as problematic with regard to the Wvggz and its compliance with the CRPD in the study by Blankman and Vermariën (2015).

The Care and Compulsion (Psychogeriatric and Intellectually Disabled Patients) Act *(Wzd)*

The second new statute, the Wzd, regulates the treatment of people with an intellectual disability or a psychogeriatric condition who a qualified doctor has identified as needing professional care in order to prevent a 'serious disadvantage' and who have an 'indication' for long-term care under the *Long-term Care Act*. The term 'serious disadvantage' has the same meaning as under the Wvggz (Wzd: Article 1(2)). The basic assumption underlying this law is 'no, unless' – meaning that coercive measures are not normally appropriate in the care of people with disabilities and elderly people, and that dangerous situations should be addressed through voluntary treatment as far as possible. Treatment is to be given in line with a care plan which has been drawn up with the individual (referred to as a 'client' in the law), or his/her representative where the client is 'mentally incompetent' (Wzd: Chapter 2). The competence of a representative to take decisions on behalf of the client is regulated in Article 3 of the Wzd. Blankman and Vermariën (2015: 34) found that this did not breach the requirements of the CRPD, since the affected individual or his/her representative can appeal against a decision of 'mental incompetence' and a totally random decision could not be made. The same study found that the Wzd provides for the wishes and preferences of the client to be taken into account, although more weight could still be given to these (Blankman and Vermariën 2015: 35). In contrast, some academics have argued that the law suggests that once a legal representative has been appointed, that representative can take decisions on behalf of the affected individual, without first checking whether they are competent to take the decision him or herself, which is contrary to the CRPD. It has accordingly been argued that the law on this point should be clarified, in order to avoid misunderstandings (Frederiks and Steen 2018: 163).

Involuntary treatment, coercion and restraint can be used under the Wzd where no other means of removing a dangerous situation exists. Article 2(1) of the Wzd provides a list of permissible involuntary treatment. Such treatment can then be provided for in the care plan subject to certain requirements. These requirements involve the client's behaviour creating a situation of 'serious disadvantage' where this is due to a psychogeriatric condition or intellectual disability; the involuntary treatment is needed to prevent (further) 'serious disadvantage'; the involuntary treatment is a suitable and proportionate means to achieve this aim; and no less intrusive measure is possible. Treatment is also subject to safeguards, including approval by another medical specialist (Wzd: Article 10). As with the Wvggz, the Wzd (Article 10) can potentially apply to involuntary treatment and restraint used in ambulant care.

Having introduced the Dutch legal framework governing the use of involuntary treatment, including restraint, in psychiatric and some other health care institutions, this chapter will now focus in more detail on one particular requirement of the law: namely the obligation to report instances of involuntary treatment and restraint to a specialised register, which can be used for benchmarking and evaluation, as well as the monitoring role of the Health Care Inspectorate more generally.

The Health Care Inspectorate and the Argus register: hopes, achievements and controversies

Overview of the tasks of the Health Care Inspectorate

The Health Care Inspectorate is responsible for supervising and monitoring the quality and safety of public health services on behalf of the government. While monitoring and supervision of health care by the state has a long history in the Netherlands, dating back to the nineteenth century, it was only in 1957 that the tasks of monitoring and supervising public health generally, and with regard to psychiatric institutions, were merged (Robbe, Bal and Grol 2012: Chapter 2). The Inspectorate's key tasks are outlined in the *Public Health Act* (*Gezondheidswet*) (1956) and involve studying public health in general and its determining factors, and supervising compliance with legal provisions in the field of public health (*Public Health Act*: Article 36(1)(a) and (b); Hout et al. 2010; Ketelaars 2011: 2–3). These statutory tasks were only formally elaborated in 1998. Prior to this a more general provision identified the tasks of the Inspectorate, but this was deemed to leave too much room for confusion and dispute (Legemaate 2001: 140).

The Inspectorate is only responsible for the supervision of laws where this power is given to it explicitly, and at present it has a supervisory role with regard to approximately 25 statutes (Hubben 2012: 97; Health Care Inspectorate [Inspectie voor de Gezondsheidszorg] 2016: 15). In October 2017 the Health Care Inspectorate merged with the Inspectorate for Youth Care and is now formally known as the Inspectorate for Healthcare and Youth (the Inspectorate) (acronym in Dutch: IGJ). The Inspectorate falls under the Ministry of Health, Welfare and Sport, but acts in a wholly independent and impartial manner (Health Care Inspectorate 2016: 18). The rest of this chapter exclusively refers to the health-related tasks of the Inspectorate.

The starting point for the Inspectorate's supervision is the assumption that health care providers are intrinsically motivated to provide good health care (Robbe, Bal and Grol 2012: 27), whilst recognising that problems can nevertheless occur (Health Care Inspectorate 2016: 22). In principle, the Inspectorate should not intervene more than necessary and adopts an approach of 'responsive regulation' (Robbe, Bal and Grol 2012: 41). Health care providers are expected to supervise themselves (Robbe, Bal and Grol 2012: 26), although Legemaate has noted that this is not uncontroversial (2001: 141). The Inspectorate accordingly only provides supervision at a distance (*toezicht op toezicht* or 'supervision of supervision'). The Inspectorate should identify problematic issues and have a general overview of developments, but supervision does not mean that every unauthorised or improper incident is sanctioned by the Inspectorate (Robbe, Bal and Grol 2012: 29). Instead, the Inspectorate should support the responsible institution to find a solution where necessary (Legemaate 2001: 142). As part of its supervisory task, the Inspectorate collects data related to various aspects of health care and analyses trends with a view to raising issues of concern with stakeholders (Health Care Inspectorate 2016: 25). Indicators can also be used as a 'steering instrument', directing attention and policy towards a particular field or risk, and to monitor progress (Health Care Inspectorate 2016: 30). While Robbe, Bal and Grol (2012: 46) identify a number of negative consequences associated with the use of indicators, they conclude that the Inspectorate has no option but to use them as part of their 'risk based monitoring'. As of the 1990s, the market has played an increasingly important role in the provision of health care in the Netherlands, and this has led to a growth in the importance of supervision (Robbe, Bal and Grol 2012: 21).

In cases where the Inspectorate decides to intervene, its actions must be proportionate and based on the scope, risk and seriousness of the problem identified (Health Care Inspectorate 2016: 23). The Inspectorate also aims to act in a transparent way (Robbe, Bal and Grol 2012: 22) and take action which is appropriate in light of the stage of development of the health care provider (Health Care Inspectorate 2016: 23). The Inspectorate uses four kinds of interventions, which vary on a scale from 'light' to 'heavy' (Health Care Inspectorate 2016: 23). These actions, as identified in the Inspectorate's current *Multi-year Plan* (Robbe, Bal and Grol 2012: 27; Health Care Inspectorate 2016: 23), are:

1. Stimulation/encouragement. These measures can involve campaigns, circular letters, journal articles, reports, motivation, or rewards.
2. Corrective measures. These measures can involve supervised improvement plans or intensified supervision, for example, in the form of additional and unannounced visits.
3. Administrative measures. These can involve a number of measures provided for under administrative law, including a closure order, the withdrawal of a license, mandatory introduction and compliance with an improvement plan, ordering a particular action, or a fine. Between 2002 and 2011 the number of administrative measures taken by the Inspectorate increased and some measures were introduced for the first time (Robbe, Bal and Grol 2012: 39).
4. Disciplinary or criminal law measures. The Inspectorate can submit a complaint about a health care provider to the recognised disciplinary bodies operating in the health care sector, and these can impose disciplinary measures. The Inspectorate can also refer cases to the public prosecutor.

As noted earlier, the Inspectorate's supervisory tasks include supervision of compulsory admissions to health care institutions as well as incidents of involuntary treatment, including use of restraint under the Bopz (now repealed). The Inspectorate also has a supervisory role under the Wvggz and Wzd. As with other Inspectorate supervision, this involves *ex ante* supervision, also known as risk oversight or 'phased supervision' (Robbe, Bal and Grol 2012: 25; Hout et al. 2010: 350), as well as *ex post* supervision or incident oversight. Those incidents can be reported to the Inspectorate by citizens, but, in principle, must be reported to the Inspectorate by the responsible health care institution. Specifically, each coercive incidence must be reported to the Inspectorate, and this information has to be related to the number of involuntary admissions (Janssen 2012: Chapter 2). However, research has suggested that the accuracy of reporting and recording has been unreliable, at least in the past (Janssen 2012: Chapter 2).

Establishment of the Argus register

In 2006 a first attempt was made to collect data on a structural basis on the use of involuntary treatment and restraint in institutions falling under the Bopz (Noorthoorn et al. 2016: 1321). Prior to this it had been argued, in the context of patients in psychogeriatric care settings, that 'there is hardly any transparency on the use of restraints, and therefore no protection in this respect' (Arends 2004: 827). Consequently a key factor in setting up what became the Argus register was that, given the absence of complete and reliable data, it was difficult to identify trends and developments in the use of coercion in mental health institutions (Voskes 2015: 19 and 35). The data that was being collected by the Health Care Inspectorate was insufficient for this purpose (Janssen 2012: Chapter 2; Noorthoorn et al. 2016: 1321), with nearly half of coercive measures not being reported to the Inspectorate (Noorthoorn et al. 2015: 1858), and data not being recorded in a standard manner to the extent that it was being recorded at all (GGZ Nederland 2012: 9). This led one academic to conclude that 'the registration of data for a legal purpose was unfit for interpretation of trends or developments at a ward or hospital level' (Janssen 2012). A national database, which could allow for benchmarking and identification of changes and trends, was important in light of the goal of reducing seclusion in Dutch hospitals by at least 10 per cent per year. A further factor prompting the establishment of the register was the possibility it would induce institutions to improve quality and demonstrate responsibility (GGZ Nederland 2012: 8).

In 2006, five psychiatric hospitals in cooperation with GGZ Nederland and the Inspectorate set up the Argus register to record instances of involuntary treatment and restraint in a standard manner. Participation was initially voluntary but, in 2012, participation became mandatory for all Bopz licensed mental health care institutions as a result of an amendment to the Bopz (GGZ Nederland 2012: 9–10; Mann-Poll et al. 2018: 741). Registration of data was required under Article 57 of the Bopz. By 2014 all 87 psychiatric hospitals in the Netherlands and psychiatric wards with involuntary admissions in general hospitals reported to the Argus register (Noorthoorn et al. 2016: 1323). However, for reasons of privacy, and after never having started substantially, from 2016 the collection of data through the register ceased altogether (Noorthoorn 2019). Institutions providing psychogeriatric care and care to people with intellectual disabilities were never obliged to report to the Argus register.

The Argus register was intended to record all 'freedom restricting' measures (*vrijheidsbeperkende interventies*) imposed on patients and became the largest database recording the use of such measures in Europe (Janssen et al. 2011: 433). The following six types of interventions had to be reported:

1 Seclusion, which involved placing a patient in a locked room specially designed for seclusion. The room was required to be officially approved by the Ministry of Health, Welfare and Sport for the use of seclusion, and had minimal facilities.
2 Isolation, which involved placing the patient in a locked low stimulus room. The room had a bed, table, chair, cupboard and sanitary facilities.
3 Mechanical or physical restraint, which could either involve mechanical devices, such as belts or straps, or physically restraining a person.
4 Parenteral medication, which was defined as medication administered intramuscularly or intravenously, where the patient displayed physical resistance.

Other forms of medication did not have to be recorded, because, in the view of GGZ Nederland, there could be a lack of certainty as to when medication was forced in other circumstances (GGZ Nederland 2012: 24). There is however a separate medication register which institutions are obliged to maintain.

5 Forced hydration and/or nutrition which was administered parenterally or through the mouth, where the patient displayed physical resistance.
6 Other freedom restricting measures, such as a mandatory stay in the patient's room (Janssen et al. 2011: 430; GGZ Nederland 2012: 19–20; Janssen et al. 2014: 10; Voskes 2015: 36–37; Noorthoorn et al. 2016: 1322).

These definitions of coercive measures are in line with international definitions (Janssen 2012: Chapter 9), and this has facilitated comparisons between hospitals and countries (Janssen 2012: Chapter 9). For each intervention, the date, start time and, except for forced medication, end time, had to be recorded (Janssen et al. 2011: 430; GGZ Nederland 2012: 21). The patient's level of resistance was also recorded: at own request, no clear resistance, or clear verbal or physical resistance (GGZ Nederland 2012: 7; Health Care Inspectorate 2015: 12; Noorthoorn et al. 2016: 1322). In 2012, 52.3 per cent of seclusion incidents involved patients who displayed resistance, 39 per cent involved no resistance and 8.6 per cent were made at the patient's own request. The relevant figures for isolation were 37.3 per cent (resistance), 53.6 per cent (no resistance) and 10.1 per cent (own request); and for mechanical or physical restraint, 23.5 per cent (resistance), 67.6 per cent (no resistance) and 8.8 per cent (own request) (Voskes 2015: 39).

An intervention occurred at the patient's own request where the initiative for the intervention came from the patient (Janssen et al. 2014: 10). A patient displayed no resistance if he or she agreed to an intervention proposed by a health care professional or displayed no visible resistance when the intervention was imposed (Janssen et al. 2014: 10). A patient displayed resistance when the initiative for the intervention was taken by a health care professional and the patient visibly resisted the intervention physically, verbally or through non-verbal means (Janssen et al. 2014: 10). In the latter two instances coercion was involved within the framework of Articles 38 or 39 of the Bopz (Janssen et al. 2014: 10), and the relevant statutory provisions and requirements were applicable. It was not necessary to report an intervention at the request of a patient in the case of parenteral medication, administration of fluids or food, or 'other freedom restricting measures'. However, all cases of seclusion, isolation and restraint had to be reported, even if made at the patient's request, and other forms of freedom restricting intervention had to be reported if the initiative for the action came from the health care provider (GGZ Nederland 2012: 19–20). Data regarding the use of consensual freedom restricting measures was collected in order to obtain a full picture of daily practices in mental health care institutions, and to facilitate full reporting by health care professionals, who were then aware that all freedom restricting measures had to be reported (Noorthoorn 2019).

The data to be registered through Argus was regarded as the minimum data set; institutions were free to collect more detailed data and data concerning other interventions (GGZ Nederland 2012: 24). The legal status of the patient was not determinative for whether information should be reported or not (GGZ Nederland 2012: 24), although it was relevant for determining whether interventions could be made without the patient's consent. Institutions had some degree of freedom to decide how to collect the data, and could, for example, collect the information in the electronic patient dossier, use separate software or collect the information in paper format before submitting it digitally (GGZ Nederland 2012: 25). The reporting institutions were responsible for ensuring the accuracy of the data submitted, although the Inspectorate could perform random inspections. Some concerns regarding accuracy of the data on seclusion were raised (Noorthoorn et al. 2015: 1866), although it has been argued that the reliability of Argus data was 'moderate to good' in the past (Janssen 2012: Chapter 9). This argument was made before the controversies surrounding data protection and the subsequent cessation of registration by institutions (see further information provided later in the chapter).

In 2012 GGZ Nederland published guidance and instructions for institutions obliged to report to the Argus register and noted a number of goals and benefits of the register: improving the quality of care, learning from one's own experience, acting responsibly and providing the basis for better academic research (GGZ Nederland 2012: 5). This guidance included a number of quotes from health care workers or managers in psychiatric institutions which were already registering data. The quotes indicate that reporting to the Argus register facilitated better internal evaluation, reflection on how to reduce the use of coercion, and was an important tool for management in identifying trends and changes (GGZ Nederland 2012: 13–14). This also reflected the view of GGZ Nederland, which noted that, by linking Argus data with individual patient records, institutions could reveal the extent to which specific individuals were exposed to coercive treatment. The data could also help institutions to identify periods in which an increased use of coercion was taking place and identify the causes. From the perspective of the Health Care Inspectorate, Argus data could identify institutions using a disproportionately high number of freedom restricting interventions, which could prompt more detailed investigation, and, for policy makers, the register could provide important information (GGZ Nederland 2012: 17).

Achievements and controversies

Undoubtedly, the aspirations of GGZ Nederland (2012: 26) for the Argus register were high:

> By carrying out regular evaluations and referring back to Argus data, developments in the application of freedom restricting interventions will be made visible. It can be established how far the goal of policies and projects relating to freedom restricting interventions are being achieved. Furthermore, the evaluations and references to the data offer the possibility to learn from one's own practice: under which conditions does a health care provider tend

> to use a freedom restricting intervention? And can that intervention perhaps be different, less intrusive, shorter or more effective? These are important questions for health care providers who look critically at their own practice when it comes to freedom restricting interventions.

To some extent these goals were achieved. The Argus register has provided a dataset which researchers have been able to use to identify trends in the use of freedom restricting interventions, including restraint. This data has been used to map changes both within institutions in the Netherlands (Vruwink et al. 2012; Janssen et al. 2014; Verlinde et al. 2014; Noorthoorn et al. 2016), and to make comparisons between the use of coercion, seclusion and restraint in the Netherlands and other countries (Noorthoorn et al. 2015; Lepping et al. 2016). Janssen and colleagues have also discussed how to analyse and make comparisons at different levels using Argus data. They identify 'five different levels of calculation over several time frames', namely, hospital, ward, patients, admission and intervention (Janssen et al. 2011: 431–32).

While documenting coercive incidents and analysing data is a quite common practice, it is relatively unusual to collect this data through a centralised agency, and for that data to be available for analysis by researchers (Lepping et al. 2016: 1302). Relatively few such datasets exist worldwide (Lepping et al. 2016: 1302), and the Argus register has allowed for benchmarking. This dataset has been used to monitor the use of seclusion, given the aforementioned target of reducing seclusion by 10 per cent on an annual basis (Noorthoorn et al. 2016). Researchers have also recognised the importance of continuing to work with Argus (Voskes 2015: 176). These findings, and the factors which have been identified as influencing changing practice, are discussed further in the final section of this chapter.

However, problems with the registration of data have arisen from a perhaps unforeseen source: data protection legislation. While GGZ Nederland initially managed the Argus register, in 2016 this responsibility was transferred to the Stichting (or Foundation) Benchmark GGZ (SBG), which undertook this task on behalf of GGZ Nederland. This was intended to bring about a professionalisation of the data collection (GGZ Nederland 2016a). GGZ Nederland is an organisation of mental health care providers, while SBG was an independent expert centre managed by representatives of patients, health care providers and health insurers, which had the task of improving the quality of mental health care by improving transparency of treatment outcomes (GGZ Nederland 2016a).

GGZ Nederland felt that the management of the register by an independent organisation was important for benchmarking and policy development and would contribute to producing credible findings, data protection and further guarantee privacy (GGZ Nederland 2016a). In order to ensure this independence, the Argus Information Centre became a separate entity within SBG (GGZ Nederland 2016a). With regard to data protection, it was argued that information collected via Argus could not be linked to other information that was being collected by SBG and that privacy of individuals would be protected through a system whereby data was first submitted to a separate organisation (*ZorgTTP* (trusted third party)) which would then 'pseudonymise' (*gepsyeuonimiseren*) the data before passing it on to SBG. This should have meant that the data could not be traced back to specific individuals (GGZ Nederland 2016a). In this way it was foreseen that legal requirements relating to data protection would be complied with. However, the data submitted to the *ZorgTTP* included personal data, including age, marital status, diagnosis and ward (Noorthoorn 2019). This meant that the information submitted could theoretically enable individual patients to be identified, especially in wards housing a small number of patients (Noorthoorn 2019), and this led to problems in the context of data protection.

At the end of 2016, GGZ Nederland wrote a letter to its members advising them to suspend temporarily the submission of data to the Argus Information Centre/SBG (GGZ Nederland 2016b). This followed a finding of the Dutch Data Protection Authority (2016) that 'pseudonymised' health data should be classified as personal data and fell under the *Law on the Protection of Personal Data* (acronym in Dutch: Wbp). This meant that the consent of patients was needed for this data to be submitted to the SBG. GGZ Nederland issued this advice to its members because, in light of the findings of the Data Protection Authority, there was no legal basis for the submission of 'pseudonymised' data, and the submission of the data could have adverse legal consequences for the organisations concerned. GGZ Nederland advised its members to stop submitting data until an exemption had been granted by the Authority or submission was legally regulated in another way. Members were however advised to continue collecting the data.

GGZ Nederland also separately advised its members to suspend the submission of data relating to Routine Outcome Monitoring (Healthcare–ICT Concerns [Zorg-ICT Zorgen] 2017a), which allowed for monitoring progress in mental health care and also involved 'pseudonymised' information concerning psychiatric treatment and results (GGZ Nederland 2017). This data was used for benchmarking and in making decisions regarding the purchase of health care by health insurers. In March 2017, the then Minister for Health, Welfare and Sport, Edith Schippers, answered a number of parliamentary questions relating to the collection of Routine Outcome Monitoring data, indicating that the Ministry was still investigating how to regulate its collection (House of Representatives of the Netherlands 2017a). In response to a second set of questions, the Minister indicated in October 2017 that 175 health care institutions had stopped submitting Routine Outcome Monitoring data (House of Representatives of the Netherlands 2017b). Elsewhere this was reported as meaning that only a third of mental health care institutions submitted data (Healthcare–ICT Concerns 2017b; van Lonkhuyzen 2017). In June 2017, it was announced that the Data Protection Authority was investigating SBG to see if the work which it did on behalf of the mental health sector complied with relevant data protection laws (van Lonkhuyzen 2017), and whether Routine Outcome Monitoring data amounted to personal data under the *Law on the Protection of Personal Data* (House of Representatives of the Netherlands 2018). This investigation was welcomed by SBG, which indicated that it would be willing to change its procedures if necessary.

In 2018 SBG ceased to function and was replaced by a new organisation, Akwa GGZ, which has the task of ensuring good quality mental health care, and works with patients, families and health care professionals. Akwa GGZ is an abbreviation of Alliantie Kwaliteit in de geestelijke gezondheidszorg (Alliance for Quality in Mental Health Care). Akwa GGZ took over the data collected by SBG, and, accordingly, the Data Protection Authority addressed its findings, when they finally came, to Akwa GGZ. Pending the publication of the Authority's report, the Secretary of State (a junior minister) for Health, Welfare and Sport advised health care providers to obtain the explicit consent of patients before submitting Routine Outcome Monitoring data (House of Representatives of the Netherlands 2018).

The Data Protection Authority finally published its report on the collection of Routine Outcome Monitoring data in the mental health sector in December 2019 (Dutch Data Protection Authority 2019). It concluded that the data received by SBG – including data related to Argus – involved the processing of personal data regarding health status which was prohibited under the European Union General Data Protection Regulation (Regulation (EU) 2016/679 of the European Parliament and of the Council (2016)) and was not covered by any of the exceptions provided for in the Regulation. As a result SBG, and now Akwa GGZ, was prohibited from processing this personal data regarding health status.

However, it seems that at least in the case of the Argus register, events superseded the investigation of the Data Protection Authority. As of October 2018, the Argus register was no longer in use and work is ongoing on the development of a new registration system in the Netherlands, which will comply with data protection legislation as well as meeting the requirements of the new mental health law, the Wvggz. Based on an interview conducted by this author with Dr Eric Noorthoorn (Noorthoorn 2019), it appears that the new register will record more forms of involuntary interventions, and interventions made at the request of the patient will not be registered. Under the new system hospitals will fully anonymise the data themselves, prior to submitting it, and there will be no possibility of an external party accessing information about individuals. Appropriate software, including business intelligence software, will be used by all institutions enabling them to submit tables containing the relevant information. The software will also allow for comparisons between institutions housing different kinds of patients, taking account of the fact that some institutions house individuals who are more likely to be subject to coercive interventions because of violent or aggressive behaviour. The submitted data can therefore still be used to identify trends in the use of coercion and make comparisons between institutions. It is anticipated that a number of institutions will begin testing the software and submitting data in 2020, with the new register being fully operational, and in use by all covered institutions, by 2022.

Trends and developments in the use of coercive and involuntary measures in psychiatric institutions

This section of the chapter identifies trends in the use of coercive measures in Dutch psychiatric institutions based on desk research. Much of the available research is based on data collected through the Argus register. In addition, again based on desk research, this section identifies the factors which seem to have influenced changes in the use of coercive measures, and particularly the use of seclusion in psychiatric institutions.

A reduction in the use of seclusion

As noted earlier, a goal of reducing seclusion in Dutch psychiatric hospitals by at least 10 per cent per year was established in 2006. Research has revealed that this goal was largely achieved, with an average annual reduction of seclusion of 9 per cent between 2008 and 2013, although some scholars have calculated slightly different figures (Steinert, Noorthoorn and Mulder 2014: 4–5; Noorthoorn et al. 2015; Voskes 2015: Chapter 2). Statistics reveal that the seclusion rate fell from 11.8 per cent in 2008 to 7.0 per cent in 2013, and the median duration of seclusion decreased from 92 to 16 hours over the same period, although these findings are somewhat unreliable because a limited number of hospitals submitted Argus data in the first three years of the period covered by the study (Noorthoorn et al. 2016: 1323). Research has also revealed that the reduction in seclusion was accompanied by an increase in the use of involuntary medication, suggesting that this coercive measure was partly used as a substitute for seclusion, although overall the total number of days on which coercive interventions took place decreased (Noorthoon et al. 2016: 1323). In 2012, the then Minister of Health, Welfare and Sport, Edith Schippers, indicated that a reduction in seclusion could not lead to an increase in the use of forced medication (Verlinde et al. 2014: 640). From a broader perspective, the number of involuntary admissions to mental health institutions under the Bopz increased between 2003 and 2013 quite significantly (Broer, Koetsier and Mulder 2014) and in 2017 there were a record number of committals to psychiatric hospitals (Kuiper 2018).

In spite of the aforementioned changes, seclusion remains more common in the Netherlands than in comparable countries, and seclusion times are also longer in the Netherlands (Noorthoorn et al. 2015: 1857). An international study found 'much higher restraint and much higher seclusion numbers per admission, per patient and per capita in the Netherlands compared to other countries' (Lepping et al. 2016: 1307). However, the study also found that other countries had higher uses of other forms of coercion, and 'in short, in some of the indicators some countries show higher figures than others, while the same countries show low figures on other indicators. In the end, the results were still much more similar than expected' (Lepping et al. 2016: 1307). Nevertheless, from a Dutch perspective, research based on Argus data does reveal that the seclusion reduction programme had some success, and an overall reduction in the use of freedom restricting measures occurred in psychiatric institutions. It is therefore interesting to explore briefly what measures could have contributed to this change.

Dutch interventions to reduce coercive and involuntary measures

A very wide range of interventions have been used in Dutch mental health institutions in an attempt to reduce the use of coercion (Vruwink et al. 2012; Hamers et al. 2013; Mann-Poll et al. 2018: 734–46). Voskes (2015: 35) gives the following overview in her PhD dissertation:

> These interventions can be grouped into five clusters: (1) care and contact, (2) prevention, (3) learning from experience, (4) participation, and (5) cooperation. Apart from new methods, structural and organisational innovations have been developed. Examples are comfort rooms, nurse stations behind accessible counters instead of in offices, and family rooms. Other structural innovations concern the adaptation of work plans and team meetings (for example, using risk assessment) and support activities (evaluation, feedback Argus data, and training). Finally, cultural changes have taken place.

It is beyond the scope of this chapter to examine the various coercion and seclusion reduction programmes which have been pursued. However, some general themes have emerged based on an analysis of the literature, and some of the themes identified in the Dutch literature correspond to the US National Technical Assistance Center for State Mental Health Planning's (2005) 'Six Core Strategies to Reduce the Use of Seclusion and Restraint' (Gooding et al. 2018: 48–49). In general staffing and staff culture 'may be the most important factors [influencing] the use of coercive measures' (Janssen 2012). Duration of the coercion reduction programme seems to be of some importance, with research indicating that institutions which have been engaged in coercion and seclusion reduction efforts over a number of years achieve greater reductions and more stable reductions on average than institutions which have only recently initiated such measures (Voskes 2015: 43 and 165; Noorthoorn et al. 2016: 1321–27).

A further theme is that new forms of intervention need to be accompanied by changes in organisational structure and culture, in order actually to lead to new practices, and that such changes require more time than that needed simply to introduce new forms of intervention (Voskes 2015: 43; Noorthoorn et al. 2016: 1324–25). This implies a need for a change in 'ethical climate' (Mann-Poll et al. 2013; Voskes 2015: 162) and having an ambitious project leader who has the backing of the organisation (Voskes 2015: 166). A change in culture should result in

> new views on the relationship with patients (from control to contact), the management of crisis (from reactive to proactive), the importance of learning from experience (from routine to learning), the role of participation (from object of care to partner in care), and the need for cooperation (from closed to open).
>
> (Voskes 2015: 64–65)

Cooperation between staff, and particularly psychiatrists and nursing staff and amongst nursing staff, also seems to be important in reducing coercion (Voskes, Theunissen and Widdershoven 2011: 41). Overall, 'in institutions in which top down and bottom up approaches are integrated, reduction of seclusion has more chance of being a success' (Voskes 2015: 166–67; Mann-Poll et al. 2018: 741). Research also indicates that the successful introduction of a new policy requires 'the active involvement of all stakeholders, including patients' representatives and administrative leaders . . . and nursing staff must be highly motivated, well-trained and sufficient in number' (Georgieva, Mudler and Noorthoorn 2013: 52). Changes to the infrastructure can enable or facilitate new approaches (Voskes 2015: 64), and cooperation with external partners, who can encourage reflection on 'taken-for-granted ideas and contribute new rationales and perspectives' (Voskes 2015: 167), are both important.

More controversially, some researchers have suggested that earlier use of (involuntary) medication can help to prevent seclusion and reduce the overall amount of coercive interventions. They also argue that, given the different nature of the two interventions (treatment versus management), involuntary medication cannot be regarded as substituting for seclusion (Verlinde et al. 2014). However, other researchers have found that, while increased use of involuntary medication can reduce the number of seclusion incidents, it does not reduce the total number of involuntary interventions or the mean time spent in seclusion (Georgieva, Mudler and Noorthoorn 2013). As noted earlier, former Minister Schippers has also expressed opposition to 'substituting' seclusion with involuntary medication.

One initiative of interest is a compilation of best practices in the reduction of coercive treatment in mental health care facilities in the Netherlands (Voskes, Theunissen and Widdershoven 2011). This inventory was commissioned by the Ministry for Health, Welfare and Sport and GGZ Nederland, and was drawn up by three academics specialised in the field. They visited 26 institutions to identify and describe best practice, some of which was adopted as part of efforts to reduce the use of seclusion and other forms of coercion within the framework of the previously mentioned nationwide programme. The study also identified bottlenecks. All institutions which were visited had been engaged in a programme to reduce coercive measures for at least a year, and a variety of different kinds of departments and wards were visited. Best practices were identified in 11 categories: contact with the client, preventative work and risk assessment, de-escalation, evaluation, reflection, cooperation, client participation, participation of close relatives, registration, intensive care and cooperation with ambulant care. Among the many examples listed, the Argus register was identified as best practice with regard to registration.

It has also been argued that it is important to measure the effects of programmes and measures aimed at reducing the use of coercion and seclusion, and that this can itself provide an incentive to improve programmes (Voskes 2015: 44). In this context, the Argus database can be regarded as an example of 'learning from experience' or 'measuring is knowing' (*meten is weten*). 'Feedback from Argus data to involved departments and discussion with staff does not only help with understanding why an intervention was or was not effective, but motivates staff to improve the intervention and to continue working to reduce coercion' (Voskes, Theunissen and Widdershoven 2011: 43). However, research by Voskes revealed that while most institutions adequately registered coercive measures, feedback and evaluation of what the data revealed received less attention (Voskes, Theunissen and Widdershoven 2011: 42; Voskes 2015: 61). Whilst the data, when registered in a central database, can provide important evidence of overall trends and allow for evaluations, it is important to also use it at an institution and ward level as part of an overall coercion reduction programme. Voskes argues 'registration of seclusion data (as a working routine) has only added value by providing structural feedback and a shared belief that the data are useful for learning' (Voskes 2015: 65). Janssen has similarly argued that 'the reported coercive measures must be embedded in a larger organisational context in which the data are used in feedback to provide information for evaluation purposes, treatment planning as well as ward and hospital policy' (Janssen 2012). Therefore, simply accurately recording data on the use and duration of coercive practices, time consuming though that is, will have no impact on reducing these practices unless it is used with this purpose in mind.

Conclusion

This chapter has provided an overview of the regulation of the use of restraint, seclusion and other forms of coercion in the Dutch mental health, psychogeriatric and intellectual disability care sectors. It has also reported on initiatives which have been taken to reduce coercion, with a particular focus on the registration of freedom-restricting incidents in a national database, the Argus register. The register was seen as a necessary tool to monitor national efforts to reduce the use of seclusion in psychiatric institutions in particular, and it allowed for benchmarking and comparisons across institutions and hospital wards in the Netherlands and internationally. However, Argus data collection has faced a perhaps unexpected challenge from data protection legislation, and this has resulted in a suspension of reporting and plans to develop a new registration system. The chapter has also revealed that while such data collection allows for benchmarking and can be a part of policy to reduce seclusion, restraint and other coercive measures within individual institutions, a conscious effort must be made to use locally collected data in this way.

References

Arends, L.A.P. (2004) 'Legal Status of Incompetent Patients in Psychogeriatric Settings from a Dutch Perspective', *Medicine and Law*, 23(4): 821–31.

Arends, L.A.P. (2010) 'Report on the Autumn Meeting of the VGR 2009 "Compulsion and Freedom Restrictions in Health Care"' ['Verslag najaarsvergadering VGR 2009 "Dwang en vrijheidsbeperkingen in de zorg"'], *Journal of Health Law* [*Tijdschrift voor Gezondheidsrecht*], 2: 94–104.

Arends, L.A.P. (2015) 'Not with a Single Comb. Psychogeriatrics, Mental Health Care and Psychiatry Need Their Own Frameworks' ['Niet over één kam, Psychogeriatrie, verstandelijk genhandicaptenzorg en psychiatrie hebben hun eigen kaders nodig'], *Journal of Health Law* [*Tijdschrift voor Gezondheidsrecht*], 39(4): 221–25.

Blankman, K. and Vermariën, V. (2015) *Conformity of the UN Convention on the Rights of Persons with Disabilities with Current and Proposed Legislation on Representation of Mentally Incompetent Persons* [*Conformiteit van het VN-Verdrag inzake de rechten van personen met een handicap met de huidige en voorgestelde wetgeving inzake vertegenwoordiging van wilsonbekwame personen*], Report Commissioned for Netherlands Human Rights Institute, Amsterdam: Vrije Universiteit Amsterdam.

Bopz Decision Means and Measures [*Besluit middelen en maatregelen Bopz*] (1993) Available https://wetten.overheid.nl/BWBR0006225/1994-01-17 (accessed 20 June 2020).

Broer, J., Koetsier, H. and Mulder, C.L. (2014) 'Increasing Use of Coercive Treatment under the Bopz Act; Implications for the New Compulsory Mental Health Care Act' ['Stijgende trend in dwangtoepassing onder de Wet Bopz; implicaties voor de nieuwe Wet verplichte geestelijke gezondheidszorg'], *Journal of Psychiatry* [*Tijdschrift voor Psychiatrie*], 57(4): 240–47.

Care and Compulsion (Psychogeriatric and Intellectually Disabled Patients) Act [*Wet Zorg en Dwang*] (Wzd) (2018). Available www.dwangindezorg.nl/wzd/wet--en-regelgeving-zorg-en-dwang (accessed 20 June 2020).

Compulsory Mental Health Care Act [*Wet verplichte geestelijke gezondheidszorg*] (Wvggz) (2018). Available https://wetten.overheid.nl/BWBR0040635/2020-01-01 (accessed 18 August 2020).

Convention on the Rights of Persons with Disabilities (CRPD) (2007) Opened for signature 30 March, 2515 UNTS 3 (entered into force 3 May 2008).

Dutch Association of Psychiatry (2008) *Guideline Decision-Making and Coercion in Mental Health Care* [*Richtlijn Besluitvorming dwang en drang in de GGZ*]. Available www.nvvp.net/stream/richtlijn-besluitvorming-dwang-opname-en-behandeling-2008.pdf (accessed 20 June 2020).

Dutch Data Protection Authority [Autoriteit Persoonsgegevens] (2016) *Letter to the Dutch Health Care Authority* [*Brief aan de Nederlandse Zorgautoriteit*]. Available https://autoriteitpersoonsgegevens.nl/sites/default/files/01_onderzoek_nza-dis.pdf (accessed 20 June 2020).

Dutch Data Protection Authority [Autoriteit Persoonsgegevens] (2019) *Report Resulting from Research into Data Processing by SBG* [*Rapport naar aanleiding van onderzoek gegevensverwerking SBG*]. Available https://autoriteitpersoonsgegevens.nl/sites/default/files/atoms/files/rapport_bevindingen_sbg_en_akwa_ggz.pdf (accessed 20 June 2020).

Frederiks, B.J.M. (2015) 'Progressive Insight, Forced Care in Psychogeriatrics and Mental Disability Care in One Legal Regulation with Psychiatry' ['Voortschrijdend inzicht, Gedwongen zorg in psychogeriatrie en verstandelijk gehandicaptenzorg in één wettelijke regeling met psychiatrie'], *Journal of Health Law* [*Tijdschrift voor Gezondheidsrecht*], 39(4): 226–31.

Frederiks, B.J.M. and Blankman, K. (2013) 'Proposed Law on Care and Coercion: Impact of Recent Changes for the Field and the Client' ['Wetvoorstel Zorg en dwang: impact van de recente wijzingen voor het veld en de cliënt'], *Journal of Health Law* [*Tijdschrift voor Gezondheidsrecht*], 37(4): 346–61.

Frederiks, B.J.M. and Steen, S.M. (2018) 'The Care and Compulsion Act Is Adopted, and Now? ['De Wet zorg en dwang is aangenomen, en nu?'], *Journal of Health Law* [*Tijdschrift voor Gezondheidsrecht*], 42(2): 156–63.

Georgieva, I., Mulder, C.L. and Noorthoorn, E.O. (2013) 'Reducing Seclusion through Involuntary Medication: A Randomized Clinical Trial', *Psychiatry Research*, 205(1–2): 48–53.

GGZ Centraal (2019) *Costs of Involuntary Care* [*kosten onvrijwillige zorg*]. Available www.ggzcentraal.nl/clienten/kosten/kosten-onvrijwillige-zorg/ (accessed 20 June 2020).

GGZ Nederland (2012) *Argus: Registration of Freedom-restricting Interventions in Mental Health Care* [*Argus: Registratie van vrijheidsbeperkende interventies in de geestelijke gezondheidszorg*]. Available www.ggznederland.nl/uploads/publication/Argus%20Registratie%20van%20vrijheidsbeperkende%20interventies%20in%20de%20ggz.pdf (accessed 20 June 2020).

GGZ Nederland (2016a) *Background Information on Locating the Argus Information Centre (AIC) with the Stichting Benchmark GGZ (SBG)* [*Achtergrondinformatie bij het onderbrengen van het Argus Informatie Centrum (AIC) bij de stichting benchmark ggz (SBG)*], Amersfoort: GGZ Nederland (On File with Author).

GGZ Nederland (2016b) *Letter of 9 November 2016 from GGZ Nederland, Subject: Temporary Stopping of Submission of Data to the Argus Information Centre* [*Subject: Tijdelijk stoppen aanlevering aan Argus Informativecentrum*], Amersfoort: GGZ Nederland (On File with Author).

GGZ Nederland (2017) *Delivering ROM Data* [*Aanlevering Rom-Gegevens*]. Available www.ggznederland.nl/actueel/aanlevering-rom-gegevens (accessed 20 June 2020).

Gooding, P., McSherry, B., Roper, C. and Grey F. (2018) *Alternatives to Coercion in Mental Health Settings: A Literature Review*, Melbourne: Melbourne Social Equity Institute, University of Melbourne. Available https://socialequity.unimelb.edu.au/news/latest/alternatives-to-coercion (accessed 20 June 2020).

Hamers, J.P.H., Gulpers, M.J.M., Bleiglevens, M.H.C., Capezuti, E. and van Rossum, E. (2013) 'A Dutch Roadmap for Care Without Belt Usage' ['De weg naar een bandenloze zorg in Nederland'], *Journal of Gerontology and Geriatrics* [*Tijdschrift voor Gerontologie en Geriatrie*], 44(6): 253–60.

Healthcare–ICT Concerns [Zorg-ICT Zorgen] (2017a) *General Audit Chamber Makes Mince of ROM in Curative Mental Health Financing* [*Algemene Rekenkamer maakt gehakt van ROM in curatieve GGZ-financiering*]. Available www.zorgictzorgen.nl/algemene-rekenkamer-maakt-gehakt-rom-curatieve-ggz/ (accessed 20 June 2020).

Healthcare–ICT Concerns [Zorg-ICT Zorgen] (2017b) *Secretary of State Assumes Giving of Explicit Permission When Continuing to Deliver ROM Data* [*Staatssecretaris veronderstelt geven van expliciete toestemming bij doorgaan leveren ROM-data*]. Available www.zorgictzorgen.nl/staatssecretaris-veronderstelt-geven-expliciete-toestemming-doorgaan-leveren-rom-data/ (accessed 20 June 2020).

Health Care Inspectorate [Inspectie voor de Gezondsheidszorg] (2015) *Mental Health Care Institutions Investing in Reducing Seclusion; Further Actions Are Needed to Achieve Ambitions* [*GGZ-instelling investeren in terugdringen van separatie; verdere acties nodig om ambities te halen*]. Available https://zoek.officielebekendmakingen.nl/blg-525986.pdf (accessed 20 June 2020).

Health Care Inspectorate [Inspectie voor de Gezondsheidszorg] (2016) *Health Care Inspectorate Multi-year Plan 2016–2019* [*IGZ Meerjarenbeleidsplan 2016–2019*], Available www.igj.nl/documenten/jaarplannen/2016/01/14/igz-meerjarenbeleidsplan-2016-2019 (accessed 20 June 2020).

House of Representatives of the Netherlands [Tweede Kamer der Staten-Generaal] Aanhangsel Handelingen 2016/17 1477 (2017a) *Response from Minister Schippers (24 March 2017) Appendix to Proceedings, 2016–2017 Session Year* [*Antwoord van Minister Schippers (24 March 2017). Aanhangsel Handelingen, vergaderjaar 2016–2017*]. Available https://zoek.officielebekendmakingen.nl/ah-tk-20162017-1477.html (accessed 20 June 2020).

House of Representatives of the Netherlands [Tweede Kamer der Staten-Generaal] Aanhangsel Handelingen 2017/18 218, (2017b) *Response from Minister Schippers to Questions Submitted by Members of Parliament Kooiman and Dieterns about the Necessity of a Study on the Coercion of Patients to Fill in ROM Lists (submitted 8 September 2017)* [*Vragen van de leden Kooiman (SP) en Diertens (D66) aan de Minister van Volksgezondheid, Welzijn en Sport over de noodzaak van een onderzoek naar de dwang bij patiënten om ROM-lijsten in te vullen (ingezonden 8 september 2017)*]. Available https://zoek.officielebekendmakingen.nl/ah-tk-20172018-218.pdf (accessed 20 June 2020).

House of Representatives of the Netherlands [Tweede Kamer der Staten-Generaal] Aanhangsel Handelingen 2017/18 1780 (2018) *Answer from Secretary of State Blokhuis (16 April 2018) Appendix to Proceedings, 2017–2018 Session Year* [*Antwoord van Secretary of State Blokhuis (16 April 2018) Aanhangsel Handelingen, vergaderjaar 2017–2018*]. Available https://zoek.officielebekendmakingen.nl/ah-tk-20172018-1780.html (accessed 20 June 2020).

Hout, F.A.G., Nienhuis, E.D., Robben, P.B., Frederiks, B.J. and Legemaate, J. (2010) 'Supervision by the Dutch Healthcare Inspectorate', *European Journal of Health Law*, 17(4): 347–60.

Hubben, J.H. (2012) 'The Health Care Inspectorate: From Silent Power to Public Watchdog' ['De IGZ: van stille kracht naar publieke waakhond'], *Journal of Health Law* [*Tijdschrift voor Gezondheidsrecht*], 2: 96–108.

Janssen, W.A. (2012) *Argus: Assessment and Use of Data Evaluating Coercive Measures in Dutch Psychiatry*, Unpublished PhD Thesis, Vrij Universiteit, Amsterdam. Available https://research.vu.nl/en/publications/argus-assessment-and-use-of-data-in-evaluating-coercive-measures- (accessed 20 June 2020).

Janssen, W.A., Noorthoorn, E.O., van de Sande, R., Nijman, H., Smit, A., Hoogendoorn, A., Voskes, Y., Mulder, N. and Widdershoven, G. (2014) 'Six Years of Argus, Freedom-restricting Interventions in Mental Health Care in 2012 and Developments Compared to Previous Years' ['Zes jaar Argus, Vrijheidsbeperkende interventies in de GGz in 2012 en ontwikkelingen ten opzichte van voorgaande jaren']. Available www.ggznederland.nl/uploads/assets/Rapport%20-%20zes%20jaar%20argus%2017062014.pdf.pdf (accessed 20 June 2020).

Janssen, W.A., van de Sande, R., Noorthoorn, E.O., Nijman, H.L., Bowers, L., Mulder, C.L., Smit, A., Widdershoven, G.A. and Steinert, T. (2011) 'Methodological Issues in Monitoring the Use of Coercive Measures', *International Journal of Law and Psychiatry*, 34(6): 429–38.

Ketelaars, C.A.J. (2011) 'Integrated Care Requires Integrated Supervision', *International Journal of Integrated Care*, 11: 1–6.

Kuiper, M. (2018) 'Record of Forced Admissions' ['Record aan gedwongen opnames'], *NRC Today*, 28 February. Available www.nrc.nl/nieuws/2018/02/28/record-aan-gedwongen-opnames-2-a1593877 (accessed 20 June 2020).

Legemaate, J. (2001) 'The Quality Control of the Health Care Inspectorate (IGZ)' ['Het toezicht van de Inspectie voor de Gezondheidszorg (IGZ) op de kwaliteit van de zorg'], *Journal of Health Law* [*Tijdschrift voor Gezondheidsrecht*], 25: 139–48.

Lepping, P., Masood, B., Flammer, E. and Noorthoorn, E.O. (2016) 'Comparison of Restraint Data from Four Countries', *Social Psychiatry and Psychiatric Epidemiology*, 51(9): 1301–09.

Mann-Poll, P.S., Smit, A., Noorthoorn, E.O., Janssen, W.A., Koekkoek, B. and Hutschemaekers, G.J.M. (2018) 'Long-Term Impact of a Tailored Seclusion Reduction Program: Evidence for Change?', *Psychiatric Quarterly*, 89(3): 733–46.

Mann-Poll, P.S., Smit, A., van Doeselaar, M. and Hutschemaekers, G.J. (2013) 'Professionals' Attitudes After a Seclusion Reduction Program: Anything Changed?', *Psychiatric Quarterly*, 84(1): 1–10.

National Technical Assistance Center for State Mental Health Planning (2005) *Six Core Strategies to Reduce the Use of Seclusion and Restraint Planning Tool*, Alexandria, VA: National Association of State Mental Health Program Directors.

Netherlands Ministry of Health, Welfare and Sport [Ministrie van Volksgezondheid, Welzijn en Sport] (2016) *The Dutch Healthcare System* [*Het Nederlandse Zorgstelsel*]. Available www.rijksoverheid.nl/documenten/brochures/2016/02/09/het-nederlandse-zorgstelsel (accessed 20 June 2020).

Netherlands National Health Care Institute [Zorginstituut Nederland] (2017) *Care and Support for People with a Mental Health Condition* [*Zorg en ondersteuningvoor mensen met een psychische aandoening*]. Available www.zorginstituutnederland.nl/Verzekerde+zorg/g/ggz-in-een-wlz-instelling/documenten/brochure/2017/08/16/zorg-en-ondersteuning-voor-mensen-met-een-psychische-aandoening (accessed 20 June 2020).

Netherlands National Health Care Institute [Zorginstituut Nederland] (2019) *Mental Health Care in an Institution Falling under the Long-term Care Act* [*GGZ in een Wlz-instelling (Wlz)*]. Available www.zorginstituutnederland.nl/Verzekerde+zorg/g/ggz-in-een-wlz-instelling (accessed 20 June 2020).

Noorthoorn, E.O. (2019) Telephone Interview with Author, 1 May.

Noorthoorn, E.O., Lepping, P., Janssen, W., Hoogendoorn, A., Nijman, H., Widdershoven, G. and Steinert, T. (2015) 'One-year Incidence and Prevalence of Seclusion: Dutch Findings in an International Perspective', *Social Psychiatry and Psychiatric Epidemiology*, 50: 1857–69.

Noorthoorn, E.O., Voskes, Y., Janssen, W.A., Mulder, C.L., van de Sande, R., Nijman, H.L., Smit, A., Hoogendoorn, A.W. and Bousardt, A. (2016) 'Seclusion Reduction in Dutch Mental Health Care: Did Hospitals Meet Goals', *Psychiatric Services*, 67(12): 1321–27.

Organisation for Economic Co-Operation and Development (2019) *Health Expenditure and Financing*. Available https://stats.oecd.org/Index.aspx?DataSetCode=SHA (accessed 20 June 2020).

Ploem, M.C. and Gevers, J.K.M. (2015) 'Legislation in Psychiatry, Psychogeriatrics and Mental Disability Care, Better Half Turned than Completely Lost' ['Wetgeving in de psychiatrie, psychogeriatrie en verstandelijk gehandicaptenzorg, Beter ten halve gekeerd dan ten hele gedwaald'], *Journal of Health Law* [*Tijdschrift voor Gezondheidsrecht*], 39(4): 203–11.

Pols, J. (2002) 'Enforcing Patient Rights or Improving Care? The Interference of Two Modes of Doing Good in Mental Health Care', *Sociology of Health and Illness*, 25(4): 320–47.

Psychiatric Hospitals (Committals) Act [*Wet bijzondere opnemingen in psychiatrische ziekenhuizen*] (Bopz) (1992). Available https://wetten.overheid.nl/BWBR0005700/2018-08-01 (accessed 20 June 2020).

Public Health Act [*Gezondheidswet*] (1956). Available https://wetten.overheid.nl/BWBR0002202/2019-02-01 (accessed 20 June 2020).

Regulation (EU) 2016/679 of the European Parliament and of the Council of 27 April 2016 on the Protection of Natural Persons with Regard to the Processing of Personal Data and on the Free Movement of Such Data, and Repealing Directive 95/46/EC (General Data Protection Regulation) (2016) OJ L 119/1.

Robbe, P.N.M., Bal, R. and Grol, R.P.T.M. (2012) *Public Sector Supervision by the Health Care Inspectorate* [*Overheidstoezicht door de Inspectie voor de Gezondheidszorg*], WRR Web Publication NR 62 [WRR Webpublicatie]. Available https://library.oapen.org/handle/20.500.12657/33947 (accessed 18 August 2020).

Steinert, T., Noorthoorn, E.O. and Mulder C.L. (2014) 'The Use of Coercive Interventions in Mental Health Care in Germany and the Netherlands. A Comparison of the Developments in Two Neighboring Countries', *Frontiers in Public Health*, 2(141): 1–10.

van Lonkhuyzen, L. (2017) 'Privacy in Mental Health Care at Issue' ['Privacy in geestelijke zorg in geding'], *NRC Today*, 13 July. Available www.nrc.nl/nieuws/2017/07/13/privacy-in-geestelijke-zorg-in-geding-12018987-a1566633 (accessed 20 June 2020).

Verlinde, A.A., Snelleman, W., van den Berg, H. and Noorthoorn, E.O. (2014) 'Effect of Compulsory Medication as an Intervention of First Choice on Separation and Applied Coercion; A Prospective Cohort Study' ['Effect van dwangmedicate als interventie van eerste keus op separatie en toegepaste dwang; een prospectief cohortonderzoek'], *Journal of Psychiatry* [*Tijdschrift voor Psychiatrie*], 56(10): 640–48.

Voskes, Y. (2015) *No Effect Without Ethics, Reduction of Seclusion in Psychiatry from a Care Ethics Perspective*, Unpublished PhD. Thesis, Vrije Universiteit Amsterdam. Available https://research.vu.nl/en/publications/no-effect-without-ethics-reduction-of-seclusion-in-psychiatry-fro (accessed 20 June 2020).

Voskes, Y., Theunissen, J. and Widdershoven, G. (2011) *Best Practices around Reducing Coercion in Mental Health Care [Best Practices rondom dwangreductie in de geestelijke gezondheidszorg*], Amsterdam: Vrije Universiteit Amsterdam. Available http://hic-psy.nl/wp-content/uploads/2012/09/Best-Practices-rondom-Dwangreductie-in-de-Geestelijke-Gezondheidszorg-2011.pdf (accessed 20 June 2020).

Vruwink, F.J., Mulder, C.L., Noorthoorn, E.O., Uitenbroek, D. and Nijman, H.L.I. (2012) 'The Effects of a Nationwide Program to Reduce Seclusion in the Netherlands', *BMC Psychiatry*, 12(231): 1–4.

Welie, S.P.K. and Widdershoven, T.P. (2018), 'CRPD and Forced Psychiatry: How to Proceed?' ['VPH and dwangpsychiatrie: hoe verder?'], *Journal of Health Law* [*Tijdschrift voor Gezondheidsrecht*], 42(1): 6–22.

World Health Organisation (2019) *European Health Information Gateway*. Available https://gateway.euro.who.int/en/ (accessed 20 June 2020).

8 Queensland's new physical restraint framework

Implementation and lessons since the commencement of the *Mental Health Act 2016*

John Allan and Amber Manwaring

Introduction

The push to decrease the use of seclusion and restraint has been prominent in Australia since it was adopted as a national safety priority in 2005 and the National Mental Health Seclusion and Restraint (Beacon) Project commenced in 2007 (National Mental Health Commission (NMHC) 2015; described in more detail by Bernadette McSherry in Chapter 11 in this volume). Since 2016 all states and territories have agreed to revise the policy goal to the *elimination of restrictive practices* (Western Australian Association for Mental Health (WAAMH) 2017). Queensland has participated in seclusion and restraint reduction efforts since these national efforts began. The fall in Queensland's seclusion rates has been significant – 24 per cent in the five years from 2009/10 to 2014/15 (Allan et al. 2017), and in 2017/18 rates for the first time fell below the national average (Australian Institute of Health and Welfare (AIHW) 2017).

There now appears to be universal acceptance of the harm and unsuitability of seclusion, but this has not always been the case (Meehan, Bergen and Fjeldsoe 2004), and efforts to convince clinical staff that there are viable alternatives continue. Until recently in Australia, much less attention has been paid to physical restraint, despite clear evidence that all forms of physical restraint have significant risks and should be used as a last resort (National Institute for Health and Clinical Excellence (NICE) 2005, 2015). National seclusion rates have been published since 2011 and were available selectively before this, but rates of physical and mechanical restraint have only been published nationally since 2016 (AIHW 2017). Although Queensland has reported mechanical restraint for some time, physical restraint rates were not collected until 2017, as there was no framework for reporting prior to the commencement of the *Mental Health Act 2016* (Qld).

The *Mental Health Act 2016* commenced on 5 March 2017, replacing the previous *Mental Health Act 2000* (Qld) which had been in operation for over 15 years. Although the new Act maintained the key structures established in its predecessor (namely, the Mental Health Court, authorised mental health services and the Mental Health Review Tribunal), an emphasis on human rights and a recovery focus were introduced among a wide range of reforms. These included a group of reforms aimed at increasing least restrictive practice, including capacity-based assessments for involuntary treatment, advanced health directives, independent patient rights advisors and stronger regulation of restrictive practices (seclusion, physical and mechanical restraint). A major advance in regard to the latter was that all the clinically oriented forms used for the *Mental Health Act 2016* were developed for electronic use and are now entered into a continuous electronic consumer record. This electronic record, the Consumer Integrated Mental Health Application (Queensland Health 2019a), has had continual refinements since it was first introduced by Queensland Health in November 2008. Besides compliance with regulation and data collection, this record also guides clinical practice and governance.

All of these measures required major implementation efforts in developing policy, education and practice. This chapter concentrates on the changes concerning physical restraint and, to a lesser extent, mechanical restraint, and the governance and data collection involved in their regulation. The present authors were extensively involved in the review, consultation, development and passage of the new *Mental Health Act 2016*, and the evaluation of its implementation. Associate Professor John Allan was the Queensland Chief Psychiatrist from July 2015 until September 2017. He was closely involved in the development of the new statute, including the consultative process; the drafting of the legislation, particularly the sections on restrictive practices; and its implementation, including responsibility for the development of the new Chief Psychiatrist's policies and practice guidelines. As discussed in this chapter, co-author Amber Manwaring was responsible for the evaluation of the *Mental Health Act 2016* implementation.

This chapter sets out how the physical restraint framework was implemented in Queensland, including barriers and learnings, and how policy and practice has supported clinician use of the new framework. It furthermore examines data regarding the use, compliance and monitoring of physical and mechanical restraint in Queensland authorised mental health services since 5 March 2017, with a focus on how the framework has increased safeguards for involuntary patients, and compares these with the use of physical restraint in other Australian states and territories.

Ultimately, we propose that there will continue to be issues raised by the use of restrictive practices. There is still a reliance upon restraint in emergency situations (not only in mental health settings but also emergency departments and general hospital wards) and as a planned part of treatment compliance, at least in Australian settings (Stedman et al. 2018). Although it is generally agreed that restraint is best avoided, what if there are situations in which physical restraint cannot be avoided? We need to be able to measure and understand reasons for restraint to implement alternatives. Although there is an argument that regulating and allowing restraint in some situations encourages overuse, the practice is still prominent; its proponents are not completely convinced that it can be eliminated, and with public reporting and changes in practice we now have a potential wealth of data to try to make sense of what actually happens in these events. In the Queensland context, the very broad extent and diversity of the reforms introduced by the *Mental Health Act 2016* may have contributed to an initial lack of awareness by staff of the new system aimed at regulating and reducing the use of physical restraint. Considerable variation was identified about what staff determine constitutes best practice and the key determinants for clinical choices. However, a regulatory framework cannot solve all practical issues or replace professional judgment and may only provide a legislative basis for clinical decision-making best practice. A better understanding of individual and service experience will contribute to better outcomes for patients. Queensland Health will therefore continue to use and refine available data to understand practice and how physical restraint fits with other choices in avoiding the use of restrictive practices.

Developing Queensland's broader mental health regulatory framework

The new regulatory framework associated with the *Mental Health Act 2016* comprises this legislation, the Queensland Chief Psychiatrist's policies and practice guidelines (Queensland Health 2019b), training and implementation of the Act, data collection, and real-time monitoring of restrictive practice events (such as mechanical restraint, seclusion and restraint plans) or a quality assurance cycle using collated data. For example, seclusion rates are a headline key performance indicator for Chief Executives of health services in their tri-monthly formal relationship management meetings with Queensland Health. Prior to such meetings, there is early, informal sharing of data by clinical improvement teams who work with services to address issues and share information about changes which have led to success elsewhere.

In practice, the Chief Psychiatrist's role is to ensure compliance with and smooth operation of the *Mental Health Act 2016* through legislative and clinical oversight. Under the Act, the Chief Psychiatrist's responsibilities include: protecting the rights of patients in authorised mental health services, balancing these rights with the rights of others; making policies and guidelines that must be adhered to by persons performing functions under the Act; ensuring, to the extent practicable, that the involuntary examination, assessment, treatment and care of persons complies with the Act; monitoring and auditing such compliance, including the power to investigate matters under the Act; promoting awareness and understanding of the legislation; and many other specific powers and responsibilities in regard to treatment, movement and safety of patients, including monitoring and authorising restrictive practices (*Mental Health Act 2016* (Qld): sections 26, 301 and 305).

While this chapter does not describe the governance of local mechanisms, readers should note the interplay of the Office of the Chief Psychiatrist providing centralised monitoring, advice and leadership with the authorised mental health services providing local authority and autonomy for mental health services. Although the Chief Psychiatrist has regulatory and legal powers (including criminal prosecution), most change is effected by pointing to evidence, partnerships and occasionally persuasion.

The governance framework is though much broader than the regulatory system (Braithwaite, Coglianese and Levi-Faur 2007: 1–7). Traditionally the governance framework is thought of as a hierarchy (Figure 8.1), but there are multiple accountabilities and potential lines of governance for each restraint event (Figure 8.2).

Mental health legislation appears to be a 'command and control' regulatory environment. In practice, although investigatory powers are often used to shed light on incidents and breaches, the powers of penalty and censure are rarely

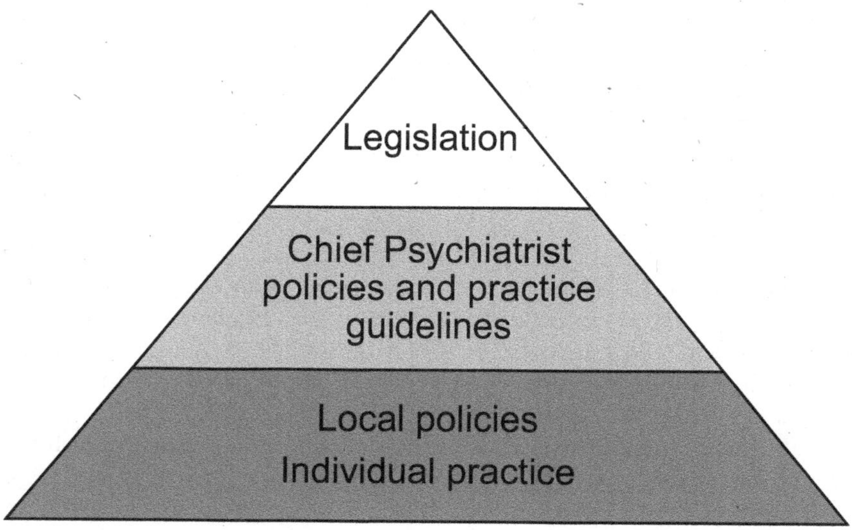

Figure 8.1 Traditional view of governance

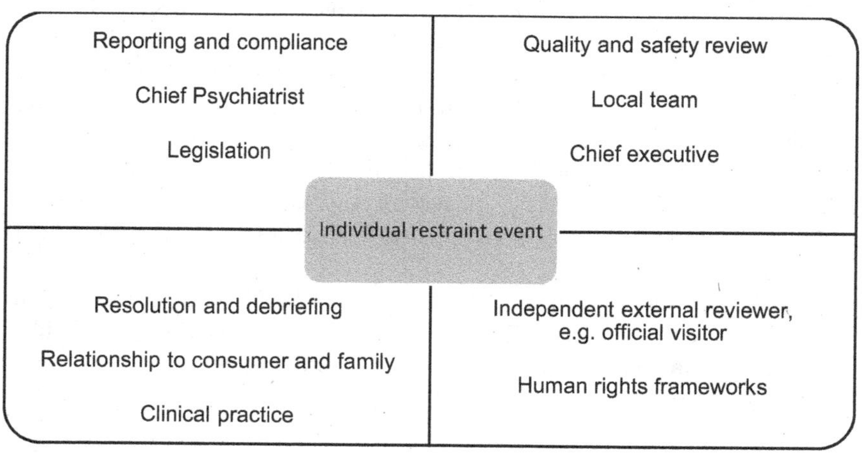

Figure 8.2 A realistic view of the different strains of governance

used, particularly where there is a desire to improve practice. Policies that are compulsory and guidelines that are not form the basis of a standard of practice but rely on their implementation at a local level. The relationship between consumer and clinician and the culture of safety and harm reduction that is promoted on the ward is very important in reducing restrictive practices and has the chance to be preventative. Censure, whether by internal mechanisms such as Chief Executives or externally by the Chief Psychiatrist or other bodies, usually occurs after the fact. Although spectacular failure can be a platform for reform (Wright et al. 2017), the goal of governance systems should be to prevent these situations arising.

A new regulatory system for physical restraint

Prior to 2017, only seclusion and mechanical restraint were regulated in Queensland, with physical restraint being unregulated. Consultation undertaken during the review of the *Mental Health Act 2000* looked to explore attitudes and new options in recovery-oriented practice which could fit with the regulatory framework (Queensland Health 2014). This review process began in 2013 with many rounds of public consultations, meetings, forums and workshops held across the State at key points, involving about 3,000 people and over 300 submissions (Parliament of Queensland 2014: 2, 2015a: 11). By these mechanisms a broad range of individuals, including service users and their families, community members and service providers, senior policy makers, government and community and not-for-profit organisations, statutory officers and advocates were all consulted. Consumers and carers were involved in the governance and decision-making process at every step until drafting and were then able to participate as part of the legislative process in parliamentary committee submissions and hearings (Parliament of Queensland 2014: 2, 2015a: 11, 2015b: 13).

These consultations indicated that physical restraint was a practice that was occurring regularly and was being recorded, but was not being adequately counted, and had a limited regulatory framework.

There were also mixed messages about its necessity. Under the new legislative regime many questions still remain to be answered about physical restraint, particularly whether it has any place in modern psychiatric care (especially beyond emergency situations). That is, whether it is a 'necessary evil' (Perkins et al. 2012: 46); and if it cannot be avoided and is used, what is the best and safest method.

The definition of physical restraint in Queensland provides that physical restraint of a patient generally refers to the use by a person of his or her body to restrict the patient's movement (*Mental Health Act 2016*: section 268). It may be authorised if there is no other reasonably practicable way to protect the patient or others from physical harm, provide treatment and care to the patient, prevent the patient from causing serious damage to property, or prevent the patient from leaving an inpatient service (*Mental Health Act 2016*: section 270). The Queensland definition for the use of physical restraint is consistent with the Mental Health Seclusion and Restraint National Best Endeavours Data Set (SECREST

NBEDS) definition which allows the application by health care staff of hands-on immobilisation or the physical restriction of a person to prevent them from harming him or herself or endangering others, or to ensure the provision of essential medical treatment (AIHW 2015a).

In the recent spate of new mental health statutes across Australian states and territories, each has introduced some form of definition of physical restraint (although there is no uniform statutory definition) and some measures to regulate its use (Royal Australian and New Zealand College of Psychiatrists (RANZCP) 2017). Two jurisdictions with older legislation however do not specifically define physical restraint. All Australian jurisdictions have though agreed to national definitions of restraint for the purposes of data collection (AIHW 2015a), but variations in requirements of individual mental health statutes have made it more difficult to standardise a national collection. Given that these definitions and the practices that surround them usually arise from a combination of local practice needs, historical governance systems and stakeholder consultation, idiosyncratic and individual views appear to be a stronger influence on the end product than a strict adherence to the literature or consideration of workable data definitions. In practical terms, Queensland Health has not yet resolved how useful the new Queensland definitions will be because it requires further experience in collection and it is not yet clear if the variations represent data errors or true variations in national practice (AIHW 2018). However, experience with the more mature companion data on seclusion, which also shows significant variation across sites, suggest differences in practice and culture can be a considerable influence (Allan et al. 2017).

Section 269 of the *Mental Health Act 2016* makes it an offence for a person to use physical restraint on a patient other than authorised under the Act. If used, it is only permissible as a last resort where less restrictive interventions have been unsuccessful or are not feasible, and where use is carefully monitored. Consultation with services and the community on the review of the *Mental Health Act 2000* suggested the need to distinguish restraint for safety in emergency situations from planned physical restraint for particular purposes, such as delivering treatment or preventing a person from leaving a mental health service. It was originally intended that the restrictive practice provisions in the *Mental Health Act 2016* would apply only to involuntary patients; however, during the drafting of the new Act it became clear that the urgent circumstances (now outlined in section 268(2)(c)) would also need to apply to voluntary patients (*Mental Health Act 2016* (Qld): section 243). This occurred because requiring a patient to be made involuntary for the purpose of defusing an emergency situation may inadvertently lead to more people becoming involuntary patients, which is against the spirit of encouraging least restrictive practice under the Act. The compromise, set out in the Chief Psychiatrist's policy, was that seclusion and mechanical restraint can only be used for involuntary patients and cannot be agreed to under an advance health directive, whereas physical restraint can be agreed to voluntarily and as part of an advance health directive (Queensland Health 2017a). The physical restraint provisions therefore cover voluntary and involuntary patients and a distinction is made between exceptions for emergency and planned physical restraint which must be authorised prior to use. Section 269 of the *Mental*

Health Act 2016 makes it an offence to use physical restraint on a patient other than as authorised by the legislation. Table 8.1 sets out practices that will not constitute such an offence, noting the relevant provisions of the *Mental Health Act 2016* and summarising the relevant descriptions in the Chief Psychiatrist's policy (Queensland Health 2017b, 2017f: 1–2).

Section 305(3) of the *Mental Health Act 2016* provides that a person performing a function under the Act must comply with the Queensland Chief

Table 8.1 Practices that will not constitute an offence under section 269 of the *Mental Health Act 2016* (Qld)

Practice	*Circumstances described in the Chief Psychiatrist policy*
Emergency physical restraint (section 268(2)(c))	Physical restraint that is required in urgent circumstances, such as managing a person who is having a seizure, restraining a patient who is physically aggressive, or where a staff member uses physical contact to defend themselves or to disarm a patient where there is an immediate risk of harm.
Planned or authorised physical restraint (section 270)	The use of physical restraint on a patient for one or more of the following purposes, if satisfied that there is no other reasonably practicable way: • to protect the patient or others from physical harm • to provide treatment and care to the patient • to prevent the patient from causing serious damage to property, or • for a patient detained in an authorised mental health service, to prevent the patient from leaving the service without permission. These uses must be authorised by an authorised doctor or a health practitioner in charge of an inpatient unit or other unit within an authorised mental health service.
Day to day care and treatment (section 268(2)(a))	• Physical restraint used as part of treatment and care with the agreement of the patient, such as to steady an arm for an injection, or • The giving of physical support or assistance reasonably necessary to enable the patient to carry out daily living activities or to redirect the patient because the patient is disoriented.
Other exceptions (section 268(2)(b))	Physical restraint that is authorised by another law.

Psychiatrist's policies and practice guidelines. These extensively describe the practice and required safeguards for the use of physical restraint (including prone restraint), which are mandated for mental health services. The relevant Chief Psychiatrist's policy, which supports the use of physical restraint as a last resort where less restrictive interventions have been unsuccessful or are not feasible (Queensland Health 2017f: 1), limits the use of prone (face down) restraint to two minutes. It further provides that physical restraint is not a substitute for other less restrictive interventions or adequate staffing levels or staff training and must not be used as a form of punishment (Queensland Health 2017f: 2 and 3). After a physical restraint event, reviews must be undertaken with the patient and all staff and support persons involved to allow open discussion about the event and circumstances leading up to it, allowing the patient to ask questions, and allowing all involved to work together to identify strategies to avoid physical restraint in the future; and reviews with the relevant staff involved to determine the methods used and triggers for the physical restraint event (Queensland Health 2017b: 4).

There is considerable evidence about the relative danger of prone restraint and several jurisdictions have taken steps to limit its use through legislation and guidelines (see Guy Cross in Chapter 6 in this volume). However, apart from avoiding restraint altogether, a practical alternative to prone restraint has not yet been agreed across Australia. Since 2003 training regarding safe use of prone restraint has been part of the Queensland training curriculum provided to all services in Queensland (Maybo 2020).

To further support the safe use of physical restraint and other restrictive practices for persons under 18 years of age (minors) the Public Guardian, a statutory office in Queensland responsible for protecting the rights of minors in the child protection system (among others), must be notified about the use of mechanical restraint, seclusion or physical restraint on minors (*Mental Health Act 2016*: section 274).

Changes to the regulation of mechanical restraint

Under the previous *Mental Health Act 2000*, mechanical restraint in Queensland could only be authorised by an authorised doctor along with direct approval by the Director of Mental Health (an equivalent former role to the Chief Psychiatrist) required in each instance (including in emergency situations). The Director of Mental Health also gave prior approval of the mechanical appliances permitted for use. In recent years the use of mechanical restraint has reduced to very low levels (AIHW 2018). However, during the legislative consultation, it was noted that episodes of mechanical restraint are still contentious and stronger regulation was needed. The *Mental Health Act 2016* expanded the Chief Psychiatrist authorisation framework for the use of mechanical restraint and introduced formal 'Reduction and Elimination Plans' to be implemented across all services (*Mental Health Act 2016* (Qld): section 264), which includes a standard form to be used (Queensland Health 2017e).

Reduction and Elimination Plans are an expansion of an administrative programme first established under the *Mental Health Act 2000* requiring the then Director of Mental Health's approval for seclusion and restraint minimisation plans for addressing episodes of prolonged seclusion in the forensic setting of high security wards. The current Reduction and Elimination Plans indicate an expectation that services will work towards cessation of restrictive interventions as early as possible to reduce the potential for trauma and harm (see Yvette Maker in Chapter 5 in this volume for further discussion of trauma and harm associated with restraint use). The process for Reduction and Elimination Plans requires a high-level review which addresses each factor hindering such cessation (*Mental Health Act 2016* (Qld): section 275). The Chief Psychiatrist's accompanying policy calls for clinical leadership, monitoring, accountability and a focus on safe, less restrictive alternatives to mechanical restraint.

Reduction and Elimination Plans can be approved by the Chief Psychiatrist for mechanical restraint only, seclusion only, or both seclusion and mechanical restraint together (*Mental Health Act 2016* (Qld): sections 264 and 267). According to the Chief Psychiatrist's policy, Reduction and Elimination Plans for seclusion are triggered whenever a patient is secluded for more than nine hours in a 24-hour period (*Mental Health Act 2016* (Qld): section 258), whereas Reduction and Elimination Plans should be made for any episode of mechanical restraint (*Mental Health Act 2016* (Qld): section 246; Queensland Health 2017c). All Reduction and Elimination Plans are overseen by local clinical directors and approval and review is sought at the same time as an application to the Chief Psychiatrist for the approval of mechanical restraint. The Chief Psychiatrist may request changes or reject a Reduction and Elimination Plan (*Mental Health Act 2016*: section 248). In addition, the Chief Psychiatrist must approve the specific type of restraint device that can be used (*Mental Health Act 2016*: section 249).

As outlined in Table 8.2, the *Mental Health Act 2016* uses a different definition of mechanical restraint to the national data collection SECREST NBEDS

Table 8.2 Definition of mechanical restraint under the *Mental Health Act 2016* (Qld) and the Mental Health Seclusion and Restraint National Best Endeavours Data Set (SECREST NBEDS)

Source	*Definition*
MENTAL HEALTH ACT 2016	'Mechanical restraint is the restraint of a person by the application of a device to the person's body, or a limb of the person to restrict the person's movement. Mechanical restraint does not include the appropriate use of a medical or surgical appliance in the treatment of physical illness or injury, or restraint that is authorised or permitted under another law' (*Mental Health Act 2016* (Qld): section 244)
SECREST NBEDS	'The application of devices (including belts, harnesses, manacles, sheets and straps) on a person's body to restrict his or her movement. This is to prevent the person from harming himself/herself or endangering others or to ensure the provision of essential medical treatment. It does not include the use of furniture (including beds with cot sides and chairs with tables fitted on their arms) that restricts the person's capacity to get off the furniture except where the devices are used solely for the purpose of restraining a person's freedom of movement' (AIHW 2015b)

definition (AIHW 2015b). While the definitions are inconsistent, both rely on the use of a device to restrict a person. This assists with consistency in reporting across jurisdictions and results in more accurate data because each restraint event relies upon the presence of a device, which is easily recognisable.

How were the reforms implemented?

Implementation activities for the *Mental Health Act 2016* began even before the new Act was passed by the Parliament of Queensland on 5 March 2016 and were concentrated in the year leading up to its legislative commencement on 5 March 2017. This involved significant collaboration and information sharing processes with external agencies, consumer and carer groups, as well as preparing the staff and administration of health services. As part of this, Queensland Health established implementation governance groups which included significant consumer and carer membership.

The development of the Chief Psychiatrist's policies and practice guidelines on restrictive practices included testing by a reference group which comprised consumers and carers, and formal consultation with mental health services. The Consumer Integrated Mental Health Application (also referred to as CIMHA), the state-wide mental health clinical information system, underwent extensive enhancements to support the *Mental Health Act 2016* and improve business efficiency by creating 'intelligent' forms and templates. These improved accuracy and reduced data entry burden and addressed other issues identified by users as key concerns for implementation.

Information and updates were distributed to staff using various mechanisms including email communications, an implementation newsletter, memoranda, meetings, workshops, Queensland Health Intranet Spotlight, the Queensland Department of Health internet site, posters, video messages and letters. The communication strategy was to create multiple levels of information, from easy-to-navigate websites and simple pamphlets, to complex policy documents available to all (Queensland Health 2017d).

In keeping with 'best practice' in cultural change, implementation committees were established in each of Queensland's 16 separate Hospital and Health Services. This ensured local resources were developed; education and training delivered to staff by *Mental Health Act 2016* administrators and administrator delegates; and compliance, data and record keeping requirements of the new statute were met. Key contacts and 'champions' were also appointed in Hospital and Health Services to assist with implementation. As there are over 30 separate inpatient services and extensive community-based services in a geographically large and diverse state, local championing and responsibility was paramount.

The Office of the Chief Psychiatrist provided training, including a compulsory online competency-based education and training package for authorised doctors and mental health practitioners called iLearn, with one module of iLearn (out of 7 or 11 modules depending on the position of the person undertaking training) devoted to seclusion and restraint (Queensland Health 2016). Face-to-face training was also provided in Consumer Integrated Mental Health Application upgrades including the documentation of restrictive practices, as well as both a face-to-face and online capacity assessment for an advanced health directive training module (Queensland Centre for Mental Health 2019).

Over 4,000 Queensland Health staff completed the seven-module iLearn online training package, and over 1,000 authorised doctors and psychiatrists completed the 11-module iLearn since being made available in early 2017. This included 100 per cent compliance for doctors (who cannot authorise any restrictive practice without completing training), although compliance was variable for inpatient nurses as not all are required to be authorised practitioners. In addition, nearly 400 external users – likely to be private hospital staff, other health care workers, consumers and carers – accessed iLearn resources (Queensland Health 2019c). Separate training and information packages including videos for consumers and carers were also developed and provided via community organisations (ADA Australia 2016).

Issues and barriers arising from the implementation of the *Mental Health Act 2016*

Two separate reviews about the implementation of the *Mental Health Act 2016* are discussed in this section. The first is the independent review undertaken by West Moreton Hospital and Health Service, which focused specifically on the practical implementation of the new physical restraint framework. The second is the broader evaluation of the implementation of the *Mental Health Act 2016* undertaken by Queensland Health (Queensland Health 2019c).

Internal review of physical restraint practices

West Moreton Hospital and Health Service (West Moreton) is one of 16 Hospital and Health Services in Queensland. It provides public hospital, health and wellbeing services to almost 290,000 people across the Somerset, Scenic Rim, Lockyer Valley and Ipswich communities, from Esk in the north, Gatton to the west, Springfield and Ipswich in the east and Boonah to the south.

From October 2017, West Moreton undertook an independent internal review of the implementation of the physical restraint changes and key barriers to their implementation (the West Moreton Review) since the commencement of the *Mental Health Act 2016*. The unpublished West Moreton Review sought to identify progress towards compliance with the *Mental Health Act 2016* and the Chief Psychiatrist's policy and practice guidelines regarding physical restraint, and to identify alternatives to prone restraint. As part of the review, West Moreton facilitated focus groups with 37 nursing staff from three hospitals and conducted a survey of West Moreton's nursing directors (of 19 nursing directors contacted, 15 responded). The West Moreton Review highlighted some of the issues and barriers that arose in the implementation of the *Mental Health Act 2016* in terms of regulating physical restraint.

When asked about changes made to their physical restraint practice since the implementation of the Act, some nursing staff noted that they had become more vigilant of the restraint duration and paid more attention to ensuring the patient's safety. Nursing directors stated that most are placing a greater emphasis on de-escalation to reduce the need for physical restraint, but few substantial changes had been made to the practice of physical restraint. The West Moreton Review also noted that when nurses were asked about their understanding and interpretation of the Chief Psychiatrist's policy and practice guidelines regarding physical restraint, it was identified that concerns of nursing staff regarding restraint time limits, raised before the commencement of the *Mental Health Act 2016*, had persisted. Staff were also concerned that mistakes could be made by rushing activities to comply with the imposed timeframe for reform. The survey of nursing directors highlighted the lack of a suitable training programme to address methods of performing restraint with minimal use of prone restraint. As all training programmes used in Queensland teach the use of prone restraint as a core part of physical practice.

The West Moreton Review noted that when asked what changes have been made to the training programme to ensure that practice complies with the *Mental Health Act 2016*, nursing directors reported that strategies had been employed to make staff more aware of the Act. However, some nursing directors had difficulty describing any specific training of alternatives to prone restraint since the *Mental Health Act 2016* was implemented. The West Moreton Review considered physical restraint events holistically, informed by staff about their understanding of the new framework and their thoughts about the training they had undertaken since the *Mental Health Act 2016* commenced. A better understanding of how physical restraint is being used requires however a more detailed examination of individual restraint events.

Evaluation of the Mental Health Act 2016 *implementation*

Due to the significant implementation efforts required in relation to several of the more significant changes introduced by the *Mental Health Act 2016*, a public commitment was made to undertake an evaluation of the Act's implementation, within two years of its commencement. This public evaluation was conducted by the Mental Health Alcohol and Other Drugs Branch within Queensland Health and commenced in July 2017. The purpose of the evaluation was to gain an understanding of the extent to which key initiatives within the *Mental Health Act 2016* have been successfully implemented; and stakeholder views of the change management processes associated with the implementation of the Act. More specifically, the evaluation considered how the changes made by the *Mental Health Act 2016* meet the objectives and principles of the Act, with particular regard to the use of less restrictive ways (including the use of advance health directives and substitute decision-making processes), patient rights focused treatment and recovery-oriented practices.

When considering the implementation of the Act, mental health service staff were asked to complete an implementation survey prior to commencement of the Act and six months post-commencement. According to the survey, the confidence of staff to implement changes arising from the Act rose from 51 per cent reporting that they were moderately or well prepared prior to commencement, to 76 per cent six months post-commencement (Queensland Health 2019c: 15).

Alongside improved safeguards for the use of restrictive practices, the *Mental Health Act 2016* requires clinicians to consider if there is a less restrictive way for a person to receive treatment and care for their mental illness instead of receiving involuntary treatment and care. The Act furthermore provides that treatment and care can be provided in the following less restrictive ways: under a person's advance health directive; with the consent of a person's personal guardian, attorney or statutory health attorney; and if the person is a minor, with the consent of the minor's parent (*Mental Health Act 2016* (Qld): section 13(1)). The evaluation indicated that, during implementation, many clinicians faced challenges in determining a less restrictive way in practice. These included knowing which options are less restrictive, identifying suitable decision-makers for providing consent to treatment and providing care to patients who are admitted to an inpatient unit under a substitute decision-maker (Queensland Health 2019c: 31).

The Less Restrictive Ways Project began one year after implementation as a collaboration between one district mental health service, the Office of the Chief Psychiatrist and a state-wide expert reference group. The purpose was to develop resources to assist clinicians across mental health services and to develop additional material to support implementation of less restrictive options. This included a guide to clinical decision-making, a range of recommendations to improve data and recording, training and education, and enhanced safeguards for people receiving treatment in less restrictive ways (Queensland Health 2019c: 31). The issues list addressed by the Less Restrictive Ways Project was led by clinicians and although many issues were identified and discussed, restraint was not raised in this project.

Data regarding the use of, compliance with, and monitoring of physical and mechanical restraint for the *Mental Health Act 2016*

One of the challenges highlighted by the evaluation was the quality of available data (Queensland Health 2019c: 81), including data to inform the specific use of physical restraint. This is the first-time physical restraint has been systematically recorded in Queensland mental health settings. The collection has now been underway for some three years and data quality issues have been identified.

In light of the challenges encountered through the implementation of the *Mental Health Act 2016*, it is useful to consider how the data can inform practice and performance. For standardisation and data system development reasons, the Consumer Integrated Mental Health Application operates using a standardised form for each physical restraint event regardless of type. Despite this, considerable data is collected and recorded for each restraint event. This includes the reasons for the restraint, particularly why there was no other reasonably practicable alternative; times and duration; number of staff involved; position (particularly prone but also standing, kneeling, sitting and the use of chairs, beds, walls or floor); the use of seclusion, medication or mechanical restraint before, after or during restraint; a verbatim report of events leading to and a description of the restraint; the clinical examination and monitoring during the event; any adverse events to patients, staff or others; and any ongoing issues post-restraint including review and debriefing (Queensland Health 2019a). While this information is collected by the Consumer Integrated Mental Health Application, the nature of the standardised form means it is not readily available for analysis and requires manual extraction prior to analysis. It is expected though that this information can be used in a quality improvement way to understand behaviours and decrease the need for restraint.

The West Moreton Review examined both data collected in the Consumer Integrated Mental Health Application and at a local level to identify reporting and monitoring issues. This review found wide variation across Queensland in the reporting of physical restraint events, suggesting significant differences in reporting practices. While Queensland Health's evaluation of the *Mental Health Act 2016* implementation found that regulation and recording of physical restraint has been well embedded across Queensland, there are opportunities for Hospital and Health Services to improve data entry for physical restraint events to ensure accuracy (Queensland Health 2019c: 42). Although at 6.3 physical restraint events per 100,000 bed days in 2017–18 (AIHW 2018), current use of physical restraint in Queensland is comparable to other Australian states including inter-hospital variation in rate. However, this measure does not account for how and why physical restraint is being used. For example, the limitations in readily available data do not allow consideration of the relationship between rates of seclusion and physical restraint to be considered. In line with safeguards introduced by the new regulatory framework for the use of physical restraint, 2,067 physical restraint events (including emergency restraint events) involving 700 patients occurred in 2017–18. Of these events, 1,750 involved 613 involuntary patients (Queensland Health 2019c: 40–42).

While changes to the regulation of mechanical restraint under the *Mental Health Act 2016* improved safeguards and oversight for its use (Queensland Health 2019c: 44), since the commencement of the new Act, there has been little change in the rate of use of mechanical restraint, which was already low (Queensland Health 2019c: 45).

The Office of the Chief Psychiatrist has advised it is considering more detailed demographic and service data for the next collection to ensure results are not confounded by data collection issues, with benchmarking of practice between units important for reducing restrictive practice.

Discussion

The *Mental Health Act 2016* represents a major step forward in recognising patient rights and safeguards, acknowledging the need for less restrictive alternatives and trying to strike balance between the competing interests of individual rights and freedoms while protecting people from potential harm. It attempts to align Queensland's mental health legislation with contemporary clinical practice including the desire to reduce and eliminate restrictive practices.

The introduction of so much reform aimed at achieving the broad range of less restrictive ways may have overshadowed the initial awareness by staff of a specific new system change aimed at understanding and reducing physical restraint. The lack of issues relating to restraint identified by staff when consulted broadly about the impact of the *Mental Health Act 2016* may be a function of other issues rather than a smooth implementation or complete satisfaction with the changes in monitoring of restraint, particularly physical restraint.

The variation in rates of restraint and a disconnect with seclusion rates presents a challenge for evaluating what has happened and planning ways forward. Was it the efforts of champions who looked to reduce restrictive practice or could a high rate be attributed to a firm leadership demanding every incident of restraint no matter how fleeting be recorded?

The process of consulting on, developing and introducing legislation brings into sharp relief the multiple ways that people and systems seek to govern and alter restrictive practices. It shows that legislation alone is not enough. What is the rationale of regulation? Is it to emphasise safety and review of current practice or is it to deliberately change practice? To make it so hard, inconvenient or too resource intense to use restrictive practice so that services need to find alternatives? To review what has happened from a different perspective or to drive change when change will not come? And what comes from driving change too hard? For example, the Queensland government has already conducted a review and introduced the legislation to require a change of practice and publicised this, but failed to appreciate that training might not catch up so easily, as was identified for prone restraint by the West Moreton Review, where it was hard for staff to find alternatives.

A regulatory framework cannot answer every question and is only a basis for ethical clinical decision-making to determine the best practice, that is, effective governance. The easiest implementations occurred when the champions were available to lead the service to a smooth change that considered local practice in relation to the requirements of the *Mental Health Act 2016* and included both doctors and nurses in their development (Queensland Health 2019c: 15). However, without new rules it is hard to imagine change occurring other than very slowly. The resistances to the multiple forces seeking change are best overcome from within.

The initial findings highlighted considerable variation for staff about what constitutes best practice and what are the key determinants for choices. It is not always clear which practice is to be considered the 'last resort' or the order of using the 'last resort' where there are multiple choices. Bak and Aggernaes (2012) compared coercive practice in Denmark to ten comparable European countries and noted considerable variation in practices that could be used and in rates of use. Of particular interest here, the researchers asked regulators and specialist clinicians which practices they considered to be the most intrusive. In most countries, the use of 'time out' or continuous observation was seen as less intrusive, followed by physical restraint which was seen as less intrusive than seclusion or mechanical restraint but the relative rankings varied. Interestingly, forced medication was viewed as preferable to physical restraint in four comparator countries and seclusion was preferred in one. The authors attributed this to culture-based differences in perceptions of coercion (Bak and Aggernaes 2012: 300). There does not appear to have been any formal testing of any such hierarchy in Australia but undoubtedly services have their preferences. Anecdotal evidence suggests individual preference by staff is often a driving force and that local leadership is the most important factor in producing change (see the discussions of culture in Part IV in this volume).

There continue to be questions about the application of physical restraint. Staff, families and service users grapple with the idea that there may be instances where something that involves holding, touching, or moving another person (which would be captured by the definition of physical restraint and may be necessary for the care and treatment of a person) is a 'restrictive practice'. Whether the definitions applied to physical restraint are correct, and reflect a consistent understanding of physical restraint, still remains to be seen.

Queensland Health's future improvement plan is to use the data to form a picture of practice and how physical restraint fits with other choices in avoiding the use of restrictive practices. There is a need to examine not just regulation, but also to consider what constitutes 'last resort' or 'necessary in emergency situations' and what does not. A hierarchy of responses should be developed rather than blanket labelling of all types of restraints together (Sethi et al. 2018). An analysis of emergency versus planned restraint practice may shed some light. What really is 'last resort' may require case by case consideration. Definitions and legislation can be improved, but practice and training must keep pace with our ambitions for restraint reduction and elimination.

The review of process and administrative data has limitations. Although Queensland Health is building a large database of events, this will not be enough without a specific understanding of patient experience (as discussed further by Grant Sara in Chapter 9 in this volume). Debriefing, surveys of individual experience or involvement in systemic review of restrictive practice can all be valuable next steps. A finer grained understanding of individual and service experience will contribute to our understanding of how to move a large health system to meet its aspirational objectives.

Regulatory change, policy definition and collection of administrative data are necessary as the bedrock on which changes to clinical practice can occur and importantly signal an intention to increase our understanding of and improvement in addressing restrictive practice events.

References

ADA Australia (2016) *Advanced Directive for Mental Health: Consumer Resources.* Available https://adaaustralia.com.au/consumer/ (accessed 20 June 2020).

Allan, J., Hanson, G., Schroder, N., O'Mahony, A., Foster, R. and Sara, G. (2017) 'Six Years of National Mental Health Seclusion Data: The Australian Experience', *Australasian Psychiatry*, 25(3): 277–81.

Australian Institute of Health and Welfare (AIHW) (2015a) *Mental Health Seclusion and Restraint (NBEDS) 2015.* Available https://meteor.aihw.gov.au/content/index.phtml/itemId/558137 (accessed 20 June 2020).

Australian Institute of Health and Welfare (AIHW) (2015b) *Restraint–Identifying and Definitional Attributes.* Available https://meteor.aihw.gov.au/content/index.phtml/itemId/558140 (accessed 20 June 2020).

Australian Institute of Health and Welfare (AIHW) (2017) *New Data Provides First Picture of the Use of Restraint in Mental Health Facilities.* Available www.aihw.gov.au/news-media/media-releases/2017/may/new-data-provides-first-picture-of-the-use-of-rest (accessed 20 June 2020).

Australian Institute of Health and Welfare (AIHW) (2018) *Mental Health Services in Australia: Web Report–Restraint.* Available www.aihw.gov.au/reports/mental-health-services/mental-health-services-in-australia/report-contents/restrictive-practices/restraint (accessed 20 June 2020).

Bak, J. and Aggernaes, H. (2012) 'Coercion Within Danish Psychiatry Compared with 10 Other European Countries', *Nordic Journal of Psychiatry*, 66(5): 297–302.

Braithwaite, J., Coglianese, C. and Levi-Faur, D. (2007) 'Can Regulation and Governance Make a Difference?', *Regulation & Governance*, 1: 1–7.

Maybo (2020) *Restrictive Physical Intervention Training (PI Training).* Available www.maybo.com.au/training/physical-intervention/ (accessed 20 June 2020).

Meehan, T., Bergen, H. and Fjeldsoe, K. (2004) 'Staff and Patient Perceptions of Seclusion: Has Anything Changed?', *Journal of Advanced Nursing*, 47(1): 33–38.

Mental Health Act 2016 (Qld). Available www.legislation.qld.gov.au/view/html/inforce/current/act-2016-005 (accessed 20 June 2020).

National Institute for Health and Clinical Excellence (NICE) (2005) *Violence: The Short-term Management of Disturbed/Violent Behaviour in Psychiatric In-patient Psychiatric Settings and Emergency Departments (NG25).* Available http://umh1946.edu.umh.es/wp-content/uploads/sites/172/2015/04/NICE-Violence-The-short-term-management-of-disturbed-violent-behaviour-in-in-patient-psychiatric-settings-and-emergency-departments.pdf (accessed 20 June 2020).

National Institute for Health and Clinical Excellence (NICE) (2015) *Violence and Aggression: Short-term Management in Mental Health, Health and Community Settings (NG10).* Available www.nice.org.uk/guidance/ng10 (accessed 20 June 2020).

National Mental Health Commission (NMHC) (2015) *A Case for Change: Position Paper on Seclusion, Restraint and Restrictive Practices in Mental Health Services.* Available www.mentalhealthcommission.gov.au/getmedia/63e1d2e6-79fe-45ea-aeab-145f1d9b269a/Position-paper-on-seclusion-and-restraint (accessed 20 June 2020).

Parliament of Queensland (2014) *Health and Ambulance Services Committee Public Briefing–Mental Health Bill, Transcript of Proceedings (11 December 2014).* Available www.parliament.qld.gov.au/documents/committees/HCSC/2014/MentalHealthB14/trns-pb11Dec2014-mhb.pdf (accessed 20 June 2020).

Parliament of Queensland (2015a) *Mental Health Bill 2015 – Explanatory Notes.* Available www.legislation.qld.gov.au/view/pdf/bill.first.exp/bill-2017-016 (accessed 20 June 2020).

Parliament of Queensland (2015b) *Report No. 9, 55th Parliament, Health and Ambulance Services Committee, Mental Health Bill 2015 and Mental Health (Recovery Model) Bill 2015.* Available www.parliament.qld.gov.au/documents/tableOffice/TabledPapers/2015/5515T1690.pdf (accessed 20 June 2020).

Perkins, E., Prosser, H., Riley, D. and Whittington, R. (2012) 'Physical Restraint in a Therapeutic Setting: A Necessary Evil?', *International Journal of Law and Psychiatry*, 35(1): 43–49.

Queensland Centre for Mental Health Learning (QCMHL) (2019) *QC40 Capacity Assessment Training and Advance Health Directives*. Available www.qcmhl.qld.edu.au/course/search.php?search=QC40+Capacity+Assessment+Training+and+Advance+Health+Directives (accessed 20 June 2020).

Queensland Health (2014) *Review of the Mental Health Act 2000 Discussion Paper–May 2014*. Available www.qmhc.qld.gov.au/sites/default/files/wp-content/uploads/2014/02/Mental-Heath-Act-Discussion-Paper.pdf (accessed 20 June 2020).

Queensland Health (2016) *Mental Health Act 2016 – Authorised Mental Health Practitioners*. Available https://ilearncatalogue.health.qld.gov.au/course/428/mhae-c-mental-health-act-2016 – authorised-mental-health-practitioners (accessed 20 June 2020).

Queensland Health (2017a) *Chief Psychiatrist Policy–Advance Health Directives and 'Less Restrictive Way' of Treatment*. Available www.health.qld.gov.au/__data/assets/pdf_file/0029/465176/cpp-advance-directives.pdf (accessed 20 June 2020).

Queensland Health (2017b) *Chief Psychiatrist Practice Guidelines–Physical Restraint*. Brisbane, Queensland Government.

Queensland Health (2017c) *Chief Psychiatrist Policy–Mechanical Restraint*. Available www.health.qld.gov.au/__data/assets/pdf_file/0033/465189/cpp-mechanical-restraint.pdf (accessed 20 June 2020).

Queensland Health (2017d) *Patient Rights and Support*. Available www.health.qld.gov.au/clinical-practice/guidelines-procedures/clinical-staff/mental-health/act/topics/patient-rights (accessed 20 June 2020).

Queensland Health (2017e) *Reduction and Elimination Plan–Seclusion and Mechanical Restraint*. Available www.health.qld.gov.au/__data/assets/pdf_file/0017/574010/f_reduce_eliminate.pdf (accessed 20 June 2020).

Queensland Health (2017f) *Chief Psychiatrist Policy–Physical Restraint*. Available www.health.qld.gov.au/__data/assets/pdf_file/0027/465174/cpp-physical-restraint.pdf (accessed 20 June 2020).

Queensland Health (2019a) *Consumer Integrated Mental Health Application (CIMHA)*. Available www.health.qld.gov.au/clinical-practice/guidelines-procedures/clinical-staff/mental-health/act/resources/consumer-integrated-mental-health-application (accessed 20 June 2020).

Queensland Health (2019b) *Chief Psychiatrist Policies*. Available www.health.qld.gov.au/clinical-practice/guidelines-procedures/clinical-staff/mental-health/act/policies-guidelines (accessed 20 June 2020).

Queensland Health (2019c) *Evaluation of the Mental Health Act 2016 Implementation–Evaluation Report*. Available www.health.qld.gov.au/__data/assets/pdf_file/0033/848517/evaluation-mha2016-report.pdf (accessed 20 June 2020).

Royal Australian and New Zealand College of Psychiatrists (RANZCP) (2017) *Restraint in Australian and New Zealand Mental Health Acts*. Available www.ranzcp.org/files/resources/college_statements/mental-health-legislation-tables/6-restraint-comparing-mental-health-acts.aspx (accessed 20 June 2020).

Sethi, F., Parkes, J., Baskind, E. and Paterson, B. (2018) 'Restraint in Mental Health Settings: Is It Time to Declare a Position?', *British Journal of Psychiatry*, 212(3): 137–41.

Stedman T., Meehan T., McGovern M., Richards G., Mansfield Y. and Keniry D. (2018) *Physical Restraint under the Mental Health Act 2016 in Queensland Health's Hospital and Health Services.* Brisbane, Australia.

Western Australian Association for Mental Health (WAAMH) (2017) *Towards Elimination of Restrictive Practices 11th National Forum (formerly Seclusion and Restraint Reduction Forum).* Available https://waamh.org.au/events-and-training/towards-elimination-of-restrictive-practices-11th-national-forum-formerly-seclusion-and-restraint-reduction-forum (accessed 20 June 2020).

Wright, M., Crowe, J., Huckshorn, K., Lenihan, K., Mooney, J. and Shields, R. (2017) *Review of Seclusion, Restraint and Observation of Consumers with a Mental Illness in NSW Health Facilities.* Available www.health.nsw.gov.au/mentalhealth/reviews/seclusionprevention/Pages/about.aspx (accessed 20 June 2020).

9 Showing restraint

The uses and limitations of data in supporting restraint reduction

Grant Sara

Introduction

Data is essential for improving health system performance. It allows for variations in services to be assessed and helps provide support and a focus for reform efforts. Data alone is rarely sufficient for change, but it is nearly always necessary. It is particularly important for complex reforms such as reducing restrictive practices, which require sustained changes in skills, practice and culture. The use of data to inform practice has been identified as one of six core strategies for seclusion and restraint reduction (Huckshorn 2004; National Technical Assistance Center for State Mental Health Planning 2005; National Association of State Mental Health Program Directors 2008). However national and international comparisons of restrictive practice have been limited by inconsistent measurement approaches (Janssen et al. 2011; Gooding et al. 2018).

This chapter has two aims. First, it aims to discuss the different stages of data development and use for seclusion and restraint reduction. The focus will be on data for comparison of services, regions or countries, rather than data development within individual organisations. Second, it aims to describe the status of data use in Australia and the data development challenges for three different areas of restrictive practices: (i) seclusion, (ii) physical and mechanical restraint and (iii) chemical restraint. The definitions of these terms are discussed in the next section and in the second half of this chapter.

Stages of data development and use

Developing data for health service indicators typically proceeds through several conceptual and technical stages (Figure 9.1). This section focuses particularly on the first three, because they are the foundation for data reporting and use.

Stage 1: Defining the construct

Measurement must start with a clear underlying construct. Most restrictive practices are defined by the specific action involved. Seclusion is typically defined by the act of confinement of a person alone in a room or area from which free exit

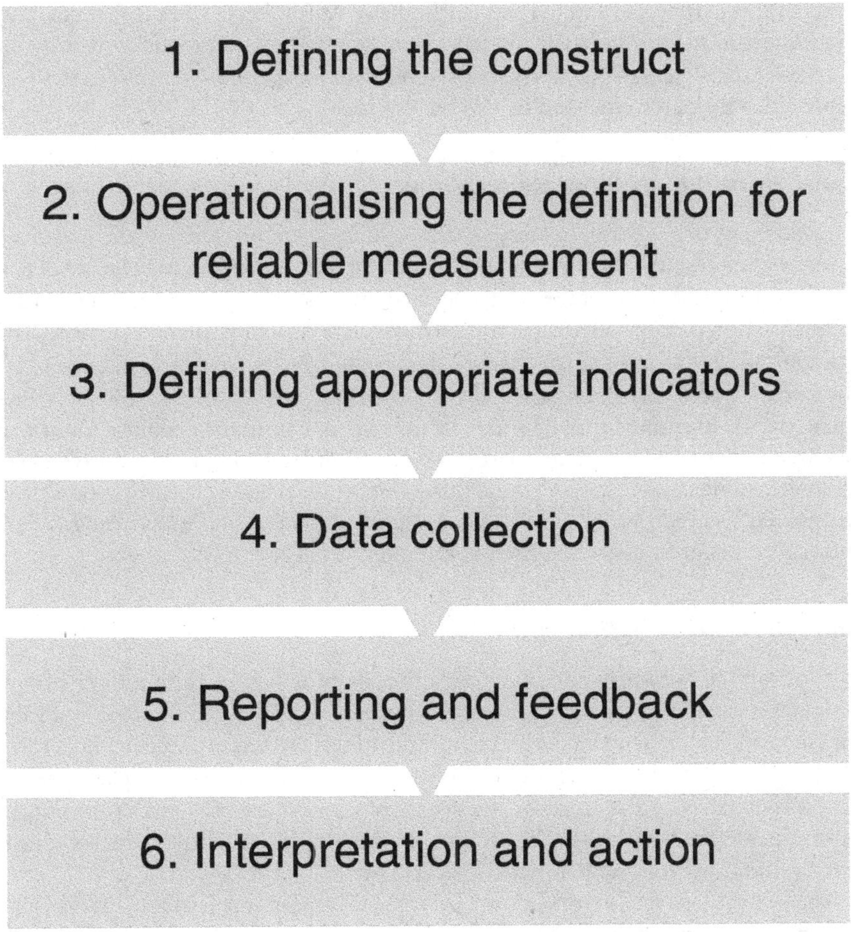

Figure 9.1 Stages of data development, collection and reporting

is prevented (see, for example, *Mental Health Act 2013* (Tas): section 3(1)). The experience of the person in seclusion does not form part of the definition. If people are confined and not free to leave at their request, this is seclusion even if they have requested to be confined or are not aware of their situation (for example if they are sleeping).

Some definitions include the additional element of the purpose or intent of the health service or practitioner. This is particularly common in definitions of chemical restraint, which is often defined to mean 'medication given *primarily to control a person's behaviour, not to treat a mental illness or physical condition*' (*Mental Health Act 2013* (Tas): section 3(1); emphasis added). The challenge that this poses in defining chemical restraint will be discussed further in the second half of this chapter.

Individual experiences of coercion are central to efforts to reduce restrictive practices, but they are rarely used as the basis for defining these practices. Lisa Waddington in Chapter 7 in this volume describes an exception to this in the Netherlands, where some forms of coercive practices are not required to be reported if they are requested by the service user.

Stage 2: Operationalising the definition

Measurement of behaviour in health systems always encounters grey zones and 'edge cases' at the boundary of the definition. Therefore, the conceptual (Stage 1) definition needs to be supplemented with a detailed operational definition which identifies frequent or predictable edge cases and provides clear counting rules for services. This is important in maximising the validity of any data (the extent to which it measures the intended concept) and its reliability (the extent to which it is free from measurement error). It ensures that different services apply consistent definitions and that services do not appear to differ merely because of different inclusions or exclusions. Examples of these edge cases include the counting of seclusion occurring outside of designated seclusion rooms, or the counting of physical restraint occurring during medical procedures. These are discussed in more detail later in the chapter.

Stage 3: Defining indicators

Operational definitions aim to ensure an accurate count of the number of episodes of seclusion or restraint. A simple count of episodes can be used as a valid measure of change in an individual unit or hospital (Azeem et al. 2011; Borckardt et al. 2011). However, a count of episodes cannot be used to compare services unless they have similar scale, or the events of interest are very rare (for example in sentinel event reporting). Therefore, it is necessary to convert these counts into an indicator for comparative measurement.

There are three main types of indicator for seclusion and restraint (Table 9.1): (i) incident or episode rate indicators, such as *seclusion episodes per 1,000 bed days*; (ii) duration-based indicators, such as *average duration of restraint*; and (iii) person-based indicators, such as *per cent of consumers experiencing at least one seclusion episode.*

No single indicator can measure all important aspects of seclusion or restraint. All involve trade-offs on issues such as ease of construction, ease of communication, extent to which they are influenced by differences in service organisation or consumer characteristics and vulnerability to influence by outliers. Therefore, more than one indicator is typically needed, providing complementary views of different aspects of practice. The choice of indicator should be specific and relevant to the purpose and the type of services being compared.

Stage 4: Data collection

Comparison of services requires accurate data collection at two levels. First, data about incidents or events must be recorded by the treating clinicians. In many

Table 9.1 Common key performance indicators for seclusion or restraint

Indicator	*Advantages*	*Disadvantages*	*Examples of use*
Incident or episode rate indicators			
Episodes per bed day	Ease and reliability of calculation Can include people still in hospital Can compare units with different length of stay	Difficult to communicate because denominator is not intuitive	Australian Key Performance Indicators set – episodes per 1,000 bed days (National Mental Health Performance Subcommittee 2013) Some service evaluations (Borckardt et al. 2011)
Episodes per hospital separation	Ease and reliability of calculation	Highly influenced by length of stay differences Capturing people whose episode of care has not yet ended	International Initiative for Mental Health Leadership (2019) Benchmarking
Episodes per capita	Allows comparison between diverse systems and countries	Influenced by differences in service organisation (e.g. beds per capita) Difficult to define populations for smaller services	International Initiative for Mental Health Leadership (2019) Benchmarking
Incidents or episodes per shift	Intuitive as a measure of change within a hospital	Influenced by size of ward, less effective as a measure of relative performance between hospitals	Safewards evaluation (Bowers et al. 2015)
Duration-based indicators			
Average duration of episodes	Ease and reliability of calculation Intuitive, easily communicated	Independent of changes in rate Highly influenced by outliers May be difficult to compare different types of practice where durations differ widely, for example, seclusion typically hours, restraint typically minutes Interpretation: for example, are many short episodes preferable to fewer long episodes?	Australian Key Performance Indicators set – average seclusion duration (National Mental Health Performance Subcommittee 2013)

(*Continued*)

Table 9.1 (Continued)

Indicator	*Advantages*	*Disadvantages*	*Examples of use*
Cumulative duration per bed day		Difficult to communicate because denominator is not intuitive	New York State (Seclusion hours per 1,000 bed days) (Sullivan et al. 2005)
Proportion of episodes longer than threshold (e.g. four hours)		May encourage more frequent but shorter episodes	
Time since last event	Intuitive as a measure of change within a unit Analogy with safety/ incident measurement in other industries	Not easily aggregated for larger scale reporting	
Person-based indicators			
Per cent of people experiencing at least one episode	Intuitive, easily communicated: conveys absolute as well as relative performance	Important to clarify whether this measures likelihood of experiencing seclusion in a single hospital episode or over a longer period (e.g. a year) involving multiple admissions Complex to calculate and allocate service responsibility over multiple episodes	Australian Key Performance Indicators set (National Mental Health Performance Subcommittee 2013)
Per cent of people experiencing multiple episodes		Insensitive in changes to base seclusion rate	Australian Council on Healthcare Standards (2019) seclusion indicators (denominator is people with at least one seclusion episode)
Per cent of people experiencing lengthy episodes		Insensitive in changes to base seclusion rate	Australian Council on Healthcare Standards (2019) seclusion indicators (denominator is people with at least one seclusion episode)

health settings these are recorded in paper or electronic registers, distinct from the clinical record. This facilitates data collation and audit, but may cause collection burden and duplication of recording. For example, some services require recording of seclusion events both in a paper register and in an electronic incident management system. Perverse incentives may be created if under-recording of incidents leads to apparently improved performance. As an alternative some Australian sites have considered using procedure codes in the medical record to identify seclusion events. However, this could be seen as legitimising seclusion or restraint as a therapeutic procedure. Ideally data collection should occur as an integrated part of clinical documentation, supporting clinical care and review. The implementation of electronic medical records in mental health services provides an important opportunity for better integrated data collection.

Second, data from individual services must be collated for comparative analysis. The more detailed the data which are pooled, the more powerful the potential analysis. If data includes details of individual episodes of seclusion or restraint, as well as information about the person and the broader episode of care, then it becomes possible to identify subgroups or time periods of greatest risk and to develop risk-adjusted comparisons of services. However, this requires both technical capacity and an appropriate framework for information-sharing and privacy. Waddington in Chapter 7 in this volume describes the development of the Argus register in the Netherlands, and the challenges posed by data protection legislation there. A single national register is not essential for national comparison. In Australia, each state and territory collates data from their services, based on local technical capacity and legislation. All these jurisdictions then pool aggregated data for individual hospitals and population groups, according to an agreed national standard (Australian Institute of Health and Welfare (AIHW) 2015).

Stage 5: Feedback and reporting

Data feedback is essential for reform and many health systems include indicators of seclusion and restraint in regular service reporting. These typically include one or more of the rate-based indicators discussed previously, aggregated by a regional provider (such as a Trust, District Health Board, or Local Health District) or individual hospital. Australian mental health services increasingly make seclusion and some forms of restraint data publicly available. National comparative data is now published comparing annual seclusion and restraint rates for all Australian public hospitals with designated mental health units (AIHW 2019).

International comparison is challenging because of significant differences in legislation, definitions and service system organisation. Several research studies have compared seclusion rates within European countries and found significant variation (Steinert et al. 2014; Noorthoorn et al. 2015). Ongoing comparative benchmarking activities facilitated by the International Initiative for Mental Health Leadership (IIMHL) are examining seclusion rates. However to date, only a handful of countries have been able to provide comparative data on these indicators (NHS Benchmarking Unit 2018).

Stage 6: Interpretation and action

Two important tensions may influence stakeholders' engagement with data. First, there may be a tension between quality improvement and performance approaches to reporting. A quality improvement focus often requires detailed review of individual incidents (Te Pou o Te Whakaaro Nui 2014), internal reporting, critical enquiry, acceptance of data imprecision and detailed peer group comparison. In the Australian context reporting on seclusion and restraint has increasingly moved to a performance framework, with specific targets and broader health system and public reporting. This is important for reform and public trust, but involves less tolerance for data error and may lead to more adversarial interactions and less space for critical reflection.

Second, there may be tension between public and clinical approaches to data quality issues. Seclusion and restraint data is collected manually by clinicians in complex, emergency situations. It will always include some errors, including variation due to differences in interpretation regarding edge cases. Consumers may prefer to err towards more inclusive reporting, and be skeptical if health services seek to exclude some potential episodes in order to improve data quality. However, clinicians may become disengaged if indicators are seen as providing inflated rates or unfair comparisons.

Action on seclusion and restraint data therefore needs to be supported by a broader framework of data literacy, reflective use of data, shared enquiry and openness to data improvement.

Measurement issues for different types of restrictive practice

The collection and use of data in Australia's mental health services is at different stages of development for different aspects of restrictive practice. There are well-developed processes for defining, collecting and reporting seclusion indicators. Physical and mechanical restraint data collections are in earlier stages of reporting, interpretation and action. However, the measurement of chemical restraint remains limited by the challenge of developing an operationally measurable definition. The following section discusses each of these issues in more detail.

Seclusion

There is broad consistency in defining seclusion in Australian state and territory mental health legislation and policy (Royal Australian and New Zealand College of Psychiatrists (RANZCP) 2017, 2018). Some 'edge cases' may arise, particularly when a person is alone in a larger multi-room space. This may occur as an intentional act by services, but may also occur inadvertently and without an intention to seclude an individual, for example a person who is temporarily the only occupant of an acute care area within a unit. Dutch definitions partly address these issues by distinguishing between 'seclusion' and 'isolation' (see Waddington in Chapter 7 in this volume). An emerging area that requires clearer operational definition is the practice of seclusion of mental health consumers in emergency departments.

Australian mental health services have adopted a consistent set of three key seclusion indicators: seclusion rate (episodes per 1,000 occupied bed days), seclusion duration (average episode duration in hours) and seclusion likelihood (proportion of people with at least one episode of seclusion). These are defined in national Key Performance Indicator specifications (National Mental Health Performance Subcommittee 2013).

Australian states and territories have a wide range of local data collection processes. However, since 2011 all have cooperated in an annual data submission for comparative reporting (Allan et al. 2017), using an agreed national data specification (AIHW 2015). This has allowed consistent national public reporting on Key Performance Indicators (KPIs), including (since 2018) reporting at an individual named hospital level (AIHW 2019). All states and territories also provide more frequent or detailed reporting to their respective health services. Many state governments make annual or quarterly data for individual hospitals publicly available (Ministry of Health (NSW) 2018; Queensland Health 2018; Bureau of Health Information (Qld) 2019; Victorian Agency for Health Information 2020), and this has been used to develop other reports focused on local consumer needs (Victorian Mental Illness Awareness Council (VMIAC) 2019).

These reporting processes have been one component of broad policy action aimed at reducing seclusion in Australian mental health services. These actions have included the adoption of national and state/territory seclusion reduction policies and targets to support reduction, the funding of a national 'Beacon Project' to build sector capacity and the publication of position statements by professional and consumer bodies (Melbourne Social Equity Institute 2014; Allan et al. 2017). In the ten years from 2008/09 to 2017/18, Australia's seclusion rate fell by 56 per cent, from 15.6 to 6.9 episodes per 1,000 bed days. Since 2013/14, when additional indicators were first reported, the likelihood of a person being secluded during a hospital stay has declined by 30 per cent (from 5.4 to 3.8 per 100 hospital episodes), and there has been a 15 per cent reduction in the average duration of seclusion episodes (AIHW 2019).

These are encouraging changes, but ongoing data and reporting are essential in maintaining change efforts. Using data to inform practice is one of six 'core strategies' for reducing seclusion and restraint use influentially proposed by the National Technical Assistance Center for State Mental Health Planning in the United States (see McSherry and Maker in Chapter 1 in this volume). Reporting of data encourages comparative benchmarking as well as signalling organisational commitment to change (Scanlan 2010). Australia has adopted consistent national data standards and recently introduced national seclusion reporting at the named hospital level. The data highlights substantial variation between sites. In 2017/18 seclusion rates for individual Australian hospitals ranged from 0 to 69 episodes per 1,000 bed days. Further work is needed to better define seclusion measures and targets for specific populations and settings, such as emergency departments and forensic mental health services. Work is also needed to ensure reliable data collection in routine practice: seclusion data is likely to be more reliable when collected from integrated electronic records (van de Sande et al. 2011), but Australian hospitals continue to collect seclusion data using a variety of paper and electronic systems.

Physical and mechanical restraint

Australia's data development for physical and mechanical restraint has followed a similar pathway to that for seclusion, but has commenced more recently and is therefore at an earlier stage. State and territory legislation and policies adopt broadly consistent definitions, such as that of the Australian Capital Territory, which defines restraint as 'the interference with, or restriction of, an individual's freedom of movement' (Australian Capital Territory Government 2016: 17). There are subtle differences in whether definitions imply an element of intent to restrict movement. For example Western Australian, Queensland and Northern Territory definitions refer to the application of force in order to restrict a person's movement (RANZCP 2018), but broadly the action or impact alone is sufficient. Most definitions distinguish between direct physical contact between staff and consumer (called 'bodily' restraint in Victoria and 'physical' restraint elsewhere) and the use of devices ('mechanical' restraint) (see McSherry and Maker in Chapter 1 in this volume for a discussion of jurisdictional differences in definitions).

Developing clear operational definitions and counting rules is more challenging for physical and mechanical restraint than for seclusion because restraint episodes are often brief and do not always have a clear boundary with other common behaviours and practices. This makes edge cases more numerous, and leads to variation in data collection and interpretation between services. Common edge cases in restraint measurement include (i) the use of tray tables, bed/cot-sides and other physical aids in Older Adult units; (ii) the use of physical restraint for medical procedures such as collection of blood samples; (iii) brief physical restraint to complete activities of daily living such as showering in persons with significant cognitive impairment or confusion; (iv) removing or limiting access to mobility aids; and (v) brief physical contact to redirect a person who is confused or disorientated.

The approach to these issues most consistent with the conceptual definition is to focus on the effect (whether a person's freedom of movement is restricted) and to consider tests such as whether the contact or restriction would be immediately ceased if requested by the consumer. However, some services have defined local counting rules for these issues by invoking clinician intent (for example, in the case of necessary medical procedures), or proposing time thresholds beyond which contact becomes restraint. These issues are likely to contribute to some unreliability in collection and comparison of services.

Key Performance Indicators can be specified for restraint using the same approaches as for seclusion. Restraint collection is included in Australia's national seclusion and restraint dataset specification (AIHW 2015). National reporting is currently available for three years to 2017/18 (AIHW 2019), however physical restraint data is not reported by all states. Physical restraint is around 20 times more common (10.3 episodes per 1,000 bed days in 2017/18) than mechanical restraint (0.5 episodes per 1,000 bed days). There is wide variation between states: average rates of mechanical restraint ranged from 0 to 1.4 episodes per 1,000 bed days and physical restraint from 2.5 to 22.0 episodes per 1,000 bed days (AIHW 2019). It is not yet known whether this variation is due to differences in counting and reporting, differences in practice or a combination of both. This underlines the developmental and iterative nature of reporting.

Chemical restraint

In mental health inpatient care, many consumers experience the use of medication as traumatic and intrusive. The term 'chemical restraint' is widely used to reflect this experience. A typical definition of chemical restraint is provided by the National Mental Health Consumer and Carer Forum (2009: 6):

> Chemical restraint occurs when medication that is sedative in effect is prescribed and dispensed to control the person's behaviour rather than provide treatment. Chemical restraint is unacceptable as a form of involuntary restraint in any circumstance.

Similar definitions exist in mental health policy or legislation in several Australian states and territories, often based on definitions used in aged care or disability sectors. All assume that it is possible to separate medication given as a treatment from medication given for the purpose of control or restriction of the individual. For example, section 3(1) of the Tasmanian *Mental Health Act 2013* defines chemical restraint as 'medication given primarily to control a person's behaviour, not to treat a mental illness or physical condition'.

The distinction between treatment and control in the intended use of medication has face validity. In policy and in law, the nature of an action is often defined by reference to the intention of the actor. However, these definitions are extremely difficult to operationalise in mental health care because the same medications may be used for both treatment and control. How can the intention of a clinician be assessed in a way that allows for reliable classification and counting of individual episodes of chemical restraint? This can only be done in one of two ways: (i) directly by asking clinicians to identify their purpose, or (ii) indirectly by using an objectively measurable aspect of the medication administration to infer the purpose.

Directly asking clinicians to identify their intentions is unlikely to produce valid or reliable data, for many reasons. First, the intentions of an individual clinician may be mixed. Many psychotropic medications are chosen for a dual purpose. For example, antipsychotic medications such as olanzapine and quetiapine are often used in acute hospital settings to treat psychosis and to provide short-term calming or sedating effects. The clinician may be unable to provide a simple binary treatment-or-control response. Second, the clinician is likely to err towards classifying episodes as treatment, because clinicians would rarely acknowledge behavioural control as their sole purpose in medication use. Third, the administration of medication typically requires action by multiple clinicians, who may have different intentions. When an individual has been administered 'PRN' (pro re nata – as needed) antipsychotic medication, *whose* intent should be assessed: the supervising psychiatrist, the junior medical officer who prescribed it, the senior clinical nurse who initiated it, the junior nurse who administered it, or a combination of these practitioners? (See Bartlett and Sampson in Chapter 3 and Breen in Chapter 13 in this volume for further discussion of psychotropic medication use and its characterisation.)

Therefore, operational definitions need to rely on indirect approaches. This is the approach taken in the aged care and disability sectors. In those sectors, chemical restraint is typically operationalised as the use of any antipsychotic medication, because those medications are not primarily treatments for intellectual disability or conditions of ageing (Department of Communities, Disability Services and Seniors (Qld) 2019; Department of Family and Community Services (NSW) 2019). The action (prescription of a specific class of drug) is taken as a sufficient measure of the purpose (behaviour control). However, this approach cannot be used in mental health settings because of the dual action of psychotropic drugs. A narrower version of the approach could be to define chemical restraint by referring to the use of specific psychotropic medications for people without indicated mental health diagnoses, such as the use of antipsychotics in people without a diagnosis of psychosis. However, this would exclude from measurement many episodes which are of central concern to consumers, such as the forced use of injectable antipsychotic medications in people with psychosis.

An alternative approach is to focus on specific forms or types of medication administration. For example, the Australian Capital Territory's *Mental Health Act 2015* does not use the term chemical restraint, and instead refers to forcible giving of medication, defined as 'the force and assistance that is necessary and reasonable to give medication' (sections 65(4)(b), 73(4)(b), 88(4)(b), 107(4)(b) and 114(4)(b)). New South Wales has developed a preliminary method of counting the use of Acute Injectable Medication, that is, the use of short acting intravenous or intramuscular antipsychotic or sedative medications. This could potentially be derived using data from hospital pharmacy or electronic prescribing systems. A national pilot study is testing the feasibility of this approach for broader national comparison (Sara et al. 2017).

A final alternative which has not been considered in detail is to ask the service user to identify the purpose for which the medication was given. This approach is inconsistent with that taken for other restrictive practices and with the conceptual definition of chemical restraint. There is likely to be frequent disagreement between the perception of clinicians as to their intentions and the experiences of service users. A preferable approach would be to see the experience of the service user as an essential but separate domain, measured and reported through systematic experience surveys.

The measurement and reporting of chemical restraint in Australia has not been able to move past the stage of operational definition. Pilot work looking at Acute Injectable Medication has developed possible methods for conversion and comparison of medication doses and construction of indicators. These show substantial variation between services and appear to correlate with other measures of restrictive practice. However further work is needed. The current method relies on a crude measure of medication supply. The widespread implementation of electronic medication prescribing and dispensing systems will allow the development of more robust methods.

Summary and conclusions

Data is necessary for health system reform but collecting data alone is insufficient. The process of data and indicator development needs to start with clear conceptual and operational definitions. Australian mental health services have reasonably mature measures of seclusion and partly developed measures of physical and mechanical restraint. However, the lack of a usable operational definition has limited data development on chemical restraint.

No single measure can capture all important aspects of seclusion or restraint. To support reform there is a need for multiple complementary measures which are as reliable as possible. These should be reinforced by a broader framework of data literacy and sharing. Ideally this would support a culture of reflective use of data, shared enquiry and openness to data improvement.

References

Allan, J.A., Hanson, G.D., Schroder, N.L., O'Mahony, A.J., Foster, R.M.P. and Sara, G.E. (2017) 'Six Years of National Mental Health Seclusion Data: The Australian Experience', *Australasian Psychiatry*, 25(3): 277–81.

Australian Capital Territory Government (2016) *Restraint of a Person–Policy.* Available www.health.act.gov.au/sites/default/files/2020-02/Restraint%20of%20a%20Person.doc (accessed 20 June 2020).

Australian Council on Healthcare Standards (2019) *Australasian Clinical Indicator Report – 20th Edition 2011–2018.* Available www.achs.org.au/media/169305/acir_2019_-_final_-_compressed.pdf (accessed 20 June 2020).

Australian Institute of Health and Welfare (AIHW) (2015) *Mental Health Seclusion and Restraint National Best Endeavours Dataset 2015.* Available https://meteor.aihw.gov.au/content/index.phtml/itemId/558137 (accessed 20 June 2020).

Australian Institute of Health and Welfare (AIHW) (2019) *Restrictive Practices–Mental Health Services in Australia 2018.* Available www.aihw.gov.au/reports/mental-health-services/mental-health-services-in-australia/report-contents/restrictive-practices (accessed 20 June 2020).

Azeem, M.W., Aujla, A., Rammerth, M., Binsfeld, G. and Jones, R.B. (2011) 'Effectiveness of Six Core Strategies Based on Trauma Informed Care in Reducing Seclusions and Restraints at a Child and Adolescent Psychiatric Hospital', *Journal of Child and Adolescent Psychiatry Nursing*, 24(1): 11–15.

Borckardt, J.J., Madan, A., Grubaugh, A.L., Danielson, C.K., Pelic, C.G., Hardesty, S.J., Hanson, R., Herbert, J., Cooney, H., Benson, A. and Frueh, B.C. (2011) 'Systematic Investigation of Initiatives to Reduce Seclusion and Restraint in a State Psychiatric Hospital', *Psychiatric Services*, 62(5): 477–83.

Bowers, L., James, K., Quirk, A., Simpson, A., Stewart, D. and Hodsoll, J. (2015) 'Reducing Conflict and Containment Rates on Acute Psychiatric Wards: The Safewards Cluster Randomised Controlled Trial', *International Journal of Nursing Studies*, 52(9): 1412–22.

Bureau of Health Information (NSW) (2019) *Reporting on Seclusion and Restraint in NSW Public Hospitals.* Available www.bhi.nsw.gov.au/__data/assets/pdf_file/0006/507669/BHI_MM_Seclusion_and_restraint.pdf (accessed 20 June 2020).

Department of Communities, Disability Services and Seniors (Qld) (2019) *Chemical Restraint Information Sheet.* Available www.communities.qld.gov.au/resources/dcdss/disability/service-providers/centre-excellence/chemical-restraint.pdf (accessed 20 June 2020).

Department of Family and Community Services (NSW) (2019) *Restrictive Practices Guidance–Chemical Restraint.* Available www.facs.nsw.gov.au/__data/assets/pdf_file/0009/636948/Restrictive-Practices-Resources-chemical-restraint-guidance.pdf (accessed 20 June 2020).

Gooding, P., McSherry, B., Roper, C. and Grey, F. (2018) *Alternatives to Coercion in Mental Health Settings: A Literature Review*, Melbourne: Melbourne Social Equity Institute, University of Melbourne. Available https://socialequity.unimelb.edu.au/news/latest/alternatives-to-coercion (accessed 20 June 2020).

Huckshorn, K. A. (2004) 'Reducing Seclusion Restraint in Mental Health Use Settings: Core Strategies for Prevention', *Journal of Psychosocial Nursing and Mental Health Services*, 42(9): 22–33.

International Initiative for Mental Health Leadership (2019) *Annual Report – 1 January to 31 December 2019.* Available www.iimhl.com/files/docs/2019_Annual_Report.pdf (accessed 20 June 2020).

Janssen, W.A., van de Sande, R., Noorthoorn, E.O., Nijman, H.L., Bowers, L., Mulder, C.L., Smit, A., Widdershoven, G.A. and Steinert, T. (2011) 'Methodological Issues in Monitoring the Use of Coercive Measures', *International Journal of Law and Psychiatry*, 34(6): 429–38.

Melbourne Social Equity Institute (2014) *Seclusion and Restraint Project: Report.* Available https://socialequity.unimelb.edu.au/__data/assets/pdf_file/0017/2004722/Seclusion-and-Restraint-report.PDF (accessed 20 June 2020).

Mental Health Act 2013 (Tas).

Ministry of Health (NSW) (2018) *NSW Health Annual Report 2017–2018: Appendix.* Available www.health.nsw.gov.au/annualreport/Publications/2018/appendix.pdf (accessed 20 June 2020).

National Association of State Mental Health Program Directors (2008) *Six Core Strategies to Reduce Seclusion and Restraint Use.* Available www.nasmhpd.org/content/six-core-strategies-reduce-seclusion-and-restraint-use (accessed 20 June 2020).

National Mental Health Consumer and Carer Forum (2009) *Ending Seclusion and Restraint in Australian Mental Health Services.* Available https://nmhccf.org.au/sites/default/files/docs/seclusion_restraint.pdf (accessed 20 June 2020).

National Mental Health Performance Subcommittee (2013) *Key Performance Indicators for Australian Public Mental Health Services*, 3rd edn. Available www.aihw.

gov.au/getmedia/f9bb1a07-a43b-458a-9b73-64ef19d8aedd/Key-Performance-Indicators-for-Australian-Public-Mental-Health-Services-Third-Edition.pdf.aspx (accessed 20 June 2020).

National Technical Assistance Center for State Mental Health Planning (2005) *Six Core Strategies to Reduce the Use of Seclusion and Restraint Planning Tool*, Alexandria, VA: National Association of State Mental Health Program Directors.

NHS Benchmarking Unit (2018) *International Mental Health Comparisons–Adult and Older Adult Services*. Available https://s3.eu-west-2.amazonaws.com/nhsbn-static/Other/2018/International%20MH%20Report%202018.pdf (accessed 20 June 2020).

Noorthoorn, E., Lepping, P., Janssen, W., Hoogendoorn, A., Nijman, H., Widdershoven, G. and Steinert, T. (2015) 'One-Year Incidence and Prevalence of Seclusion: Dutch Findings in an International Perspective', *Social Psychiatry and Psychiatric Epidemiology*, 50(12): 1857–69.

Queensland Health (2018) *Chief Psychiatrist Annual Report 2017–2018*. Available www.health.qld.gov.au/__data/assets/pdf_file/0042/729969/CP-Annual-Report-2017-2018_FINAL.pdf (accessed 20 June 2020).

Royal Australian and New Zealand College of Psychiatrists (RANZCP) (2017) *Powers and Duties of Psychiatrists in Australian and New Zealand Mental Health Acts: A Literature Review*. Available www.ranzcp.org/files/resources/college_statements/mental-health-legislation-tables/powers-and-duties-of-psychiatrists-in-australian-a.aspx (accessed 20 June 2020).

Royal Australian and New Zealand College of Psychiatrists (RANZCP) (2018) *Mental Health Legislation–Australia and New Zealand*. Available www.ranzcp.org/publications/Guidelines-and-resources-for-practice/Mental-health-legislation-Australia-and-New-Zealan (accessed 20 June 2020).

Sara, G., Hanson, G.D., McCaul, D., Schelling, K., Young, A. and Allan, J.A. (2017) 'Acute Injectable Medication: Can We Develop a Method for National Comparison?', *Towards Elimination of Restrictive Practice 11th National Forum*, 4–5 May, Perth, Western Australia.

Scanlan, J.N. (2010) 'Interventions to Reduce the Use of Seclusion and Restraint in Inpatient Psychiatric Settings: What We Know So Far a Review of the Literature', *International Journal of Social Psychiatry*, 56(4): 412–23.

Steinert, T., Noorthoorn, E.O. and Mulder, C.L. (2014) 'The Use of Coercive Interventions in Mental Health Care in Germany and the Netherlands: A Comparison of the Developments in Two Neighboring Countries', *Frontiers in Public Health*, 2: 141.

Sullivan, A., Bezmen, J., Barron, C., Rivera, J., Curley-Casey, L. and Marino, D. (2005) 'Reducing Restraints: Alternatives to Restraints on an Inpatient Psychiatric Service–Utilizing Safe and Effective Methods to Evaluate and Treat the Violent Patient', *Psychiatric Quarterly*, 76(1): 51–65.

Te Pou o Te Whakaaro Nui (2014) *Debriefing Following Seclusion and Restraint: A Summary of Relevant Literature*. Available www.tepou.co.nz/uploads/files/resource-assets/debriefing-following-seclusion-and-restraint-281014.pdf (accessed 20 June 2020).

van de Sande, R., Nijman, H.L., Noorthoorn, E.O., Wierdsma, A.I., Hellendoorn, E., van der Staak, C. and Mulder, C.L. (2011) 'Aggression and Seclusion on Acute Psychiatric Wards: Effects of Short-term Risk Assessment', *British Journal of Psychiatry*, 199(6): 473–78.

Victorian Agency for Health Information (2020) *Adult Mental Health Services–Rate of Seclusion Episodes for Adult Mental Health Services, per 1,000 Bed Days.* Available https://vahi.vic.gov.au/mental-health/adult-mental-health-services (accessed 20 June 2020).

Victorian Mental Illness Awareness Council (2019) *Seclusion Report: How Safe Is My Hospital?* Available www.vmiac.org.au/seclusion-report-how-safe-is-my-hospital/ (accessed 20 June 2020).

10 The Court, the law and German psychiatry's slow progress towards human rights

Margret Osterfeld and Martin Zinkler

Introduction

The ratification of the United Nations (UN) *Convention on the Rights of Persons with Disabilities* (CRPD) by Germany in 2009 raised hopes among users of psychiatry and progressive professionals that German mental health care would move quickly towards less coercive treatment, but over ten years later there is still a long way to go (Steinert 2019: 45–46). The aim of the CRPD is to promote and protect the 'full and equal enjoyment of all human rights and fundamental freedoms . . . and to promote respect for their inherent dignity' for all citizens with severe impairments (CRPD: Article 1). All severe and chronic mental illnesses, such as dementia, addiction, schizophrenia and mood disorders fall within the inclusive definition of long-term 'mental impairments' set out in Article 1 of the CRPD. Although the CRPD does not differentiate between physical, sensory, intellectual and mental 'impairments', academic psychiatry in the Western world still perceives the CRPD as a threat to its traditional medical and biological approach to mental disorders or disabilities. This is demonstrated by a recent editorial in the journal of the World Psychiatric Association entitled 'Saving the UN CRPD – from itself' (Appelbaum 2019).

In 2011 – only two years after Germany's ratification of the CRPD – Germany's Federal Constitutional Court decided in the case 2 BvR 882/09 that there must be strict legal limitations on the use of coercive medication in forensic hospital care. This decision was based on a complaint against compulsory medical treatment lodged by a person committed to a psychiatric hospital. The Federal Constitutional Court does not serve as a regular appellate court on violations of federal laws from lower courts or the Federal Supreme Courts. Any person may raise a complaint that his or her constitutional rights have been violated by the state, especially by a court decision. The Federal Constitutional Court has the competence to set aside judgments or to refer the case back to the court to which it was originally allocated and to ask for clear and specific legal regulations.

Soon after the Constitutional Court's 2011 decision, the German Association for Psychiatry, Psychotherapy and Psychosomatic Medicine, known as the DGPPN, criticised the decision in an official statement. The DGPPN clearly asserted that psychiatry is unable to work with less coercion and interpreted the decision as meaning psychiatrists were stopped by the Constitutional Court from treating mental illness (Zinkler 2012: 62–63). For about five years, this statement was to be found on the webpage of the DGPPN and only a minority of German psychiatrists took a different view publicly (Osterfeld 2012; Zinkler 2012).

This situation made it seem impossible to re-think psychiatric theory and practice in German psychiatric hospital care at that time. The cognitive bias of clinicians, discussed by Nathan Gibson in Chapter 14 in this volume, appeared strong and the use of physical restraints like belts (known in other jurisdictions as mechanical restraints) increased in many German hospitals. In July 2018, a long overdue Federal Constitutional Court decision on the use of physical restraints was published (cases 2 BvR 309/15 and 2 BvR 502/16), finding that the use of physical restraints – in that case, five-point or seven-point restraints where all limbs and other parts of the body are strapped to a bed – for more than approximately 30 minutes constitutes a deprivation of liberty which requires judicial authorisation. While a less coercive approach may encourage the reduction of physical restraints in psychiatric hospital care, its implementation will need significant political support.

In this chapter, we place this 2018 court judgment in historical context and identify barriers and opportunities for implementing the decision and other human rights-compliant approaches to restraint across Germany. We first describe German mental health laws and the insurance-driven nature of psychiatric hospital care. We then discuss the role and limitations of state supervisory bodies in implementing legal changes, using the example of the state of North Rhine-Westphalia's state inspectorate, the Visiting Commission. We then turn to the meaning and implications of the 2018 Federal Constitutional Court decision and examine reasons for the legal and professional resistance to its implementation. We conclude by identifying the strategies necessary to introduce a CRPD-compliant approach in Germany, as well as discussing how the UN *Convention Against Torture and Other Cruel, Inhuman or Degrading Treatment or Punishment* and its *Optional Protocol* may be of additional assistance in reducing restraints.

From Prussian psychiatric law to the legal and economic basis of modern German mental health care

More than two centuries ago, in 1794, the first mental health law was introduced under the Prussian monarchy. It aimed to remove 'odd' citizens with strange behaviour from the streets and from public view. Large asylums were built all over the country. At the beginning of the twentieth century, psychiatric science, driven by ideas from social Darwinism, began to construct ideas about lives not worth living. For example, in 1920 Alfred Hoche, a professor of psychiatry, and Karl Binding, a professor of law, published a paper advocating the 'destruction of unworthy lives' (Binding and Hoche 1920). With direct support from the legal profession, these ideas grew fast and led to the humanitarian disaster of mass murder with involuntary euthanasia of persons with severe psychiatric diagnoses or mental disabilities during World War II.

The horrors of World War II led to the adoption of the *Universal Declaration of Human Rights* in 1948, and in 1949, only a few months later, the Federal Republic of Germany established a constitution (known as the *Basic Law*), which follows the same ideas and ideals. However, it took more than three decades after the war had ended for political attention to be drawn to persons with psychiatric diagnoses in institutional care. A process of reform confirmed the right of these persons to medical care on the same basis as persons with somatic diseases, instead of just custodial placement and housing. This reform led to significantly more funding for mental health care, but the support system remained hospital-centred.

A major change of legal norms occurred with the introduction of the *Legal Guardianship Law* in 1992. This law permits substitute decision-making, deprivations of liberty, coercive medication and restraints if a person with a psychiatric diagnosis is medically assessed to be a danger to himself or herself (also known as risk of self-harm) and lacks capacity to consent. The wording of the associated legal norm – any person who 'due to a mental (or somatic) disorder' is unable to 'declare a free will' (*Civil Law Code*: Article 1896) – raises the possibility that any chronic mental health condition could be considered a disorder that might necessitate substitute decision-making, thereby leading to discrimination on the basis of a psychiatric diagnosis.

Additionally, each of the 16 German states has a *Law on Support and Protective Measures for Persons with Mental Illnesses* called *Psychisch-Kranken-Gesetze*, abbreviated as 'PsychKG'. These laws permit detention, the use of restraints and coercive medication if an individual is confirmed by the police or his or her carers and a psychiatrist to be a danger to self or others. The name of the law is already discriminatory, as it pertains only to persons with a diagnosed or presumed mental illness. Historically, these laws belong to police legislation. In fact, any person who is regarded by the police as committing a public offence can be taken to hospital on the basis of these laws (Voellm et al. 2017).

In contrast to the United Kingdom's state-driven National Health Service (NHS), Germany's health care system is insurance-driven (see also Lisa Waddington's discussion of the Dutch system in Chapter 7 in this volume). All German citizens are required to have health care insurance. However, unlike in Britain, a widespread and well-developed psychiatric community care system, including outreach and treatment in the home paid by health insurance, does not yet exist in Germany. Instead Germany still has more psychiatric hospital beds than many other comparable countries (Eurostat 2020). Due to the murders and other cruelties inflicted on those with psychiatric conditions in the name of science during the Nazi era, coercive medication is only legally permitted in hospitals. Inpatient care in Germany is paid for on a per-day basis by insurance companies. Like general hospitals, psychiatric hospitals compete with each other and are required to be profitable. In many hospitals, minimising coercive measures is not a care quality goal and may even conflict with the goals of profit-driven hospital management, as the treatment and care of patients perceived to be a risk to themselves or others attract higher daily tariffs than standard inpatient treatment. The use of restraint during inpatient care is one of several criteria for the higher 'intensive care' tariff, which can be twice as high as the standard tariff (Horter et al. 2016).

The state inspectorate for psychiatry in the German state of North Rhine-Westphalia: Personal reflections on the role and limits of this body

An amendment to the PsychKG in the state of North Rhine-Westphalia in 1999 gave users of psychiatry and their family members the opportunity to become members of the state inspectorate for psychiatry, the so-called Visiting Commission. The Visiting Commission provides the statutory supervision of hospitals registered to detain and treat persons with psychiatric disorders, and it is the Commission's duty to visit more than 100 premises at least once a year. As a member of the Visiting Commission representing users of psychiatry for more than 15 years, the first author of this chapter frequently witnessed the willingness of psychiatric hospitals to implement the higher demands of newer legal norms. However, there were always some hospitals that circumvented new regulations, often at the expense of the patients and to the detriment of the protection of their basic human rights. For example, as a result of technological advances, but also politically driven pressure to economise and save on staff expenses, an increasing number of psychiatric hospitals in North Rhine-Westphalia resorted to using only video surveillance to monitor restrained patients. Thus, restraints turned into a measure that eased the staff's workload, offering a way of cutting personnel costs and increasing economic profit.

In the past 20 years the PsychKG of North Rhine-Westphalia, compared to mental health laws in other German states, has turned into one of the more progressive of these regional laws. At the end of 2011, an amendment of the law forbade video surveillance of restrained patients (PsychKG of North Rhine-Westphalia: section 20(3)); constant staff attendance is now required during the entire time a patient is held in restraint. However, even today, a number of hospitals still complain to the Visiting Commission about the fact that they are no longer allowed to use video surveillance. Even worse is the fact that these places continue to use video surveillance for involuntarily committed patients on the basis of guardianship law. The Visiting Commission is not and does not see itself as formally responsible for the legal supervision of this federal law. In practical terms, and contrary to the constitutional norm of Article 3 of the German Constitution regarding equality and non-discrimination, different standards of protection of civil and human rights are applied to patients in the same hospital depending on the legal grounds for detention. In a further example, the last amendment to the PsychKG of North Rhine-Westphalia, dated 1 January 2017, stipulates in paragraph 16(1): '[t]he hospital is obliged to facilitate a stay outside generally daily for at least one hour' (translation by authors). The state of North Rhine-Westphalia was the first to introduce this standard, which has long been an implicit right in detention under criminal law, into a legal norm for persons deprived of liberty for mental health reasons. But this has yet to be implemented for involuntary patients in psychiatric hospitals in North Rhine-Westphalia.

The Visiting Commission's main purpose is to control the conduct of hospitals, meaning it has the potential to play an important role in the implementation of the PsychKG and other protections of patients' human rights. In some cases, however, it is hesitant to deploy strict measures to protect these rights. Three negative, anonymised examples are given here from the first author's personal experience as a member of the Visiting Commission to illustrate how substandard practice can lead to poor outcomes and traumatisation as a consequence of physical restraints.

One patient diagnosed with 'borderline disorder' was hospitalised voluntarily but was made an involuntary patient on the legal basis of PsychKG of North Rhine-Westphalia after incidences of self-harm. She was restrained with belts on her body, arms and legs, and she complained to the Visiting Commission about this procedure. She reported extremely degrading treatment such as being bound to the bed with her legs and hips spread. There is not a small likelihood that she – as many persons diagnosed with borderline disorder – experienced sexual assault or other serious psychological traumatisation in her younger life (Linehan 1987) as this has been associated with self-harming behaviour in adult life. There is an inherent risk that physical restraint in such a case could lead to severe re-traumatisation. The facts that the patient was restrained in the same room as male patients and not constantly attended to by staff were also compelling reasons for her to complain, and she experienced these circumstances as particularly degrading. Even worse, by not providing constant nursing care, the hospital clearly violated applicable law. However, it was only after multiple visits by the Visiting Commission that an official hospital complaints procedure was put in motion.

From a psychiatric point of view, the alarming part of this story is the fact that, for a long time, the treatment team did not question whether these restraint procedures would improve the health situation of this young woman and never considered other, less drastic safety measures. There is no scientific evidence of restraints reducing self-harming behaviour. Whether and in what amount this woman deserves legal compensation and whether those responsible for restraining her are liable for prosecution for deprivation of liberty is a question for the courts.

Further obstacles may arise for those subjected to long hospitalisation and poor mental health, in terms of difficulties obtaining information about their legal options. Psychiatric hospital care in North Rhine-Westphalia still does not have a stringent procedure of informing patients about their rights in this regard, and a proper and independent complaints mechanism does not exist. This needs to be urgently addressed along with sufficient powers given to supervising bodies to respond to complaints. Lisa Waddington in Chapter 7 in this volume indicates how supervising bodies can apply a range of measures to address complaints.

Another patient who had previously been diagnosed with a severe mental health condition was hospitalised again under the PsychKG of North Rhine-Westphalia a few days before the visit of the State Inspectorate. The psychiatrist responsible for his care reported that the patient was now completely altered; he appeared confused and disoriented and a diagnosis of dementia was suspected. For this reason, the hospital staff began restraining him as soon as he entered other patients' rooms. This was not a safety measure for an acute danger towards himself or others but was essentially a 'pedagogical restraint' – the team was merely trying to change the person's undesirable behaviour with the harshest form of deprivation of liberty and without any up-to-date diagnostic clarity. According to law, restraint for therapeutic reasons like these is not permitted. The PsychKG of North Rhine-Westphalia (section 20) clearly states that restraint can only be used as '[s]pecial safety measures for avoidance of a present substantial danger of self-harm or a present substantial danger of particular rights of third parties' (translation by authors). Obliviousness to other patients' privacy is not a danger that legally or ethically justifies restraints.

Not uncommon is the practice of restraining a known patient immediately after hospital admission (and thereby under the German *Civil Law Code*) for the sole purpose of injecting them with a long-lasting antipsychotic drug. This is unauthorised forced medication and a covert form of forced community treatment, which is not permitted in Germany. In one such case identified by the Visiting Commission, the medical management on site gave the vague explanation that the patient had voluntarily accepted the injection. However, informed consent for an injection while being in full restraint appears rather implausible. The restrained patient knows there is no choice anymore.

The German Federal Constitutional Court's 2011 judgment on forced medication effected legal changes with a much higher threshold for coercive treatment. Psychiatrists mainly responded defensively, complaining that as a result of these legal changes they would have to use more frequent mechanical restraint measures to control their patients' behaviour (Zinkler 2012: 62–63). The examples just given also raise questions about whether the ruling had any positive effects on clinical practice. For legal developments to effect corresponding changes in clinical practice, supervising authorities with strong powers to address complaints are needed. Legal norms that fail to control their implementation are ineffective and undermine the credibility of the legal system. In a strong 2013 statement on coercive measures in psychiatry, the Central Committee for Observance of Ethical Principles in Medicine and its Adjacent Fields (ZEKO) of the German Medical Association identified the need for proportionality and legitimacy in the use of coercive measures and the need to develop alternative milder measures; it further admitted that confidence in the psychiatric health care system had been lost (ZEKO 2013).

The German Federal Constitutional Court's decision on the use of physical restraints in psychiatric care (July 2018)

This resistance to implementing the 2011 judgment meant a Federal Constitutional Court ruling on restraint was overdue. In the mid-2010s, two patients – one from the state of Bavaria and the other from Baden-Württemberg – made constitutional complaints that the respective mental health acts of the two states did not comply with the constitutional requirements regarding deprivation of liberty for the use of physical restraints in psychiatric hospitals. The complaints concerned the use of physical (known elsewhere as mechanical or bodily) restraints – strapping the persons concerned on their back to a hospital bed using a special type of belt to largely or completely restrict their ability to move. The additional legal question was whether authorisation for such deprivation of liberty was covered by coercive admission under the PsychKG or if a further judicial decision was needed as well as a doctor's order. The 2018 judgment of the Federal Constitutional Court stated:

> [64] The use of physical restraints on patients constitutes an interference with their fundamental right to freedom of the person (Art. 2(2) second sentence in conjunction with Art. 104 [of the *Basic Law*] . . .). Both five-point and seven-point restraint measures that go beyond mere short-term application constitute a deprivation of liberty within the meaning of Art. 104(2) [of the *Basic Law*] . . . . This also applies in cases where the persons concerned are already subject to a deprivation of liberty by way of confinement in a psychiatric hospital . . . .
>
> [68] . . . A short-term application can generally be presumed where it is foreseeable that the measure will not last longer than approximately half an hour . . . .
>
> [94] Art. 104(2) fourth sentence [of the *Basic Law*] . . . obliges the legislature to enact provisions that specify the requirement of a judicial decision in procedural terms . . . . In order to give consideration to the specific characteristics of the different contexts in which such measures are applied, the legislature must provide for a procedural regime that is tailored to the respective measure of deprivation of liberty.

This 2018 judgment referred to the need for constant supervision by nursing staff of patients in restraints and emphasised the need to carefully document the specific risks of a patient to be restrained (para 110). The Constitutional Court further held that justification and proportionality for all restraints must be documented in a transparent way.

Implementation of the new restraint ruling: A challenge for lawmakers, psychiatric staff and society as a whole

While the PsychKG of North Rhine-Westphalia now specifies 'safety measures to prevent current and significant self-harm or present significant threat to special legally protected rights of third parties' (section 20), other regional mental health laws are less precise and must still be amended to incorporate the Federal Constitutional Court's decision. German guardianship law does not yet have similar safeguards, so significant amendments are needed there as well. Whether and how this will help to reduce the frequency of physical restraint is discussed later.

Our own experience indicates that the Court's 2018 decision is also yet to be implemented at the state level. At present, particularly in cases of emergency admissions at night, patients are still restrained as soon as they are transferred from an ambulance stretcher to a hospital bed. Observations from the Visiting Commission in North Rhine-Westphalia suggest that the specific justification for restraint is not always transparent in the medical records; rather, the need for restraint is based on a particular diagnosis (for example, intoxication or psychosis).

The Bavarian complainant before the Federal Constitutional Court was brought to the hospital in an emotional state with a blood alcohol level of 2.68 per ml. The police had also recorded 'assumed suicidal tendencies'. This alone led to an automatic medical conclusion that the patient was dangerous and needed to be restrained for eight hours. He had no previous record of mental illness; there was no other reason, except for his condition of having drunk too much, for hospital treatment, and he was released from hospital 12 hours after being admitted. The hospital had simply taken on a security assignment from the police. The expenses for the person's 'disorderly behaviour' which led to this forcible confinement were shifted to the solidarity fund of the health insurance company. Psychiatric staff also shirked their own professional responsibility by not compiling an individual risk justification specific to this admitted person, but instead coming only to a generalised conclusion: 'Someone arriving in handcuffs must be dangerous'. Quite to the contrary, the authors of this chapter suggest that, in their experience, the majority of involuntarily committed people who are drunk peacefully sleep off their intoxication in hospital.

As we discuss in the next section, extra measures are likely to be needed to support the implementation of the Federal Constitutional Court's 2018 decision and other aspects of a human rights-compliant approach to restraint. The major players attempting to avoid such extra measures – and the expenses they incur – in psychiatric hospital care are the health insurance companies. The German Hospital Federation (DKG), is the federation of national and state associations of hospital owners and represents hospitals in the self-governance of health care. Just a few weeks after the 2018 restraint ruling, this body made several recommendations in its guidelines (DKG 2018) for addressing the Constitutional Court's judgment that might undermine the implementation of this decision.

The first recommendation was that video surveillance may be viewed as a milder measure, as long as this is not explicitly prohibited in the law of the relevant state (point 4 of the guidelines). In our view, this may lead to more video surveillance in many states of the Federal Republic of Germany. The second recommendation was that only five-point and seven-point restraints are dealt with in the Constitutional Court's decision (points 11 and 12 of the guidelines). While this is technically correct, it raises concerns that hospitals may be encouraged to use more three-point restraints or cage beds to avoid the judicial review of five-point restraints. The DKG's third recommendation was that the provision of information on the option for a legal review to the restrained person must be documented, but confirmation of the information by the patient is not needed. In our view, this is insufficient to ensure that restrained persons have access to their legal rights.

Such guidelines create the impression that this federal association does not wish to change its practices. Considering the reluctance within the psychiatric profession and the management teams of psychiatric hospitals to change clinical practice, we can only conclude that the fight for rights-based psychiatry in Germany will need significant patience and civil society engagement to be successful. Numerous civil society organisations representing persons with disabilities are helpful stakeholders for the implementation of the Federal Constitutional Court's decisions and other measures necessary to comply with the CRPD.

Milder measures and a change of traditions: What is needed

Further progress on human rights-compliant approaches will not be easy (see McSherry and Maker in Chapter 1 in this volume for a further discussion of human rights requirements in this regard). As in other parts of the world, mental health services in Germany reflect the prevailing biological model of mental illness combined with a defensive approach towards the disability rights agenda (for a detailed critique, see Weinmann 2019). Only a small number of university hospitals, such as The University Hospital of Hamburg-Eppendorf (Universitätsklinikum Hamburg-Eppendorf, UKE), carry out research on interventions to reduce the use of coercive medication, seclusion and restraint (see for example, Mahlke et al. 2017). Medical schools and teaching hospitals pay little attention to the problem of coercion in hospital settings. Doctors are legally responsible for coercive interventions (only they can authorise coercive measures, and now, after 30 minutes, a further authorisation needs to be granted by a court of law), but they do not know enough about these measures and their legal background.

Coercion is common in Germany's psychiatric hospitals. Between 3 and 17 per cent of inpatients experience one or more coercive interventions during their inpatient treatment (Flammer and Steinert 2018), involving mostly being tied with belts to a bedframe or, less frequently, seclusion (being locked inside a room) or coercive medication. Milder measures, like de-escalation, offering listening to music or going for a walk, withdrawing to a quiet room, taking a bath, one-to-one nursing care, having some food, or finding a place to smoke, are not used as frequently as they could be (Heumann, Bock and Lincoln 2017).

However, there have previously been successful efforts to reduce the use of restraint. For example, in the 1990s a decree by the management of a large hospital where the first author of this chapter worked meant that physical restraint had to be accompanied by a constant presence of nursing staff. If the doctor did not make sure this was adhered to, any unwanted consequences would be his or her personal responsibility. This rule provided an opportunity for nursing staff to enter into communication with the restrained patient, to provide assistance and comfort, but also to suggest options to end the coercive measure.

For an effective strategy to reduce coercion in mental health care institutions across Germany we suggest a number of core elements:

1 Establish a register of all coercive measures within an institution and its units, including the type of intervention, age group and diagnosis of the patient, reason for the intervention and duration;
2 Benchmark the register with other institutions in a similar domain, for example, other psychiatric hospitals or departments;
3 Eliminate restraint of elderly patients;
4 Eliminate restraint in cases of self-harm; and
5 Increase the staff-patient ratio to deal with incidents of violence.

The register of coercive interventions for all psychiatric hospitals and hospital departments in Baden-Württemberg was introduced through its regional mental health statute in 2015 and yields data on coercive interventions from 32 hospitals and hospital departments in the south-west of Germany (Flammer et al. 2018). While, overall, 6.7 per cent of inpatients experience coercive interventions during their hospital stay, the frequency of coercion in those institutions within a defined catchment area (and regional responsibility for emergency admissions) varies from 3 to 17 per cent. A breakdown of this data reveals that most institutions use coercion when treating elderly patients with dementia, people who self-harm, people with substance abuse disorders and those with psychosis. Some use coercion only in situations of severe violence for patients who are intoxicated or suffering from psychosis or both.

One of these hospitals with a defined catchment area (and regional responsibility for emergency admissions) has stopped using coercion on elderly patients and patients with self-harm or suicidal crises (Zinkler and Waibel 2019). Instead of coercion, patients receive one-to-one care. In dementia care, this consists of 'being with' the patient in their daily activities or in their nightly wanderings. For people who self-harm, it consists of individual psychotherapy, individual skills training or sports, but also 'being with' the patient when they are resting or consoling them during sleepless nights. Restraints are only used in situations of actual physical harm to others arising from a patient's behaviour (Zinkler and Waibel 2019).

This change has brought the rate of inpatients who undergo coercive interventions down to 2 per cent (obtained from routine hospital data via personal communication, Anonymous 2018). The hospital in question does not use seclusion and has almost completely stopped coercive medication with antipsychotics (only two cases in eight years). The situations in which coercive interventions are still used involve patients who become violent in intoxicated or psychotic states.

However, an in-depth analysis of all coercive interventions in the first six months of 2018 revealed that all of them could have been avoided with an increased staff-patient ratio (Zinkler and Waibel 2019). Currently, this hospital can arrange for one-to-one care involving not just nursing staff but all professions, including doctors and psychologists. Two-to-one or even three-to-one care (where two or three nurses, doctors, psychologists, social workers and/or occupational therapists spend time with one patient exclusively for a number of hours) cannot be arranged with the current level of staffing. The additional staff required to cover this extra care would amount to 5.4 WTE (whole-time-equivalents) or an increase of 4 per cent in the hospital budget. For the community as a whole, this would mean an extra cost of 2.65 euros per municipal resident each year.

Thus, inpatient care without physical (mechanical) or chemical restraint and without seclusion appears a realistic goal and could conceivably be achieved with moderately increased staffing levels. This would also not involve any changes in Germany's mental health law but would empower those working in the system to strive for human rights-based mental health care.

Summary and outlook

As a highly developed nation priding itself on its constitution and respect for the rule of law, Germany has reformed its mental health care in terms of accessibility and availability of community services. However, in terms of human rights, Germany's mental health care system remains something of a darkroom (Prantl 2018). Decisions by its Federal Constitutional Court have spurred legislative reform, yet the implementation appears patchy and incomplete.

Substitute decision-making remains common in guardianship proceedings and coercive interventions are still stubbornly frequent across regions and institutions. Reform projects to move towards coercion-free service provision exist, but without rigorous evaluation and political or professional support. User organisations advocate for CRPD-compliant service provision (for example Berlin Manifesto 2019), while professional organisations and hospital management teams remain sceptical about the scope for rights-based mental health care and support the status quo.

The CRPD is not the only United Nations treaty which has been viewed as calling for rights-based psychiatry. Another core treaty is the 1984 *Convention against Torture and Other Cruel, Inhuman or Degrading Treatment or Punishment*. In 2006, the *Optional Protocol to the Convention against Torture and other Cruel, Inhuman or Degrading Treatment or Punishment* (the Optional Protocol) came into force and was ratified by Germany at the same time as the CRPD. The Optional Protocol establishes a new kind of treaty body with a preventive mandate focused on an innovative, sustained and proactive approach to the prevention of torture and ill treatment, the Subcommittee on Prevention of Torture or Degrading Treatment or Punishment (Article 2). The Optional Protocol is not well known globally in the medical and caring professions, even though its requirements have been in place for over ten years. Ratifying states are obliged to establish visiting bodies known as National Preventive Mechanisms for the prevention of torture, inhuman or degrading treatment or punishment (Article 3), and it is expected that these bodies will help to develop standards regarding physical restraints. Such independent supervising bodies have an important role to play in implementing legal protection and changing practice about physical restraints. Without independent supervising bodies such as National Preventive Mechanisms, protective laws and court decisions, like those regarding physical restraints of Germany's Federal Constitutional Court, are unlikely to be fully implemented and institutions like psychiatric hospital care are likely to persist in their traditional behaviour.

References

Anonymous (2018) 'Personal Communication to Martin Zinkler'.

Appelbaum, P.S. (2019) 'Saving the UN Convention on the Rights of Persons with Disabilities–From Itself', *World Psychiatry*, 18(1): 1–2.

Berlin Manifesto (2019) *Berlin Manifesto for Humane Psychiatry [Berliner Manifest einer menschenwürdigen Psychiatrie]*. Available http://berliner-manifest.de/wp-content/uploads/2019/10/2019-10-08-Berlin-Manifesto-of-a-Humane-Psychiatry.pdf (accessed 20 June 2020).

Binding, K. and Hoche, A. (1920) *The Approval of the Extermination of Unworthy Life. Its Degree and Form [Die Freigabe der Vernichtung lebensunwerten Lebens. Ihr Maß und ihre Form]*, Leipzig: Meiner.

Bundesverfassungsgericht [German Constitutional Court], 2 BvR 309/15, 24 July 2018.

Bundesverfassungsgericht [German Constitutional Court], 2 BvR 502/16, 24 July 2018.

Bundesverfassungsgericht [German Constitutional Court], 2 BvR 882/09 23 March 2011.

Central Committee for Observance of Ethical Principles in Medicine and Its Adjacent Fields (ZEKO) (2013) *Statement–Coercive Treatment in Psychiatric Illness [Stellungnahme–Zwangsbehandlung bei psychischen Erkrankungen]*. Available https://www.zentrale-ethikkommission.de/fileadmin/user_upload/downloads/pdf-Ordner/Zeko/ZwangsbehandlungPsych2013.pdf (accessed 20 June 2020).

Deutsche Krankenhausgesellschaft (2018) *5-point and 7-point Restraints in Involuntary Commitment Subject to Public Law [5-Punkt und 7-Punkt-Fixierungen in der öffentlich-echtlichen Unterbringung, Leitfaden]*. Available www.neuroreha-bayern.de/images/Urteile/180907-DKG-Leitfaden_Fixierung_von_Patienten.pdf (accessed 20 June 2020).

Eurostat (2020) *Psychiatric Care Beds in Hospitals*. Available https://ec.europa.eu/eurostat/databrowser/view/tps00047/default/table?lang=en (accessed 18 August 2020).

Federal Constitutional Court (2011) *Successful Constitutional Complaint Lodged by a Person Committed to a Psychiatric Hospital against Compulsory Medical Treatment–Legislation in Baden-Württemberg Held Unconstitutional–Press Release No. 63/2011 of 20 October 2011*. Available www.bundesverfassungsgericht.de/SharedDocs/Pressemitteilungen/EN/2011/bvg11-063.html (accessed 20 June 2020).

Federal Constitutional Court (2018) *Constitutional Requirements Regarding the Use of Physical Restraints on Patients Confined Under Public Law in Psychiatric Hospitals–Press Release No. 62/2018 of 24 July 2018*. Available www.bundesverfassungsgericht.de/SharedDocs/Pressemitteilungen/EN/2018/bvg18-062.html (accessed 20 June 2020).

Flammer, E. and Steinert, T. (2018) 'The Case Register for Coercive Measures According to the Law on Assistance for Persons with Mental Diseases of Baden-Württemberg: Conception and First Evaluation' ['Das Fallregister für Zwangsmaßnahmen nach dem baden-württembergischen Psychisch-Kranken-Hilfe-Gesetz: Konzeption und erste Auswertungen'], *Psychiatrische Prax*, 46(2): 82–89.

Heumann, K., Bock, T. and Lincoln, T.M. (2017) 'Please Do Something–No Matter What! A Nationwide Online Survey of Mental Health Service Users About the Use of Alternatives to Coercive Measures' ['Bitte macht (irgend)was! Eine bundesweite Online-Befragung Psychiatrieerfahrener zum Einsatz milderer Maßnahmen zur Vermeidung von Zwangsmaßnahmen'], *Psychiatrische Prax*, 44(2): 85–92.

Horter, H., Zapp, W. and Driessen, M. (2016) 'System-Immanent Incentives in the Remuneration for Psychiatry and Psychosomatics', *Der Nervenarzt*, 87(7): 760–69.

Linehan, M.M. (1987) 'Dialectical Behavioural Therapy for Borderline Personality Disorder Theory and Method', *Bulletin of the Menninger Clinic*, 51(3): 261–76.

Mahlke, C.I., Priebe, S., Heumann, K., Daubmann, A., Wegscheider, K. and Bock, T. (2017) 'Effectiveness of One-To-One Peer Support for Patients with Severe Mental Illness–A Randomised Controlled Trial', *European Psychiatry*, 42: 103–10.

Osterfeld, M. (2012) 'DGPPN Against Precedent Setting Decision of Federal Constitutional Court' ['DGPPN gegen richtungsweisendes Urteil des Bundesverfassungsgerichts'], *Sozjale Psychiatrie*, 12: 34–35.

Prantl, H. (2018) 'Mental Health Care Mustn't Be a Legal Darkroom' ['Psychiatrie darf keine Dunkelkammer des Rechts sein'], *Süddeutsche Zeitung*, 31 January. Available www.sueddeutsche.de/panorama/fixierung-psychiatrie-darf-keine-dunkelkammer-des-rechts-sein-1.3847901 (accessed 20 June 2020).

Steinert, T. (2019) 'The UN Committee's Interpretation of "Will and Preferences" Can Violate Human Rights', *World Psychiatry*, 18(1): 45–46.

Voellm, B., Schanda, H., Haenggi, S. and Zinkler, M. (2007) 'Human Rights in Mental Health Care–Recommendations from the Council of Europe, Civil and Penal Law Relevant to Compulsory Measures in Psychiatry in Austria, Germany and Switzerland', *Recht & Psychiatrie*, 25(3): 132–40.

Weinmann, S. (2019) *Surveying Psychiatry–Deception and Self-Deception of a Medical Speciality [Die Vermessung der Psychiatrie–Täuschung und Selbsttäuschung eines Fachgebiets]*, Cologne: Psychiatrieverlag.

Zinkler, M. (2012) 'Incitement to Breach of Law? The Statement of the German Association for Psychiatry, Psychotherapy and Neurology About Coercive Medication in Forensic Psychiatric Care' ['Aufforderung zum Rechtsbruch? Die Stellungnahme der Deutschen Gesellschaft für Psychiatrie, Psychotherapie und Nervenheilkunde zum Urteil des Bundesverfassungsgerichts zur Zwangsbehandlung im Maßregelvollzug'], *Recht & Psychiatrie*, 30(2): 62–63.

Zinkler, M. and Waibel, M. (2019) 'Inpatient Mental Health Care Without Mechanical Restraint, Seclusion or Compulsory Medication' ['Auf Fixierungen kann in der klinischen Praxis verzichtet werden – ohne dass auf Zwangsmedikation oder Isolierung zurückgegriffen wird'], *Psychiatrische Prax*, 46(Supp 1): 4–6.

Part IV

Changing culture and practice

Introduction to Part IV

The chapters in Part IV explore a question that arises throughout this volume, namely, why does the use of restraint and other restrictive practices persist and, in some cases, increase even in the face of the growing recognition of their harms and concerted efforts to reduce or eliminate them? The authors of these chapters explore the importance of institutional and organisational cultures in converting – or failing to convert – regulatory frameworks for restraint use into practice in Australian mental health and aged care contexts.

Several authors describe the pressures on clinical and other members of staff that may precipitate – or be cited to justify – the use of restraint. These include concerns about the potential risk of harm individuals pose to themselves or others, and fear of being injured, blamed or held responsible if something goes wrong. Bernadette McSherry in Chapter 11 and Lisa Brophy, Justine Fletcher and Bridget Hamilton in Chapter 12 highlight the dominance of risk management culture in health and care settings, while noting the lack of strong evidence for such risk-based approaches. Brophy, Fletcher and Hamilton also note the influence of wider contextual factors, such as the intensification of acuity in mental health inpatient units and pressures associated with limited staffing and bed numbers. McSherry notes that concerns about the potential risk of harm are echoed in regulatory instruments that permit restraint use. She points to major inquiries into harmful restrictive practices in Australia and England and argues that the concept of risk may be interpreted very broadly to justify restraint use for the convenience of members of staff, meaning restraint becomes the measure of first, not last, resort.

Juanita Breen in Chapter 13 and Nathan Gibson in Chapter 14 focus on the role of clinicians in the authorisation and use of restraint. Breen points to cultural forces influencing the high rates of psychotropic medication use in Australian aged care facilities, despite guidelines recommending their use only when non-pharmacological approaches fail. Her research suggests that, while clinicians make prescribing decisions, nursing and care staff have considerable influence in these decisions but are not necessarily aware of relevant guidelines or the potential negative consequences. Again, the lack of available guidance on alternatives, and insufficient awareness of the issues among all staff, including clinicians, appears to play a role here. Gibson describes the multitude of internal and external factors that are at play whenever a clinician makes a decision to authorise or use restraint. He suggests that greater clinical leadership and engagement – supported by research to understand the factors contributing to clinician decision-making – are essential to reduction and elimination efforts.

All the authors suggest that these cultural barriers and points of resistance must be addressed before meaningful change can occur. A role for formal statements (whether in regulation or elsewhere) is contemplated. For example, Gibson proposes that clinicians' ethical codes and other guiding statements – which have not usually mentioned restraint and other restrictive practices and do not appear to influence practice in this regard – should be amended to clarify the role of clinicians in eliminating restraint and other restrictive practices. As has been explored throughout this volume, such formal statements will not be sufficient on their own. Breen notes the persistence of high rates of psychotropic use in Australian care homes despite the introduction of professional guidelines, prescribing restrictions and multiple reviews and interventions. As Brophy, Fletcher and Hamilton observe in Chapter 12, an excess of paperwork or other formal regulatory requirements might interfere with practices that can contribute to restraint avoidance. These authors describe some well-established initiatives that can give front-line staff the confidence and support they need to transform systems and practices. These include the Safewards model and interventions, post-incident reviews, environmental changes and improving staff capabilities.

Gibson in Chapter 14 notes that many contemporary strategies have a long history, offering cause for both optimism that change is possible and concern about the sporadic nature of progress to date. Again, the importance of research, and the need for more research on good practice and good implementation, is highlighted throughout this part. Several authors suggest that the voice of consumers has been a missing component of prior restraint minimisation or elimination initiatives. They argue that all activity in this area must be preceded by comprehensive and systematic involvement of consumers and service users at all stages in developing, implementing, monitoring and evaluating measures to reduce and eliminate restraint.

The chapters in this part indicate that reforms will need to be ongoing because of dynamic factors such as leadership change, high staff turnover in some sectors and the potential for small groups of staff to resist and impede reform. McSherry suggests in Chapter 11 that the rationales for the use of restraint found in regulatory instruments and in practice may reflect prejudicial attitudes and discrimination towards people with mental health conditions and others considered to be inherently dangerous or disruptive. This again recalls Cath Roper and colleagues' contention in Chapter 2 that reform efforts cannot be confined to restraint use specifically and must challenge the very bases on which mental health and other services are designed, regulated and delivered.

11 The intractable use of restraint, organisational culture and 'othering'

Lessons from the Oakden scandal

Bernadette McSherry

Introduction

There have been multiple attempts at a national level to reduce, if not eliminate, the use of seclusion and different forms of restraint in Australian health care settings. For example, in 2005, as part of the National Mental Health Strategy, all Australian Health Ministers agreed to a set of national safety priorities in mental health. One of the key priority areas they identified was '[r]educing [the] use of, and where possible eliminating, [the use of] restraint and seclusion' (National Mental Health Working Group 2005: 17–19).

A national mental health seclusion and restraint project (known as the Beacon project) was established two years later and ran until 2009 (Australian Institute of Health and Welfare 2012). The Beacon project targeted 11 key sites around Australia, all of which were charged with developing and implementing 'best practice' with the aim to reduce and, where possible, eliminate the use of seclusion and restraint in public mental health services. The project developed a set of key principles and guidelines for the use of seclusion and restraint by mental health services but did not recommend any specific legislative changes (Kumble and McSherry 2010).

In 2012, one of ten key recommendations made by the National Mental Health Commission (NMHC) was to 'reduce the use of involuntary practices and work to eliminate seclusion and restraint' (NMHC 2012: 13). It commissioned a research project to investigate and identify instances of 'best practice' in reducing and eliminating the practices of seclusion and restraint in relation to people with mental health conditions (Melbourne Social Equity Institute 2014). This resulted in a report that set out several options for reform including uniformity in regulatory frameworks, changing reporting and oversight, filling the gaps in existing literature and the adoption of multi-intervention strategies (Melbourne Social Equity Institute 2014: Chapter 7).

The disability and aged care sectors in Australia have been somewhat slower than the mental health sector in providing national guidance for reducing seclusion and restraint. In 2014, Australian Disability Ministers endorsed the *National Framework for Reducing and Eliminating the Use of Restrictive Practices in the Disability Service Sector*.

The national Aged Care Quality Assessment and Accreditation Framework was reviewed in 2017 (Carnell and Paterson 2017) and the Senate's Community Affairs References Committee (2019) has recommended a range of regulatory mechanisms to protect aged care residents from abuse and poor practices. This included extending the *National Framework for Reducing and Eliminating the Use of Restrictive Practices in the Disability Service Sector* to the aged care sector. The Committee stated (2019: para 5.47):

> [T]he high rates of restrictive practice within the aged care sector cannot be tolerated any longer. The current practice of light-touch regulation of restrictive practice has been proved a failure.

A Royal Commission into Aged Care Quality and Safety (the Royal Commission) was established by the Australian government in October 2018 to inquire into

> the quality of aged care services provided to Australians, the extent to which those services meet the needs of the people accessing them, the extent of sub-standard care being provided, including mistreatment and all forms of abuse, the causes of any systemic failures, and any actions that should be taken in response.
> (Royal Commission into Aged Care Quality and Safety (RCACQS) 2018)

In its Interim Report, the Royal Commission found that the prevalence of physical restraint is 'very poorly documented' (RCACQS 2019: 198) and that prescription rates of antipsychotics for people in residential aged care 'are significant and well above what might be expected' (RCACQS 2019: 200). It concluded (RCACQS 2019: 216):

> The prevalence of restrictive practices in residential aged care is unacceptable. The Royal Commission can only conclude, on the evidence before us, that the ongoing and common use of restrictive practices in aged care represents severely substandard and unsafe care.

It also pointed to a lack of limitations on the use of restrictive practices, despite a 'plethora of guidelines' (RCACQS 2019: 209).

While there has been a national focus on reducing and eliminating restrictive practices and improvements in many health services, the use of physical, mechanical and chemical restraints in health care settings appears intractable. The ongoing, highly concerning use of these practices that occurred over a period of years at the Oakden Older Person's Mental Health Service (Oakden) in the state of South Australia, provides but one example of the difficulties in controlling the excessive use of restraint. The next section discusses what occurred at Oakden and the outcomes of several inquiries that followed.

The chapter then provides an overview of some of the reasons for the use of physical, mechanical and chemical restraint with a focus on how preventing the risk of harm to self or others has become a major justification for the use of these forms of restraint. Drawing on social psychology, the chapter posits that the cultural practices within services may reflect wider cultural beliefs about certain groups within society.

The Oakden scandal

In 2015, Robert Spriggs was treated at the Repatriation General Hospital in Adelaide for Parkinson's disease and Lewy body dementia before moving to Oakden as a permanent resident. Oakden, located in the north-eastern suburbs of Adelaide, provided mental health services for older people, thereby bringing into play both state-based mental health and federally funded aged care regulatory systems.

Following his move to Oakden, Mr Spriggs' wife and family noted a rapid deterioration in his condition (Gage 2017). In February 2016, Mr Spriggs was taken to the Royal Adelaide Hospital with unexplained and significant bruising on his hip and thighs. With the help of Maurice Corcoran, South Australia's Principal Community Visitor, Mr Spriggs' family made a formal complaint to the state's aged care and mental health officials about Mr Spriggs' treatment at Oakden (Senate Community Affairs References Committee 2018: 2).

Mr Spriggs died on the 18th July 2016, aged 66. His family subsequently learned that while a resident at Oakden he had been given 500mg of the antipsychotic medication Seroquel, instead of the prescribed 50mg, and that the bruising he had experienced was likely caused by his being strapped into a chair (Senate Community Affairs References Committee 2018: 12–13). It was only after Mr Spriggs' family went to the media that the full extent of what had been occurring at Oakden over decades finally became public.

South Australia's then Chief Psychiatrist and his colleagues (Groves et al. 2017) and the state's Independent Commissioner Against Corruption (Lander 2018), both issued damning reports about the quality and management of care provided at Oakden. Those inquiries, and a third Commonwealth review (Carnell and Paterson 2017) which examined failures in the aged care quality regulation process, criticised many aspects of the service at Oakden and the behaviour of those charged with its administration. The Senate Community Affairs References Committee (2018, 2019) within the Australian Parliament was also asked to investigate 'the adequacy of medication handling practices and drug administration methods specific to aged care delivered at Oakden' (Senate Community Affairs References Committee 2017).

The Chief Psychiatrist's review (Groves et al. 2017: 105) found that the use of mechanical restraint, particularly the use of pelvic restraint to keep people in chairs, was excessive and there was 'a significant failure to appreciate the seriousness of restraint as stated by the UN and as agreed in Australia'. The review further determined (Groves et al. 2017: 109) that:

> most incidents of restrictive practice commenced in the early morning (around breakfast time) and or around dinner time. The Review believes this

> strongly suggests the use of Restrictive Practices is not 'as a last resort' as required, but as a routine management tool.

The review (Groves et al. 2017: 104) also criticised the failure to record and report each instance of restraint use, despite such reporting being mandatory from the 1st July 2013.

The Oakden case presented shocking evidence of the mistreatment of residents in one mental health and aged care facility. Amongst many concerns, it highlights the issue of the (over)use of various forms of restraint in health care settings across Australia. Many of these settings are 'closed environments' where oversight may be limited. While it would be comforting to believe that this was a one-off situation, the Royal Commission stated in its Interim Report (RCACQS 2019: 5) that:

> the combined impact of the evidence, submissions and stories provided to the Royal Commission leads us to conclude that substandard care is much more widespread and more serious than we had anticipated.

The next section considers organisational culture and how it may contribute to staff members relying on the use of restraint as a 'normal' way of managing clients rather than viewing it as a last resort.

Organisational culture: Beyond last resort to convenience

An organisation's culture refers to the pattern of values and underlying assumptions of the different members within it as well as rules and practices (Banaszak-Holl et al. 2011: 46–47). Organisations may have a dominant culture as well as one or more sub-cultures. The Chief Psychiatrist's Review of Oakden (Groves et al. 2017: 93) pointed out that there may be different cultures within organisations, such as 'Cultures based on fear; Cultures based on bullying; Tribal Cultures; which were considered by the review as being of important consideration'. The review (Groves et al. 2017: 94) referred to a dominant organisational culture that revolved around the idea that there was 'no money' to provide adequate staffing or high-quality care. This led to many staff members 'feeling despondent' as well as 'diminished opportunity for positive change' (Groves et al. 2017: 94).

There was also a tendency to hide everyday practices from external scrutiny (Groves et al. 2017: 93–94):

> Early on in the Review, we came across use of the phrase 'boss on floor' as a distinctive form of insider communication. As a cultural practice, 'boss on floor' is a phrase used by nursing staff to communicate to each other that a person in authority (for example, an external assessor, official visitor, protected person's guardian or senior SA Health employee) was in the building and/or on the ward. Upon hearing the phrase staff would be expected to act in ways that would reduce the likelihood of being scrutinised.

The review also pointed out (Groves et al. 2017: 95) that interpersonal difficulties between staff led to bickering, low morale and a 'toxic culture'. Many of the nurses had been trained overseas and spoke English as a second language which sometimes gave rise to difficulties in communication with Australian born nurses. There was tension between staff and a manager because of broken equipment not being replaced and some staff had simply stopped talking to one another (Groves et al. 2017: 96). The Senate Community Affairs References Committee (2018: 26, para 2.57) pointed to evidence of 'consistent understaffing' and the fact that between 2016 to 2017, the only allied health professional working at Oakden was a part-time dietician, noting that 'there was no occupational therapist, physiotherapist, psychologist, speech pathologist or social worker employed by Oakden' (2018: 25, para 2.53).

The Chief Psychiatrist's Review (Groves et al. 2017: 97) received information about 'rough handling' of residents. Some within Oakden justified this in a distorted interpretation of occupational health and safety concerns. They said (Groves et al. 2017: 98):

> the rough handling and other aggressive actions are needed in order to keep the upper hand. These staff also viewed these actions as an effective way to get the job done. In many instances, the 'job to be done' was to prevent falls using pelvic restraint.

There was also evidence of 'verbal abuse and demeaning behaviour from staff towards clients' (Groves et al. 2017: 98). In all, the Chief Psychiatrist's Review (Groves et al. 2017: 100) found that the dominant culture was:

> characterised by, poor morale, disrespect and bickering, secrecy, an inwardly looking approach, control, a sense of entitlement and indifference. This culture led to a loss of dignity and rights for those in Oakden, both consumers and staff.

It also pointed out (Groves et al. 2017: 100) that there was a sub-culture of caring staff, but the dominant culture was such that it generally led them to leave rather than become 'acculturated'.

The findings of the Chief Psychiatrist's Review concerning organisational culture reflect other inquiries into poor health care practice. For example, an inquiry in England into the operations of the Mid Staffordshire National Health Service (NHS) Foundation Trust discovered appalling treatment of patients and another example of toxic culture (Francis 2013: 13):

> The culture at the Trust was not conducive to providing good care for patients or providing a supportive working environment for staff; there was an atmosphere of fear of adverse repercussions; a high priority was placed on the achievement of targets; the consultant body largely dissociated itself from management; there was low morale amongst staff; there was a lack of openness and an acceptance of poor standards.

The Mid Staffordshire NHS review (Francis 2013: 64) found that external bodies were able to avoid responding to complaints about poor practice for several reasons:

> The responsibilities and accountabilities of external agencies were not well defined, often resulting in 'regulatory gaps' or failure to follow up warning signs.

This review found (Francis 2013: 64) that these 'regulatory gaps', lack of effective communication and constant reorganisation led to a broader, systemic culture where organisations could avoid carrying out sufficient scrutiny of complaints.

This suggests that there are levels of complexity in both internal and external organisational culture(s) that can give rise to poor practice or worse and allow these practices to continue.

The Carnell and Paterson (2017) review of Australian aged care quality regulatory processes considered the question as to whether the Oakden situation should be considered an exceptional one. Oakden was the only specialist mental health facility for older people in South Australia and one of only a handful of like facilities among the 2,500 residential services in Australia. Having the dual purpose of state based mental health care and Commonwealth regulated aged care gave rise to an argument that Oakden may have more easily fallen between the cracks than had it been subject to one jurisdictional system. However, Carnell and Paterson (2017: 39) found that the issues of care could be 'attributable to failures that any service could be vulnerable to' and that 'Oakden is not unique, because the characteristics and needs of its residents were not unique'. They also found that patterns in aged care complaints data indicated Oakden was not an exceptional case (Carnell and Paterson 2017: 41), with the most common complaints across Australia being about the administration and management of medication, the prevention and management of falls and personal and oral hygiene which were all issues considered by the Oakden inquiries.

Justifications for the use of restraint

The preceding section examined the organisational culture in Oakden that led to restraint being justified to 'get the job done' (Groves et al. 2017: 98). This section provides an overview of the various justifications that have been proffered in relation to when restraint should be used.

Where regulation of restraint exists, it is often permitted 'as a last resort' in order to prevent the risk of harm to self or others. The control of behaviour is thus justified because of the risk of what might otherwise occur. Lisa Brophy, Justine Fletcher and Bridget Hamilton in Chapter 12 in this volume outline how a culture of risk management, an emphasis on staff safety and a shift towards locked door wards can all serve to justify the continued use of restraint.

An analysis of 1,150 responses to a survey on the use of seclusion and restraint in mental health settings (Kinner et al. 2017) found that many participants, particularly mental health practitioners, believed that some forms of restraint were likely to produce some benefits, including increasing consumer safety, increasing the safety of staff and others and setting behavioural boundaries.

A comparison between consumer and mental health practitioner responses to the perceived benefits of restraint is revealing (Kinner et al. 2017: 541). Nearly 72 per cent of mental health practitioners agreed that physical restraint often or always increases consumer safety, whereas only 46.5 per cent of consumers agreed with this statement. Sixty-one per cent of mental health practitioners agreed that mechanical restraint often or always increases consumer safety, whereas 39 per cent of consumers agreed with this statement. The figures were somewhat closer in relation to whether chemical restraint often or always increases consumer safety (77.3 per cent of mental health practitioners; 55.2 per cent of consumers).

While most participants agreed that it was feasible to eliminate mechanical restraint, only a small minority of mental health practitioners believed that it was feasible to eliminate physical restraint (14 per cent) or chemical restraint (13 per cent) (Kinner et al. 2017: 539).

Perhaps the main reason for this acceptance of restraint lies in the perception that it is necessary to deal with the risk of harm to others. Just on 72 per cent of mental health practitioners agreed that physical restraint often or always increases staff or others' safety (Kinner et al. 2017: 541). Around 75 per cent agreed that mechanical restraint and almost 86 per cent agreed that chemical restraint had the same effect. Risk management culture can lead to defensive practice by mental health and allied staff, despite defensive practice detracting from therapeutic engagement (Slemon et al. 2017).

This idea that restraint can increase the safety of staff and others is closely related to occupational health and safety concerns. Peter Bartlett and Stephanie Sampson outline in Chapter 3 in this volume how rapid tranquillisation and/or chemical restraint policies in England refer to the reduction of violence on wards and are underpinned with concerns about staff safety. As Bartlett and Sampson point out, this indicates a tension between the occupational health and safety of staff and the human rights of those subjected to these practices.

In Australia, each state and its two self-governing territories have legislation dealing with occupational health and safety. Section 4(1) of Victoria's *Occupational Health and Safety Act 2004*, for example, states as a key principle:

> The importance of health and safety requires that employees, other persons at work and members of the public be given the highest level of protection against risks to their health and safety that is reasonably practicable in the circumstances.

Section 20(1) of the same Act sets out certain matters that may be taken into account in determining what is 'reasonably practicable':

(a) the likelihood of the hazard or risk concerned eventuating;
(b) the degree of harm that would result if the hazard or risk eventuated;
(c) what the person concerned knows, or ought reasonably to know, about the hazard or risk and any ways of eliminating or reducing the hazard or risk;
(d) the availability and suitability of ways to eliminate or reduce the hazard or risk;
(e) the cost of eliminating or reducing the hazard or risk.

Jeffrey Chan (2016: 209) has argued that occupational health and safety laws have been misinterpreted and implemented in such a way as to hold that the behaviour of individuals with disabilities in closed environments constitute an 'occupational hazard'. He argues that such laws and human rights are viewed by some services as mutually exclusive. This view may exist despite the protection of human rights being emphasised in disability (and mental health) legislation.

Even where human rights are perceived as integral to the provision of health services, human rights are not absolute and the right to safety of staff and patients may be viewed as trumping the right to physical and mental integrity of the individual. Western liberal theory generally holds that human rights may entail duties and there is a complex relationship between the two (Dudley, Silove and Gale 2012: 15–16). The concept of balancing human rights is one that has become central to judicial decision-making in some countries and, in particular, by the European Court of Human Rights (Çali 2007). Often this is expressed in terms of balancing individual human rights with communal interests and involves a commitment to 'the principle of proportionality' (Çali 2007: 253). Balancing the competing interests of the individual and others may lead to placing more weight on occupational health and safety than the dignity of those residing in health care settings, particularly in situations where there is a power differential and where residents have not traditionally been viewed as rights-holders.

This argument seems to be borne out with the Oakden example of restraint being used in order to 'get the job done' (Groves et al. 2017: 98). The use of different forms of restraint were viewed as a 'reasonably practicable' means of preventing falls and presumably behavioural expressions of distress (on appropriate terms to describe such behaviour, see Markwell 2016). In their review, Carnell and Paterson (2017: 115) pointed out that 'restrictive practices' are 'explained and justified as protecting the restrained person or others from harm during episodes of "challenging behaviours", such as striking themselves or other people or wandering'.

In aged care settings, risk management culture may emphasise that restraint is justifiable to prevent falls or disruption to other residents. Risk management culture in other settings such as psychiatric facilities may focus on the use of restraint to prevent harm to others. In both cases, what international human rights law requires (as explored in other chapters in this volume) can be unjustifiably dismissed because of a perception that preventing harm, however interpreted, trumps individual rights. This perception may reflect the societal context surrounding risk of harm which is explored in the next section.

Societal culture: Risk of harm and common beliefs and practices

One area that was not fully explored in the Oakden inquiries is the societal context within which the (over)use of restraint and poor practice in health care can persist. This section discusses societal culture in relation to how restraint continues to be justified on the grounds of occupational health and safety as a means of preventing harm.

The risk of harm justification for the use of restraint may reflect beliefs about certain individuals. Outside the emergency context, restraint use may be targeted at certain individuals in marginalised groups such as those with physical and/or cognitive disabilities, the elderly and those with severe mental health conditions. In relation to the latter, it has proved difficult to counter stereotypical perceptions equating 'madness' with 'dangerousness' and violence (see e.g. Jorm and Oh 2009; Jorm, Reavley and Ross 2012; Jorm and Reavley 2014).

Using David Garland's (1996) words, those most subject to restraint may be viewed as the 'alien other' whose risky behaviour can only be addressed by removing them from circulation in order to manage and control them. He writes that certain individuals are targeted as 'dangerous members of distinct . . . social groups which bear little resemblance to "us"' and that the rhetoric of the 'alien other' leads to the perspective that '[t]he only practical and rational response to such types is to have them "taken out of circulation" for the protection of the public' (Garland 1996: 461).

While this chapter is concerned with practices in health care settings, there may indeed be an element of moving beyond treatment to social control of those whose behaviour is deemed too difficult, too 'risky' to manage in the community.

The cultural anthropologist Mary Douglas (1982, 1985, 1992) has explored notions of risk in terms of shared cultural beliefs and practices that are based on social expectations and responsibilities. Notions of risk are viewed as shared within communities and as part of an historical continuum rather than the result of any distinctive social, political or economic conditions. What a community selects as embodying risk is that which is seen to threaten the community's moral principles. This in turn helps maintain social order.

To some extent, as indicated earlier, the culture of members of staff in the Oakden facility can be perceived as controlling 'risky' individuals for their own convenience to enable orderly daily activities. An emphasis on efficiency through the 'marketisation of care' may also mean that 'staffing ratios are reduced, or less qualified staff are employed' (Brennan et al. 2012: 5). Individuals being subject to restraint may be perceived as 'childish' or less than human. For example, the Chief Psychiatrist's Review (Groves et al. 2017: 98) heard evidence that:

> [S]taff would say to a client who was often left on the floor [so called 'floor time']: 'only children behave like that' . . . . 'Get up off the floor, don't be so childish'; 'Do you want dinner . . . well grow up and get up off the floor'.

The concepts of 'prejudice', 'stigma' and 'discrimination' are central to explanations as to why certain groups are marginalised.

Prejudice means prejudgment (from the Latin 'prae' and 'judicium') and while it is generally linked to derogatory social attitudes or beliefs, there are many studies indicating that most individuals are prejudiced in the sense of making assumptions about certain groups (Hogg and Vaughan 2011: 376ff). Susan Fiske (1998) refers to 'gut level' prejudices which stem from anticipated threats, thus affecting the ways in which a certain group is seen to threaten the goals or interests of the person concerned. Such prejudices may provoke emotions such as anger, fear, anxiety or sadness. Most research on prejudice has focused on sexism and racism rather than disability or sexual orientation (Hogg and Vaughan 2011: 378–79). Instead, the concept of 'stigma' has been used primarily in studies focusing on exclusion and mental illness (Thornicroft 2006), although Michael Perlin's work on 'sanism' and the law offers a way of understanding prejudicial attitudes towards individuals with mental health conditions and their effect on compulsory treatment and criminal laws (for example, Perlin 1999).

The term 'stigma' derives from the Greek for 'mark' or 'tattoo' and in Ancient Greece the term referred to the mark placed on those worthy of contempt by burning with a hot iron. The plural form 'stigmata' in the Christian tradition referred to the marks that appeared on the devout that resembled the wounds of the crucified Christ. Erving Goffman (1963: 3) used the term to refer to an attribute that discredited an individual, reducing him or her 'from a whole and usual person, to a tainted, discounted one'. He distinguished three categories of stigmatising conditions: 'blemishes of individual character' which are assumed to reflect immoral or deviant behaviour; 'abominations of the body' arising from physical disfigurements or deviations from what is considered 'normal'; and 'tribal stigmas' that are based on the membership of a despised racial, ethnic or religious group. Goffman states (1963: 5) that there is a belief that 'the person with a stigma is not quite human'.

Social exclusion is closely related to stigmatisation. Cheryl Kaiser and Carol Miller (2001) observe that stigma is so interconnected with rejection and exclusion that prejudice towards members of stigmatised groups is often measured by asking people to indicate the social distance they want to keep between themselves and the stigmatised group. Brenda Major and Collette Eccleston (2005: 66) point out that there are three essential elements of stigma-based exclusion. First, it is consensual in that '[t]here is general agreement within a culture that certain types of people should be excluded'. Second, exclusion is shared with others who have the same attribute so that it can be seen as based on social rather than individual identity. Third, the exclusion of stigmatised groups is viewed by members of the group doing the excluding as justified or legitimate.

Stigmatisation and social exclusion are so pervasive that some researchers have posited that these processes serve to enhance personal or group self-esteem for those doing the excluding, as well as serving to alleviate discomfort and anxiety (Wills 1981; Tajfel and Turner 1986). For example, Robert Brooks (2000) has pointed out that 'almost all cultures have viewed mental illness as a deviant form, subject to negative social sanctions'. In Michel Foucault's (1965) terminology, those with 'mental illness' are seen as 'the other'. Not all members of society, however, stigmatise those with mental health conditions. Marie Yeh and colleagues (2017) pointed to different segments of society: allies, who consistently endorse positive beliefs and feelings toward people with mental health conditions; adversaries, who consistently endorse negative beliefs and feelings; ambivalents, who have mixed beliefs and feelings; blamers, who endorse the belief that people with mental health conditions are responsible for their conditions; and shamers, who believe mental health conditions should be kept secret.

There is some research suggesting that those with mental health conditions have thus been subjected to social exclusion because people tend to feel uncomfortable around those who they know or believe to be 'mentally ill' in part because they are perceived to be unpredictable and dangerous (Farina and Ring 1965; Farina 1998). This then serves to alleviate the feelings of anxiety within the excluding group.

In relation to those with disabilities and elderly individuals, there is some research suggesting that they are subject to social exclusion because they remind those carrying out the exclusion of their own vulnerability and mortality (Major and Eccleston 2005). Some studies indicate that nurses may have 'ageist' beliefs in perceiving older patients as mentally or physically dependent (Cooper and Coleman 2001; Eymard and Douglas 2012) and prefer to work with those considered 'mentally intact' (Cooper and Coleman 2001: 401). There may therefore be self-protective motives at play both at an individual and also a group level when certain groups are excluded and denigrated (Reed and Aquino 2003).

There are also 'system justification' theories that view stigma as a method of justifying existing social inequalities and maintaining the status quo (Sidanius and Pratto 1993; Jost and Banaji 1994), as well as evolutionary theories that view stigma as a method of excluding individuals who are perceived to be poor partners in order to preserve reproductive fitness (Neuberg, Smith and Asher 2000; Kurzban and Leary 2001).

In recent years, there has been a move away from the concept of stigma towards that of discrimination to explain the experiences of those who are excluded. This is because the term stigma is seen as locating the problem within the individual who is excluded rather than focusing on the negative attitudes of those carrying out exclusory practices. Graham Thornicroft (2006: 191) argues that much of the work on stigma 'has been beside the point' because it has concentrated on the attitudes of 'normal' people to certain groups of individuals and has focused on hypothetical situations, rather than examining the actual experiences of those who have been 'shunned'. He argues that shifting the focus from stigma to discrimination has the advantage of focusing on actual behaviour rather than just attitudes and can lead to much needed research on interventions to change discriminatory behaviour.

In her foreword to Graham Thornicroft's book (2006: xii), Judi Chamberlin defines discrimination as 'the societal codification of [negative] attitudes, as expressed in laws and customs that result in [certain individuals] having a lower social status and fewer rights than non-labelled people'. She makes the point (2006: xiii, emphasis in original) that '[w]hile "changing attitudes" may have a warm, fuzzy appeal, changing discriminatory *behaviour* is, I believe far more important'.

Health care that is provided in closed environments such as locked mental health wards and aged care or disability residential facilities may exacerbate negative perceptions about those treated within such settings (Chan 2016). They may be seen as the 'alien other' who can be treated differently because of their perceived risky behaviour. This hostile form of 'othering' may reflect 'simplistic and self-serving representations that gloss over the complexity and diversity of people's lives' (Grey 2016: 243). Certainly, in long-term care settings, it appears that staff may 'consciously or unconsciously discriminate against residents who are impaired, or refer to residents' families for decisions about care rather than dealing directly with the resident' (Zimmerman et al. 2016: 536).

There is also the added complexity of 'stigma by association' (Goffman 1963), whereby those who work in mental health and aged care facilities may be viewed negatively. Margaret Halter (2008) conducted a survey of nurses which found that psychiatric nursing was the least preferred specialty of ten areas and that psychiatric nurses were least likely to be described as skilled, logical, dynamic and respected.

The complex dynamics of institutional cultures reflect broader societal concerns. The rise of risk management and prevention has permeated organisations in many societies (McSherry 2014) and the concepts of prejudice, stigma and discrimination may go some way towards explaining why it is that an 'us and them' perspective can permeate mental health and aged care facilities, reinforcing the apparent intractable use of restraint.

Conclusion

The (over)use of physical, mechanical and chemical restraints in health care settings has led to many attempts to restrict when and how restraint may be used. Elimination, however, remains elusive.

Lisa Brophy, Justine Fletcher and Bridget Hamilton point out in Chapter 12 in this volume that 'risk management continue[s] to influence the culture and practices within mental health service delivery even without strong evidence, maintaining a high tolerance for the restrictive interventions that are characterised as necessary responses to risk and safety fears'.

This chapter has argued that the perceived need to prevent any risk of harm to others along with occupational health and safety issues are used to justify the continued use of restraint. These justifications are influenced by negative attributes associated with those with mental health conditions, persons with disabilities and older adults, leading to their devaluation and an 'othering' mentality. Exclusion and discrimination at a societal level may be mirrored in the institutional context of mental health and aged care facilities, enabling practices such as physical, mechanical and chemical restraint to continue. In turn, because the use of restraint is permitted to prevent the risk of harm, individuals subject to restraint may in themselves be seen as inherently 'risky', thereby reinforcing discriminatory beliefs and practices.

Because of the pervasiveness of stigmatisation and social exclusion, as Judi Chamberlin in her foreword to Thornicroft (2006: xiii) has pointed out, focusing on discriminatory behaviour rather than attitudes may indeed be a starting point for cultural change in health care settings. It would be comforting to consider Oakden as an outlier in the (over)use of various forms of restraint. However, while good efforts continue to reduce these practices, it must be recognised that organisational culture focused too much on the risk of harm to self and others, together with beliefs that individuals with mental health conditions are unpredictable and dangerous, can lead to different forms of restraint being used as a first rather than a last resort.

Lisa Waddington has pointed out in Chapter 7 in this volume that staffing and staff culture may be the most important factors affecting the use of restraint and other coercive measures. Reflecting this, the Chief Psychiatrist's Review (Groves et al. 2017: 100) recommended that there needed to be

> the significant introduction of people in senior leadership positions at Oakden that can drive the change in culture required to one that has as its core principles the values of dignity, respect, care and kindness for both consumers and the staff that work there.

This recommendation reflects the first strategy within the six core strategies for reducing seclusion and restraint as developed by the United States National Association of State Mental Health Program Directors (National Technical Assistance Center for State Mental Health Planning 2005; National Association of State Mental Health Program Directors 2008). This first strategy is leadership towards organisational change. As outlined in Chapter 1 in this volume, the other strategies are:

- Using data to inform practice;
- Supporting the workforce through developing procedures, practices and training that are based on knowledge and principles of mental health recovery;
- Using restraint reduction 'tools' such as assessments and resources to individualise aggression prevention;
- Consumer roles in inpatient settings; and
- Using 'debriefing' techniques (National Technical Assistance Center for State Mental Health Planning 2005; National Association of State Mental Health Program Directors 2008).

Nathan Gibson points out in Chapter 14 in this volume that these strategies reflect those that date back nearly two centuries. Without senior leaders driving respectful practices, such strategies are unlikely to gain traction. The World Health Organisation's QualityRights initiative includes a training course guide entitled *Transforming Services and Promoting Human Rights* (2019) which sets out techniques to transform organisational cultures to ensure human rights are promoted.

Other chapters in this volume explore systemic 'top-down' efforts to reduce, if not eliminate, the use of restraint in health care settings. What the Oakden scandal reveals, however, is that these efforts will not be enough in the absence of support for respectful workplace cultures. Systemic reforms will eventuate only when organisational cultures which reflect negative perceptions of certain 'out' groups are identified and appropriately addressed.

References

Australian Institute of Health and Welfare (AIHW) (2012) *Admitted Patient Mental Health-Related Care–Use of Restricted Practices During Admitted Patient Care.* Available www.aihw.gov.au/getmedia/71900b8a-fe09-4a6b-9b3c-350698cc82c9/Mental-health-related-admitted-patient-care-2011–12.pdf.aspx (accessed 20 June 2020).

Banaszak-Holl, J., Nembhard, I.M.E., Taylor, L. and Bradley, E.H. (2011) 'Leadership and Management: A Framework for Action', in L.R. Burns, E.H. Bradley and B.J. Weiner (eds) *Shortell and Kaluzny's Health Care Management: Organisation Design and Behaviour*, New York: Delmar Cengage Learning, 33–62.

Brennan, D., Cass, B., Himmelweit, S. and Szebehely, M. (2012) 'The Marketisation of Care: Rationales and Consequences in Nordic and Liberal Care Regimes', *Journal of European Social Policy*, 22(4): 377–91.

Brooks, R. (2000) 'Official Madness: A Cross-Cultural Study of Involuntary Civil Confinement Based on Mental Illness', in J. Hubert (ed.) *Madness, Disability and Social Exclusion: The Archaeology and Anthropology of 'Difference'*, New York: Routledge, 9–28.

Çali, B. (2007) 'Balancing Human Rights? Methodological Problems with Weights, Scales and Proportions', *Human Rights Quarterly*, 29(1): 251–70.

Carnell, K. and Paterson, R. (2017) *Review of National Aged Care Quality Regulatory Processes.* Available www.health.gov.au/sites/default/files/review-of-national-aged-care-quality-regulatory-processes-report.pdf (accessed 20 June 2020).

Chan, J. (2016) 'Challenges to Realizing the Convention on the Rights of Persons with Disabilities (CRPD) in Australia for People with Intellectual Disability and Behaviours of Concern', *Psychiatry, Psychology and Law*, 23(2): 207–14.

Cooper, S.A. and Coleman, P.G. (2001) 'Caring for the Older Person: An Exploration of Perceptions using Personal Construct Theory', *Age and Ageing*, 30(5): 399–402.

Douglas, M. (1982) *In the Active Voice*, London: Routledge.

Douglas, M. (1985) *Risk Acceptability According to the Social Sciences*, New York: Russel Sage Foundation.

Douglas, M. (1992) *Risk and Blame: Essays in Cultural Theory*, London: Routledge.

Dudley, M., Silove, D. and Gale, F. (2012) 'Mental Health, Human Rights, and Their Relationship: An Introduction', in M. Dudley, D. Silove and F. Gale (eds) *Mental Health and Human Rights: Vision, Praxis, and Courage*, Oxford: Oxford University Press, 1–49.

Eymard, A.S. and Douglas, D.H. (2012) 'Ageism Among Health Care Providers and Interventions to Improve Their Attitudes Toward Older Adults: An Integrative Review', *Journal of Gerontological Nursing*, 38(5): 26–35.

Farina, A. (1998) 'Stigma', in K.T. Meuser and N. Tarrier (eds) *Handbook of Social Functioning in Schizophrenia*, Boston: Allyn and Bacon, 247–79.

Farina, A. and Ring, K. (1965) 'The Influence of Perceived Mental Illness on Interpersonal Relations', *Journal of Abnormal Psychology*, 70(1): 47–51.

Fiske, S.T. (1998) 'Stereotyping, Prejudice, and Discrimination', in D.T. Gilbert, S.T. Fiske and G. Lindzey (eds) *The Handbook of Social Psychology*, Boston: McGraw-Hill, 357–411.

Foucault, M. (1965) *Madness and Civilization: A History of Insanity in an Age of Reason*, New York: Pantheon Books.

Francis, R. (2013) *Report of the Mid Staffordshire NHS Foundation Trust Public Inquiry–Executive Summary.* Available https://assets.publishing.service.gov.uk/

government/uploads/system/uploads/attachment_data/file/279124/0947.pdf (accessed 20 June 2020).

Gage, N. (2017) 'Spriggs Family Searches for Answers After Father Was Overmedicated at Oakden Mental Health Facility', *ABC News*, 18 January. Available www.abc.net.au/news/2017-01-18/sa-father-overmedicated-at-oakden-mental-health-family-says/8191428 (accessed 20 June 2020).

Garland, D. (1996) 'The Limits of the Sovereign State: Strategies of Crime Control in Contemporary Society', *The British Journal of Criminology*, 36(4): 445–71.

Goffman, E. (1963) *Stigma: Notes on the Management of Spoiled Identity*, Englewood Cliffs, NJ: Prentice-Hall.

Grey, F. (2016) 'Benevolent Othering: Speaking Positively About Mental Health Service Users', *Philosophy, Psychology and Psychiatry*, 23(3–4): 241–324.

Groves, A., Thomson, D., McKellar, D. and Procter, N. (2017) *The Oakden Report: The Report of the Oakden Review*, Adelaide: SA Health, Department for Health and Ageing. Available www.sahealth.sa.gov.au/wps/wcm/connect/4ae57e8040d7d0d58d52af3ee9bece4b/Oakden%2BReport%2BFinal%2BEmail%2BVersion.pdf?MOD=AJPERES&CACHE=NONE&CONTENTCACHE=NONE (accessed 20 June 2020).

Halter, M.J. (2008) 'Perceived Characteristics of Psychiatric Nurses: Stigma by Association', *Archives of Psychiatric Nursing*, 22(1): 20–26.

Hogg, M.A. and Vaughan, G.M. (2011) *Social Psychology*, Harlow: Prentice Hall.

Jorm, A.F. and Oh, E. (2009) 'Desire for Social Distance from People with Mental Disorders', *Australian & New Zealand Journal of Psychiatry*, 43(3): 183–200.

Jorm, A.F. and Reavley, N.J. (2014) 'Public Belief That Mentally Ill People Are Violent: Is the USA Exporting Stigma to the Rest of the World?', *Australian & New Zealand Journal of Psychiatry*, 48(3): 213–15.

Jorm, A.F., Reavley, N.J. and Ross, A.M. (2012) 'Belief in the Dangerousness of People with Mental Disorders: A Review', *Australian & New Zealand Journal of Psychiatry*, 46(11): 1029–45.

Jost, J.T. and Banaji, M.R. (1994) 'The Role of Stereotyping in System-Justification and the Production of False Consciousness', *British Journal of Social Psychology*, 33(1): 1–27.

Kaiser, C.R. and Miller, C.T. (2001) 'Stop Complaining! The Social Costs of Making Attributions to Discrimination', *Personality and Social Psychology Bulletin*, 27(2): 254–63.

Kinner, S.A., Harvey, C., Hamilton, B., Brophy, L., Roper, C., McSherry, B. and Young, J.T. (2017) 'Attitudes Towards Seclusion and Restraint in Mental Health Settings: Findings from a Large, Community-based Survey of Consumers, Carers and Mental Health Professionals', *Epidemiology and Psychiatric Sciences*, 26(5): 535–44.

Kumble, S. and McSherry, B. (2010) 'Seclusion and Restraint: Rethinking Regulation from a Human Rights Perspective', *Psychiatry, Psychology and Law*, 17(4): 1–11.

Kurzban, R. and Leary, M.R. (2001) 'Evolutionary Origins of Stigmatization: The Functions of Social Exclusion', *Psychological Bulletin*, 12(2): 187–208.

Lander, B. (2018) *Oakden: A Shameful Chapter in South Australia's History*, Adelaide: Independent Commission Against Corruption. Available https://icac.sa.gov.au/system/files/ICAC_Report_Oakden.pdf (accessed 20 June 2020).

Major, B. and Eccleston, C.P. (2005) 'Stigma and Social Exclusion', in D. Abrms, M.A. Hogg and J.M. Marques (eds) *The Social Psychology of Inclusion and Exclusion*, New York: Psychology Press, 63–87.

Markwell, H. (2016) 'Loaded Meanings: The Narrative of Behaviour', *Australian Journal of Dementia Care*, 5(3): 12–16.

McSherry, B. (2014) *Managing Fear: The Law and Ethics of Preventive Detention and Risk Assessment*, New York: Routledge.

Melbourne Social Equity Institute (2014) *Seclusion and Restraint Project: Report*, Melbourne: University of Melbourne. Available https://socialequity.unimelb.edu.au/__data/assets/pdf_file/0017/2004722/Seclusion-and-Restraint-report.PDF (accessed 20 June 2020).

National Association of State Mental Health Program Directors (2008) *Six Core Strategies to Reduce Seclusion and Restraint Use*. Available www.nasmhpd.org/content/six-core-strategies-reduce-seclusion-and-restraint-use (accessed 20 June 2020).

National Mental Health Commission (NMHC) (2012) *A Contributing Life: The 2012 National Report Card on Mental Health and Suicide Prevention*. Available www.mentalhealthcommission.gov.au/monitoring-and-reporting/national-reports/2012-national-report (accessed 20 June 2020).

National Mental Health Working Group (2005) *National Safety Priorities in Mental Health: A National Plan for Reducing Harm*, Canberra: Department of Health and Ageing. Available www.mindbank.info/item/400 (accessed 20 June 2020).

National Technical Assistance Center for State Mental Health Planning (2005) *Six Core Strategies to Reduce the Use of Seclusion and Restraint Planning Tool*, Alexandria, VA: National Association of State Mental Health Program Directors.

Neuberg, S.L., Smith, D.M. and Asher, T. (2000) 'Why People Stigmatize: Toward a Biocultural Framework', in T.F. Heatherton, R.E. Kleck, M.R. Hebk and J.G. Hull (eds) *The Social Psychology of Stigma*, New York: Guildford Press, 31–61.

Perlin, M. (1999) 'Half-Wracked Prejudice Leaped Forth: Sanism, Pretextuality, and Why and How Mental Disability Law Developed as It Did', *Journal of Contemporary Legal Issues*, 10: 3–36.

Reed, A. and Aquino, K.F. (2003) 'Moral Identity and the Expanding Circle of Moral Regard Toward Out-Groups', *Journal of Personality and Social Psychology*, 84(6): 1270–86.

Royal Commission into Aged Care Quality and Safety (RCACQS) (2018) *Terms of Reference*. Available https://agedcare.royalcommission.gov.au/Pages/Terms-of-reference.aspx (accessed 20 June 2020).

Royal Commission into Aged Care Quality and Safety (RCACQAS) (2019) *Interim Report: Neglect–Vol 1*. Available https://agedcare.royalcommission.gov.au/publications/interim-report-volume-1 (accessed 18 August 2020).

Senate Community Affairs References Committee (2017) *Effectiveness of the Aged Care Quality Assessment and Accreditation Framework for Protecting Residents from Abuse and Poor Practices, and Ensuring Proper Clinical and Medical Care Standards Are Maintained and Practised–Terms of Reference*. Available www.aph.gov.au/Parliamentary_Business/Committees/Senate/Community_Affairs/AgedCareQuality/Terms_of_Reference (accessed 20 June 2020).

Senate Community Affairs References Committee (2018) *Effectiveness of the Aged Care Quality Assessment and Accreditation Framework for Protecting Residents from Abuse and Poor Practices, and Ensuring Proper Clinical and Medical Care Standards Are Maintained and Practised–Interim Report*. Available www.aph.gov.au/Parliamentary_Business/Committees/Senate/Community_Affairs/AgedCareQuality/Interim_report (accessed 20 June 2020).

Senate Community Affairs References Committee (2019) *Effectiveness of the Aged Care Quality Assessment and Accreditation Framework for Protecting Residents from Abuse and Poor Practices, and Ensuring Proper Clinical and Medical Care Standards Are Maintained and Practised–Final Report.* Available www.aph.gov.au/Parliamentary_Business/Committees/Senate/Community_Affairs/AgedCareQuality/Report (accessed 20 June 2020).

Sidanius, J. and Pratto, F. (1993) 'The Inevitability of Oppression and the Dynamics of Social Dominance', in P. Sniderman, P.E. Tetlock and E.G. Carmines (eds) *Prejudice, Politics, and the American Dilemma*, Stanford, CA: Stanford University Press, 173–211.

Slemon, A., Jenkins, E. and Bungay, V. (2017) 'Safety in Psychiatric Inpatient Care: The Impact of Risk Management Culture on Mental Health Nursing Practice', *Nursing Inquiry*, 24(4): e12199.

Tajfel, H. and Turner, J.C. (1986) 'The Social Identity Theory of Intergroup Behavior', in S. Worchel and W.G. Austin (eds) *The Psychology of Intergroup Relations*, Chicago, IL: Nelson-Hall, 7–24.

Thornicroft, G. (2006) *Shunned: Discrimination against People with Mental Illness*, Oxford: Oxford University Press.

Wills, T.A. (1981) 'Downward Comparison Principles in Social Psychology', *Psychological Bulletin*, 90(2): 245–71.

World Health Organisation (2019) *Transforming Services and Promoting Human Rights: WHO Quality Rights Training and Guidance–Mental Health and Social Services.* Available https://apps.who.int/iris/bitstream/handle/10665/329611/9789241516815-eng.pdf (accessed 20 June 2020).

Yeh, M.A., Jewell, R.D. and Thomas, V.L. (2017) 'The Stigma of Mental Illness: Using Segmentation for Social Change Marie', *Journal of Public Policy and Marketing*, 36(1): 97–116.

Zimmerman, S., Dobbs, D., Roth, E.G., Goldman, S., Peeples, A.D. and Wallace, B. (2016) 'Promoting and Protecting Against Stigma in Assisted Living and Nursing Homes', *The Gerontologist*, 56(3): 535–47.

12 Being recovery-oriented and reducing the use of restrictive interventions in mental health care

The challenges in achieving transformation

Lisa Brophy, Justine Fletcher and Bridget Hamilton

Introduction

In Australia and internationally there is commitment to the principle of providing mental health care in the least restrictive environment. For most people, the community is the preferred place of care, meaning less effort should be focused on the restrictive environment of the inpatient unit and compulsory treatment (World Health Organisation 1996) than on developing comprehensive support in the community. Even so, hospitals continue to care for people in acute mental health wards and in many jurisdictions a high proportion of admissions are involuntary. For example, in Australia for 2016/17 almost half of admissions (45.4 per cent) were involuntary, under the provisions of Australia's mental health laws (Australian Institute of Health and Welfare 2019). This often leads to consumers experiencing a contained and controlling environment in which restriction of movement is commonplace, based on a judgment that this will minimise risk of harm to self and others.

In this chapter, we incorporate a focus on the practices of restraint, but recognise the close relationship between those and a full spectrum of restrictive interventions (for a further discussion, see Roper et al. in Chapter 2 in this volume). Beginning with detention itself, many restrictive interventions flow from admission without consent (or detention) in psychiatric hospital settings. Practices include restricting exits by locking hospital doors, hands-on restraint, administering medication without consent and sometimes by intramuscular injection while restrained, mechanical restraint and sole confinement to a room or other enclosed space that a person cannot choose to leave (seclusion). As Grant Sara discusses in Chapter 9 in this volume, effective comparisons of rates of restrictive interventions across countries are hampered by varied definitions and poor levels of routine reporting (see also Stienert et al. 2010). These practices are regulated in different ways and utilised at varying rates in different jurisdictions. There is also considerable variation in the use of compulsory detention and restrictive interventions within and between jurisdictions (Raboch et al. 2010). Some people, particularly those with a diagnosis of a psychotic disorder, are at higher risk of coercive intervention (Schmitz-Buhl et al. 2019).

Making efforts to improve the experience of consumers on inpatient units and decreasing the associated harms has been an imperative in Australia and elsewhere for at least two decades (Huckshorn 2004; Victorian Department of Health and Human Services 2016; Fletcher et al. 2019a). As summarised by Brophy and colleagues (2016a), consumers in Australia reported overwhelmingly negative views about restraint and seclusion including being humiliated, traumatised and feeling punished (see also Robins et al. 2005; Mayers et al. 2010; Akther at al. 2019; Fletcher et al. 2019a; Maker in Chapter 5 in this volume). Consumers and their informal supporters have identified numerous examples of poor practice by staff that they believe contributes to the use of these practices or worsens the associated harms (Brophy et al. 2016a). Knowing these harms raises concerns that the ongoing high risk of suicide, both within inpatient units and post discharge, may be related to these experiences (Chung, Ryan and Hadzi-Pavlovic 2017; Large et al. 2017).

Multiple forces are now driving a movement to reduce the use of coercion. A recovery-oriented approach to mental health service delivery focuses on the person's values and preferences and supports them in relation to their personal recovery goals. It does not depend on clinical recovery or the reduction of symptoms (Slade et al. 2014; Byrne, Happell and Reid-Searl 2015). Key concepts of recovery are social inclusion, citizenship and agency. Thus, a recovery-oriented approach is directly challenged by the ongoing use of restrictive interventions (Huckshorn 2004; Curie 2005; Fletcher et al. 2019a). The United Nations *Convention on the Rights of Persons with Disabilities* (2007), which can be seen as compatible with the recovery paradigm, reframes these practices as fundamentally challenging the human rights and citizenship of people with disabilities (McSherry 2017; and see Bartlett and Sampson in Chapter 3 in this volume).

Despite efforts at law reform, recovery-oriented practice frameworks and policy development, there is ongoing use of restrictive and coercive interventions. For example, there has been an ongoing trend towards routine locking of acute mental health wards, such as occurred in Queensland in 2016 (Fletcher et al. 2019a). The Victorian Mental Illness Awareness Council (VMIAC), a peak body for mental health consumers across the Australian state of Victoria, reported on rates of seclusion in individual hospitals across Victoria and found substantial differences between wards. VMIAC also found that services in Victoria seclude people at a higher rate than in Australia overall. The seclusion of adolescents has been trending upward and there has been minimal change for adult inpatients in the previous three years (VMIAC 2019). Bowers and colleagues (2007) previously indicated that rates of seclusion and restraint varied between international jurisdictions and also between mental health facilities within individual countries.

How can this persisting practice and variation be explained? Why, despite now long-standing evidence that restrictive and coercive practices are harmful and may be creating more problems than they resolve, do these practices persist? This chapter explores these questions, mainly from the authors' own research in this area. We consider the drivers of change, who they are influencing and how. We also present information about the emerging evidence and its impact and finally explore the key common themes in qualitative literature and how that might guide what happens next. Our overall findings suggest that there are 'micro cultures' that continue to support the use of restrictive interventions while others have successfully embraced change. This is important to consider in ongoing efforts, especially those designed to support front-line workers to be confident about the potential for system and practice transformation.

The drivers of and barriers to change

The overall policy stance in Australia is that mental health services, including inpatient units, need to take a recovery-oriented approach and adopt a stronger human rights focus. This means, among other things, working towards the reduction, if not elimination, of restrictive interventions (Victorian Department of Health and Human Services 2013; Australian Commission on Safety and Quality in Health Care 2018). However, many mental health professionals continue to see seclusion and restraint as having some benefits in managing risk and promoting safety for patients and staff (Kinner et al. 2017; Fletcher et al. 2019c). Hence there are both driving and restraining factors at play in establishing the feasibility and desirability of reducing and/or eliminating these practices.

Factors driving less restriction

Recovery-oriented practice

Key policies devote considerable space to both recovery-oriented practice and least restrictive care (Commonwealth of Australia 2009a, 2009b, 2013). Davidson and colleagues (2009: 326) have defined recovery-oriented practice as:

> person-centered, strengths-based, collaborative and empowering. Consistent with the goals of self-determination and enabling people to pursue meaningful lives in the community despite the lack of a cure for their condition, advances in psychiatric rehabilitation focus on enhancing functioning and supporting people in taking part in routine adult roles in the community such as employment, education, and socialization.

Policies requiring recovery orientation sit alongside policies requiring reduction in restrictive interventions. Significant investment has been made in Australia to attempt to reduce restrictive interventions over the past two decades through law, policy and practice change. The National Mental Health Commission in 2012 recommended that services 'reduce the use of involuntary practices and work to eliminate seclusion and restraint' (Brophy et al. 2016b: 600). However, these policies on restrictive interventions do not directly speak to recovery-related policies.

Inpatient units are a particularly challenging environment in which to reduce coercion and embed recovery-oriented practice. Wyder and colleagues (2016: 338) have investigated this tension and concluded that:

> for coercive treatment to aid, rather than disrupt recovery, treatment services need to focus on: the provision of rights; the creation of a sense of safety; establishing supportive relationships; carrying hope and finding ways to foster a strong sense of agency and empowerment.

Though the notion that coercion can be recovery-oriented is contested, this statement is consistent with findings of Fletcher and colleagues (2019a), in a study investigating the impact of locked doors in Queensland. All study participants (consumers, staff and carers) endorsed the recommendation that acute wards should take a recovery-oriented approach and expressed views about how this could be achieved, even in locked wards.

Structured intervention programmes, such as Safewards (Bowers 2014), have gone some way to changing the tenor of 'limit setting' interactions between staff and consumers, recognising the provocations of restrictions and promoting consumer agency. Fletcher and colleagues (2019b, 2019c) have argued that, although Safewards was not initially developed as a recovery-oriented practice, it provides a pathway to reducing restrictive interventions which also appears to enable a move towards recovery-oriented practice (Kennedy et al. 2019) while more generally improving consumer experiences (Fletcher et al. 2019b).

United Nations Convention on the Rights of Persons with Disabilities

The United Nations *Convention on the Rights of Persons with Disabilities* (CRPD) (2007) raises expectations that signatory countries, like Australia, will reduce the use of coercive practices and restrictive interventions. Applying the human rights lens that the CRPD encourages, seclusion and restraint are restrictions of liberty and breaches of bodily integrity, and potentially abuses of power and privilege, rather than justifiable clinical interventions that are undertaken in the best interests of the person and others. The CRPD requires a radical reinterpretation of consumer participation in decision-making within signatory countries. It puts the person with disability at the centre of decision-making while rejecting a 'best interests' approach that privileges the opinions and power of clinicians and services (Brosnan 2018). Supported decision-making is a process whereby consumers are provided with the supports they need to exercise choice and control and express their views and preferences in decision-making on an equal basis with others. Supported decision-making contrasts with the substitute decision-making processes currently enabled by mental health law.

While the CRPD may be viewed as not introducing any new rights, it reinforces the need for all persons to have their views and preferences heard and respected. The safeguards or mechanisms for supported decision-making that have been encouraged by the CRPD, such as Advance Directives or statements, advocacy and other strategies to enable supported decision-making, can be understood as attempts to restrict the use of coercive interventions and involuntary orders (Callaghan and Ryan 2016; Brosnan 2018). The CRPD also encourages increased sensitivity to the importance of the rights of people with disabilities, including psychosocial disabilities, to be free from torture or cruel, inhuman or degrading treatment. Considering the feedback from consumers about the high level of distress associated with restraint and seclusion, as well as forced medication, the potential that mental health services in Australia are in breach of these rights can be considered to be additional drivers for reducing the use of restrictive interventions.

Factors driving the ongoing use of restriction

In our research, several common themes have emerged to help explain the persistent use of coercive and restrictive interventions.

Risk management culture

Preventing or reducing the risk of harm to self or others is a primary driver of restrictive interventions (Paterson, McIntosh and Mason 2011). However, this is alternatively viewed as a perpetuation of the stigma-based belief that people living with mental illness are aggressive, or potentially aggressive, and need to be contained and controlled (Slemon et al. 2017). As Bernadette McSherry discusses in more detail in Chapter 11 in this volume, an emphasis on risk mitigation and managerialism drives staff to prioritise the safety and control of everyone on the ward, even at the risk of breaching individuals' rights, legitimising the use of restrictive interventions with no consideration of long-term psychological impacts (Happell et al. 2010; Slemon et al. 2017). A managerial mindset also privileges efficient processes and routines in wards, undermining potentially slower interpersonal processes, such as the careful communication required to enable supported decision-making (Holttum 2016). One obvious example and a common moment of conflict arises from the routine expectation that medications are given as prescribed and on time (Bowers et al. 2014).

Staff safety

Mental health professionals are at higher risk of being subjected to physical aggression than many other health care practitioners (Bilici, Sercan and Izci 2016). Restrictive interventions may be perceived as necessary when mental health nurses are fearful about being injured at work (Larsen and Terkelsen 2013). Even in the context of some staff experiencing cognitive dissonance (Chambers et al. 2015) and feelings of guilt associated with forcing consumers to take medication and using other restrictive interventions, alternative safety-promoting practices may be elusive (Larsen and Terkelsen 2013). Kinner and colleagues (2017) found that mental health professionals were the group most likely to support restrictive interventions, although they found that some consumers and carers were also concerned about safety and supported the use of restrictive interventions for this reason.

The context of service delivery

There is currently an intensification of acuity in inpatient units, as lengths of inpatient stay are reducing across most countries (Newman et al. 2018). With community-based treatment preferred, only those with the most severe mental health issues are admitted, often involuntarily, and they are usually experiencing acute distress. This distress may also be a product of the admission process to hospital itself, including responding to the involvement of emergency services (including the police) and the emergency department (Allison and Bastiampillai 2015). Furthermore, pressure on a limited number of beds may lead to relatively short stays (Allison and Bastiampillai 2015). A shift towards locked doors, and difficulties in reducing other restrictive interventions, is potentially an unintended consequence of this changing population of people admitted to acute wards.

The limited evidence for interventions to reduce restrictions

Considering the breadth of concern about restrictions, there is a lack of strong evidence suggesting the best strategies for reducing reliance on restrictive interventions. In the context of the driving and restraining factors identified earlier, more evidence is needed to guide innovation and to resolve some of the inherent difficulties in trying to reduce restrictive interventions. However, highly valued evidence, such as is produced through rigorous research trials, can be difficult for researchers to produce and for practitioners to obtain. Accessing evidence for the locking (or not) of wards is an example of this difficulty, as we found in our review of the literature on this practice (Fletcher et al. 2019a). Advantages of locking were identified in the literature, including protection from outside and a sense of safety for consumers, more time for nurses to spend with patients and relief for families concerned about safety (Haglund and von Essen 2005; Fletcher et al. 2019a). However, disadvantages of locking doors were also apparent – consumers reported lower self-esteem, a sense of being excluded from the world, confinement and associated irritability (Bowers et al. 2010; Haglund and von Essen 2005; Muir-Cochrane et al. 2011; Fletcher et al. 2019a). Research has indicated that locking wards can lead to more aggressive behaviours among patients, increased awareness by people of losing their autonomy, higher rates of medication refusal and lower satisfaction with treatment (Middelboe et al. 2001; Müller et al. 2002; Baker et al. 2009; Fletcher et al. 2019a). Staff have expressed concerns about the potential for increased workload and the need to manage disputes when undertaking surveillance of entry and exit in the context of locked doors (Haglund et al. 2007; van der Merwe et al. 2009; Muir-Cochrane et al. 2011; Fletcher et al. 2019a). There is also minimal evidence about whether locked wards can prevent absconding even though this might be the primary purpose of imposing this restriction (Huber et al. 2016; Fletcher et al. 2019a).

Research regarding seclusion has found that it is not therapeutic (Sailas and Fenton 2000). However, as described earlier, a view persists among service providers in particular that seclusion and restraint are necessary interventions and potentially of benefit to the safety of particular patients and others around them (Larsen and Terkelsen 2013; Kinner et al. 2017).

As also mentioned earlier, Safewards is one evidence-based intervention that reduces restrictive interventions and aims to improve therapeutic relationships between direct care staff and consumers on inpatient units (Bowers et al. 2014). Evidence has been found supporting its effectiveness in decreasing conflict and containment events, as well as helping staff feel safer and reducing the use of forced sedation (Bowers et al. 2013; Maguire et al. 2018; Stensgaard et al. 2018; Fletcher et al. 2020). However, some studies indicate problems in staff acceptance of Safewards and in achieving fidelity of interventions when implemented (Price et al. 2016; Higgins et al. 2018). A trial in Victoria, where relatively high fidelity has been achieved, found a significant reduction in seclusion rates, from 14.1 seclusions per 1,000 occupied bed days prior to Safewards implementation, to 10.1 seclusions per 1,000 occupied bed days at 12-months follow up, representing a 36 per cent reduction (Fletcher et al. 2017).

Research evidence relating to consumers' experiences on inpatient units indicates that consumers feel safer and more respected when they are listened to about their own preferences during care (Gilburt, Rose and Slade 2008; Stenhouse 2013; Berg, Rørtveit and Aase 2017). The Safewards model can also contribute to feelings of safety by enabling a calm and predictable environment where there is less use of restrictive interventions (Gilburt, Rose and Slade 2008; Rise et al. 2014; Fletcher et al. 2019a).

Post-incident review following restraint in mental health care is a very promising practice but there has not been any 'gold standard' research on whether it contributes to any reduction in restraint and seclusion. Using a before and after study design, Fisher (2003) found that there was a 67 per cent decline in seclusion and restraint following implementation of a post-incident review programme. There is also some more recent evidence from post-incident review pilot studies demonstrating a reduction in seclusion (Goulet, Larue and Lemieux 2018). Furthermore, various practices involving staff talking to consumers about their experience after incidents of restraint are generally highly regarded in the qualitative literature when the practice is respectful and collaborative (Petti et al. 2001; Bonner and Wellman 2010; Goulet, Larue and Lemieux 2018). There is a belief that this will lead to more reflective practice and a reduction in the use of restrictive interventions. Evidence suggests that it may contribute to less restrictive and more ethical practice but findings from other studies indicate that post-incident review is not consistently implemented (Goulet and Larue 2016).

The invisibility of restraint and other restrictive interventions in policy and practice guidance

Another source of guidance may exist in government and service-based policy. However, a search of Australian state and national policies and guidelines revealed little mention of restrictive interventions in policies and procedures in services (Fletcher et al. 2019a). By contrast, these key state and national policies devote considerable space to recovery-oriented practice and least restrictive care in principle (Commonwealth of Australia 2009a, 2009b, 2013). It appears that this overarching policy position is not always reflected in local policy and practice that might guide the reduction of restrictive practices. Staff have expressed frustration that the rhetoric of recovery-oriented practice does not necessarily translate into any practical guidance for inpatient settings or the organisational commitment and leadership that is required (McKenna et al. 2014; Slade et al. 2014). As observed by a consumer participant in Brophy and colleagues' (2016a: 6) study:

> Seclusion and restraint, the very practices themselves, are sort of very anti-recovery . . . . [Recovery is] all about self-responsibility, self-direction, and then seclusion and restraint is all about someone else's control, so it doesn't actually sit with recovery at all.

As harms of restriction are increasingly recognised, the justificatory term that commonly emerges is 'last resort', whereby these practices are permitted as a last resort, rather than affirmed (Riahi, Thomson and Duxbury 2016). However, in the absence of explicit policy direction, practitioners and teams are left to determine where the threshold of last resort lies, what is the best practice use of a restriction in a given situation, and how these practices can align with recovery-orientation or with upholding of human rights, if indeed they can.

Common themes in qualitative findings regarding restrictive interventions

Another contribution to the question of how services can be transformed to be more recovery-oriented and reduce the use of restrictive interventions in mental health care can be drawn from listening directly to those involved, through qualitative studies. This involves hearing the valuable perspectives of consumers, carers and staff. Common themes in qualitative findings are often intersecting and many appear to be linked to stigma and discrimination, in particular the 'othering' of consumers, leading to disrespect and human rights violations.

The need to reduce boredom in wards

Consumers in mental health wards report feeling lonely, bored and in need of engaging activity (Donald et al. 2015) and they frequently feel unsafe (Novak et al. 2012; Brophy et al. 2016a). Many express sadness that there is no opportunity to talk and are troubled that staff don't have time for therapeutic engagement (Donald et al. 2015; Brophy et al. 2016a).

The need to reduce boredom among consumers who are under-occupied was the highest priority recommendation in the Queensland locked doors study, based on rankings by staff, consumers and carers. As described by one consumer:

> [Y]ou know you might be having a really crappy day, but you can sit and get lost in [an activity] and you don't want to sit in a group, and you don't want

> to sit in the courtyard and talk, you don't want to converse with a nurse or whoever, but you want to get lost in whatever you're doing, whether you're beading or drawing or painting or, and it might be a dark painting but hey this is how I feel on the day.
>
> (Fletcher et al. 2019a: 543)

Addressing the issue of boredom may be key to providing a safe and recovery-oriented environment on acute mental health wards.

The value of peer support workers

According to our qualitative research findings, there is general agreement among consumers, their families and other supporters and staff that wards need to have peer support workers who spend time with consumers and their families (Brophy et al. 2016b; Fletcher et al. 2019a, 2019c). For example, the words of one mental health worker interviewed highlight the value placed on having someone who has their own lived experience to support consumers (Fletcher et al. 2019a: 543):

> I think it's the lived experience that you cannot get from staff. The staff get their knowledge from their training but they don't have the experience of it and sometimes what you want to hear is someone who's actually experienced this.

In focus groups conducted by Brophy and colleagues (2016b: 602), peer support and advocacy were suggested as strategies to enable elimination or reduction of seclusion and restraint. There was strong consensus across these focus groups that peer support is vital to ensuring that understanding, empathy and recovery-oriented practice occur in the inpatient setting. Research elsewhere also highlights that the addition of peer support workers to wards can support a shift to recovery-oriented services (Holmes et al. 2013; see also Roper et al. in Chapter 2 in this volume). Further, 'leadership towards organisational change' and 'consumer roles in inpatient settings' are two of six strategies recommended by the United States National Association of State Mental Health Program Directors for reducing restrictive interventions, including restraint, in inpatient settings (National Association of State Mental Health Program Directors 2008; see McSherry and Maker in Chapter 1 in this volume).

Choice and control

As Slemon and colleagues (2017) suggest, moving from a strongly risk averse culture to one more prepared to tolerate risk and promote safety and therapeutic relationships is an important foundation for enabling more consumer choice and empowerment. Fletcher and colleagues (2019a: 543) accordingly found that consumers value being able to make choices in what can be a highly restrictive environment:

> I probably look at it that you've got a choice, you could sit and watch telly if you want, you can sit out in the courtyard, but a lot of the time when you're on a ward your choices are taken away from you, you know you're medicated, you know you're there sometimes under your, you don't want to be there, so it's about having that choice.
>
> (*Consumer*)

Continuity, quality and experience of staff

Positive relationships between consumers on the ward, and between staff and consumers, contribute to a safe, therapeutic environment and reduce the potential that consumers will abscond (Muir-Cochrane et al. 2011). Fletcher and colleagues (2019a: 544) found that participants wanted consistent, well-trained nursing staff who had the kind of experience that led to advanced skills – not just more of the same:

> I want to qualify that, you know, saying you want quality and experience of nursing staff doesn't mean you want someone who's been doing it for 40 years and very dated because some of the best experiences that I've had either as a patient or as a carer when family have been in has been actually from quite young and passionate and enthusiastic and really caring young new staff.
>
> (*Carer*)

For some staff in Victoria, implementing Safewards was reported to be consistent with their professional training. It enabled them to refresh their thinking about providing more holistic care and offered a renewed focus on building therapeutic relationships (Fletcher et al. 2019c).

Consumer perspectives on Safewards in the Victorian trial (Fletcher et al. 2019b) included doubts about some staff having the ability to carry out all components of the intervention, with consumers stating that 'full time staff are usually better at it than casual/part time staff, in my experience'; and 'night staff are not very good at this, day staff are'.

Brophy and colleagues (2016b: 602) found that:

> improving staff culture was strongly linked to education and training, but also to steps such as 'weeding out' staff who appeared to lack skills and compassion and introducing more consumer feedback and involvement in services was likely to be helpful in reducing restraint and seclusion. Greater recognition of staff skills to calm and defuse situations was seen as a positive contribution to culture change.

Addressing problems with inpatient environments

Consumers have reported feeling a loss of freedom and control (Wood et al. 2019) in what are often custodial inpatient environments (Bower, McCullough and Timmons 2003). Other issues include the environment being sterile (Donald et al. 2015), with stringent and arbitrary rules (Baker, Bowers and Owiti 2009), a lack of collaboration in care (Wood et al. 2019) and consumers not feeling heard and respected (Robins et al. 2005). Wards can also be poorly designed as some aspects of the physical environment, such as crowding, excess noise and lack of privacy, have been found to contribute to higher rates of aggression and increased risk of restrictive interventions (Ulrich et al. 2018).

In the Queensland locked wards study, Fletcher and colleagues (2019a: 544) found that some staff identified the custodial features of the ward as having a negative impact on consumers. These features may have perpetuated stigma:

> [T]he custodial features of the ward is a huge thing, it's probably the biggest, is [comments made by consumers] 'I feel I've been in prison', 'I feel like I'm being punished', 'why am I being treated this way', yeah that's probably – if I was going to start anywhere it would definitely be there.
>
> (*Staff*)

In Brophy and colleagues' (2016a: 5) study, participants discussed how seclusion and restraint were used by staff to gain control over consumers and to manage the environments they found themselves in, with one supporter observing, 'that's just routine, doesn't matter what the individual's state of mind is, so then they have to be kind of contained within that routine'.

This accords with our earlier analysis that the organisational emphasis in inpatient settings is often on managing people within the space and routine, rather than on forming relationships.

Tolerating risk and addressing fear

In qualitative studies, staff and organisations making the shift away from a 'risk averse' orientation is commonly described as a significant challenge. This shift to being more prepared to tolerate risk and enable consumers (including compulsory patients on inpatient units) to have the opportunity of the 'dignity of risk' requires clear leadership. Concerns about people being at risk of suicide, self-harm or absconding plays an important role in why inpatient units are locked. But Fletcher and colleagues (2019a) found that singling out people who are considered to be 'high risk', and making decisions around them, was not necessarily endorsed by participants in their study. They proposed 'that a locked ward could be available for consumers who are either in crisis or at risk of harming others, but that this should be for as short a time as possible' (Fletcher et al. 2019a: 545).

The perspective of being risk averse, fearful of potential harms and being persistently focused on safety may interfere with meaningful therapeutic engagement between consumers and staff and encourage harmful practices (O'Hagan 2004; Slemon et al. 2017; Fletcher et al. 2019a). It also poses a barrier to recovery-oriented practice (Commonwealth of Australia 2013). This is reflected in a consumer's comment in Brophy and colleagues' (2016a: 8) study that:

> Staff are frightened, police officers are probably frightened too, like people don't necessarily have those connections, like staff in hospitals don't always have connections with people that are like deep enough to, or like genuine enough to talk to people when they're in really bad distress.

Recognising trauma

In Brophy and colleagues' study (2016a: 5), participants made a link between the trauma experienced as a result of seclusion and restraint, and the subsequent impact this had on the person's recovery, sense of trust in the world and relationships with service providers:

> So what I've seen with people who've felt, when they've had even a single 24 hour experience of seclusion and restraint under the mental health system, which is the door, the police, the medication, down into the whatever, the taking of the clothes, the whole lot – that person's changed forever in their feeling and their relationship to the society around them. To every other state agency they're changed, and that allows, that's again that learned helplessness.
>
> (*Consumer*)

Acknowledging dehumanisation and 'othering'

Brophy and colleagues (2016a: 5) discuss how seclusion and restraint was viewed by consumers and their supporters as an experience of 'othering', in that people had to cope with times in their lives when people treated them as though they were 'sub-human'. In another study, Brophy and colleagues' (2016a: 6) study participants – including both consumers and their informal supporters – described the use of excessive force, lack of empathy and paternalistic attitudes among some staff:

> I've seen people, patients . . . knocking on windows when nurses close them off . . . because they couldn't get heard, and therefore they'd start kicking the window and they'd be injected and taken off to seclusion.
>
> (*Supporter*)

Attempts to reduce restrictive interventions need to acknowledge that these underlying attitudes and values form barriers to changing practice.

Listening, respect, compassion and hope

The importance of listening well and talking respectfully to consumers while engaging in person-centred care was identified as central to conflict prevention and reducing restrictive interventions in the Victorian Safewards trial (Fletcher et al. 2019c). Staff found that Safewards affirmed their engagement in positive practice, such as being caring, compassionate and valuing consumers, which has been found to decrease the likelihood of conflict and containment (Papadopoulos et al. 2012; Gudde et al. 2015; Fletcher et al. 2019c). These themes were also endorsed by consumer feedback about the Victorian Safewards trial (Fletcher et al. 2019b). Respect was a key theme, and this is consistent with findings from other studies that being respected impacts on how engaged people are in their care and the quality of care they receive (Rise et al. 2014; Fletcher et al. 2019b). Similarly the concept of hope has been endorsed as making an essential contribution to moving towards more recovery-oriented service delivery (Wyder, Bland and Crompton 2015). Again, in the Safewards trial study, consumers reported feeling more hopeful about being on the ward (Fletcher et al. 2019b).

Addressing the culture of wards and overall organisational culture

Working in organisations that are highly risk-averse was described as difficult for staff in both the locked wards and Safewards projects described previously (Fletcher et al. 2019a, 2019c). Participants commonly described an apparently competing expectation that staff and organisations will be more recovery-oriented while also having a high level of tolerance of restrictive interventions. One participant in the locked wards study (Fletcher et al. 2019a: 545) described this tension as follows:

> On one hand, [the government is] saying we need to give people freedom to experience recovery to make mistakes to learn from those mistakes and on the other hand they're saying lock the doors put monitors on people make sure nobody escapes because the Minister doesn't like it. And so as a result of all of that we've got this very risk-averse organisation that we work for. So there's mixed messages one day we're recovery-orientated and the next day lock the doors.
>
> (*Staff*)

Fletcher and colleagues (2019c) found that the Safewards interventions had some success in supporting staff to have less social distance from patients on the ward and enhanced mutual regard. This appeared to be related to more shared responsibility and increased collaboration between staff and patients. According to the staff participants in the study, Safewards helped to facilitate a more recovery-oriented environment because it was linked to enhancing consumer involvement in their care and treatment, hope and peer support, choice, dignity and staff taking a more respectful stance towards consumers (Fletcher et al. 2019c). These outcomes potentially contributed to cultural change that is required to reduce restrictive interventions. According to Larsen and Terkelson (2013) the process of reducing the distance between staff and consumers is one element that enables a more individualised, person-centred approach, challenging the potential for continuing to 'other' patients and define them as a category of people who need control and restriction.

More staff, more resources and more money

In Victoria, staff in all wards participated in Safewards training prior to the model's implementation, with evaluation surveys revealing significant increases in staff knowledge, confidence and motivation to implement Safewards (Fletcher et al 2020). This provides a possible explanation of staff understanding of the Safewards model and interventions and may explain the high fidelity scores achieved. However, Brophy and colleagues (2016a: 9) heard from consumer participants that staff in services were too stressed and busy to attend to the needs of consumers:

> You'll go talk to them and they seem run off their feet and angry and stuff, and they take it, then their mood affects everyone else, because they're usually carrying on. Sometimes they're just as bad as people on the ward.
>
> (*Consumer*)

Hence without appropriate investment in training and everyday support, and in situations where staff are overworked, restrictive interventions may flourish.

Conclusion

Despite mounting evidence about the potential for practices such as Safewards, post-incident reviews, environmental changes and staff improvements in preventing and reducing seclusion and restraint, there is a lack of consistent implementation of this evidence. This extends to other restrictive and coercive interventions such as locking ward doors, where evidence promotes caution and reduction in use while other research suggests increased and expanding day-to-day use (Fletcher et al. 2019a).

Other drivers, particularly risk management, continue to influence the culture and practices within mental health service delivery even without strong evidence, maintaining a high tolerance for the restrictive interventions that are characterised as necessary responses to risk and safety fears.

Brophy and colleagues (2016a: 8) concluded that their findings indicate that:

> consumers and supporters view 'poor practice' as indicative of a system which expects and condones mental health practitioners to use seclusion and restraint to manage behaviour, despite consumers experiencing such practices in an overwhelmingly negative way. This suggests that it is institutional cultures and norms that require addressing.

Consumers, staff and carers have all made important contributions to suggesting how to move to more recovery-oriented service delivery and reduce the use of restrictive interventions. Qualitative research reveals many consistent themes around the importance of reducing boredom on inpatient units, improving the treatment environment, care that is compassionate and respectful and having staff more prepared for their roles.

Research and evaluation efforts that are informed by implementation science, enabling consideration of process, implementation and outcome data are necessary to understand potential practice change in complex mental health service systems. It is also important for research findings, including lived experience perspectives, to reach the desired recipients. More effort to link and embed a range of evidence will be important for achieving practice, policy change and innovation in mental health service delivery and realising human rights (Redfern et al. 2003).

Management and leadership are also key to system transformation. Unfortunately, they are potentially most influenced by the drivers encouraging more risk aversion and accountability practices that appear to get in the way of working well with people in distress. An abundance of paperwork does not appear to have had the desired effect of changing practice; instead, it is frequently blamed for staff having less time to build positive and trusting relationships. However, it is inevitably an important challenge to have both accountability and sufficient staff time and resources to be with people and support their recovery. Peer workers appear to have an important role to play here, although there is a danger that this forms a proxy for more significant system transformation involving all staff.

Despite these challenges, transformation appears to be possible. On inpatient units Safewards is offering a pathway to reducing restrictive interventions and enabling a move towards recovery-oriented practice, while also improving consumer experiences (Fletcher et al. 2019b, 2019c). However, practices such as Safewards, post-incident reviews and the unlocking of doors need ongoing attention to remain relevant. The consumer voice is often missing in the initial development of these new practices and interventions. It is essential that staff are encouraged to be reflexive and value the critical perspective of consumers in order to ensure practices focused on reducing restrictive interventions are relevant and recovery-oriented. Co-design, co-production and consumer perspectives being valued in the ongoing development, evaluation and evolution of these practices may be the key to the credibility of the next stage of intervention refinements (Hoddinott et al. 2018). This has the potential to raise the credibility of these practices and increase expectations about change and improved engagement with new ways of working.

References

Akther, S., Molyneaux, E., Stuart, R., Johnson, S., Simpson, A. and Oram, S. (2019) 'Patients' Experiences of Assessment and Detention Under Mental Health Legislation: Systematic Review and Qualitative Meta-Synthesis', *BJPsych Open*, 5(3): E37.

Allison, S. and Bastiampillai, T. (2015) 'Mental Health Services Reach the Tipping Point in Australian Acute Hospitals', *Medical Journal of Australia*, 203(11): 432–34.

Australian Commission on Safety and Quality in Health Care (2018) *National Safety and Quality Health Service (NSQHS) Standards–Action 5.3 Minimising Restrictive Practices: Restraint.* Available www.nationalstandards.safetyandquality.gov.au/5.-comprehensive-care/minimising-patient-harm/minimising-restrictive-practices-restraint (accessed 20 June 2020).

Australian Institute of Health and Welfare (2019) *Mental Health Services in Brief 2018.* Available www.aihw.gov.au/getmedia/0e102c2f-694b-4949-84fb-e5db1c941a58/aihw-hse-211.pdf.aspx?inline=true (accessed 20 June 2020).

Baker, J.A., Bowers, L. and Owiti, J.A. (2009) 'Wards Features Associated with High Rates of Medication Refusal by Patients: A Large Multi-Centred Survey', *General Hospital Psychiatry*, 31(1): 80–89.

Berg, S. V., Rørtveit, K. and Aase, K. (2017) 'Suicidal Patients' Experiences Regarding their Safety During Psychiatric In-patient Care: A Systematic Review of Qualitative Studies', *BMC Health Services Research,* 17(1): [73].

Bilici, R., Sercan, M. and Izci, F. (2016) 'Levels of the Staff's Exposure to Violence at Locked Psychiatric Clinics: A Comparison by Occupational Groups', *Issues in Mental Health Nursing*, 37(7): 501–06.

Bonner, G. and Wellman, N. (2010) 'Postincident Review of Aggression and Violence in Mental Health Settings', *Journal of Psychosocial Nursing and Mental Health Services*, 48(7): 35–40.

Bower, F.L., McCullough, C.S. and Timmons, M.E. (2003) 'A Synthesis of What We Know About the Use of Physical Restraints and Seclusion with Patients in Psychiatric and Acute Care Settings: 2003 Update', *Online Journal of Knowledge Synthesis for Nursing*, 10(1): 1–29.

Bowers, L. (2013) 'The Safewards Model and Cluster RCT', *International Journal of Mental Health Nursing*, 22(S1): 2.

Bowers, L. (2014) 'Safewards: A New Model of Conflict and Containment on Psychiatric Wards', *Journal of Psychiatric and Mental Health Nursing*, 21(6): 499–508.

Bowers, L., Haglund, K., Muir-Cochrane, E., Nijman, H., Simpson, A., and Van der Merwe, M. (2010) 'Locked Doors: A Survey of Patients, Staff and Visitors', *Journal of Psychiatric and Mental Health Nursing*, 17(10): 873–880.

Bowers, L., Alexander, J., Bilgin, H., Botha, M., Dack, C., James, K., Jarrett, M., Jeffery, D., Nijman, H., Owiti, J.A., Papadopoulos, C., Ross, J., Wright, S. and Stewart, D. (2014) 'Safewards: The Empirical Basis of the Model and a Critical Appraisal', *Journal of Psychiatric and Mental Health Nursing*, 21(4): 354–64.

Bowers, L., van der Werf, B., Vokkolainen, A., Muir-Cochrane, E., Allan, T. and Alexander, J. (2007) 'International Variation in Containment Measures for Disturbed Psychiatric Inpatients: A Comparative Questionnaire Survey', *International Journal of Nursing Studies*, 44(3): 357–64.

Brophy, L.M., Roper, C.E., Hamilton, B.E., Tellez, J.J. and McSherry, B.M. (2016a) 'Consumers and Their Supporters' Perspectives on Poor Practice and the Use of Seclusion and Restraint in Mental Health Settings: Results from Australian Focus Groups', *International Journal of Mental Health Systems*, 10(6): 1–10.

Brophy, L.M., Roper, C.E., Hamilton, B.E., Tellez, J.J. and McSherry, B.M. (2016b) 'Consumers' and Their Supporters' Perspectives on Barriers and Strategies to Reducing Seclusion and Restraint in Mental Health Settings', *Australian Health Review*, 40(6): 599–604.

Brosnan, L. (2018) 'Who's Talking About Us Without Us? A Survivor Research Interjection into an Academic Psychiatry Debate on Compulsory Community Treatment Orders in Ireland', *Laws*, *7*(4): 33.

Byrne, L., Happell, B. and Reid-Searl, K. (2015) 'Recovery as a Lived Experience Discipline: A Grounded Theory Study', *Issues in Mental Health Nursing*, 36(12): 935–43.

Callaghan, S. and Ryan, C.J. (2016) 'An Evolving Revolution: Evaluating Australia's Compliance with the Convention on the Rights of Persons with Disabilities in Mental Health Law', *University of New South Wales Law Journal*, 39(2): 596–624.

Chambers, M., Kantaris, X., Guise, V. and Valimaki, M. (2015) 'Managing and Caring for Distressed and Disturbed Service Users: The Thoughts and Feelings Experienced by a Sample of English Mental Health Nurses', *Journal of Psychiatric and Mental Health Nursing*, 22(5): 289–97.

Chung, D.T., Ryan, C.J. and Hadzi-Pavlovic, D. (2017) 'Suicide Rates After Discharge from Psychiatric Facilities: A Systematic Review and Meta-Analysis', *JAMA Psychiatry*, 74(7): 694–702.

Commonwealth of Australia (2009a) *Fourth National Mental Health Plan: An Agenda for Collaborative Government Action in Mental Health 2009–2014*. Available https://www1.health.gov.au/internet/main/publishing.nsf/Content/mental-pubs-f-plan09 (accessed 20 June 2020).

Commonwealth of Australia (2009b) *National Mental Health Policy 2008*. Available https://www1.health.gov.au/internet/main/publishing.nsf/Content/mental-pubs-n-pol08 (accessed 20 June 2020).

Commonwealth of Australia (2013) *A National Framework for Recovery-oriented Mental Health Services: Policy and Theory*. Available www.health.gov.au/internet/main/publishing.nsf/Content/mental-pubs-n-recovpol (accessed 20 June 2020).

Convention on the Rights of Persons with Disabilities (2007) Opened for signature 13 December, 2515 UNTS 3 (entered into force 3 May 2008).

Curie, C.G. (2005) 'SAMHSA's Commitment to Eliminating the Use of Seclusion and Restraint', *Psychiatric Services*, 56(9): 1139–40.

Davidson, L., Drake, R.E., Schmutte, T., Dinzeo, T. and Andres-Hyman, R. (2009) Oil and Water or Oil and Vinegar? Evidence-based Medicine Meets Recovery', *Community Mental Health Journal*, 45(5): 323–32.

Donald, F., Duff, C., Lee, S., Kroschel, J. and Kulkarni, J. (2015) 'Consumer Perspectives on the Therapeutic Value of a Psychiatric Environment', *Journal of Mental Health*, 24(2): 63–67.

Fisher, W.A. (2003) 'Elements of Successful Restraint and Seclusion Reduction Programs and Their Application in a Large, Urban, State Psychiatric Hospital', *Journal of Psychiatric Practice*, 9(1): 7–15.

Fletcher, J., Buchanan-Hagen, S., Brophy, L., Kinner, S. and Hamilton, B. (2019b) 'Consumer Perspectives of Safewards Impact in Acute Inpatient Mental Health Wards in Victoria, Australia', *Frontiers in Psychiatry*, 10: 461 (1–11).

Fletcher, J., Hamilton, B., Kinner, S. and Brophy, L. (2019c) 'Safewards Impact in Inpatient Mental Health Units in Victoria, Australia: Staff Perspectives', *Frontiers in Psychiatry*, 10: 462 (1–10).

Fletcher, J., Hamilton, B., Kinner, S., Sutherland, G., King, K., Tellez, J.J., Harvey, C. and Brophy, L. (2019a) 'Working Towards Least Restrictive Environments in Acute Mental Health Wards in the Context of Locked Door Policy and Practice', *International Journal of Mental Health Nursing*, 28(2): 538–50.

Fletcher, J., Reece, J., Kinner, S., Brophy, L. and Hamilton, B. (2020) 'Safewards Training in Victoria: A Descriptive Analysis of Two Training Methods and Subsequent Implementation', *Journal of Psychosocial Nursing and Mental Health Services* (forthcoming).

Fletcher, J., Spittal, M., Brophy, L., Tibble, H., Kinner, S.A., Elsom, S. and Hamilton, B. (2017) 'Outcomes of the Victorian Safewards Trial in 18 Wards: Impact on Seclusion Rates and Fidelity Measurement', *International Journal Mental Health Nursing*, 26(5): 461–71.

Gilburt, H., Rose, D. and Slade, M. (2008) 'The Importance of Relationships in Mental Health Care: A Qualitative Study of Service Users' Experiences of Psychiatric Hospital Admission in the UK', *BMC Health Services Research*, 8(92): 1–12.

Goulet, M.H. and Larue, C. (2016) 'Post-Seclusion and/or Restraint Review in Psychiatry: A Scoping Review', *Archives of Psychiatric Nursing*, 30(1): 120–28.

Goulet, M.H., Larue, C. and Lemieux, A.J. (2018) 'A Pilot Study of "Post-Seclusion and/or Restraint Review" Intervention with Patients and Staff in a Mental Health Setting', *Perspectives in Psychiatric Care*, 54(2): 212–20.

Gudde, C.B., Olso, T.M., Whittington, R. and Vatne, S. (2015) 'Service Users' Experiences and Views of Aggressive Situations in Mental Health Care: A Systematic Review and Thematic Synthesis of Qualitative Studies', *Journal of Multidisciplinary Healthcare*, 8: 449–62.

Haglund, K., van der Meiden, E., von Knorring, L. and von Essen, L. (2007) 'Psychiatric Care Behind Locked Doors. A Study Regarding the Frequency of and the Reasons for Locked Psychiatric Wards in Sweden', *Journal of Psychiatric and Mental Health Nursing*, 14(1): 49–54.

Haglund, K. and von Essen, L. (2005) 'Locked Entrance Doors at Psychiatric Wards–Advantages and Disadvantages According to Voluntarily Admitted Patients', *Nordic Journal of Psychiatry*, 59(6): 511–15.

Happell, B. and Harrow, A. (2010) 'Nurses' Attitudes to the Use of Seclusion: A Review of the Literature', *International Journal of Mental Health Nursing*, 19(3): 162–68.

Higgins, N., Meehan, T., Dart, N., Kilshaw, M. and Fawcett, L. (2018) 'Implementation of the Safewards Model in Public Mental Health Facilities: A Qualitative Evaluation of Staff Perceptions', *International Journal of Nursing Studies*, 88: 114–20.

Hoddinott, P., Pollock, A., O'Cathain, A., Boyer, I., Taylor, J., MacDonald, C., Oliver, S. and Donovan, J.L. (2018) 'How to Incorporate Patient and Public Perspectives into the Design and Conduct of Research', *F1000Research*, 7: 752 (1–33).

Holmes, D., Molloy, L., Beckett, P., Field, J. and Stratford, A. (2013) 'Peer Support Workers Hold the Key to Opening Up Recovery-Orientated Service in Inpatient Units', *Australasian Psychiatry*, 21(3): 282–83.

Holttum, S. (2016) 'How Included Are Mental Health Service Users in Decisions About Their Medication?', *Mental Health and Social Inclusion*, 20(3): 141–48.

Huber, C., Huber, C.G., Schneeberger, A.R., Kowalinski, E., Froehlich, D., Walter, M., Zinkler, M., Beine, K., Heinz, A., Borgwardt, S. and Lang, U.E. (2016) 'Suicide Risk and Absconding in Psychiatric Hospitals with and Without Open Door Policies: A 15 year, Observational Study', *Lancet Psychiatry*, 3(9): 842–49.

Huckshorn, K.A. (2004) 'Reducing Seclusion and Restraint Use in Mental Health Settings: Core Strategies for Prevention', *Journal of Psychosocial Nursing and Mental Health Services*, 42(9): 22–33.

Kennedy, H., Roper, C., Randall, R., Pintado, D., Buchanan-Hagen, S., Fletcher, J. and Hamilton, B. (2019), 'Consumer Recommendations for Enhancing the Safewards Model and Interventions', *International Journal of Mental Health Nursing*, 28(2): 616–26.

Kinner, S.A., Harvey, C., Hamilton, B., Brophy, L., Roper, C., McSherry, B. and Young, J.T. (2017) 'Attitudes Towards Seclusion and Restraint in Mental Health Settings:

Findings from a Large, Community-based Survey of Consumers, Carers and Mental Health Professionals', *Epidemiology and Psychiatric Sciences*, 26(5): 535–44.

Large, M.M., Chung, D.T., Davidson, M., Weiser, M. and Ryan, C.J. (2017) 'In-Patient Suicide: Selection of People at Risk, Failure of Protection and the Possibility of Causation', *BJPsych Open*, 3(3): 102–105.

Larsen, I.B. and Terkelsen, T.B. (2013) 'Coercion in a Locked Psychiatric Ward: Perspectives of Patients and Staff', *Nursing Ethics*, 21(4): 426–36.

Maguire, T., Ryan, J., Fullam, R. and McKenna, B. (2018) 'Evaluating the Introduction of the Safewards Model to a Medium- to Long-Term Forensic Mental Health Ward', *Journal of Forensic Nursing*, 14(4): 214–22.

Mayers, P., Keet, N., Winkler, G. and Flisher, A. J. (2010) 'Mental Health Service Users' Perceptions and Experiences of Sedation, Seclusion and Restraint', *International Journal of Social Psychiatry*, 56(1): 60–73.

McKenna, B., Furness, T., Dhital, D., Ennis, G., Houghton, J., Lupson, C. and Toomey, N. (2014) 'Recovery-Oriented Care in Acute Inpatient Mental Health Settings: An Exploratory Study', *Issues in Mental Health Nursing*, 35(7): 526–32.

McSherry, B. (2017) 'Regulating Seclusion and Restraint in Health Care Settings: The Promise of the Convention on the Rights of Persons with Disabilities', *International Journal of Law and Psychiatry*, 53: 39–44.

Middelboe, T., Schjødt, T., Byrsting, K. and Gjerris, A. (2001) 'Ward Atmosphere in Acute Psychiatric In-Patient Care: Patients' Perceptions, Ideals and Satisfaction', *Acta Psychiatrica Scandinavica*, 103(3): 212–19.

Muir-Cochrane, E., van der Merwe, M., Nijman, H., Haglund, K., Simpson, A. and Bowers, L. (2011) 'Investigation into the Acceptability of Door Locking to Staff, Patients, and Visitors on Acute Psychiatric Wards', *International Journal of Mental Health Nursing*, 21(1): 41–49.

Müller, M.J., Schlösser, R., Kapp-Steen, G., Schanz, B. and Benkert, O. (2002) 'Patients' Satisfaction with Psychiatric Treatment: Comparison Between an Open and a Closed Ward', *Psychiatric Quarterly*, 73(2): 93–107.

National Association of State Mental Health Program Directors (2008) *Six Core Strategies to Reduce Seclusion and Restraint Use*. Available www.nasmhpd.org/content/six-core-strategies-reduce-seclusion-and-restraint-use (accessed 20 June 2020).

Newman, L., Harris, V., Evans, L.J., and Beck, A. (2018) 'Factors Associated with Length of Stay in Psychiatric Inpatient Services in London, UK', *Psychiatric Quarterly*, 89(1), 33–43.

Novak, T., Scanlan, J., McCaul, D., MacDonald, N. and Clarke, T. (2012) 'Pilot Study of a Sensory Room in an Acute Inpatient Psychiatric Unit', *Australasian Psychiatry*, 20(5): 401–406.

O'Hagan, M. (2004) 'Force in Mental Health Services: International User and Survivor Perspectives', *Mental Health Practice*, 7: 12–17.

Papadopoulos, C., Bowers, L., Quirk, A. and Khanom, H. (2012) 'Events Preceding Changes in Conflict and Containment Rates on Acute Psychiatric Wards', *Psychiatric Services*, 63(1): 40–47.

Paterson, B., McIntosh, I. and Mason, T. (2011) 'Mental Health Policy Making in England the Risk Society: A Political Discourse Analysis', *Journal of Risk and Governance*, 2(3): 147–58.

Petti, T.A., Mohr, W.K., Somers, J.W. and Sims, L. (2001) 'Perceptions of Seclusion and Restraint by Patients and Staff in an Intermediate-Term Care Facility', *Journal of Child and Adolescent Psychiatric Nursing*, 14(3): 115–27.

Price, O., Burbery, P., Leonard, S. and Doyle, M. (2016) 'Evaluation of Safewards in Forensic Mental Health', *Mental Health Practice*, 19(8): 14–21.

Raboch, J., Kalisová, L., Nawka, A., Kitzlerová, E., Onchev, G., Karastergiou, A., Magliano, L. Dembinskas, A., Kiejna, A., Torres-Gonzales, F., Kjellin, L., Prieve, S. and Kallert, T.W. (2010) 'Use of Coercive Measures During Involuntary Hospitalization: Findings from Ten European Countries', *Psychiatric Services*, 61(10): 1012–17.

Redfern, S., Christian, S. and Norman, I. (2003) 'Evaluating Change in Health Care Practice: Lessons from Three Studies', *Journal of Evaluation in Clinical Practice*, 9(2): 239–49.

Riahi, S., Thomson, G. and Duxbury, J. (2016) 'An Integrative Review Exploring Decision-Making Factors Influencing Mental Health Nurses in the Use of Restraint', *Journal of Psychiatric Mental Health Nursing*, 23(2): 116–28.

Rise, M.B., Westerlund, H., Bjorgen, D. and Steinsbekk, A. (2014) 'Safely Cared for or Empowered in Mental Health Care? Yes, Please', *International Journal of Social Psychiatry*, 60(2): 134–38.

Robins, C.S., Sauvageot, J.A., Cusack, K.J., Suffoletta-Maierle, S. and Frueh, B.C. (2005) 'Consumer's Perceptions of Negative Experiences and "Sanctuary Harm" in Psychiatric Settings', *Psychiatric Services*, 56(9): 1134–38.

Sailas, E.E.S. and Fenton, M. (2000) 'Seclusion and Restraint for People with Serious Mental Illnesses', *Cochrane Database of Systematic Reviews*, 1: 1–17.

Schmitz-Buhl, M., Gairing, S.K., Rietz, C., Häussermann, P., Zielasek, J. and Gouzoulis-Mayfrank, E. (2019) 'A Retrospective Analysis of Determinants of Involuntary Psychiatric In-Patient Treatment', *BMC Psychiatry*, 19(127): 1–15.

Slade, M., Amering, M., Farkas, M., Hamilton, B., O'Hagan, M., Panther, G., Perkins, R., Shepherd, G., Tse, S. and Whitley, R. (2014) 'Uses and Abuses of Recovery: Implementing Recovery-Oriented Practices in Mental Health Systems', *World Psychiatry*, 13(1): 12–20.

Slemon, A., Jenkins, E. and Bungay, V. (2017) 'Safety in Psychiatric Inpatient Care: The Impact of Risk Management Culture on Mental Health Nursing Practice', *Nursing Inquiry*, 24: e12199.

Steinert, T., Lepping, P., Bernhardsgrutter, R., Conca, A., Hatling, T., Janssen, W., Keski-Valkama, A., Mayoral, F. and Whittington, R. (2010) 'Incidence of Seclusion and Restraint in Psychiatric Hospitals: A Literature Review and Survey of International Trends', *Social Psychiatry and Psychiatric Epidemiology*, 45(9): 889–97.

Stenhouse, R. C. (2013). 'Safe Enough in Here?': Patients' Expectations and Experiences of Feeling Safe in an Acute Psychiatric Inpatient Ward', *Journal of Clinical Nursing*, 22(21-22): 3109–3119.

Stensgaard, L., Andersen, M.K., Nordentoft, M. and Hjorthøj, C. (2018) 'Implementation of the Safewards Model to Reduce the Use of Coercive Measures in Adult Psychiatric Inpatient Units: An Interrupted Time-Series Analysis', *Journal of Psychiatric Research*, 105: 147–52.

Ulrich, R.S., Bogren, L., Gardiner, S.K. and Lundin, S. (2018) 'Psychiatric Ward Design Can Reduce Aggressive Behavior', *Journal of Environmental Psychology*, 57: 53–66.

van der Merwe, M., Bowers, L., Jones, J., Simpson, A. and Haglund, K. (2009) 'Locked Doors in Acute Inpatient Psychiatry: A Literature Review', *Journal of Psychiatric and Mental Health Nursing*, 16(3): 293–97.

Victorian Department of Health and Human Services (2013) *Providing a Safe Environment for All: Framework for Reducing Restrictive Interventions.* Available https://www2.health.vic.gov.au/about/publications/researchandreports/Providing-a-safe-environment-for-all-Framework-for-reducing-restrictive-interventions (accessed 20 June 2020).

Victorian Department of Health and Human Services (2016) *Victoria's Mental Health Services Annual Report 2015–2016.* Available https://www2.health.vic.gov.au/about/publications/annualreports/mental-health-annual-report-2015-16 (accessed 20 June 2020).

Victorian Mental Illness Awareness Council (2019) *Seclusion Report: Accessible Information on Seclusion in Victorian Mental Health Services.* Available www.vmiac.org.au/wp-content/uploads/Seclusion-Report_VMIAC_Vic-mental-health-hospital-services_APRIL_2019_FINAL.pdf (accessed 20 June 2020).

Wood, L., Williams, C., Billings, J. and Johnson, S. (2019) 'The Therapeutic Needs of Psychiatric In-Patients with Psychosis: A Qualitative Exploration of Patient and Staff Perspectives', *BJPsych Open*, 5(E45): 1–9.

World Health Organisation (1996). *Mental Health Care Law: Ten Basic Principles.* Available www.who.int/mental_health/media/en/75.pdf (accessed 20 June 2020).

Wyder, M., Bland, R. and Crompton, D. (2016) 'The Importance of Safety, Agency and Control During Involuntary Mental Health Admissions', *Journal of Mental Health*, 25(4): 338–42.

Wyder, M., Bland, R., Herriot, A. and Crompton, D. (2015) 'The Experiences of Legal Processes of Involuntary Treatment Orders: Tension Between the Legal and Medical Frameworks', *International Journal of Law and Psychiatry*, 38: 44–55.

13 Psychotropic use in Australian aged care homes

What can be done to ensure appropriate use?

*Juanita Breen**

Introduction

In 2017, approximately 85 per cent of all residents in Australian aged care homes were diagnosed with at least one mental health condition, with depression top ranked at 47 per cent (Australian Institute of Health and Welfare (AIHW) 2018). Anxiety and sleep disorders are estimated to affect up to 20 per cent and 30 per cent of residents respectively (Creighton, Davison and Kissane 2016; Ye et al. 2018). It is important to recognise that around 53 per cent of all residents are also estimated to have dementia (AIHW 2018); most of whom will experience 'changed behaviour', or 'behavioural and psychological symptoms of dementia' (BPSD) at some stage, including mental health symptoms of anxiety, agitation, depression and insomnia (Royal Australian and New Zealand College of Psychiatry (RANZCP) 2016). Given this high burden of poor mental health it is no surprise that some experts have declared aged care homes to be 'modern mental institutions for the elderly' (Rovner and Katz 1993: 84).

For common old age mental health conditions (mild-moderate depression, anxiety, insomnia and 'changed behaviour'), guidelines advocate non-pharmacological approaches as first-line treatment (Malhi et al. 2015; Royal Australian College of General Practitioners (RACGP) 2015; RANZCP 2016). Although there is some evidence to support using psychotropic medications to treat these conditions, for most older people their effect size is modest, and they can cause severe adverse effects such as falls, pneumonia and stroke (Glass et al. 2005; Schneider, Dagerman and Insel 2006; Gambassi, Sultana and Trifirò 2015; Johnell et al. 2016; RANZCP 2016; Taipale et al. 2017). Given this unfavourable risk/benefit ratio, guidelines now recommend that psychotropics are trialled only after non-pharmacological approaches fail, when symptoms cause distress or confer risk of harm (RACGP 2015; RANZCP 2015, 2016).

High rates of psychotropic medication use in Australian aged care homes indicate over-reliance on pharmacological therapy (Westaway et al. 2018; Westbury et al. 2019). This issue is not new. Evidence of inappropriate use has been reported for 20 years, with concern expressed about extended duration of treatment (Westbury et al. 2010a), unlicensed indications (New South Wales (NSW) Ministerial Taskforce 1997), limited review (Westbury et al. 2010a; Harrison et al. 2019) and a lack of monitoring for adverse effects (NSW Ministerial Taskforce 1997; Westaway et al. 2018).

Psychotropic medications

Psychotropic medications are 'capable of affecting the mind, emotions, and behaviour, and are used to treat mental illnesses' (Farlex 2012). The three main classes of psychotropic medications used in aged care are antidepressants (for example, citalopram, mirtazapine, sertraline), anxiolytics/hypnotics, mostly benzodiazepines (for example, diazepam, temazepam, oxazepam) and antipsychotics (for example, risperidone, olanzapine, quetiapine). Other psychotropic classes include anticonvulsants (Westbury et al. 2019). These psychotropic classes are outlined in turn.

Antidepressants are the most commonly prescribed psychotropic medications in aged care, taken by over 40 per cent of residents (Harrison et al. 2019; Westbury et al. 2019). The majority of those (80 per cent) diagnosed with depression are prescribed such medications as first-line treatment (Gaboda et al. 2011; Bourgeois et al. 2012). Ironically, despite this high use, overall rates of uncontrolled depression have not declined. The reasons for this lack of treatment effect are complex. First, reviews suggest that antidepressants only offer modest benefit in older people, at best, particularly in people with dementia (Farina, Morrell and Banerjee 2017). Second, antidepressants are often requested as first-line treatment by aged care staff who have inadequate knowledge about how to recognise depression and manage it (Iden, Hjorleifsson and Ruths 2011). When these medications are prescribed, monitoring for response rarely occurs (Shah et al. 2012). Finally, there is a recognised deficit in Australian aged care regarding the provision of psychology services and training in psychosocial management (Davison et al. 2017).

Benzodiazepines are endorsed for short-term use only for anxiety and insomnia after non-drug approaches are trialled (RACGP 2015). They are also prescribed to treat 'changed behaviour' in people with dementia, despite limited evidence of beneficial outcomes (Loi et al. 2015). Due to side effects of drowsiness, language impairment, cognitive impairment and falls, they are considered to offer more risks than benefits in most older people (Glass et al. 2005). Falls in aged care homes are associated with substantial mortality; over a third of residents with a hip fracture will die within six months, and among those who survive six months, approximately 28 per cent will become totally disabled (Neuman et al. 2014). Another issue with long-term benzodiazepine use is that users often become dependent and tolerant to their effects meaning that they lose effectiveness and higher doses are needed to relieve symptoms. Tolerance to the hypnotic effects of benzodiazepines develops within a few weeks of use, whereas tolerance to the anxiolytic effects develops over a few months (Madhusoodanan and Bogunovic 2004).

The Royal Australian College of General Practitioners (RACGP) now recommends that older people presenting with anxiety should be treated initially with psychological therapies, then with antidepressants, if anxiety symptoms do not abate. Benzodiazepines should be used only intermittently, and chronic use avoided to lessen the risk of tolerance and dependence. In insomnia, the RACGP notes that although benzodiazepine treatment has shown statistically significant improvements in sleep in the short-term, 'the magnitude of effect is small, and the benefits of these drugs may not justify the increased risk'. If hypnotics are to be used for treating insomnia, it is recommended that treatment is short-term (that is, not more than four weeks) and at the lowest possible dose (RACGP 2015).

Antipsychotics are licensed for use for schizophrenia and other severe mental health conditions. In dementia, only one antipsychotic, risperidone, is subsidised by the Pharmaceutical Benefits Scheme (commonly known as the PBS) for use in Australia, and only then for 12 weeks, in moderate to severe Alzheimer's disease (not vascular dementia or Lewy Body dementia), for severe agitation and psychosis when non-drug treatments have failed (Department of Health (Australia) 2019a, 2019b). When taken by people with dementia, antipsychotics increase the risk of stroke, death from any cause, heart arrhythmias and pneumonia and cause metabolic and movement disorders (RANZCP 2016). For this reason, the RANZCP endorses that

> the first-line approach to management of BPSD is a person-centred, psychosocial, multidisciplinary treatment plan. Indications for antipsychotic medications in patients with dementia include: severe agitation and aggression associated with risk of harm; delusions and hallucinations and comorbid pre-existing mental health conditions.
>
> (RANZCP 2016)

In the United States, antipsychotics are not licensed for use in people with dementia at all and have a black box warning of severe adverse effects (Maust et al. 2018).

Prevalence of psychotropic use in Australia

For several decades, high prevalence rates and inappropriate use of psychotropic medication in aged care homes have been reported, particularly for antipsychotics and benzodiazepines (NSW Ministerial Taskforce 1997; Westaway et al. 2018). Researchers from the United States were the first to draw attention to high rates and dubious quality of psychotropic use in aged care. In 1988, Beers and colleagues reported that over a quarter of residents in United States nursing homes were taking antipsychotics and around 40 per cent were taking hypnotics. Beers and colleagues also drew attention to the high rate of 'prn' or 'as required' prescribing of antipsychotics and benzodiazepines, meaning that nursing staff were often deciding when and which residents would take this medication (Beers et al. 1988).

The first major Australian study of aged care home psychotropic use was conducted in a group of 46 homes in Sydney during 1993 and was led by Professor John Snowdon. The rates of regular antipsychotic (27 per cent) and benzodiazepine (35 per cent) use were 'among the highest reported in the world' (Snowdon et al. 1995). Consequently, Snowdon's study attracted considerable media attention, resulting in the establishment of the New South Wales Ministerial Taskforce into Psychotropic Medication Use in Aged Care during which concerns were raised regarding high rates of combination psychotropics, excessive dosages and extended duration of use (NSW Ministerial Taskforce 1997).

Comprehensive data on overall psychotropic use in aged care homes in Australia is limited. Most studies focus on antipsychotic use and measure prevalence through varying methods, such as obtaining data from medication charts and medication reviews. There is also wide variation in the resident case mix and number of homes assessed in each study. Respecting these limitations, the rate of antipsychotic use in Australian aged care homes varies from 13 to 42 per cent of residents (Westaway et al. 2018).

The first national prevalence study conducted in Australian residential care was published in 2019. This study examined psychotropic use in a large sample of 139 aged care homes across six states and the Australian Capital Territory in 2014/15, involving over 11,500 residents (Westbury et al. 2019). Nearly a quarter (22 per cent) of residents were taking antipsychotics every day and the same percentage (22 per cent) were taking daily doses of benzodiazepines. 'Prn' or 'when needed' use of sedative psychotropics was the highest reported in an Australian study to date, with 32 per cent and 11 per cent of all residents charted for 'prn' benzodiazepines and antipsychotics, respectively (Westbury et al. 2019). The national rates of benzodiazepine use were almost identical to those observed in a 2014 study of six South Australian homes, where 25 per cent of residents were prescribed regular doses and 32 per cent 'prn' doses (Chen et al. 2016).

Regarding duration of use, several Australian studies have highlighted that many residents are prescribed antipsychotics for longer periods than guidance recommends (Westaway et al. 2018). In 2007 research, we found that 58 per cent of residents prescribed an antipsychotic were taking the same drug for at least one year, and only 27 per cent of residents originally receiving one had their dose reduced or medication ceased during that time (Westbury et al. 2010a). Similarly, the average duration of antipsychotic use in a 2017 study across 24 homes in New South Wales was 416 days (Pont et al. 2017). In baseline data for the Halting Antipsychotic use in Long-Term care (HALT) intervention targeting 23 New South Wales aged care homes, residents were prescribed an antipsychotic for an average duration of 2.1 years and with an unchanged dose for 1.2 years. Verbal consent to prescribe an antipsychotic was recorded in only 15 per cent of residents' files and written consent was recorded in only one (Brodaty et al. 2018).

There is little data on benzodiazepine utilisation in Australian aged care homes. When we compared the dosages of benzodiazepines in the same group of residents of aged care homes in 2006 and 2007, we found that nearly two-thirds of residents taking benzodiazepines were taking exactly the same drug, at the same dose. Less than a quarter of the residents had their dose reduced, or medication ceased, as recommended by guidelines (Westbury et al. 2010a).

High rates of sustained antipsychotic and benzodiazepine use suggest non-adherence to guidelines. In general, antipsychotic and benzodiazepine medications are prescribed too often and for too long to aged care residents. Less is known about antidepressant utilisation in Australian aged care homes.

International psychotropic medication use

In general, rates of psychotropic use observed in Australian homes are similar to rates recorded overseas, although comparisons are difficult due to differences in aged care systems and study methodologies. For reference, Australia's national prevalence rates for antipsychotic, benzodiazepine and antidepressant prescribing were estimated to be 22 per cent, 22 per cent and 41 per cent, respectively (Westbury et al. 2019). The regular antipsychotic prevalence (22 per cent) we observed in our national Australian nursing home prevalence study is almost identical to rates recorded using large databases from the United States (22.7 per cent) (Department of Health and Human Services (US) 2016) and England (21.0 per cent) (Szczepura et al. 2016) in the same time frame.

The 2014–15 benzodiazepine and antidepressant prevalence rates recorded in US nursing homes were approximately 25 per cent and 54 per cent, respectively (Department of Health and Human Services 2016). Benzodiazepine prevalence data for English homes is unavailable. However, a 2011 Scottish study reported that 28 per cent of a sample of residents received benzodiazepines or other sleeping medication (Johnson et al. 2016). A large English nursing home survey conducted between 2010 and 2012 found that 41 per cent of residents were prescribed antidepressant medication (Stewart et al. 2014).

Factors underlying psychotropic use

As part of my doctoral thesis I conducted qualitative research to understand the drivers and key influences underlying psychotropic prescribing practice. This research was based in five aged care homes in Hobart, in the Australian state of Tasmania during 2008 to 2009. After in-depth interviewing of 20 aged care nurses, five doctors delivering care to residents, five directors of care, five pharmacists providing services to aged care homes and ten relatives of residents, I found that the drivers affecting psychotropic use are complex and multi-factorial.

Although nursing and care staff cannot legally prescribe, they were the most influential of all the groups interviewed in requesting that psychotropic medication be started. Many of the staff interviewed believed that these medications are a lot more beneficial than the evidence suggests. Further, aged care staff were often not aware of side effects associated with use, often attributing these as related to 'getting old' or a 'part of the dementia'. They were also not aware of any professional guidelines relating to psychotropic use. Many of the staff stated that they felt these medications improved resident quality of life and that they were necessary to 'calm and comfort' them. Several directors of care also felt they were required to improve the care that other residents experienced and that relatives often asked staff to 'do something' about behaviours such as calling out (Westbury 2011).

In one-to-one interviews, all of the general practitioners interviewed said they were asked to prescribe these medications primarily by the staff. None of the general practitioners could recall being asked for these medications by relatives. They reported that they assumed that non-drug strategies had been trialled before being asked to prescribe. Half of the general practitioners interviewed said that by using low doses they minimised side effects and would justify use by stating they only used just a 'small amount'. The interviewees suggested that comprehensive assessment of a resident's symptoms as recommended by most professional guidelines occurred infrequently; review of psychotropic medications did not occur routinely, if at all. There was marked reluctance shown by staff to alter medications or doses due to the possibility that behavioural or psychological symptoms would worsen or reappear (Westbury 2011).

Although pharmacists are funded by the Australian government to review medications of residents in aged care homes, they reported resistance from general practitioners and staff to suggestions to reduce psychotropic use. All pharmacists interviewed said that other medication classes were much easier to alter. Over half of the relatives reported that the only time they knew about medications being started was when they noted them on a pharmacy bill. Consent to start, or alter, existing psychotropic medication was rarely sought from 'persons responsible' despite the legal obligation to do so (Westbury 2011).

Kieran Walsh and colleagues conducted a systematic review of international qualitative studies determining factors influencing antipsychotic use in people with dementia (Walsh et al. 2017). Of 18 studies meeting inclusion criteria from inception to July 2016, reasons for prescribing these medications included:

- Understaffing and insufficient time to engage with residents, for thorough assessment and to perform non-drug strategies;
- Staff inability to deal with the severity of behaviour of residents;
- Lack of training on non-drug ways to manage 'changed behaviour', leading to pressure on prescribers from staff to initiate antipsychotics;
- Inadequate knowledge of prescribers and staff on the risks and benefits of antipsychotics;
- Poor communication within health care teams and with families;
- Uncertainty regarding roles and responsibilities in relation to antipsychotic prescribing;
- Poor organisational culture within the home; and
- Fear of behaviour recurrence if medication was altered (Walsh et al. 2017).

Chemical restraint? The term is very much open to interpretation

Over the decade I have researched this issue, approximately ten Directors of Care that I consulted have claimed that there was no chemical restraint (or restrictive practice) used in their home. Their understanding was that the use of psychotropic medication was legally justified if a resident had a medical or mental health diagnosis. Thus, if there was a diagnosis of anxiety, sleep disorder or dementia then psychotropic medication was considered to be an acceptable treatment. As explored by Grant Sara in Chapter 9 in this volume, chemical restraint may be the most difficult form of restraint to define because of its openness to interpretation.

Strategies to reduce psychotropic use

This section provides an overview of regulatory, safety and policy strategies designed to reduce the use of psychotropic medication.

Regulation and mandatory public reporting

Of all countries, the United States has made the most concerted effort to address inappropriate use of psychotropic medications in nursing homes, especially with antipsychotic prescribing. After several reports in the 1980s highlighting poor quality of nursing home care, the United States Congress passed the *Nursing Home Reform Amendment* in 1987 as part of the *Omnibus Budget Reconciliation Act 1987* (OBRA). This Act sets national minimum standards of care and rights for residents, one of which protects them from 'medically unnecessary physical or chemical restraints imposed for purposes of discipline or convenience' (OBRA 1987: section 7(c)(1)(A)(ii)). After the amendment, the United States government regulated standards of care for psychotropic medication that homes must follow, publishing interpretive guidelines to assist them to follow the law and surveyors to enforce it (Department of Health and Human Services 2016). Nursing homes that do not meet these regulations are subject to a series of sanctions, ranging from financial penalties to closure (Ellis et al. 2015). Mandatory public reporting of each home's antipsychotic use was introduced in the United States in 2012, along with a five-star rating system (Department of Health and Human Services 2016).

By 2012, in response to concerns about persistently high rates of antipsychotic use, the United States government launched the National Partnership to Improve Dementia Care in Nursing Homes, with its aim of reducing antipsychotic use in residents with dementia by 30 per cent by the end of 2016 (Ellis et al. 2015). Marked reductions in use were observed and publicised, but there has been recent criticism that aged care staff have been under-reporting use (reporting is all self-reported) and that residents have been 'intentionally diagnosed' with schizophrenia as this diagnosis is exempt from mandatory reporting (Department of Health and Human Services 2016). There is also concern that decreases in antipsychotic use may be accompanied by compensatory shifts to other psychotropics with sedating properties, notably benzodiazepines, sedating antidepressants and anticonvulsants, as these medications are not legislated nor part of mandatory reporting. A recent study revealed that use of antipsychotics was falling but that this trend started before the partnership. The authors expressed concern that benzodiazepine and anticonvulsant (or mood stabilisers) prescribing had risen since the partnership commenced (Maust et al. 2018).

Safety warnings and policy

After several studies linking antipsychotic use in older people to stroke and death, the United States Food and Drug Administration issued a black box warning in 2005, and again in 2008 (Ellis et al. 2015). The impact of these warnings was mixed, with doctors attending nursing homes reporting reducing antipsychotic doses and consulting with mental health specialists but no substantial decline in the rates of antipsychotic use (Lester et al. 2011).

Unlike the United States, England does not adopt a punitive regulatory approach nor monitor and report psychotropic use in their nursing homes, although care home legislation and minimum standards were introduced in the early 2000s (Hughes, Roughead and Kerse 2008). England has highlighted excessive use of antipsychotics in relation to people with dementia more generally through safety warnings and public policy, which are outlined later in the chapter.

The first English safety warning about prescribing antipsychotics in this patient group was released in 2004 (Medicines Healthcare Products Regulatory Agency (MHRA) 2004) and updated again in 2009 (MHRA 2009). Although the two safety warnings reduced antipsychotic prescribing temporarily, it is noteworthy, like in the United States, that benzodiazepine and antidepressant use increased significantly as antipsychotic use declined (Guthrie et al. 2013).

Persistent concerns over the safety of antipsychotics in dementia led to the release of the English Department of Health's *Time for Action* report (Banerjee 2009). The government committed to reducing antipsychotic prescribing in people with dementia by two-thirds in two years; recommending audit/feedback cycles and education for nursing home staff (Banerjee 2009).

Two years on, an English national prescribing audit indicated a marked reduction of over 50 per cent in antipsychotic use in people with dementia from 2006 to 2011. However, this reduction claim has to be treated with caution as the number of people in England with recorded dementia, especially those at early stages and therefore much less likely to be given antipsychotics, more than doubled since 2006 (Smith 2011). Further, the audit did not provide information on the residential setting of people with dementia, thus data did not come only from aged care homes. Another study conducted in British nursing homes reported that the government pledge had limited impact on antipsychotic prescribing rates (Szczepura et al. 2016). Critics of the *Time for Action* initiative say that it fails on two fronts; specifically, that it neither identifies who is responsible for reviewing antipsychotic use, nor adopts systematic approaches to do so (Smith 2011).

Australian initiatives to address psychotropic use

Australia has not relied on public reporting, setting targets or safety warnings to address the issue of high psychotropic use in its aged care homes. Despite repeated international safety warnings, the first Australian safety update about risperidone in dementia was only released in August 2015 by the Therapeutic Goods Administration, following data linking the use of risperidone to a five times higher risk of stroke in people with vascular and mixed dementia

(Department of Health 2015). The warning advised that risperidone only be prescribed in people with a diagnosis of Alzheimer's disease and that use be restricted to a maximum period of 12 weeks. The warning was later incorporated into the Pharmaceutical Benefits Scheme entry for risperidone (Department of Health 2019a). Although these warnings appear to have reduced the number of risperidone prescriptions, the use of alternative medications markedly increased, particularly quetiapine and oxazepam. By 2018 levels of risperidone prescribing had rebounded to pre-warning levels. Figure 13.1 shows the number of scripts issued over a five year period.

The Australian government first identified excessive psychotropic use in aged care homes in 1995 when a Senate committee report, *Psychotherapeutic Medication in Australia*, suggested that 'the lack of monitoring, or review of psychotropic agents, led to high levels of antipsychotics and benzodiazepines being prescribed for excessive periods, for little apparent benefit'. One of the report's recommendations was that pharmacists become more involved in the review of psychotropic medication (Australian Senate 1995). This was reinforced in 1997 when the *New South Wales Ministerial Taskforce on Psychotropic Medication in Nursing Homes* report also recommended that pharmacists become involved by providing regular medication reviews and nurse education in homes as potential strategies to reduce psychotropic use.

In 2001, the Australian government introduced national *Standards for Aged Care Facilities* which reflect the quality management and services expected in

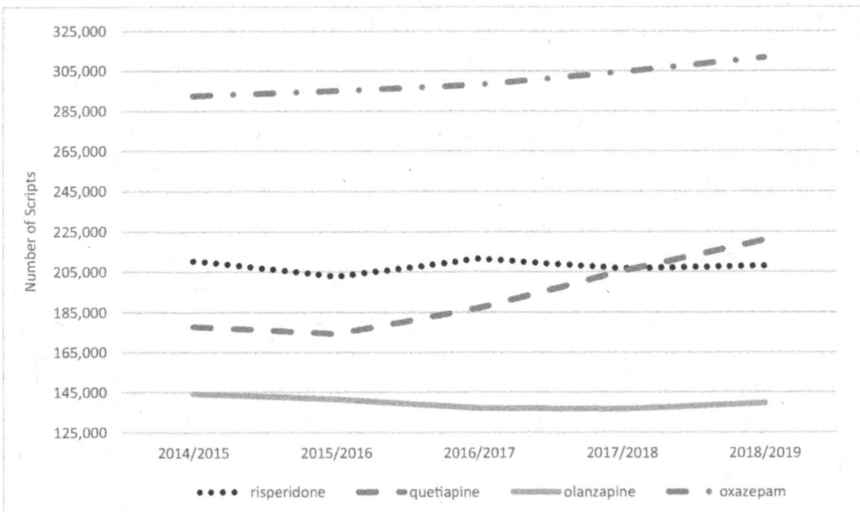

Figure 13.1 Low dose risperidone, quetiapine, olanzapine and oxazepam prescribing in Australia over financial years 2014–2019 derived from Pharmaceutical Benefits Scheme (PBS) data

Source: Department of Health (Australia) 2019a, 2019b

homes and determine suitability for accreditation. Although the standards do not stipulate appropriate psychotropic use directly, they include key outcomes on medication management, sleep and behaviour management (Aged Care Quality and Safety Commission 2019a). New standards replaced the accreditation standards from 1 July 2019. The new standards do not provide guidance for 'chemical restraint' directly, instead requiring the reporting of restrictive practices as part of Standard 8 (Aged Care Quality and Safety Commission 2019b).

Residential medication management review and quality use of medicines programme

A pioneering trial in 52 aged care homes in Queensland and northern New South Wales found that the combination of pharmacist-led medication review and nursing staff education offered the potential to significantly reduce inappropriate medication use, including that of benzodiazepines, and generate significant cost savings (Roberts et al. 2001). The findings of this study and recommendations from the reports discussed previously led the Australian government to fund pharmacist-led Residential Medication Management Reviews in homes, starting from 1997 (Pharmaceutical Society of Australia (PSA) 2017). A Residential Medication Management Review is defined (PSA 2017) as:

> a comprehensive medication review, by an accredited pharmacist, that is resident-focused involving the systematic evaluation of the resident's complete medication regimen and management of that medication.

A Residential Medication Management Review fosters good quality use of medicine at a resident level, however, medication use is also influenced at the aged care home level (PSA 2017). The Quality Use of Medicine service is a separate service provided by a registered pharmacist and focuses on improving practices and procedures as they relate to the quality use of medicines in homes. From 2002, Quality Use of Medicine services, including strategies such as nursing education and psychotropic audits, were incorporated into the existing Residential Medication Management Reviews programme (PSA 2017).

The Residential Medication Management Reviews programme appears to have affected psychotropic use in Australia, although specific evidence to support this is not available. A 2011 study reported that most accredited pharmacists highlighted inappropriate psychotropic use when conducting Residential Medication Management Reviews. However, the recommendations from these reviews involved monitoring for adverse effects rather than recommending withdrawal attempts and only half of the recommendations relating to mental health medications were agreed to and implemented by general practitioners (Nishtala et al. 2011). A study conducted in 17 New South Wales homes during 2014 reported that only 53 per cent of psychotropic medication was clinically reviewed over a 6-month period. Less than eight per cent of reviews led to a dosage reduction. The authors concluded that practices were not effective in reducing the use of psychotropic medicines, nor were they compliant with current guidance (Yang et al. 2014). Disappointingly, in mid-2014, funding for Residential Medication Management Reviews was changed to once every two years per resident, instead of yearly as under the previous agreement; meaning that reviews are now done half as frequently (PSA 2017).

The Quality Use of Medicine programme was independently evaluated by Campbell Research in 2010, which reported that although Quality Use of Medicine services were generally well received, some directors of homes were 'almost entirely unaware of what they could and indeed, should, anticipate from the pharmacist and what services they could request' (Campbell Research 2010). Another issue highlighted related to the types and quality of Quality Use of Medicine services delivered to the home as these are not mandated, nor audited. When homes were surveyed, over 25 per cent had not received any in-service education from pharmacists throughout a 12-month period and less than half were offered a medication audit (Campbell Research 2010).

Despite the Residential Medication Management Reviews and Quality Use of Medicine service programme, the problem of overuse of psychotropic medication in homes continues as evidenced by persistently high use of antipsychotics and benzodiazepines.

Focused interventions

Although there is a plenitude of studies describing inappropriate psychotropic use in aged care homes, only a few intervention projects have addressed this issue. Like regulation and policy approaches, most are targeted at reducing inappropriate antipsychotic use. Thompson-Coon and colleagues' (2014) international systematic review examined projects aimed to improve antipsychotic prescribing. Twenty-two quantitative studies (reported in 23 articles) were included evaluating the effectiveness of educational programmes (n = 11), in-reach services (n = 2), medication review (n = 4) and multicomponent interventions (n = 5). Eleven studies were randomised or controlled in design; the remainder were uncontrolled before and after studies. Beneficial effects were seen in nine of the 11 studies, with the most robust study design involving reductions in antipsychotic prescribing levels of between 12 and 20 per cent (Thompson-Coon et al. 2014).

In the Australian context, a recent review, again focused solely on antipsychotic prescribing, concluded that '[m]ultidisciplinary, multi-strategic approaches have demonstrated effectiveness' (Westaway et al. 2018: Abstract). Four Australian interventions aimed to reduce the use of antipsychotics among aged care home residents were included. A six-month controlled trial which aimed to reduce the use of antipsychotics and benzodiazepines in 25 Tasmanian residential aged care facilities during 2008 and 2009 used comprehensive educational strategies (including educational sessions for staff), promotional materials and guidelines, academic detailing for doctors and interdisciplinary reviews of sedative medicine use to guide prescribing. Results of the study indicated initial reductions in antipsychotic use of 8 per cent in the intervention homes as opposed to increased rates of use in control homes (Westbury et al. 2010b). The use of benzodiazepines in intervention homes also declined significantly by 13%, whereas use in control homes remained static (Westbury et al. 2010b). The sustainability of the intervention was assessed 12 months post-intervention. Benzodiazepine use continued to decline in the year after the intervention. However, in the absence of active strategies, the rates of antipsychotic use rebounded slightly (Westbury et al. 2011).

An expansion of this project, the 'RedUSe' (Reducing Use of Sedatives) programme, was implemented in 150 aged care homes across Australia, involving 12,157 residents between 2014 and 2016. The multi-strategic, multidisciplinary six-month intervention which encompassed strategies such as audits and feedback, and educational sessions to doctors, nurses and pharmacists, reduced antipsychotic use by 13 per cent without increasing 'prn' or as required psychotropic drug use. Of over 2,000 residents taking antipsychotic medication at the beginning of the project, 40 per cent had their doses ceased outright or reduced. Notably, over two-thirds of all 150 participant homes recorded reductions in antipsychotic prescribing (Westbury et al. 2018).

The 'Halting Antipsychotic use in Long-Term care' (HALT) study, conducted from 2014–2017, aimed to examine the conditions under which antipsychotics were prescribed to better understand inappropriate prescribing in residents with dementia and to evaluate the feasibility of a multidisciplinary approach to reduce antipsychotic use. The study involved educating nurses, pharmacists, general practitioners and psychologists about managing dementia and changed behaviours and reducing antipsychotic use (Brodaty et al. 2018). Residents taking a regular antipsychotic for three or more months without a psychotic illness or severe BPSD were recruited into the study after agreeing to withdraw their antipsychotic medication. The intervention required nurse 'champions' at the participating facilities to be trained in how to manage behavioural symptoms using person-centred, non-drug approaches. General Practitioners reviewed antipsychotic use and followed an individualised de-prescribing protocol established by pharmacists to reduce the dose or cease where appropriate. Results of the intervention indicated that of the 133 residents taking a regular antipsychotic at the start of the study, almost 95 per cent (126 residents) had ceased antipsychotic use at the 12-month assessment. However, some residents re-started their medication. Withdrawal of the regular antipsychotic was not substituted with prn antipsychotic use or benzodiazepine use and there was little change in BPSD or adverse outcomes (Brodaty et al. 2018).

The Veterans' Medicine Advice and Therapeutics Education Services (Veterans' MATES) programme, which is funded by the Australian Department of Veterans' Affairs and provides educational materials and patient-specific audit and feedback to general practitioners, was shown to be effective in reducing antipsychotic use in older Australian veterans with dementia. An intervention in 2007 and 2008 that targeted 3,884 general practitioners, 6,690 veterans aged 65 years or older (dispensed an oral antipsychotic) and 8,089 pharmacists across Australia, resulted in a significant change in antipsychotic use. Risperidone decreased in use by 14.3 per cent at the time of the intervention and the rate of use continued to decrease by 2.7 per cent per month relative to the pre-intervention trend for the period from February 2008 to September 2009 (for example, overall use continued to increase, but only by 0.9 per cent per month) (Roughead et al. 2013).

Thompson-Coon and colleagues' systematic review concludes:

> [i]nterventions to reduce inappropriate prescribing of antipsychotic medications to people with dementia resident in care homes may be effective in the short term, but longer-term, more robust studies are needed. For prescribing levels to be reduced. . . the culture and nature of care settings and feasibility of nondrug alternatives needs to be addressed.
>
> (Thompson-Coon et al. 2014: 717)

Conclusions

Despite numerous governmental investigations in Australia (both state and federal), prescribing restrictions, professional guidelines, a pharmacist-led review and Quality Use of Medicine programme and several government-funded interventions, psychotropic use in Australian aged care homes continues to be high and inappropriate in terms of duration of use, lack of monitoring and review.

Continued inappropriate and high levels of use attest to the complexity of this issue. Of all approaches, multi-strategy, multidisciplinary programmes appear to offer the most potential to improve psychotropic use. However, given funding constraints and high staff turnover in aged care homes, as well as poor access to health practitioner services, such programmes need to be provided in the long-term rather than as a one-off intervention. They need to be reinforced by both policy and regulation approaches which limits chemical restraint and ensure that informed consent is gained before use. When utilised, such programmes must be monitored closely with defined time limits.

References

Aged Care Quality and Safety Commission (Australia) (2019a) *Old Standards.* Available www.agedcarequality.gov.au/providers/standards/old-standards (accessed 20 June 2020).

Aged Care Quality and Safety Commission (Australia) (2019b) *Quality Standards.* Available www.agedcarequality.gov.au/providers/standards (accessed 20 June 2020).

Australian Institute of Health and Welfare (AIHW) (2018) *GEN Fact Sheet 2016–17: People's Care Needs in Aged Care.* Available www.gen-agedcaredata.gov.au/www_aihwgen/media/2017-Factsheets/People-s_care_needs_in_aged_care_factsheet_2016%E2%80%9317.pdf?ext=.pdf (accessed 20 June 2020).

Australian Senate (1995) *Psychotherapeutic Medication in Australia: Report of the Senate Community Affairs References Committee*, Canberra: Australian Government Printing Service.

Banerjee, S. (2009) *The Use of Antipsychotic Medication for People with Dementia: Time for Action–A Report for the Minister of State for Care Services (England).* Available www.jcpmh.info/wp-content/uploads/time-for-action.pdf (accessed 20 June 2020).

Beers, M., Avorn, J., Soumerai S., Everitt, D.E., Sherman, D.S. and Salem, S. (1988) 'Psychoactive Medication Use in Intermediate-Care Facility Residents', *JAMA*, 260(20): 3016–20.

Bourgeois, J., Elseviers, M., Van Bortel, L., Petrovic, M. and Vander Stichele, R.H. (2012) 'The Use of Antidepressants in Belgian Nursing Homes: Focus on Indications and Dosages in the PHEBE Study', *Drugs & Aging*, 29(9): 559–69.

Brodaty, H., Harrison, F., Jessop, T., Cations, M., Chenoweth, L., Shell, A., Popovic, G.C., Heffernan, M., Hilmer, S., Sachdev, P.S. and Draper, B. (2018) 'Antipsychotic Deprescription for Older Adults in Long-Term Care: The HALT Study', *Journal of the American Medical Directors Association*, 19(7): 592–600.

Campbell Research (2010) *Evaluation of the Residential Medication Management Review Program, Prepared for the Department of Health and Ageing*. Available www1.health.gov.au/internet/main/publishing.nsf/Content/F520A0D5EDEA0172CA257BF0001D7B4D/$File/RMMR%20Report.pdf (accessed 18 August 2020).

Chen, L., Bell, J.S., Visvanathan, R., Hilmer, S.N., Emery, T., Robson, L., Hughes, J.M. and Tan, E.C. (2016) 'The Association Between Benzodiazepine Use and Sleep Quality in Residential Aged Care Facilities: A Cross-Sectional Study', *BMC Geriatrics*, 16(196): 1–9.

Creighton, A., Davison, T. and Kissane, D. (2016) 'The Prevalence of Anxiety Among Older Adults in Nursing Homes: A Systematic Review', *International Journal of Geriatric Psychiatry*, 31(6): 555–66.

Davison, T.E., Koder, D., Helmes, E., Doyle, C., Bahr, S., Mitchell, L., Hunter, C., Knight, B. and Pachana, N. (2017) 'Brief on the Role of Psychologists in Residential and Home Care Services for Older Adults', *Australian Psychologist*, 52(6): 397–405.

Department of Health (Australia) (2015) 'Risperidone and Risk of Cerebrovascular Adverse Events in Dementia Patients', *Medicines Safety Update*, 6(4). Available www.tga.gov.au/publication-issue/medicines-safety-update-volume-6-number-4-august-2015 (accessed 20 June 2020).

Department of Health (Australia) (2019a) *Pharmaceutical Benefits Scheme General Schedule 2019 – Risperidone 8100H-9293D*. Available www.pbs.gov.au/medicine/item/8100H-9293D (accessed 20 June 2020).

Department of Health (Australia) (2019b) *Pharmaceutical Benefits Scheme General Schedule 2019 – Risperidone 8787L-8869T*. Available www.pbs.gov.au/medicine/item/8787L-8869T (accessed 20 June 2020).

Department of Health and Human Services (US) (2016) *Update Report on the National Partnership to Improve Dementia Care in Nursing Homes, Centers for Medicare & Medicaid Services*. Available www.cms.gov/Medicare/Provider-Enrollment-and-Certification/SurveyCertificationGenInfo/Downloads/SC-Letter-16-28-Partnership-Update-Report.pdf (accessed 20 June 2020).

Ellis, M., Molinan, V., Dobbs, D., Smith, K. and Hyer, K. (2015) 'Assessing Approaches and Barriers to Reduce Antipsychotic Use in Florida Nursing Homes', *Aging & Mental Health*, 19(6): 507–16.

Farina, N., Morrell, L. and Banerjee, S. (2017) 'What Is the Therapeutic Value of Antidepressants in Dementia? A Narrative Review', *International Journal of Geriatric Psychiatry*, 32(1): 32–49.

Farlex Partner Medical Dictionary (2012) *Psychotropic*. Available https://medical-dictionary.thefreedictionary.com/psychotropic (accessed 20 June 2020).

Gaboda, D., Lucas, J., Siegel, M., Kalay, E. and Crystal, S. (2011) 'No Longer Undertreated? Depression Diagnosis and Antidepressant Therapy in Elderly Long

Stay Nursing Home Residents, 1999–2007', *Journal of the American Geriatrics Society*, 59(4): 673–80.

Gambassi, G., Sultana, J. and Trifirò, G. (2015) 'Antipsychotic Use in Elderly Patients and the Risk of Pneumonia', *Expert Opinion on Drug Safety*, 14(1): 1–6.

Glass, J., Lanctôt, K.L., Herrmann, N., Sproule, B.A. and Busto, U.E. (2005) 'Sedative Hypnotics in Older People with Insomnia: Meta-Analysis of Risks and Benefits', *The BMJ*, 331(7526): 1169.

Guthrie, B., Clark, S., Reynish, E., McCowan, C. and Morales, D.R. (2013) 'Differential Impact of Two Risk Communications on Antipsychotic Prescribing to People with Dementia in Scotland', *PLOS One*, 8(7): e68976.

Harrison, S.L., Cations, M., Jessop, T., Hiler, S.N., Sawan, M. and Brodaty, H. (2019) 'Approaches to Deprescribing Psychotropic Medications for Changed Behaviours in Long-Term Care Residents Living with Dementia', *Drugs & Aging*, 36(2): 125–36.

Hughes, C.M., Roughead, E. and Kerse, N. (2008) 'Improving Use of Medicines for Older People in Long-Term Care: Contrasting the Policy Approach of Four Countries', *Health Care Policy*, 3(3): e154–67.

Iden, K., Hjorleifsson, S. and Ruths, S. (2011) 'Treatment Decisions on Antidepressants in Nursing Homes: A Qualitative Study', *Scandinavian Journal of Primary Health Care*, 29(4): 252–56.

Johnell, K., Jonasdottir Bergman, G., Fastbom, J., Danielsson, B., Borg, N. and Salmi, P. (2016) 'Psychotropic Drugs and the Risk of Fall Injuries, Hospitalisations and Mortality Among Older Adults', *International Journal of Geriatric Psychiatry*, 32(4): 414–20.

Johnson, C.F., Frei, C., Downes, N., McTaggart, S.A. and Akram, G. (2016) 'Benzodiazepine and Z-Hypnotic Prescribing for Older People in Primary Care: A Cross-Sec tional Population-based Study', *British Journal of General Practice*, 66(647): e410–5.

Lester, P., Kohen, I., Stefanacci, R. and Feuerman, M. (2011) 'Antipsychotic Drug Use Since the FDA Black Box Warning: Survey of Nursing Home Policies', *Journal of the American Medical Directors Association*, 12(8): 573–77.

Loi, S.M., Westphal, A., Ames, D. and Lautenschlager, N.T.L. (2015) 'Minimising Psychotropic Use for Behavioural Disturbance in Residential Aged Care', *Australian Family Physician*, 44(4): 180–84.

Madhusoodanan, S. and Bogunovic, O. (2004) 'Safety of Benzodiazepines in the Geriatric Population', *Expert Opinion on Drug Safety*, 3(5): 485–93.

Malhi, G.S., Bassett, D., Boyce, P., Bryant, R., Fitzgerald, P.B., Fritz, K., Hopwood, M., Lyndon, B., Mulder, R., Murray, G., Porter, R. and Singh, A.B. (2015) 'Royal Australian and New Zealand College of Pyschiatrists Clinical Practice Guidelines for Mood Disorders', *Australian and New Zealand Journal of Psychiatry*, 49(12): 1–185.

Maust, D., Kim, H.M., Chiang, C. and Kales, H.C. (2018) 'Association of the Centers for Medicare & Medicaid Services' National Partnership to Improve Dementia Care with the Use of Antipsychotics and Other Psychotropics in Long-term Care in the United States From 2009 to 2014', *JAMA Internal Medicine*, 178(5): 640–47.

Medicines Healthcare Products Regulatory Agency (MHRA) (2004) *New Advice Issued on Risperidone and Olanzapine*. Available http://webarchive.nationalarchives.gov.uk/20141205150130/http://mhra.gov.uk/printpreview/defaultsp/con002047 (accessed 20 June 2020).

Medicines Healthcare Products Regulatory Agency (MHRA) (2009) 'Antipsychotics: Use in Elderly Patients with Dementia', *Drug Safety Update*, 2(8): 5–6. Available http://webarchive.nationalarchives.gov.uk/20091114175357/http://mhra.gov.uk/Publications/Safetyguidance/DrugSafetyUpdate/CON041211 (accessed 20 June 2020).

Neuman, M.D., Silber, J.H., Magaziner, J.S., Passarella, M.A., Mehta, S. and Werner, R.M. (2014) 'Survival and Functional Outcomes After Hip Fracture Among Nursing Home Residents', *JAMA Internal Medicine*, 174(8): 1273–80.

New South Wales (NSW) Ministerial Taskforce (1997) *Report on Psychotropic Medication Use in Nursing Homes*, Sydney: NSW Department of Health, Public Health Division.

Nishtala, P.S., McLachlan, A.J., Bell, J.S. and Chen, T.F. (2011) 'A Retrospective Study of Drug-Related Problems in Australian Aged Care Homes: Medication Reviews Involving Pharmacists and General Practitioners', *Journal of Evaluation in Clinical Practice*, 17(1): 97–103.

Omnibus Budget Reconciliation Act 1987 (OBRA) P.L. 100–203 (US). Subtitle C. Nursing Home Reform Act. Available www.congress.gov/bill/100th-congress/house-bill/3545 (accessed 20 June 2020).

Pharmaceutical Society of Australia (PSA) (2017) *Guidelines for Pharmacists Providing Residential Medication Management Review (RMMR) and Quality Use of Medicines (QUM) Services*. Available https://my.psa.org.au/s/article/Guidelines-for-pharmacists-providing-RMMR (accessed 20 June 2020).

Pont, L., Raban, M., Siette, J., Mitchell, R., Georgious, A. and Westbrook, J. (2017) 'Antipsychotics Are Forever? De-Prescribing of Antipsychotics in Residential Aged Care', *Pharmacoepidemiol Drug Safety*, 26(Suppl 2): 329–30.

Roberts, M.S., Stokes, J.A., King, M.A., Lynne, T.A., Purdie, D.M., Glasziou, P.P., Wilson, D.A., McCarthy, S.T., Brooks, G.E., de Looze, F.J. and Del Mar, C.B. (2001) 'Outcomes of a Randomised Controlled Trial of a Clinical Pharmacy Intervention in 52 Nursing Homes', *British Journal of Clinical Pharmacology*, 51(3): 257–65.

Roughead, E.E., Kalisch Ellett, L.M., Ramsay, E.N., Pratt, N.L., Barratt, J.D., LeBlanc, V.T., Ryan, P., Peck, R., Killer, G. and Gilbert, A.L. (2013) 'Bridging Evidence-Practice Gaps: Improving Use of Medicines in Elderly Australian Veterans', *BMC Health Services Research*, 13(514): 1–14.

Rovner, B.W. and Katz, I.A. (1993) 'Psychiatric Disorders in the Nursing Home', *International Journal of Geriatric Psychiatry*, 8(1): 75–87.

Royal Australian College of General Practitioners (RACGP) (2015) *Prescribing Drugs of Dependence in General Practice, Part B – Benzodiazepines*. Available www.racgp.org.au/download/Documents/Guidelines/Addictive-drugs/Addictive-drugs-guide-B.pdf (accessed 18 August 2020).

Royal Australian and New Zealand College of Psychiatrists (RANZCP) (2015) *Position Statement 81: Use of Antidepressants to Treat Depression in Dementia*. Available www.ranzcp.org/news-policy/policy-and-advocacy/position-statements/use-of-antidepressants-to-treat-depression-in-deme (accessed 20 June 2020).

Royal Australian and New Zealand College of Psychiatrists (RANZCP) (2016) *Professional Practice Guideline 10: Antipsychotics as a Treatment of Behavioural and Psychological Symptoms of Dementia*. Available www.ranzcp.org/files/resources/college_statements/practice_guidelines/pg10-pdf.aspx (accessed 20 June 2020).

Schneider, L.S., Dagerman, K. and Insel, P.S. (2006) 'Efficacy and Adverse Effects of Atypical Antipsychotics for Dementia', *American Journal of Geriatric Psychiatry*, 14(3): 191–210.

Shah, S., Schoenbachler, B., Streim, J. and Meeks, S. (2012) 'Antidepressant Prescribing Patterns in the Nursing Home: Second-Generation Issues Revisited', *Journal of the American Medical Directors Association*, 13(4): 406.e13–406.e18.

Smith, T. (2011) 'Antipsychotics in Dementia–Mortality Risks and Strategies to Reduce Prescribing', *Evidence-based Mental Health*, 14: 35–36.

Snowdon, J., Vaughan, R., Miller, R., Burgess, E.E. and Tremlett, P. (1995) 'Psychotropic Drug Use in Sydney Nursing Homes', *Medical Journal of Australia*, 163(2): 70–72.

Stewart, R., Hotopf, M., Dewey, M., Ballard, C., Bisla, J., Calem, M., Fahmy, V., Hockly, J., Kinley, J., Pearce, H., Saraf, A. and Begum, A. (2014) 'Current Prevalence of Dementia, Depression and Behavioural Problems in the Older Adult Care Home Sector: The South East London Care Home Survey', *Age and Ageing*, 43(4): 562–567.

Szczepura, A., Wild, D., Khan, A.J., Owen, D.W., Palmer, T., Muhammad, T., Clark, M.D. and Bowman, C. (2016) 'Antipsychotic Prescribing in Care Homes Before and After Launch of a National Dementia Strategy: An Observational Study in English Institutions Over a 4-Year Period', *BMJ Open*, 6(9): 1–10.

Taipale, H., Tolppanen, A.M., Koponen, M., Lavikainen, P., Sund, R., Tihonen, J. and Hartkainen, S. (2017) 'Risk of Pneumonia Associated with Benzodiazepine Use Among Community Dwelling Adults with Alzheimer Disease', *Canadian Medical Association Journal*, 189(14): E519–29.

Thompson-Coon, J., Abbott, R., Rogers, M., Whear, R., Pearson, S., Lang, I., Cartmell, N. and Stein, K. (2014) 'Interventions to Reduce Inappropriate Prescribing of Antipsychotic Medications', *Journal of the American Medical Directors Association*, 15(10): 706–18.

Walsh, K.A., Dennehy, R., Sinnott, C., Browne, J., Byrne, S., McSharry, J., Coughlan, E. and Timmons, S. (2017) 'Influences on Decision-Making Regarding Antipsychotic Prescribing in Nursing Home Residents with Dementia: A Systematic Review and Synthesis of Qualitative Evidence', *Journal of the American Medical Directors Association*, 18(10): 897.e1–e12.

Westaway, K., Sluggett, J., Alderman, C., Moffat, A., Procter, N. and Roughead, E. (2018) 'The Extent of Antipsychotic Use in Australian Residential Care Facilities and Interventions Shown to Be Effective in Reducing Antipsychotic Use: A Literature Review', *Dementia*, 19(4): 1189–202.

Westbury, J. (2011) *Roles for Pharmacists in Improving the Quality Use of Psychotropic Medicines in Residential Aged Care Facilities*, PhD. Thesis, University of Tasmania.

Westbury, J., Beld, K., Jackson, S. and Peterson, G. (2010a) 'Review of Psychotropic Medication in Tasmanian Residential Aged Care Facilities', *Australasian Journal of Ageing*, 29(2): 72–76.

Westbury, J., Gee, P., Jackson, S. and Peterson, G. (2010b) 'An Effective Approach to Decrease Antipsychotics and Benzodiazepine Use in Nursing Homes: The RedUSe Project', *International Psychogeriatrics*, 22(1): 26–36.

Westbury, J., Gee, P., Ling, T., Brown, D.T., Franks, K.H., Bindoff, I., Bindoff, A. and Peterson, G.M. (2018) 'RedUSe: Reducing Antipsychotic and Benzodiazepine Prescribing in Residential Aged Care Facilities', *Medical Journal of Australia*, 208(9): 398–403.

Westbury, J., Gee, P., Ling, T., Kitsos, A. and Peterson, G. (2019) 'More Action Needed: Psychotropic Prescribing in Australian Residential Aged Care Facilities', *Australian and New Zealand Journal of Psychiatry*, 53(2): 136–47.

Westbury, J., Tichelaar, L., Peterson, G., Gee, P. and Jackson, S. (2011) 'A 12-Month Follow-Up Study of "RedUSe": A Trial Aimed at Reducing Antipsychotic and Benzodiazepine Use in Nursing Homes', *International Psychogeriatrics*, 23(8):1260–69.

Yang, Y.J., Chen, T.F., Beazley, B. Hannan, P. and Schneider, C.R. (2014) 'An Audit of Psychotropic Medication Monitoring in Australian Aged Care Facilities', Paper Presented at the Australian Pharmaceutical Sciences Association Conference, Brisbane, December.
Ye, L. and Richards, K.C. (2018) 'Sleep and Long-Term Care', *Sleep Medicine Clinics*, 13(1): 117–25.

Note

* Formerly Westbury

14 Engaging doctors to reduce restraint

Practice and pragmatics around restraint in clinical care

Nathan Gibson

Introduction

In Australia, each state and territory has legislation and policies aimed at reducing certain types of restrictive practices, including restraint, in mental health settings. Regulation through legislation and policies has a central and vital role to play in reducing restrictive practices. Regulation can be effective, but its mechanism is complex and varied (Smithson et al. 2018).

The focus of this chapter is on the reduction of restraint in inpatient mental health services, but this is inevitably intertwined with reduction of other restrictive practices. The following discussion focuses on restraint wherever possible, but at times more broadly references other or all restrictive practices. It considers several questions that may inform regulatory drivers to reduce restrictive practices. These are:

1 What are the lessons from specific examples of historical models, set up by doctors, that worked to reduce restraint?
2 What do doctors' value sets (oaths, charters, ethical codes) say about restraint and other restrictive practice, and how do they influence doctors?
3 What are some of the individual factors that influence clinicians, particularly doctors, in the context of their actions around restraint reduction?
4 What are useful, contemporary ways to engage with and change medical behaviours around restraint and other restrictive practices?

The next section provides an overview of what restrictive practices are, how they are regulated and the interplay between that regulation and clinical practice. The chapter then turns to a model from the nineteenth century for reducing restraint and what can be learned from it, before considering the other three questions.

The regulation of restrictive practices and clinical practice

Restrictive practices cover a range of actions, including seclusion, physical, bodily or mechanical restraint and chemical restraint, among others. There are agreed definitions of seclusion, and physical, bodily and mechanical restraint at state and national levels in Australia (see McSherry and Maker in Chapter 1 in this volume for an overview). There is not however an agreed definition of chemical restraint, despite the work that has taken place over several years to identify one by the Safety and Quality Partnership Standing Committee, an interjurisdictional mental health group that seeks to drive a cohesive and effective approach to safety and quality in the Australian mental health sector.

Currently only a minority of Australian jurisdictions have defined chemical restraint in their respective mental health legislation. Other circumstances or acts are identified by various stakeholders as sitting within the realm of restrictive practices in mental health settings, for example, emotional restraint (National Mental Health Consumer and Carer Forum 2009), although concepts like these are less well developed in literature and policy.

A myriad of pragmatic issues influences the success of a change process to reduce restrictive practices. In particular, there is a critical, organic aspect to achieving reform that relies on individual clinician engagement. If it was as simple as passing a law or writing a policy, restraint would have been consigned to the dustbin of history. Equally, millennia of clinical practice which have seen significant advances in intervention options across health care have not resulted in the extinguishing of restraint within mental health, or indeed in other sectors.

There are numerous examples throughout history where programmes – often driven by individuals – have successfully removed restraints from people with mental illness in asylums, but the influence of these programmes and sites has waned or has been unable to be generalised. How do we know this? The situation remains that restraint, seclusion and other forms of restrictive practices are still used in contemporary mental health care across cultures and geography.

There are more recent examples of services that have taken significant steps to reduce restrictive practices, and yet they have been unable to sustain the levels of reduction which previously had been the envy of other services. In Australia, the Fourth National Mental Health Plan committed to public reporting of seclusion in 2009, and the Australian Health Ministers Advisory Committee in 2013 approved the annual collection and public reporting of jurisdictional seclusion data. For many years, the Australian Capital Territory had the lowest rate of seclusion comparative to all other Australian states and territories (Australian Institute of Health and Welfare (AIHW) 2020). This was in the context of an older piece of mental health legislation, the *Mental Health (Treatment and Care) Act 1994* (ACT), which has since been replaced by the *Mental Health Act 2015* (ACT). Recently, however, the Australian Capital Territory has seen increases in restrictive practices such as seclusion (AIHW 2020). There has been no weakening of legislation or policies – quite the contrary – and the mental health leadership remains committed to working towards eliminating restrictive practices. There are clearly other factors at play that have an impact upon the effectiveness of legislation and policies.

The interplay between legislation and clinical practice can appear direct. National cross-jurisdiction comparative figures for restraint rates and average time in restraint are relatively new in Australia. However, cross-jurisdiction seclusion rates and average time in seclusion have had several years' worth of comparison. Following the commencement of Western Australia's *Mental Health Act 2014*, the average seclusion time for the 2016/17 recording period in this state reduced to two hours (AIHW 2020). It appeared to be no coincidence that the Act included a legislated maximum time of two hours in seclusion (reduced from four hours under the previous statute), after which medical review was required.

Considered in isolation, this reduction in average seclusion time might appear to be a direct result of legislative change. Two hours is, of course, not a clinically determined or 'best practice' time. There is not necessarily any automatic relationship between the time of two hours and potential seclusion 'requirements' of any individual. What is not explicit in the cross-sectional Western Australian average seclusion figures is that seclusion rates had been falling over several years, even in advance of the 2014 legislation, which formally commenced in November 2015. The average seclusion times in other Australian jurisdictions in 2016/17 ranged from 1.8 hours (Tasmania) to 6.4 hours (Northern Territory) (AIHW 2020). Many other mental health laws describe longer maximum seclusion times that do not correspond to their comparative rates of use in the data – the Tasmanian *Mental Health Act 2013* for example establishes a legislated maximum time in seclusion of seven hours. Thus, respective state and territory statutes may be viewed as framing desired clinical actions, but other factors also play a significant role in leading to – or not leading to – restrictive practice reduction.

Reducing restraint was done a long time ago

Hill's 1839 treatise on 'Total Abolition of Personal Restraint'

At the age of 28, Dr Robert Gardiner Hill (1839) published his treatise *Total Abolition of Personal Restraint in the Treatment of the Insane: A Lecture on the Management of Lunatic Asylums and the Treatment of the Insane, with Statistical Tables* based on his time as the House-Surgeon at Lincoln Asylum in the United Kingdom. He referred at length to the earlier work of Dr Philippe Pinel at the Bicêtre Hospital in Paris removing chains from long-term patients with mental illness (although still using straightjackets), and William Tuke at his York Retreat, both of whom had implemented 'moral' (humane) care for the mentally ill. This was the context to Hill's work, who said he 'wished to complete that which Pinel began' (Hill 1839: 21).

As its central principle, Hill (1839: 24) noted that 'the violence (by patients) is much oftener the result of coercion than of the malady'. Although Pinel's *Treatise on Insanity* (1806) had been published prior, Hill's work has been preferred as an important and very comprehensive early dataset with the aim of supporting a more humane model of care. It also sought to establish more quantitative proof that it was indeed possible to abolish restraint and sustain this abolition. Hill's treatise importantly also considered the role of staff skillsets to enable his model to work.

Hill (1839: Appendix C) described that in 1830 there were 92 patients in the 'House' (the asylum), with 54 patients restrained that year. In 1830 there were in total 2,364 instances of restraint, with 27,113¾ hours passed under restraint. He further documented that in 1837 there were 130 patients in the House, with two patients restrained that year, three instances in total of restraint, with 28 hours passed under restraint (Hill 1839: Appendix C). Assuming they are accurate, these figures speak to Hill's attention to detail. Hill (1839: Appendix D) also noted that there were no suicides at the Lincoln Asylum in the three and a half years following his reforms. Suicides were uncommon over the subsequent two decades at Lincoln, and Hill sought to link the reform process of restraint abolition with cessation of suicides.

Hill's model for restraint reduction

In his treatise, acknowledging the collaboration with Dr Edward Parker Charlesworth, who was also a physician driving this approach at the Lincoln Asylum (demonstrating the value of collegial support), Hill (1839: 22–23) described a model of 'undivided personal attention towards the patients', 'improved construction of the building', 'night-watching' and 'attentive supervision'. Specifically, this was a heightened responsiveness to patients' needs and welfare, described as getting the right 'classification' (Hill 1839: 38) of each patient in order to determine their specific needs. For those who required it, this might include 'watchfulness – vigilant and unceasing attendance by day and by night – kindness, occupation, and attention to health, cleanliness, and comfort, and the total absence of every description of other occupation of the attendants' (Hill 1839: 37–38).

There were four 'essential requisites' according to Hill (1839: 39–40):

1 A suitable building with extensive grounds (courtyards, gardens);
2 Proper classification of the patients (especially those requiring increased supervision at night);
3 A 'sufficient number' of 'tall, strong, and active attendants', appropriately remunerated to 'secure persons of character and trust' whose attention is focused solely on the needs of the patient, who do 'not speak angrily' but must otherwise be firm – noting 'the laws of France assign one keeper to every ten patients' (Hill 1839: 44); and
4 The House-Surgeon (attendant doctor) to 'exercise an unremitting control and inspection' to prevent deviation from the plan even 'in the slightest degree' (Hill 1839: 38–39).

'Proper classification' (Hill 1839: 38) is perhaps a primitive precursor to identifying patient needs in the context of current concepts around patient-centred care (see Pelzang 2010).

The focus on kindness, comfort, dignity (implied in a sense by Hill's prioritisation of 'cleanliness') and meaning (which can be potentially linked to Hill's 'occupation') are also suggestive of fragments of a contemporary recovery paradigm in mental health care (Simpson and Penney 2011). Recovery has been defined as 'a set of ideas and principles derived from the experiences of people with mental health problems' (Boardman and Shepherd 2012: 6) and is an important contextual driver for reduction of restrictive practice (see Brophy, Fletcher and Hamilton in Chapter 12 in this volume). Interestingly, Hill (1839: 49) appeared to still use intermittent seclusion and there was a degree of inherent coercion in the imposing stature and nature of the attendants (see Szmukler and Appelbaum 2008) and the described autocratic style of internal institutional leadership characterised by 'unremitting control and inspection'. In practice, sustaining Hill's four 'essential requisites' is difficult. For better outcomes in a contemporary health care setting, regulation must be combined with a quality improvement focus owned by staff. Smithson and colleagues' (2018) review of the impact of the Care Quality Commission's regulatory model in England in the context of provider performance identified that the provider's capacity and willingness for change was a central determinant of the impact of the regulatory function.

It is important to note there are other limitations of this example. Hill, while referencing Pinel, did not provide a comprehensive background of the other attempts to reduce restraint to a similar level in order to identify issues of sustainability or learning. Furthermore, Hill arguably did not sufficiently credit other key pioneering work that had been done, such as Tuke's work in York. He did not describe in detail the impact of injury or trauma on staff, which has become a significant practical issue in addition to the well-established trauma to patients (see Brophy, Fletcher and Hamilton in Chapter 12 in this volume for more on this issue). Notwithstanding these limitations, Hill is an important figure in the history of reducing restrictive practice. Reform under Hill and Charlesworth, as well as Pinel, Tuke and other activists beginning more than 200 years ago, highlights that restraint in psychiatric services has long been an issue of serious concern.

The long history of contemporary challenges

Hill's treatise also flags, with irony and frustration in a contemporary reading, those aspects of the principles of 'best practice' mental health care aimed at eliminating restrictive practice that are so hard to either achieve or sustain in current systems. Hill's work either began to explore or thematically considered contemporary issues including therapeutic infrastructure, sufficient numbers of staff, a skilled workforce, a focus on compassionate and trauma-informed care, medical and clinical engagement, an organisational learning culture and sufficiently supported and capable leadership – all of which are challenging to either develop or sustain in contemporary mental health, and most other health, settings. Hill's treatise – which is over 180 years old – also identifies the power in providing data to evidence value, seek funding and maximise sustainability.

Huckshorn's (2004) more recent six core strategies to reduce restrictive practice are well known (see McSherry and Maker in Chapter 1 in this volume). These include leadership towards organisational change, use of data to inform practice, workforce development, use of seclusion and restraint prevention tools, consumer roles in inpatient settings and debriefing techniques. It is interesting to note their consistency with certain strategies that were recognised nearly two centuries ago. Both the right staff and staff working within the defined model was central to the integrity of Hill's model and is today reflected in contemporary concerns about workforce skills. The role of leadership in organisational change has also long been recognised. There were two key leaders within the Lincoln Asylum – Hill and Charlesworth – who, with a fervent drive for change, successfully convinced the hospital governors, at least for a defined period, of the value of their model. The use of specific tools was also recognised by Hill, where within the Lincoln Asylum this was the use of occupation. The definition and grouping of different patient groups drove the specifics of care, together with the subsequent use of meticulous data in Hill's treatise were used as primary evidence for the effectiveness of the model and as a driver for more widespread system change. Because resource limitations often affect the development of therapeutic infrastructure and potentially sufficiency of staff numbers, both Hill's and Huckshorn's strategies suggest that factors including leadership, data and different workforce strategies (for instance, around culture and clinical engagement) are increasingly important to reduce restraint and other restrictive practices.

There are significant points of difference in the consideration of restrictive practices across this time frame of almost two centuries, with restraint being viewed in the nineteenth century as the critical event to extinguish and Hill using seclusion in pursuit of this goal. There were few effective or safe pharmacological options in the 1830s and this represents another stark point of difference to today, although this makes the achievement of the reduction of restraint at Lincoln Asylum all the more significant.

It is interesting to consider this in the context of the embryonic English mental health legislation during Hill's time at the Lincoln Asylum. The serial laws then dealing with the poor in England had been around for some centuries and individuals with mental illness, in the context of homelessness, vagrancy or poverty, sometimes fell within the remit of these statutes. Although these laws were not primarily for care of the mentally ill, the *Vagrancy Act of 1744* for example had referred to people with mental illness (the 'furiously mad'), but only in the context of facilitating incarceration (Hamilton 1983). The English *Madhouses Act 1774* provided for licensing of asylums, notification of admissions and a system of visits and inspections of doctors, but only initially in London. The *County Asylums Act 1808* was driven by the relative failures of the *Madhouses Act 1774* and the need to ensure the provision of asylums primarily for the poor. While there may have been some legislative context to ensure appropriate contemporary care, there were severe statutory penalties for 'keepers' who allowed patients to escape (Hamilton 1983). In some ways, these penalties for escape would have been antithetical to reducing restrictive practice, as it could have easily encouraged restraint to prevent such escape. It is therefore difficult to imagine this English legislation directly driving a reduction in restraint and Hill in his treatise does not identify the existing legislation at the time as a significant component of his developed model. Equally, Hill did not place significant weight on the role of oaths, charters or ethical codes as part of his strategy.

The residual question is: if there are such historical examples of effective restraint reduction, why are clinicians in the third decade of the twenty-first century still using restraint in mental health settings?

The significance of oaths, charters and ethical codes in the use and reduction of restraint

Could the treatment of restraint in codes of ethics and other charters make a difference to clinicians', especially doctors', behaviours?

Ethical codes and charters for clinicians have been around for a long time. The Hippocratic Oath, possibly not written by Hippocrates himself, was written sometime in the fourth or fifth century BCE. It states, 'I will follow that system of regimen which, according to my ability and judgment, I consider for the benefit of my patients, and abstain from whatever is deleterious or mischievous'. It refers to being 'bound by Oath and Covenant according to the Law of Medicine'.

The Declaration of Geneva, as a more contemporary version of the Hippocratic Oath, was adopted by the General Assembly of the World Medical Association in 1948. In 2017, in Chicago, the World Medical Association adopted the most recent revision of the Declaration of Geneva (Parsi-Parsi 2017). The 2017 version added two new components relevant to the consideration of restrictive practice:

- 'I will respect the autonomy and dignity of my patient'; and
- The existing statement, 'I will practise my profession with conscience and dignity' had the following words added, 'and in accordance with good medical practice'.

The Declaration also says, 'I will not use my medical knowledge to violate human rights and civil liberties, even under threat'.

Oaths such as these are not universally taken by doctors and they are interpreted liberally and variably by individuals (Oxtoby 2016). They do not usually contemplate mental health specifically and they do not seek to resolve the uncertainty when different parts of these oaths and ethical frameworks appear to conflict with one another. Additionally, the issue of restraint is not usually considered directly by such oaths, charters and codes. There are some exceptions. In the context of restraint, the American Medical Association Code of Medical Ethics (2016) states:

> All individuals have a fundamental right to be free from unreasonable bodily restraint. At times, however, health conditions may result in behavior that puts patients at risk of harming themselves. In such situations, it may be ethically justifiable for physicians to order the use of chemical or physical restraint to protect the patient.

This potentially sits in tension with the statement in the Declaration of Geneva that physicians should not use their 'medical knowledge to violate human rights and civil liberties' and should respect patients' 'autonomy and dignity'. Where a doctor believes restraint is preventing harm, 'in the best interest' of a patient and meets 'good medical practice', how is this weighed with other aspects of such codes?

Given the present author's origins, Australian frameworks are now considered in more depth. The Royal Australian and New Zealand College of Psychiatrists (RANZCP) is a fellowship-structured professional body that provides training in psychiatry, credentialing and ethical/professional guidance, as well as seeking to influence mental health care more broadly. It is not a regulator. Its Code of Ethics (2018) does not define or address specific restrictive practices such as restraint. It instead notes (RANZCP 2018: Principle 1.3) that 'compulsory treatment may be justified where a less restrictive intervention cannot achieve safe and adequate care; its purpose is ultimately to promote and re-establish patients' autonomy and welfare'. This principle appears to be intentionally left to clinician interpretation or clinical judgment. Principle 5 states that treatment can be provided 'in accordance with the law' in emergencies where life is at risk and consent cannot be obtained (RANZCP 2018: Principle 5.10). Principle 11 notes the responsibility of psychiatrists to work to improve mental health services. It could therefore be extrapolated that this applies to reducing trauma and re-traumatisation within mental health services, but it remains sufficiently vague as to be open to a range of interpretation.

The RANZCP (2016a) does have a position statement entitled *Minimising the Use of Seclusion and Restraint in People with Mental Illness.* There has been a steady decline in Australian jurisdictional seclusion rates since the commencement of the Beacon Project, a restrictive practice reduction project which was established in 2007 and ran until 2009 (AIHW 2012). The Beacon project targeted 11 key sites around Australia, all of which were charged with developing and implementing 'best practice' with the aim to reduce and, where possible, eliminate the use of seclusion and restraint in public mental health services. Since the release of the RANZCP's (2016a) position statement concerning restraint, two jurisdictions in Australia have seen an increase in their own jurisdictional seclusion rates (AIHW 2020). While it is acknowledged that there can be a lag period between commencing a strategy and the actual real reduction, and the factors governing increases and decreases in restrictive practices are often complex, it does not appear that the release of the position statement has had an impact on further reduction, at least in these two Australian jurisdictions. The RANZCP (2017) has also released a subsequent position statement entitled *Mental Health Legislation and Psychiatrists: Putting the Principles into Practice* where it states, 'we support government policy in Australia and New Zealand to reduce and, where possible, eliminate their [restrictive practices] use altogether', and discusses drivers for the reduction of such seclusion and restraint.

The Australian Medical Association (commonly known as the AMA) is a broad professional body for medical practitioners. It acts as an advocacy and support body for individual doctors and as a health influencing body both publicly and politically at the Australian national and state levels. It is not a regulator or credentialing agent. The Australian Medical Association's Code of Ethics (2016) makes no specific comment on restraint or restrictive practices. In its section on patients with limited, impaired or fluctuating decision-making capacity it does not contemplate the restrictive complexities of involuntary care or substitute decision-making. It focuses primarily on the consideration of consent and associated support processes.

The Australian Medical Association (2015) does have a position statement dealing with restraint in the care of people in residential aged care facilities. That statement focuses on the potential physical risk of restraint use but does not consider any potential broader impact of psychological trauma. The final statement in that document says '[m]edical practitioners have an educative and mentoring role in minimising the use of restraint' (Australian Medical Association 2015).

The question remains as to whether the various oaths, charters, codes of ethics and other statements have driven reduction in restraint or restrictive practice by doctors more broadly. The duration of existence of some oaths (such as the Hippocratic Oath), the lack of specificity relating to restraint or restrictive practices in many of these texts, the apparently purposeful ambiguity in their drafting and the focus on restrictive practices (including restraint) that appears to be generally temporally independent of modification of these documents must all be acknowledged. It is therefore reasonable to postulate that, while these broader frameworks might provide a 'moral compass', they have not been a primary influence on doctors and psychiatrists as a broad group compelling the issue of restraint or other restrictive practices to be addressed.

Individual factors for doctors

There has been a survey of Australian mental health professionals, in addition to consumers and carers, regarding their perspectives on seclusion and restraint (Kinner et al. 2016). A large majority of surveyed clinicians (including doctors) believed that seclusion and restraint practices were likely to cause harm, breach human rights, compromise trust and potentially cause or trigger past trauma (see McSherry in Chapter 11 in this volume for further details). Yet at the same time, the survey indicated that clinicians were very likely to consider restrictive practices to confer benefits of safety to consumers, staff and others, and set appropriate boundaries. It is reasonable to assume clinicians, and in this case doctors, have similar cognitive biases to the rest of the population and their behaviour is impacted by a complex range of influences.

The *National Mental Health Survey of Doctors and Medical Students* (Beyond Blue 2019) identified Australian doctors as having higher rates of mental distress and minor mental disorders than the general population. The RANZCP (2016b) has issued a position statement on this issue entitled *The Contribution to Practice Made by Psychiatrists who have a Personal Experience of Mental Illness.* It states:

> [p]sychiatrists with personal experience of mental illness have the potential to add value to the knowledge of the profession and its practices. How the impact of lived experiences can benefit the practice of psychiatry, and the best way to go about this, requires further exploration and research.
>
> (RANZCP 2016b)

Other than published stories of individual, personal narratives, with anonymity common, there has been very little research regarding doctors – or their family members – who have had severe mental illness or who have been subject to restrictive practices themselves. Given the prevalence of serious mental illness and the historical frequency of restrictive practices, it would seem likely that many doctors will also have been aware of restrictive practices experienced in mental health settings by extended family members.

While regulation has been a core strategy to address restrictive practices embedded in contemporary mental health legislation, fluctuations in data has continued. A majority of mental health clinicians may agree with the principle to reduce seclusion (Kinner et al. 2016), but there are pragmatic and dynamic barriers – as well as facilitators – to the application of this. Consider the following hypothetical clinical scenario, which, while the names and exact circumstances are fictional, might occur on any given day in any mental health inpatient unit in any Australian jurisdiction.

A young man in his early 20s, Jerome, has been admitted late in the evening to a secure mental health unit, having been referred under mental health legislation. He is experiencing distressing psychotic symptoms in the context of overwhelming paranoia and possibly fleeting, directive voices. He is extremely fearful, having been restrained during a prior admission to the same hospital. His family are not with him and have not been contacted yet. He was brought from the community into the hospital emergency department by the police and his difficult experience with the police and the somewhat rushed approach of the emergency department have raised his levels of vigilance and fear.

The on-duty doctor, Byron, assesses him. This doctor is a relatively junior psychiatric trainee, who is tired and hungry, having worked a double shift. Byron was assaulted on the mental health unit a few weeks prior (not by Jerome) and remains somewhat anxious and sensitised. Another patient waiting to be seen by the doctor in the admission area of the mental health unit has been noted by staff to be very suicidal and the admission area nursing staff are pushing for Byron to finish with Jerome very quickly and see the other person for admission. Nursing staff from another ward within the mental health unit have also telephoned to ask Byron to promptly review the sleeping medication of another patient who is agitated and becoming increasingly distressed. There is only one on-duty doctor and the consultant psychiatrist is on-call, but lives 30 minutes away from the hospital.

While the nursing and medical leadership of the unit are championing restrictive practices elimination strategies, the nursing staff on this particular night shift are ambivalent about the value of these strategies. Senior nurses on this night shift have been part of a small group of staff who have approached the nurses' union in recent months to raise concerns that the restrictive practices elimination approach, driven by the unit leadership, is placing nursing staff at higher risk of assault by patients. This is motivated by a prevailing view within this group that restrictive practices are essential to keep staff and patients safe. There is also one nurse short on this current night shift and there has been delay in finding a replacement nurse from a nursing agency.

Byron interviews Jerome as part of the ward admission procedure. Jerome remains wary and fearful and begins to appear irritated with the assessment questions. He asks to leave. Byron is also becoming increasingly anxious himself and says brusquely that Jerome cannot leave. Jerome stands and becomes increasingly insistent on leaving the ward immediately.

Contextually, the nursing staff member in the room observing the interview, Kathy, has a mixed opinion of Byron, believing him to be routinely anxious and somewhat naïve and junior. She is uncertain as to whether she can fully trust him to keep staff safe in an escalating and potentially violent situation. Kathy gestures through the window of the room to a colleague, Mike, and he moves quickly to stand at the door to the interview room. Jerome recognises Mike as one of the staff members who was involved in restraining him during a prior admission.

At this point, Jerome feels that this sudden increase in the number of staff means they are planning to overpower him. He feels vulnerable and increasingly overwhelmed, at which point he picks up his chair and threatens to smash his way out of the room. Byron reflexively stands, backs away and presses the duress alarm on the security pendant he is carrying. The duress alarm triggers a number of other staff to attend the interview room within a short period of time.

What are the possible outcomes here and what is the likely outcome?

While there may be other systemic processes in place at this service aimed at the elimination of restrictive practices, pragmatically there is a significant chance Jerome will be physically restrained, secluded, or given medication against his will – in the context of chemical restraint – or a combination of any of these. There are, of course, a myriad of variables that might change or alter the outcome in this scenario, many of which are discussed in other chapters in this volume. Staff engagement, staffing levels, staff training, support and supervision, on-the-ground (shift) leadership, practice around family engagement and peer worker availability are but some that may be relevant.

In addition, there are the immediate stakeholder issues. Can Byron understand his likely cognitive bias about the level of risk given the recency of his assault and his probable heightened fear that an assault by Jerome is highly likely? Does Byron have the conflict resolution skills to manage the escalating interpersonal tension? Does he have the skills and gravitas to assuage the escalating concerns of the nursing staff? Will Kathy, Mike or other nursing leaders on this shift – individually and as a group – take steps to seek to support Jerome and manage his spiraling fear? What capacity does Jerome himself have at this point to engage with the staff to try to de-escalate this situation?

Some variables are easier to modify than others, but as this narrative suggests, there are multiple variables and no single strategy is likely to be the most important or effective. Accordingly, a multipronged approach will inevitably be needed to prevent restrictive practices here. It will depend on the combination of local barriers – in this hypothetical case, barriers related to variations in staff readiness to change, resourcing and possibly ward-level leadership – and will therefore require a targeted, context-specific response. Service leaders need to be cognisant of strategies to deal with multiple variables that prevent elimination of restrictive practices, and some may be less easy to control than others. For example, it is not necessarily possible for a service to control the potentially myriad personal stressors for staff (both due to or unrelated to work) that may have an impact on their relational therapeutic capacity on any given day. But a service can certainly provide a clinical supervision structure to help identify when staff are having a difficult time and provide better on-the-ground support for staff during those periods.

While the preceding may appear to some to be designed as an extreme example, these dynamic variables play out across Australian mental health services on a daily basis. Those issues that can be controlled and facilitated will drive restraint reduction, such as the strong regulatory drivers, leaders championing restrictive practice reduction and workforce development proposed as part of the 'six core strategies' (Huckshorn 2004). However, there are multiple barriers, both pragmatic and interpersonal that will have an impact on clinician behaviour on a case by case basis. In addition to such personal and situational variables, there are intrinsic and recognisable cognitive processes that impact on restrictive practice outcomes. It is important at this point to note that doctors and other clinicians as a group are not inherently unethical, unprofessional, or lacking compassion or empathy. While there are well known examples of doctors who have committed heinous crimes (for example, the English doctor Harold Shipman who was found guilty of the murder of 15 patients under his care, but who was estimated to have killed up to 250 patients), there is no evidence to suggest that doctors as a group have a preponderance of problematic or pathological personalities (Bucknall et al. 2015). There are, however, identifiable unhelpful practices that can occur without reflection and oversight.

Deviation of practice

Over time, deviations from standards of practices can become normalised in health care delivery systems (Banja 2010). This is termed 'normalisation of deviance', meaning a process where a substandard practice becomes embedded as routine and part of acceptable practice over time. This is not related to specific maleficence of practitioners, or one-off breaches of standards that may have a range of contributing or associated factors, but rather represents unchecked drift of practice over time.

Consider this example of deviation relating to restrictive practice. The Western Australian *Mental Health Act 1996* (in effect from 1997 to 2015) defined seclusion within psychiatric hospitals as 'sole confinement in a room that is not within the control of the person confined to leave' and prescribed conditions on its use. A practice known as 'time-out' emerged where a patient was directed by staff (explicitly or implicitly) to enter a side room by him or herself. The door was left ajar or open, but the individual was given no indication that they could leave the room, nor were they given pre-emptive indication of the consequences should they leave the room, and in some cases patients were also explicitly being redirected back into the room when they expressed a wish to leave.

The Chief Psychiatrist, a statutory position in Western Australia who under the *Mental Health Act 1996* had a responsibility to oversee standards of care, formally wrote to services specifying that this practice of 'time-out' met the statutory definition of seclusion and should be reported and managed as such. It was specified by the Chief Psychiatrist that 'time-out' should only be used to refer to a personal request by the patient to enter a quiet room, with that room being a therapeutic space, with pre-emptive verbally explicit advice to the person by staff that they could leave the room at any time and consequent actions which confirmed to the patient that they could leave when they wished.

Over the ensuing years, the Western Australian Chief Psychiatrist received further reports that some services had drifted in their practice. They had reverted to a practice of having a distressed or agitated person in a seclusion room with the door open, at times only ajar. They were calling this 'time-out' and not recording this as seclusion. There appeared to be, at times, implicit coercion in this context. It was clearly implied that the person was not allowed to leave this room because a staff member was standing at or just outside the door. At times this requirement was made explicit, when the person was directed back into the room when they sought to leave. This was not voluntary or therapeutic 'time-out', as the person had no capacity to leave the room.

When the Chief Psychiatrist raised this matter with clinical staff at those services, they expressed genuine surprise that this constituted seclusion and reported no knowledge of the previous advice from the Chief Psychiatrist. Despite further clarifying discussion between the Chief Psychiatrist and the staff at these services, a small cohort of staff maintained a personal view that they had no statutory requirement to advise the person of their right to leave the room and that this represented true voluntary 'time-out' rather than seclusion.

In this example, a number of reasons might be postulated as to why this 'normalisation of deviance' from agreed practice had occurred. Two considerations relate to operational processes for embedding policy. First, it is possible the original formal clarifying advice from the Chief Psychiatrist was not effectively disseminated at the service level. Secondly, with natural changeover of staff at services, the new staff may not have been aware of the appropriate translation of the statute as previously clarified by the Chief Psychiatrist. An alternate 'cultural' postulate is that the small group of staff with specific, unmodified idiosyncratic views may have exerted influence over the broader cohort. Interestingly, the issue of 'seclusion is not seclusion if the door is open' again resurfaced in clinical practice with Western Australia's implementation of its superseding *Mental Health Act 2014*.

In this subsequent example, involving the actual practical introduction of the *Mental Health Act 2014* in Western Australia in November 2015, a robust training package involving both online and face-to-face components for the new Act was implemented for clinicians within mental health services, broader health services and primary care. Area Health Services, which then ran public sector mental health services, including hospitals and clinics, approximated full roll-out of the training package for public sector mental health service clinicians in Western Australia, with significantly lesser coverage for broader public sector health services (such as emergency department staff and junior general hospital doctors). The uptake of this training by primary health care clinicians (targeted primarily toward General Practitioners, who are predominantly not public sector employees in Australia) was unknown, despite a rigorous dissemination and implementation process. This training package included Standards of Clinical Care (Chief Psychiatrist of Western Australia 2015: 19–21) which included a Seclusion and Bodily Restraint Reduction Standard.

In July/August 2017, a survey was taken of clinicians across Western Australia's public sector health services to understand clinician awareness of the Chief Psychiatrist's Standards of Clinical Care. Eighty-seven per cent of respondents indicated they were aware of these Standards. After this 2017 survey, the importance of clinician understanding of the *Mental Health Act 2014* was discussed with all of the Chief Executives of the Health Service Providers (the new terminology for Area Health Services) in Western Australia, with a request they follow-up with staff training.

In June/July 2018 the survey was repeated. Seventy-nine per cent of respondents indicated they were aware of the Chief Psychiatrist's Standards. Acknowledging methodological (including sampling) limitations in both surveys, there was still a cohort of clinical staff who were not aware of the statutory standards relating to seclusion and restraint reduction. Thus, despite multiple processes for awareness-raising for relevant staff, there remained a cohort who appeared to be unaware of these standards.

These examples highlight the issues of implementation and sustainability even where 'best practice' statutory drivers are in place to pursue reduction in restrictive practices (a topic also discussed by Allan and Manwaring in Chapter 8 in this volume). Practice deviations are common and clinicians who deviate from agreed practice are not usually intending harm (Banja 2010). There is nevertheless an inherent responsibility on service leaders to acknowledge this and take steps to not only sustain improvements, but to actively prevent return to default clinical behaviours.

Medical engagement and behaviour change

Engagement in a work setting, in this case clinician (specifically medical) engagement, has multitudinous definitions, but can usefully be defined as a measure of how people connect in their work and feel committed to their organisation and its goals – practically, it might be interpreted as involvement in managerial decision-making and in implementing change (West and Dawson 2012). Clinician service performance, including lower patient mortality, is linked to clinician engagement (Spurgeon, Mazelan and Barwell 2011; West and Dawson 2012). When clinical services identify that organisational cultural problems are at the heart of poor patient outcomes, clinician engagement is an important strategy to facilitate improved service culture and improved patient outcomes (Clark and Nath 2014). Clark and Nath highlight the key factors of successful services, noting that clinical engagement is an essential part of high-quality services. They note that real engagement takes time, an organisation genuinely committed to clinician engagement, a governance structure that values clinical leadership and a rigorous approach to appointing medical leaders. Such high-quality services also support a leadership learning pathway and invest well in leadership development, with education being treated as central to the service's culture. Along these lines, Ham (2014) suggested that transforming the National Health Service (NHS) in England depended much less on bold strokes and big gestures by politicians than on engaging doctors, nurses and other staff in improvement programmes.

At a granular level, Robertson and Jochelson (2006) mapped the literature around the effectiveness of various interventions to change clinician behaviour, noting that actual clinical practice often differs from that recommended by evidence or guidelines for care. Seeking the most powerful strategies that may affect clinician behaviour change, they identified that regulation was clearly associated with improvements in health care quality. Certification status (including re-certification processes) of doctors was linked to improved quality of care. There is significant evidence that the skills and knowledge of medical professionals erode over time, with potentially serious consequences for the quality of care.

For the individual, educational materials provided to practitioners may only bring modest effect. Robertson and Jochelson (2006) identified that large didactic meetings may be ineffective, but smaller scale meetings might potentially be more effective. Specific outreach visits to clinicians were also found to be powerful, but more costly. The role of opinion leaders within organisations in behaviour change was less clear. Using auditing of service performance had variable benefit but appeared to be more effective when the audit focused on the issues that were problematic at a local service level. Thus, there may be nationally important performance issues to track across services, but each service will generally have its own local performance issues. Reminders were likewise variable, but often useful for clinicians. Robertson and Jochelson (2006) noted that good organisational communication channels were important in complex change, which would include change to reduce restrictive practice. Locally focused, multifaceted strategies were more likely to be effective, but potentially also more costly.

While there has been broad work on high-performing services and the role of changing behaviours, there is still uncertainty about the relative effectiveness of the components of each of these strategies when it comes to changing medical behaviour around restraint and other restrictive practice.

Conclusion

Legislation and policies remain essential to frame an ongoing process towards eliminating restrictive practices, including restraint, in inpatient mental health units. Historical experience indicates the achievability of significant practice change regarding restraint reduction, but the ongoing variability in restrictive practices rates in Australia highlights difficulties in sustaining and generalising restraint reduction, among other restrictive practices.

Oaths, broad charters, ethical codes and equivalent documents are important statements, but have not to-date provided a consistent message about the contemporary understanding of the impact of restraint and other restrictive practices.

They appear to have done little to reduce the use of restrictive practices. Given the evidence of the impact of restraint, professional bodies, such as general medical associations and professional psychiatric bodies, have a responsibility via their ethical codes and equivalent guiding statements to minimise ambiguity and to directly communicate more with their members on the role of doctors in the elimination of restraint, among other restrictive practices.

The external and internal drivers for clinicians to meet their statutory and ethical requirements under mental health legislation are complex. All clinicians, including doctors, are subject to a range of personal factors and broader cognitive biases which may have an impact on their drive to apply restraint reduction and elimination strategies. More work needs to be done to understand how this is best managed to maximise the sustainability of restrictive practices elimination. It is clear for services that are seeking to successfully reduce and move towards the elimination of restraint and other restrictive practices – and sustain this – that the regulatory components must be complemented with a strong focus on clinical leadership and clinician engagement.

The strategies to change clinician behaviour around restraint and restrictive practices in most cases cannot be single-pronged interventions. Instead they must include a locally tailored and targeted mix of educational strategies, engagement with clinical leaders, audit processes and other systemic approaches. It is likely, although not always the case, that a multifaceted approach to changing behaviour will be more expensive than a single strategy. The almost inevitable corollary to this is that if change management is to be effective, it requires strategic resourcing.

The value of the engagement of medical staff in improving quality and safety outcomes for patients has a growing evidence base. Given the burgeoning understanding of the broader importance of reducing trauma and re-traumatisation within inpatient mental health units, there is an onus on service and system leaders to both engage clinicians more rigorously and also engage with improvement science to change clinician behaviour.

References

American Medical Association (AMA) (2016) *Code of Medical Ethics Opinion 1.2.7 – Use of Restraints*. Available www.ama-assn.org/delivering-care/ethics/use-restraints (accessed 20 June 2020).

Australian Institute of Health and Welfare (AIHW) (2012) *Use of Restricted Practices During Admitted Patient Care*, Canberra: Commonwealth of Australia.

Australian Institute of Health and Welfare (AIHW) (2020) *Mental Health Services in Australia–Restrictive Practices 2018–19 Tables*. Available www.aihw.gov.au/getmedia/5359b4f0-3de5-4864-815b-3c801159dc91/Restrictive-practices-tables-2018-19.xls.aspx (accessed 20 June 2020).

Australian Medical Association (2015) *Restraint in the Care of People in Residential Aged Care Facilities 2001, Revised 2015*. Available https://ama.com.au/position-statement/restraint-care-people-residential-aged-care-facilities-2015 (accessed 20 June 2020).

Australian Medical Association (2016) *Code of Ethics 2004, Editorially Revised 2006, Revised 2016*. Available https://ama.com.au/position-statement/code-ethics-2004-editorially-revised-2006-revised-2016 (accessed 20 June 2020).

Banja, J. (2010) 'The Normalization of Deviance in Healthcare Delivery', *Business Horizons*, 53(2): 139.

Beyond Blue (2019) *National Mental Health Survey of Doctors and Medical Students.* Available https://www.beyondblue.org.au/docs/default-source/research-project-files/bl1132-report-%2D-nmhdmss-full-report_web (accessed 20 June 2020).

Boardman, J. and Shepherd, G. (2012) 'Implementing Recovery in Mental Health Services', *International Psychiatry*, 9(1): 6–8.

Bucknall, V., Burwaiss, S., MacDonald, D., Charles, K. and Clement, R. (2015) 'Mirror Mirror on the Ward, Who's the Most Narcissistic of Them All? Pathological Personality Traits in Health Care', *Canadian Medical Association Journal*, 187(18): 1359–63.

Chief Psychiatrist of Western Australia (2015) *Chief Psychiatrist's Standards for Clinical Care: As Required Under Section 547 of the Mental Health Act 2014.* Available www.chiefpsychiatrist.wa.gov.au/wp-content/uploads/2015/12/CP_Standards_2015.pdf (accessed 20 June 2020).

Clark, J. and Nath, V. (2014) *Medical Engagement: A Journey Not an Event.* Available www.kingsfund.org.uk/sites/default/files/field/field_publication_file/medical-engagement-a-journey-not-an-event-jul14_0.pdf (accessed 20 June 2020).

Ham, C. (2014) *Reforming the NHS from Within: Beyond Hierarchy, Inspection and Markets.* Available www.kingsfund.org.uk/sites/default/files/field/field_publication_file/reforming-the-nhs-from-within-kingsfund-jun14.pdf (accessed 20 June 2020).

Hamilton, J.R. (1983) 'Mental Health Act 1983', *British Medical Journal (Clinical Research Edition)*, 286(6379): 1720–25.

Hill, R.G. (1839) *Total Abolition of Personal Restraint in the Treatment of the Insane: A Lecture on the Management of Lunatic Asylums and the Treatment of the Insane, with Statistical Tables*, London: Simpkin, Marshall and Co.

Huckshorn, K.A. (2004) 'Reducing Seclusion Restraint in Mental Health Use Setting: Core Strategies for Prevention', *Journal of Psychosocial Nursing and Mental Health Services*, 42(9): 22–33.

Kinner, S.A., Harvey, C., Hamilton, B., Brophy, L., Roper, C., McSherry, B. and Young, J.T. (2016) 'Attitudes Towards Seclusion and Restraint in Mental Health Settings: Finding from a Large, Community-based Survey of Consumers, Carers and Mental Health Professionals', *Epidemiology and Psychiatric Sciences*, 26(5): 535–44.

National Mental Health Consumer and Carer Forum (2009) *Ending Seclusion and Restraint in Australian Mental Health Services*, Deakin West: National Mental Health Consumer and Carer Forum.

Oxtoby, J. (2016) 'Is the Hippocratic Oath Still Relevant to Practicing Doctors Today?', *British Medical Journal*, 355: i6629.

Parsi-Parsi, R.W. (2017) 'The Revised Declaration of Geneva: A Modern-Day Physician's Pledge', *JAMA*, 318(20): 1971–72.

Pelzang, R. (2010) 'Time to Learn: Understanding Patient-Centred Care', *British Journal of Nursing*, 19(14): 912–17.

Pinel, P.H. (1806) *A Treatise on Insanity: In Which Are Contained the Principles of a New and More Practical Nosology of Maniacal Disorders*, Sheffield: W. Todd.

Robertson, R. and Jochelson, K. (2006) *Interventions That Change Clinician Behaviour: Mapping the Literature.* Available www.kingsfund.org.uk/publications/articles/interventions-change-clinician-behaviour-mapping-literature (accessed 20 June 2020).

Royal Australian and New Zealand College of Psychiatrists (RANZCP) (2016a) *Minimising the Use of Seclusion and Restraint in People with Mental Illness–Position Statement 61.* Available www.ranzcp.org/news-policy/policy-and-advocacy/position-statements/minimising-the-use-of-seclusion-and-restraint-in-p (accessed 20 June 2020).

Royal Australian and New Zealand College of Psychiatrists (RANZCP) (2016b) *The Contribution to Practice Made by Psychiatrists Who Have a Personal Experience of Mental Illness.* Available www.ranzcp.org/news-policy/policy-and-advocacy/position-statements/the-contribution-to-practice-made-by-psychiatrists (accessed 20 June 2020).

Royal Australian and New Zealand College of Psychiatrists (RANZCP) (2017) *Mental Health Legislation and Psychiatrists: Putting the Principles into Practice–Position Statement 92.* Available www.ranzcp.org/news-policy/policy-and-advocacy/position-statements/mental-health-legislation-and-psychiatrists-putti (accessed 20 June 2020).

Royal Australian and New Zealand College of Psychiatrists (RANZCP) (2018) *Code of Ethics.* Available www.ranzcp.org/files/about_us/code-of-ethics.aspx (accessed 20 June 2020).

Simpson, A.I.F. and Penney, S.R. (2011) 'The Recovery Paradigm in Forensic Mental Health Services', *Criminal Behaviour and Mental Health*, 21: 299–306.

Smithson, R., Richardson, E., Roberts, J., Walshe, K., Wenzel, L., Robertson, R., Boyd, A., Allen, T. and Proudlove, N. (2018) *Impact of the Care Quality Commission on Provider Performance: Room for Improvement?* Available www.kingsfund.org.uk/sites/default/files/2018-09/cqc-provider-performance-report-september2018.pdf (accessed 20 June 2020).

Spurgeon, P., Mazelan, P.M. and Barwell, F. (2011) 'Medical Engagement: A Crucial Underpinning to Organisational Performance', *Health Services Management Research*, 24(3): 114–20.

Szmukler, G. and Appelbaum, P.S. (2008) 'Treatment Pressures, Leverage, Coercion, and Compulsion in Mental Health Care', *Journal of Mental Health*, 17(3): 233–44.

West, M.A. and Dawson, J.F. (2012) *Employee Engagement and NHS Performance.* Available www.kingsfund.org.uk/sites/default/files/employee-engagement-nhs-performance-west-dawson-leadership-review2012-paper.pdf (accessed 20 June 2020).

Part V

Conclusions

15 Regulating restrictive practices

Challenges and possibilities

Bernadette McSherry and Yvette Maker

Introduction

The chapters in this volume have raised several common themes regarding the regulation of practices to control health care and disability service users' behaviour. Offering perspectives from a range of personal and disciplinary standpoints, contributors have identified significant barriers to regulating the use of the different forms of restraint and developing mechanisms to reduce or eliminate such use.

Students of legal theory may be familiar with a lecture by the renowned legal scholar, Herbert Hart, entitled *The Nightmare and the Noble Dream* (1977). Hart compared the nightmare of unrestrained judicial discretion with the noble dream of judges simply finding and declaring what the law is. The chapters in this volume suggest that the regulation of restraint and other restrictive practices raises an analogous dichotomy. The nightmare is exemplified by the unrestricted use of physical and chemical restraint in the Oakden scandal as outlined in Chapter 11 and the Noble Dream set out in Chapter 2 that restraint will be eliminated and the human rights of all those in health and social care contexts upheld by the year 2050.

The original aim of the Australian Research Council Discovery Project which gave rise to this volume was to develop model laws and guidelines in order to regulate and reduce, with a view to eliminating, the use of various forms of restraint. That aim now seems otiose given the central insight offered by the chapters in this volume – that no matter how ideal the laws and guidelines, it will only be through supportive and therapeutic procedures that restrictive practices will be reduced, if not eliminated, in mental health, disability, aged care and other contexts. In order to support reform endeavours, law and policymakers must be aware of both the contributions and the limits of regulation, as well as the practical challenges outlined in many of these chapters.

This concluding chapter describes some of the volume's main themes relating to challenges and possibilities for positive change. It also highlights promising alternatives to the use of restrictive practices in the regulatory and non-regulatory spheres and proposes future directions for research.

Main themes

Many of the chapters in this volume deal with the advantages and shortcomings of different approaches to regulation in mental health, disability and/or aged care services, many of which are common to multiple sectors. Legislation has the advantage of providing clear definitions of restrictive practices, setting processes for oversight (including time frames for monitoring and reporting and clarifying the circumstances in which a breach occurs), setting penalties for such breaches and setting complaints procedures. Regulation through legislation may also make the regulatory framework easy to locate. In practice, as many of the authors in this volume discuss, regulation through legislation can be patchy and inconsistent across sectors and jurisdictions (see Chandler in Chapter 4 and Maker in Chapter 5), may have limited practical impacts if not supported by concerted efforts and resources for implementation (see Allan and Manwaring in Chapter 8 and Gibson in Chapter 14), and cannot necessarily provide definitive and universally understood definitions to support data collection (see Sara in Chapter 9).

Policies, procedures, standards and guidelines can be more detailed than legislation and more easily adapted to local conditions. They are also easier to amend to incorporate the latest developments. However, the multitude of policies, standards, guidelines and procedures aimed at managing or reducing the use of restrictive practices in many jurisdictions means there can be confusion about which are relevant and/or legally binding (see Bartlett and Sampson in Chapter 3 and Cross in Chapter 6), and effective dissemination, education and training of staff can be challenging (see Breen in Chapter 13). Accreditation has the advantage of providing a financial incentive to comply with regulations but decisions relating to accreditation must be based on continual and rigorous inspection and monitoring processes, the challenges of which are touched on by Waddington in Chapter 7. Other mechanisms for change, such as the German Federal Constitutional Court decisions discussed by Osterfeld and Zinkler in Chapter 10, may necessitate urgent and sweeping changes but may nevertheless be met with resistance.

This points to an overriding theme in the chapters in this volume, namely, that restrictive practices have proved difficult to eliminate – or in many cases meaningfully reduce – despite the introduction of one or more of these models of regulation. The approach taken to reform is one possible barrier here. For example, several contributors have identified situations where one practice has been driven downwards through strong regulation (as has occurred with seclusion in some jurisdictions, such as the Netherlands), only for the frequency of another practice (such as chemical restraint) to increase in its place (see Waddington in Chapter 7, Osterfeld and Zinkler in Chapter 10 and Brophy, Fletcher and Hamilton in Chapter 12). This alludes to another tension in the regulation of restraint use. While regulation can protect against the arbitrary use of these practices and specify procedural safeguards, it also arguably normalises their use and necessitates the assessment and labelling of 'risky' service users (see Bartlett and Sampson in Chapter 3 and Sara in Chapter 9).

Organisational cultures are identified as an important factor in the persistence of certain practices despite attempts to reduce them. Here, risk-based rather than recovery and human rights-based decision-making appears to contribute to a tolerance for restrictive practices and resistance to change (see McSherry in Chapter 11 and Brophy, Fletcher and Hamilton in Chapter 12). Inadequate attention to restraint reduction and elimination in clinical guidelines, codes of ethics and other clinician-focused initiatives also appear to be significant barriers to change (see Breen in Chapter 13 and Gibson in Chapter 14). Many authors note that the practical challenges of implementing regulatory reform are not insignificant, requiring resources, leadership, data and data literacy, goodwill and clear and practical guidance on how to implement alternatives to existing practices. The chapters in this volume highlight many points of commonality across mental health, disability and aged care services. There is, for example, a range of potential harms and rights concerns raised by the use of restraint, a lack of consultation and involvement of service users in developing and implementing interventions and a common emphasis on risk avoidance. Several authors do, however, highlight the need for interventions that are tailored to specific service settings and to the roles and responsibilities of particular actors (see Breen in Chapter 13 and Gibson in Chapter 14).

Several chapters in this volume stress the small or non-existent evidence base for many current practices and regulatory guidance such as, for example, the use of medications for rapid tranquilisation or chemical restraint and the determination of an 'appropriate' duration for the use of prone restraint (see Bartlett and Sampson in Chapter 3, Cross in Chapter 6 and Breen in Chapter 13). This points to the absolute necessity of reforms being driven by evidence.

Future directions for research

In terms of mapping and monitoring current practices and tracking the effects of reform, several research gaps are evident. For example, while data collections on the use of some forms of restraint – such as physical and mechanical restraint in Australia – are growing, there remain significant gaps in recording and reporting on the use of other forms, especially chemical restraint. There are undoubtedly challenges in measuring and reporting on these and other restrictive practices, but the idea that chemical restraint cannot be clearly defined and is therefore immeasurable must be addressed, as Grant Sara discusses in Chapter 9.

There is a clear need for more research into which interventions reduce the use of restrictive practices and how those interventions can be enacted through changes to regulation and practice. In relation to the *Six Core Strategies* discussed in Chapter 1 (National Technical Assistance Center for State Mental Health Planning 2005; National Association of State Mental Health Program Directors 2008), the most tested strategy is that of leadership. Much of the literature on this topic deals with the importance of top-down organisational leadership in conjunction with local level leadership (for example, at ward level) in order to create and maintain culture change. While multiple chapters in this volume explain why this is an important factor in restraint reduction, it may be that the overwhelming focus on leadership as a strategy for change reflects the fact that much of the research in the field is driven by management concerns rather than by consumers.

This highlights arguably the most significant gap in existing research, namely, the lack of consumer-led and consumer-endorsed initiatives that aim to eliminate restrictive practices. Cath Roper, Mary O'Hagan, Hamilton Kennedy and Helena Roennfeldt have provided examples of such initiatives in Chapter 2. It is timely now to evaluate and expand on these initiatives and to consider how they may be supported by regulation (see also Brophy, Fletcher and Hamilton in Chapter 12). This should also present an opportunity to address the superficial extent to which regulation and practice recognises the relevance of a range of dimensions of difference – including, but not limited to, gender, gender identity, sexuality, class, 'race', ethnicity, religion and disability status – in the treatment, experiences, requirements and views of service users (discussed by Roper et al. in Chapter 2; Bartlett and Sampson in Chapter 3 and Maker in Chapter 5). While the emphasis of many chapters in this volume has been on the experiences of mental health consumers and their role in working towards reducing and eliminating restraint, an equally strong argument can be made for the greater involvement of users of disability and aged care services in research and in the development, implementation and monitoring of reform.

Promising alternatives

Several chapters in this volume have emphasised that there is some research evidence identifying promising alternatives that may assist in reducing the use of these practices across contexts.

Re-thinking the design of service settings themselves through, for example, implementing recovery-oriented and human rights-based approaches, as well as ensuring co-production, co-design and peer support throughout service design and delivery are two particularly promising alternatives to the status quo (see Roper et al. in Chapter 2, Maker in Chapter 5 and Brophy, Fletcher and Hamilton in Chapter 12). Borckhardt and colleagues (2011) have observed that physical changes to the environment are some of the easiest changes to implement. Changes to the environment that helped reduce the use of seclusion and restraint by over 82.3 per cent in a state run hospital in the south-eastern United States included 'repainting walls with warm colors, placement of decorative throw rugs and plants, and rearrangement of furniture . . . along with replacing worn-out furniture and continuing with environmental changes' (Borckardt et al. 2011: 479; see also Brophy et al. 2020). There is also some indication that sensory approaches such as the use of sensory modulation rooms can help reduce levels of distress (Champagne and Sayer 2003; Te Pou o te Whakaaro Nui 2010; Chalmers et al. 2012) thereby preventing the need to use restrictive interventions. Sensory modulation tools can include the use of audio and video equipment, weighted blankets, soft materials and pleasant aromas (Te Pou o te Whakaaro Nui 2010: 3).

Many attempts to reduce the use of restrictive interventions feature the strategy of staff training and the use of new assessment, review and debriefing tools. Several chapters in this volume have emphasised that such interventions will only be successful if they are adequately resourced, extend to all those who might be involved in authorising or applying restraint, disseminated effectively and on an ongoing basis and tailored to the context and audience. The wide variety of approaches that exist across Australia, New Zealand, England, Germany and the Netherlands suggests that 'suites of options' for reform may be the most useful way forward for different sectors and jurisdictions.

Many chapters in this volume emphasise the importance of broader societal culture in the persistent use and acceptance of restraint and other restrictive practices in spite of the recognition and acknowledgment of their harms. Specifically, dominant discourses or models of mental illness and disability emphasise medical diagnosis and treatment, draw hard distinctions between acceptable and unacceptable behaviour, and define certain people as inherently risky due to their diagnosis (see Osterfeld and Zinkler in Chapter 10, McSherry in Chapter 11 and Brophy, Fletcher and Hamilton in Chapter 12). Observations by several contributors about the lack of clarity – and indeed inquiry – about the lawfulness or otherwise of restraint use in particular circumstances or for particular purposes lends support to the notion that approaches based on containment and control are so culturally normalised that there is little space to consider the perspectives, rights and dignity of service users. Roper and colleagues in Chapter 2 note the building chorus of international voices arguing that we cannot hope to reduce (let alone eliminate) the use of restraint without challenging the broader systems of coercion and disenfranchisement in which it is practised.

Conclusion

The recognition of restrictive practices as breaches of human rights and the growing consensus that such practices are not therapeutic has led to many attempts to regulate them, although mostly with the intention of reducing or minimising, rather than totally eliminating, their use. The chapters in this volume suggest that regulatory reform has the potential to support such attempts in mental health, disability and aged care sectors, but only in combination with effective implementation and monitoring and with wider transformation of the culture of services and societies more generally.

Reform efforts are likely to be effective if they are coordinated, consistent and informed by clearly formulated and stated rationales, such as trauma-avoidance or human rights compliance. This also requires agreement on the purpose and goal of reform which, as several authors have indicated, is not a straightforward matter.

Regulatory instruments to support reform efforts must be designed to strike a balance between giving enough detail to ensure consistent, lawful practice and avoiding 'regulatory overload' for staff and services, which can undermine good relationships and other practices that contribute to restraint avoidance. These instruments must not only prohibit bad practice but must also identify and encourage alternatives. The voices of people who have been, or may be, subject to restraint have been critical in challenging prevailing practices on the basis of the harms and disempowerment they produce, and such individuals and systemic advocates should continue to be at the heart of reform efforts.

Formal regulatory change must be supported by well-resourced and comprehensive implementation, with agreement from all parties concerned. This is likely to require new or renewed efforts at coalition-building, including intersectoral, multidisciplinary efforts to challenge the 'safety versus rights' dichotomy that continues to dominate health settings. Achieving real reform will rely on strong leadership, culture change and a willingness by staff and services to consider how things can be done differently. Often the least powerful and influential staff members are the ones required to apply restraint and they are the ones at risk of being hurt or blamed if things go wrong. Any regulatory change must therefore ensure that workers have adequate resources, support, training and autonomy.

Perhaps most fundamentally, reform efforts must tackle the discriminatory notions that people with mental health or disability diagnoses, and older people, inherently pose a risk or danger to themselves or others. Other forms of prejudice or stigma that dehumanise and undermine the dignity of service users must be addressed.

Ultimately it will only be through reform endeavours on multiple fronts that the Noble Dream of eliminating restrictive practices inches closer to reality.

References

Borckardt, J.J., Madan, A., Grubaugh, A.L., Danielson, C.K., Pelic, C.G., Hardesty, S.J., Hanson, R., Herbert, J., Cooney, H., Benson, A. and Frueh, B.C. (2011) 'Systematic Investigation of Initiatives to Reduce Seclusion and Restraint in a State Psychiatric Hospital', *Psychiatric Services*, 62(5): 477–83.

Brophy, L., Oostermeijer, S., Minshall, C., Harvey, C., Hamilton, B., Roper, C., Martel, A. and Fletcher, J. (2020) *Designing Mental Health Facilities That Prevent the Use of Seclusion and Restraint: An Evidence Check Rapid Review Brokered by the Sax Institute for the NSW Ministry of Health*. Available www.saxinstitute.org.au/wp-content/uploads/2020.06_Designing-mental-health-facilities-that-prevent-the-use-of-seclusion-and-restraint_Evidence-Check.pdf (accessed 29 June 2020).

Chalmers, A., Harrison, S., Mollison, K., Molloy, N. and Gray, K. (2012) 'Establishing Sensory-based Approaches in Mental Health Inpatient Care: A Multidisciplinary Approach', *Australasian Psychiatry*, 20(1): 35–39.

Champagne, T. and Sayer, E. (2003) *The Effects of the Use of the Sensory Room in Psychiatry: A Quality Improvement Study*. Available www.ot-innovations.com/clinical-practice/sensory-modulation/sensory-rooms-in-mental-health-3/qi_study_sensory_room/ (accessed 20 June 2020).

Hart, H.L.A. (1977) 'American Jurisprudence Through English Eyes: The Nightmare and the Noble Dream', *Georgia Law Review*, 11(5): 969–89.

National Association of State Mental Health Program Directors (2008) *Six Core Strategies to Reduce Seclusion and Restraint Use*. Available www.nasmhpd.org/content/six-core-strategies-reduce-seclusion-and-restraint-use (accessed 20 June 2020).

National Technical Assistance Center for State Mental Health Planning (2005) *Six Core Strategies to Reduce the Use of Seclusion and Restraint Planning Tool*, Alexandria, VA: National Association of State Mental Health Program Directors. Available https://www.ot-innovations.com/wp-content/uploads/2014/09/2._six_core_sr20plan20template20with20cover207-05.pdf (accessed 18 August 2020).

Te Pou o te Whakaaro Nui (2010) *Impact of Sensory Modulation in Mental Health Acute Wards on Reducing the Use of Seclusion*. Available www.tepou.co.nz/download/asset/159 (accessed 20 June 2020).

Index